The Essential Wrapped In Plastic: Pathways to Twin Peaks

John Thorne

Library of Congress Control Number: 2016904537
John Thorne, Dallas, TX

ISBN-13: 978-0-9971081-0-1

To Laura

To Sarah and Daniel

.

CONTENTS

Introduction:

Rapt

In 2005, Craig Miller and I published our final issue of *Wrapped In Plastic* magazine. For over thirteen years and seventy-five issues, we studied and wrote about the television series, *Twin Peaks,* and its prequel film, *Fire Walk With Me.* Producing *Wrapped In Plastic* was a rewarding and memorable chapter in our lives; over the years we interviewed *Twin Peaks* co-creators, David Lynch and Mark Frost, as well as dozens of other people associated with the show—from actors and writers, to musicians and cinematographers. We wrote about all aspects of the series: the history of its production, its cultural impact, and its rich thematic content. We made some great discoveries along the way and brought a keen critical eye to a television series that was—and is—unlike any other.

What was it about *Twin Peaks* that compelled us to devote so much time and energy on one short-lived television show?

Twin Peaks surprised us. Before the days of cable channels and edgy start-up networks and streaming services, a show like *Twin Peaks* was unheard of. When the *Twin Peaks* pilot aired on April 8, 1990, we wanted to watch it again as soon as it ended. Then, when Dale Cooper's dream closed episode 2, we were floored (literally). Nothing like this had ever been on television.

Twin Peaks worked in an abstract, unconventional manner. It was challenging, subversive, and unpredictable. Most casual viewers were unaccustomed to such unusual television; they expected programs to supply all the answers. What many didn't realize was that *Twin Peaks* was offering viewers an opportunity to supply their own. As scholar Brad Chisholm has noted, *Twin Peaks* was the kind of show designed for those viewers who "presumed to relish or at least respect the kind of challenge posed" by a narrative. This was exactly the kind of viewer Mark Frost had in mind when developing the series, the kind of audience who watches television in order to engage their minds.

Frost deliberately (and Lynch intuitively) designed *Twin Peaks* to be a subjective experience for viewers—one that would allow them to develop their own interpretation of the text, to supply their own meaning to what they heard and saw. The fact that *Twin Peaks* attempted the ambitious task of throwing off the shackles of passivity made the series an artistic success. The show proved that television was capable of much more than least-common-denominator content. As such, it made an enduring cultural impact and stirred the minds of countless writers, producers, critics and scholars. Few series have provided so much rich narrative and discursive material on which to study. The content and the format of *Twin Peaks* has been deconstructed, re-interpreted, and subjected to various forms of analyses. Much of this analysis appeared in *Wrapped In Plastic*. Hopefully, the magazine helped sustain some of the enthusiasm for *Twin Peaks* over the years.

When *Wrapped In Plastic* ceased publication, the material contained within went out of print. And while some of the later issues were still available online from Win-Mill Productions, many of the older issues became increasingly scarce. Fans of *Twin Peaks* who wanted those rare back issues had to seek them out from second-hand sources, usually from other collectors or on eBay.

Much of the *Twin Peaks* material in *Wrapped In Plastic* was scattered through the seventy-five issues. (The magazine did more than focus on *Twin Peaks*; *Wrapped In Plastic* closely examined significant works from Mark Frost and David Lynch, and it kept up with the ongoing work of many of the actors associated with the show.) Our *Twin Peaks* episode guide was spread across four non-consecutive issues; our script analysis ("The Unseen *Twin Peaks*") appeared in nine different issues; and interviews with the various actors and other creative talent appeared throughout the thirteen-year run.

There was a great deal of material about *Twin Peaks* packed into those many pages of *Wrapped In Plastic*. With a new *Twin Peaks* series on the horizon, it seemed important to collect the dispersed—but essential—writings about the original series into book-form. Rather than simply reprint the issues, however, I decided to reassemble the important *Twin Peaks* material from *Wrapped In Plastic* into one place. The result is *The Essential Wrapped In Plastic: Pathways to Twin Peaks*, a book that features in-depth essays, thorough reviews of every episode, and—perhaps most importantly—commentary about the show and film from all the principal players we interviewed. There are many great pathways to explore, here, each leading to a new, and hopefully valuable, perspective on *Twin Peaks*.

The Essential Wrapped In Plastic collects some good writing about *Twin Peaks*, but it is a subset of a larger work. Much of the great writing from *Wrapped In Plastic* was done by other authors who contributed to the magazine over the years (and that includes some exceptional work by Craig Miller, who was primary author on many *Twin Peaks* and David Lynch-related essays). Those works belong to their respective authors and could not be reproduced here. So, while this book presents some essential writings about *Twin Peaks*, there is a still a great deal more to be found in the original magazine. Back issues are worth seeking out for the insightful work they contain.

In the process of gathering this material from the pages of *Wrapped In Plastic* I started to see the magazine in a way I hadn't considered before: *Wrapped In Plastic* presented various kinds of conversations about *Twin Peaks*. First and foremost, *Wrapped In Plastic* conversed with its readers, usually through the letters pages where ideas about *Twin Peaks* were bandied back and forth. Second, *Wrapped In Plastic* represented a conversation between Craig and me—one where we debated our specific takes on the show (and the other works of Lynch and Frost) in a public, albeit discreet way. Finally—and here most uniquely—*Wrapped In Plastic* represented a conversation that all of us, readers and writers alike, had with the show. *Twin Peaks* was a living work of art; it was idiosyncratic, elusive, baffling and boundless. It invited viewers to argue with it, to challenge it. *To imagine with it.* In the pages of *Wrapped In Plastic* we addressed *Twin Peaks* directly and spoke with it as best we could. We never got all the answers we sought but we never tired of having those conversations.

Now I find myself talking with *Twin Peaks* once more. After all these years, the series and film continue to speak loudly and strongly. Re-engaged by the work, I found that *Twin Peaks* could still surprise me. That was good; the show was keeping me on my toes. In the course of preparing this book I did far more re-writing than I thought I would. I tweaked some of my arguments, re-oriented a few of my theses, and revised a great deal of text.

I've attempted to reassemble pieces of *Wrapped In Plastic* into an organized and sensible structure. But I recognize that this work isn't seamless. This book is a collection of pieces, carefully placed together to provide a logical flow. But the seams do show from time to time. The essays in this book were written as stand-alone works, and there is a degree of repetition to them. This results in perhaps a certain fragmented feel to the book. But I thought it better to keep the essays as intact as possible when reprinting them here. In that way they can be read separately (or out of order) and still function as effective reference works.

The Essential Wrapped In Plastic is a work of critical analysis and historical reporting. It studies each episode of *Twin Peaks* in order to better understand the series as a whole. These studies are supplemented by comments from actors, writers, producers and other creative personnel from the series, who provide intimate and first-hand remarks about the work. In addition, each critique includes discussion of scripted scenes that were either deleted from the final version, or changed in some important way. This examination allows for a deeper understanding of how the series was being crafted as it went along. The final episode of *Twin Peaks* is studied in-depth, with a chapter that focuses on the installment's final, mesmerizing act—an essay that hopefully sheds light on what really happened to the series' enigmatic protagonist, Dale Cooper.

The film, *Fire Walk With Me*, garners the most critical attention with two lengthy (and a few short) essays in which I struggle to make sense of a hermetic movie that is both independent of, yet vitally connected to, the larger work. The first essay delves into the character of Laura Palmer, and attempts to show how David Lynch transformed the *idea* of Laura (from the series) into a fully realized character (in the film), a difficult task that Lynch undoubtedly struggled with. The second essay, one of *Wrapped In Plastic*'s more controversial pieces, radically challenges the idea of the *Fire Walk With Me* prologue, arguing that Dale Cooper is a more prominent and vital presence in the story than might first (or second, or third . . .) appear.

In addition to providing essays, *The Essential Wrapped In Plastic* also functions as a guide book. Story details, cast lists, ratings data, and contemporary reviews serve to aid students of *Twin Peaks* who are looking for specifics about what happened in the story as well as what happened behind-the-scenes on the production.

Finally, this book renews the argument we made in the pages of *Wrapped In Plastic*: *Twin Peaks* is an enduring work. It is singular and important and worth writing about. For years, *Wrapped In Plastic* offered a way for Craig Miller and me (and our readers) to study *Twin Peaks*. But the magazine was also a place to celebrate it. *The Essential Wrapped In Plastic* continues that celebration.

Welcome back to the party.

John Thorne,

January 31, 2016

CULT BUSTER

How many times have you heard *Twin Peaks* referred to as a *cult* show? All the time, right? After all, *Twin Peaks* seems the like the ultimate cult series—a quirky TV show with a handful of episodes and a die-hard fan-base. Cult seems like the *only* way to describe it.

But, really, to call *Twin Peaks* a cult show is to do it an injustice. There's something inexplicably more to the series, a subtle, sublime quality that makes the term "cult" seem inappropriate and inadequate.

In his book, *Full of Secrets*, editor David Lavery explains how *Twin Peaks* is "explicitly formulated as cult TV."[1] Lavery's argument is convincing, but it only provides a narrow way of addressing the show. Defining *Twin Peaks* is an elusive proposition: just as the show explores the concept of duality we find that *Twin Peaks*, itself, is an *example* of duality. While it satisfies all the cultic characteristics described by Lavery, it also rejects them. In so doing, *Twin Peaks* reveals itself as something more—a work of art.

To Be or Not to Be: How Twin Peaks is—and is not—Cult

Although there are various meanings of the term "cult," the most concise and satisfying definition originates from author, Umberto Eco (a professor of semiotics at the University of Bologna, and best known for his novel, *The Name of the Rose*). Eco observes that a cult work exhibits specific qualities: First, it will present a comprehensive, make-believe world, rich with background detail and minutiae. Second, it will typically be of uneven quality yet manage to contain magnificent moments—vivid scenes that make indelible impressions. Third, it will seem familiar to an audience; it will be a work that is comfortable and understandable and one that does not reveal the particular style of any individual creator. In his introductory essay to *Full of Secrets*, David Lavery supplies labels to Eco's cult characteristics. These are: "a completely furnished world;" "detachability;" and "living textuality." *Twin Peaks* exhibits all these qualities. But, as we will see, it also *defies* them.

1

A Completely Furnished World

According to Eco, a cult object must provide "a completely furnished world" from which "fans can quote characters and episodes [and] can make up quizzes and play trivia games so that adepts of the sect recognize through each other a shared expertise."[2]

Lavery describes how the various pieces of *Twin Peaks* tie-in merchandise (*The Secret Diary of Laura Palmer, The Autobiography of FBI Special Agent Dale Cooper, The Twin Peaks Access Guide*, etc.) satisfy this cultic characteristic. But even without that material *Twin Peaks* fulfills Eco's definition. David Lynch and Mark Frost created *Twin Peaks* with great attention to detail. Starting with a map they carefully laid out the fictional setting of the series. From there, they created complex characters and character inter-relationships and a rigid timeline within which the *Twin Peaks* storyline would take place. This wealth of detail was ideal for "quizzes and trivia games." *Twin Peaks*, with its character histories and detailed setting, makes for a fully-furnished, definable world—a bounded domain of exactness that lends itself to fan "expertise."

And yet can anyone be an expert on the Red Room? Does anyone know the definitive fate of Dale Cooper? *Twin Peaks* is filled with ambiguity. Its narrative wanders out of the three-dimensional reality of a corporeal small-town and into a surreal landscape of dreams and elastic time. The Red Room is a place that has its own ambiguous rules—or no rules at all. According to David Lynch it's a place where "things get kind of slippery."[3] Time becomes nonlinear and unreliable; events appear disordered, misleading and incomplete. But this place—this "waiting room"—is an essential element to the *Twin Peaks* narrative. The story leads to and away from the Red Room, and Agent Cooper and Laura Palmer—the two most important characters in the narrative—are connected to it in significant, albeit puzzling, ways.

The Red Room is but one example of *Twin Peaks'* ambiguity. Other curious events include Sarah Palmer's vision of a white horse and Josie Packard's anguished visage in a wooden drawer pull. And mysterious characters such as the Log Lady and Major Briggs play an unpredictable and enigmatic role in the story.

All these obscure elements—these characters, places and events—are open to interpretation; they defy the precision and boundedness required to construct a "fully furnished world" which lends to "shared expertise" among fans. There can be no consensus among followers of *Twin Peaks* as to what certain characters represent or what particular events signify. "The bottom line, hard to digest, is that the central theme of *Twin Peaks* is whatever each one of the viewers wants to name it."[4] *Twin Peaks* fulfills—and then thwarts—Eco's first cultic condition.

Detachability

Eco's second characteristic is detachability: "one must be able to break [a cult object], dislocate it, unhinge it so that one can remember only parts of it, irrespective of their original relationship to the whole." Lavery explains how *Twin Peaks* was filled with memorable "images, details, bits of dialog" that stood out from the rest of the series. Without doubt, *Twin Peaks* contained striking, beguiling images—prominent moments that recur in the memories of viewers. The series had "major" memorable moments—Cooper's dream (episode 2), the death of Maddy (episode 14), the haunting image of Bob's face in the broken bathroom mirror (episode 29)—and it had "minor" moments—a dancing, flashlight-wielding Louise Dombrowski (episode 15), Leland's leap onto Laura's coffin (episode 3), Audrey Horne's trick with the cherry stem (episode 6).

Eco argues that these moments occur because a cult show "does not reveal a coherent philosophy of composition," and that the cult object is "ramshackle, rickety, unhinged in itself." In other words, the work is uneven and unrefined.

To be sure, *Twin Peaks* varied in quality from episode-to-episode. This was the result of two important factors: First, *Twin Peaks* was subject to the inherent nature of TV production; episodes of any series must be produced on-budget and on-time. Inevitably there are lapses in quality (although *Twin Peaks* maintained a remarkable visual and literate excellence throughout its run). Second, there are typically many different creative personnel guiding a TV series, and *Twin Peaks* was no exception; each writer or director on the series brought a different storytelling style and sensibility to the work (just a quick example: writer/producer Mark Frost had a keen sense of story structure; writer/producer Harley Peyton wrote sharp, distinct dialog; director David Lynch imbued the series with moody, surreal imagery; director Tim Hunter created precise, elegant visuals). With so many different creative people working on such a demanding production, *Twin Peaks* arguably exhibited "an incoherent philosophy of composition."

And yet David Lynch's authorial presence cannot be ignored, especially since he directed some of the most significant "chapters" in the narrative: the pilot, a critical mid-series episode (Bob kills Maddy), the final episode, and the post-series film "prequel," *Fire Walk With Me*. Initially, Lynch's artistic sensibilities were complemented by Mark Frost's storytelling skills, and neither creator was forced to compromise his vision: "At the beginning of the series, Frost's knowledge of the classics and of the literature of mysticism worked brilliantly with Lynch's instincts."[5] As the series progressed Frost's creative approach temporarily supplanted Lynch's authorial presence, due, in part, to Lynch's brief absence from the series. But Lynch re-exerted control of the narrative by re-writing and directing

Twin Peaks' crucial final episode. Lynch's changes "created the conditions for an organic coherence [to the series] despite the periodic glitches."[6]

David Lynch had a consistent philosophy of composition, even if that philosophy was occasionally diluted by other contributing artists. Lynch ensures coherence with the film, *Fire Walk With Me*, a movie that is neither prequel or sequel, but a fascinating blend of both. *Fire Walk With Me* is Lynch's successful effort at connecting *Twin Peaks'* final episode with its first (the pilot). The film creates in *Twin Peaks* a hermetic narrative—one that encompasses the entirety of the series. Without *Fire Walk With Me*, the *Twin Peaks* narrative is a graceful arc. With the film, the narrative becomes a perfect circle. As Gregg Rickman has so cogently observed, "*Twin Peaks*, film and series, can together be thought of as . . . an elegantly constructed whole complete unto itself."[7] Rickman makes an acute point—under David Lynch's guidance *Twin Peaks* is structurally sound, and here, again, it defies Eco's definition of cult.

Living Textuality

David Lavery identifies Eco's third cultic characteristic as "living textuality." According to Eco, a cult work appears to be "outside the conscious control of its creators." To the audience, the creative forces behind a cult show are hidden or inconsequential. The fictional milieu has its own momentum, forcing characters to behave, and storylines to move, in a specific way, regardless of who is writing or directing. In short, a cult work seems to have a life of its own.

This component of Eco's definition is the least applicable to *Twin Peaks*. In his essay, Lavery acknowledges that *Twin Peaks* was "more authored than most in the inherently anonymous 'producer's' medium of television."[8] Rather than directly address Eco's definition, Lavery chooses to focus on the "intertextual" nature of *Twin Peaks*; that is, the way the series acknowledged its own medium and others. *Twin Peaks* incorporated elements of "precedent texts." For example, some character names (Phillip Gerard, Gordon Cole, Madeleine Ferguson) originated from past TV series and classic movies. Lavery argues that these elements "invited cultic participation" with *Twin Peaks*,[9] the audience acknowledged that pieces of the show were deliberate "winks and nudges" from the show's creative personnel.

So what did Eco mean by "living textuality" and why did *Twin Peaks* fail to fulfill this aspect of the cult definition? Eco discuss the presence of archetypes in the cult object, defining an archetype as "a pre-established and frequently reappearing narrative situation, cited or in some way recycled by innumerable other texts, and provoking in the addressee a sort of intense emotion accompanied by a vague feeling of déjà vu." This windy definition is another way of saying "cliché," a term which Eco equates with "archetype."

Clichés are abundant in cult objects, whether they be narrative situations (the hero fights the villain and wins, true love triumphs over adversity) or character types (the tough guy, the self-made businessman, the canny detective). Cult science fiction series commonly feature clichés such as the "warrior-leader" (Captain Kirk in *Star Trek*) or the "truth seeker" (Fox Mulder in *The X-Files*), and cult mystery series commonly feature the "rational detective" (Columbo in *Columbo*) or the "no-nonsense cop" (Joe Friday in *Dragnet*), among others. Even when these characters are tweaked with idiosyncratic behavior or embellished with unique backgrounds, they usually conform to a basic cliché. No matter how you dress them up, most characters on TV are circumscribed by certain rules which make them easier for writers to write, and for audiences to identify.

When archetypes function properly, cult TV storylines will move in satisfying, if not predictable directions to deliver expected denouements. In this way the cult show does, indeed, seem an autonomous text that is "outside the control of a creator."

Superficially, *Twin Peaks* presented a plethora of standard archetypes. Cooper constituted the traditional rational detective; Sheriff Truman was an able partner (archetypal roles explicitly acknowledged by the text when, in episode 1, Truman says, "I'm starting to feel like Dr. Watson"); Laura Palmer was the not-so-innocent teenager; Bobby Briggs was the jealous, hot-headed boyfriend; Ben Horne was the ruthless businessman. Such a list could go on and on; almost every character in *Twin Peaks* initially appeared to be a stereotype (not surprising, really, since *Twin Peaks* was envisioned by Mark Frost as, among other things, a parody of traditional prime-time soap operas).

But almost instantly the "stereotypical-ness" of the *Twin Peaks* characters dissolves; their status as clichés become challenged as the characters evolve through the narrative (Cooper displays a child-like, naïve quality, coupled with an element of self-doubt; Truman becomes passive and confused, etc.). Granted, these changes in character could be viewed as nothing more than the exchange of one stereotype for another, but the *Twin Peaks* characters undergo constant change and revision as the narrative proceeds. Most remain puzzling, unique, unclassifiable characters. They have an enigmatic quality. Is there any simple way to define Dale Cooper? Is he a failed or triumphant hero? Did he rely on logic or intuition (or both)? And what really happened to Laura Palmer? Was she victim or victor? In the end, none of these questions can be definitively and objectively answered. *Twin Peaks* remains open to interpretation primarily because of David Lynch's authorship and Mark Frost's effort to undermine viewer expectation. Refusing to rely on predictable archetypes and clichés, the series subverts the third component of Eco's definition of cult.

It should be no surprise that *Twin Peaks*, which explored duality and contradiction with an open, indeterminate narrative, would, as a cultural product, both comply with and thwart the definition of cult object. The definition is simply not enough to encompass the complexity of the work. It is inadequate to label *Twin Peaks* as "cult TV." Instead, *Twin Peaks* should be viewed as a transcendent, sublime achievement—a piece of art—that will be appreciated for generations to come.

The Path to Transcendence

There are dozens (if not hundreds) of network TV series which can be precisely described by Umberto Eco's definition of cult. (A few examples from the SF/Fantasy genre: *Star Trek, The X-Files, Fringe, Lost, Battlestar Galactica.*) Most—but not all—of these shows remain firmly embedded in the cult substratum, destined to remain cultural artifacts whose appeals are limited each to a particular audience.

Those who create commercial TV programs are typically trying to do two things: One, create art that has its own intrinsic aesthetic value; and two, create a product that will attract a sizable audience to whom to advertise. Accomplishing both goals is often a difficult balancing act made more complicated by the usual interference from networks, advertisers and other business entities to whom profit is paramount. Most TV productions are handicapped by constraints and limits placed on them by outside influence—someone other than the show's creator. These outsiders want to sell products and believe they are more apt to persuade audiences to buy if those audiences are relaxed, placid and open to suggestion. Hence, network TV programs are often familiar and repetitive—predictable fare that will not make audiences uncomfortable or confused.

When David Lynch and Mark Frost developed *Twin Peaks* they, too, hoped their series would have aesthetic value and mass appeal. But mass appeal was much less important. They wanted to create *art*, and they were indifferent to the media forces surrounding their production.

Twin Peaks reflected the indulgence of its creators, the willingness of Lynch and Frost to let their imaginations run free with little regard for the economic forces of network TV. Frost, who knew the TV industry as well as anyone, was determined to produce an undiluted vision. In fact, Frost may have considered *Twin Peaks* an experiment, one that would last a few short episodes and then be gone. If Frost took this attitude during *Twin Peaks'* initial seven episodes he may have felt free to indulge his artistic whims. In so doing he ignored network input: "I was not very responsive to ABC's notes all the way through, particularly that first season . . . . [We] stuck by our guns and did exactly what we wanted to do."[10]

Where Mark Frost may have been deliberately ignoring the economic constraints of commercial TV, David Lynch was naïve to the realities of the industry. Unaware or unconcerned with the forces that drive network television production, Lynch created *Twin Peaks* exactly according to his vision. He felt free to indulge and to follow his intuition just as he always had when making feature films. According to Martha Nochimson, Lynch "frees himself to receive ideas, images and impulses . . . during the directing process."[11] As a result, *Twin Peaks* was pure, uncalculated expression—an observation echoed by Lynch: "I guess what made *Twin Peaks Twin Peaks* is hard to talk about. I don't think we even knew what it was."[12]

Lynch later became aware of the importance of ratings and the need for commercials; media fixtures he felt damaged his artistic vision. For Lynch, ratings were arbitrary, "based on absurdity,"[13] and commercials, "break up the show . . . . They're ruining everything . . . . I don't know how anything can work when they're so destructive."[14] But even after Lynch became aware of television's restrictive environment he continued to follow his own artistic path, directing an unconventional final episode of *Twin Peaks*—an episode that featured an extended segment of Agent Cooper in the Red Room. This segment contained a relentless series of unusual images and encounters, from the terrifying visage of a screaming Laura Palmer to the intense pursuit of Agent Cooper by his own doppelgänger. Lynch's final *Twin Peaks* episode was bold, cryptic and disturbing—hardly prime-time TV fare.

A Detour Down Mulholland Drive

Lynch's refusal to acknowledge the inherent artistic limitations of creating network programming continued long after his work on *Twin Peaks*. In 1999, Lynch wrote and directed the pilot for *Mulholland Drive* with hopes it would air on ABC Television as the first installment in a potential new on-going series. Lynch again indulged his artistic vision, creating exactly the kind of show he wanted with little regard to network protocols. The final product—a hypnotic, enthralling introductory episode—ran two hours and five minutes (without commercials), an unwieldy and unusual length. Most "two hour" TV pilots run less than ninety minutes, leaving room for commercials to fill out the rest of the scheduled two-hour timeslot.

Writing for *The New Yorker*, essayist Tad Friend accurately described the full, two-hour cut of *Mulholland Drive* as "spooky, funny, and absorbing" with "a handful of indelible images: a boy with metal crutches and piercing blue eyes; a bloated corpse floating in a sea of blood; and, particularly, the sepulchral appearance of the pinheaded Mr. Roque."[15] Not surprisingly, ABC balked at Lynch's extended version, and demanded edits, not only to shorten the work to a standard 88-minute run-time, but also because they wanted to quicken the pilot's pace and remove "objectionable" content such as explicit violence, language, and, peculiarly, a close-up shot of dog feces. In addition, they made the baffling demand that Lynch remove any character who appeared only once. Lynch reluctantly made the edits hoping that ABC would agree to a series and thereby give him the opportunity to restore the deleted material in later episodes.

The resulting 88-minute version of *Mulholland Drive* was a diluted, compromised production. According to Friend, "what had distinguished it was gone: scenes that weren't immediately fathomable, pauses and puzzles and lingerings, a pervading senses of a powerful and idiosyncratic mind at work."[16] Lynch considered it a "butchered version," like a "bad traffic accident." Ironically, ABC still rejected the show, despite the edits they extorted from Lynch.

The case of *Mulholland Drive* illustrates the unique nature of *Twin Peaks*. Unencumbered by network interference, Lynch and Frost developed the pilot and initial seven episodes according to their own plan. If ABC—the network that commissioned the *Twin Peaks* pilot—suggested any significant changes, Mark Frost ignored them. For his part, Lynch was satisfied to create for creation's sake, even if nothing were to become of the *Twin Peaks* project: "I had a sense of freedom making that pilot. The euphoria of 'this probably isn't going to go anywhere, let's really do it.'"[17]

The result of Lynch and Frost's combined effort is exactly what Tad Friend saw in the uncut *Mulholland Drive* pilot: pauses and puzzles and lingerings, a pervading sense of powerful and idiosyncratic minds at work. The *Twin Peaks* pilot was brilliant and beguiling and timeless.

Timeless and Transcendent Art

To categorize *Twin Peaks* as nothing more than a cult show is to do it an injustice. As we've seen, *Twin Peaks* defies Umberto Eco's definition of cult object. It lacks the "ramshackle, rickety qualities" which Eco insists must be present and which typically result from the clash between creator impulse and network interference. What's more *Twin Peaks* eschews the concept of "living textuality." Where cult shows are "outside the conscious control" of their creators, *Twin Peaks* was firmly *inside* the conscious control of its makers. *Twin Peaks* toys with clichés and discards them, forging into original and unexpected narrative territory. Cult TV depends on cliché for success—clichés seduce the cult audience with comfort and predictability, they "manage to be particularly appealing to a given cultural area or a historical period" (according to Eco).

Granted, *Twin Peaks* has its cult followers, those fans who relish its palpable otherworldliness, its singular images, its comfortable oddball character and idyllic setting (its "quirky allure" as John Leonard, writing for *New York Magazine* so aptly put it). These are the fans who loved the series but spurned the film, *Fire Walk With Me*. But *Twin Peaks* has another set of admirers: those who not only relish the show's cultic characteristics, but who revel in its contradictions, its raw imaginative power, its everlasting openness to interpretation, its enduring ability to stimulate. The first set of fans may fade over time, but the second set will always exist—replenished by each new generation that discovers *Twin Peaks*.

TWIN PEAKS FIRST SEASON CREDITS

Kyle MacLachlan - *FBI Special Agent Dale Cooper*
Michael Ontkean - *Sheriff Harry S. Truman*
Sherilyn Fenn - *Audrey Horne*
Richard Beymer - *Benjamin Horne*
Ray Wise - *Leland Palmer*
Dana Ashbrook - *Bobby Briggs*
Mädchen Amick - *Shelly Johnson*
Peggy Lipton - *Norma Jennings*
Lara Flynn Boyle - *Donna Hayward*
James Marshall - *James Hurley*
Sheryl Lee - *Laura Palmer/Madeleine Ferguson*
Joan Chen - *Josie Packard*
Jack Nance - *Pete Martell*
Piper Laurie - *Catherine Martell*
Kimmy Robertson - *Lucy Moran*
Harry Goaz - *Deputy Andy Brennan*
Warren Frost - *Doctor Will Hayward*
Grace Zabriskie - *Sarah Palmer*
Charlotte Stewart - *Betty Briggs*
Don Davis - *Garland Briggs*
Gary Hershberger - *Mike Nelson*
Michael Horse - *Deputy Tommy "Hawk" Hill*
Everett McGill - *Big Ed Hurley*
Wendy Robie - *Nadine Hurley*
Russ Tamblyn - *Doctor Lawrence Jacoby*
Jan D'Arcy - *Sylvia Horne*
Robert Bauer - *Johnny Horne* (episodes 1-7)
Eric Da Re - *Leo Johnson*
Mary Jo Deschanel - *Eileen Hayward*
David Patrick Kelly - *Jerry Horne*
Chris Mulkey - *Hank Jennings*
Catherine Coulson - *Margaret Lanterman, The Log Lady*
Al Strobel - *Phillip Gerard/Mike, the One Armed Man*

Created by Mark Frost & David Lynch
Music Composed & Conducted by Angelo Badalamenti
Produced by Gregg Fienberg
Executive Producers: Mark Frost & David Lynch
Associate Producer: Philip Neel
Director of Photography: Frank Byers
Production Designer: Richard Hoover

DREAMS, DONUTS, AND DANCING MEN:

TWIN PEAKS SEASON ONE

The first season of *Twin Peaks* has two distinct stages. The first stage (comprising the pilot through episode 2) is an "establishing phase" that introduces most of the characters and lays the groundwork for the investigation into Laura Palmer's murder. This segment of *Twin Peaks* is marked by the authorial presence of David Lynch (who co-wrote the first three installments and who directed the pilot and episode 2). The first phase of the series culminates with Agent Cooper's cryptic dream (episode 2), a powerful, hypnotic sequence that, according to Lynch, "may or may not relate to anything else."[1] Upon waking from the dream, Cooper believes he knows the identity of Laura Palmer's murderer.

The second stage of the first season can be thought of as the "post-dream phase" comprising the remaining five episodes (3-7). In this part of the series Cooper attempts to break his dream's code in order to find the murderer (the identity of whom he has forgotten).

The second half of the first season is the most accessible, unambiguous section of the early *Twin Peaks* narrative. In it, Mark Frost's authorial style takes control; the narrative is unmistakably earthbound, the story is forensic, and the plot is conveyed with purposeful momentum. Frost attempts the near impossible: translating the perplexing elements of Cooper's dream into a legible story (i.e., to assign meaning to Lynchian abstraction).

Pilot (Episode 1000; First televised April 8, 1990)

Guest Starring: John Boylan (Mayor Dwayne Milford), Phoebe Augustine (Ronette Pulaski), Robert Davenport (Johnny Horne), Andrea Hays (Heidi), Tawnya Pettiford-Waites (Dr. Shelvy), Diane Caldwell (Julie), Julee Cruise (singer at Roadhouse), Rick Tutor (Janek Pulaski), Roberta Maguire (Maria Pulaski), Jessica Wallenfels (Harriet Hayward), Ben DiGregorio (football coach), Troy Evans (Principal Wolchezk), Dorothy Roberts (Mrs. Jackson), Jane Jones (Mrs. Honeycutt), Marjorie Nelson (Janice Hogan)

Written by Mark Frost and David Lynch; Directed by David Lynch; Edited by Duwayne Dunham

Friday, February 24, 1989:

Act 1: Outside the Blue Pine Lodge in Twin Peaks, Pete Martell notices a body, wrapped in plastic, by the lakeshore. Sheriff Harry S. Truman and Doc Hayward identify the body as Laura Palmer. At the Palmer home, Sarah Palmer can't find her daughter. At the Great Northern Hotel, Benjamin Horne and Leland Palmer discuss Ben's pending real-estate deal with a Norwegian investment group. Leland takes a call from Sarah. Truman arrives and tells Leland there's "been an incident." Leland tells Ben, "My daughter is dead." Over the phone, Sarah wails uncontrollably.

Act 2: Bobby Briggs offers Shelly Johnson a ride home from the Double R Diner. Shelly says her husband, Leo Johnson, is still away. But when they get to Shelly's house, Leo's truck is parked outside. At the hospital, Leland identifies Laura's body. Donna Hayward, Audrey Horne, and James Hurley arrive at school. A sheriff's deputy speaks with Laura's teacher and Donna and James realize something is wrong. Truman arrests Bobby. The school principal announces that Laura Palmer is dead and dismisses school for the day.

Act 3: Deputy Hawk finds a diary and video camera in Laura's room. Deputy Andy Brennan tells Truman that another girl, Ronette Pulaski, has been reported missing. On the edge of town, a stunned and brutalized Ronette wanders out of the mountains along a railroad track. James tells his uncle, Ed Hurley, that Laura is dead. FBI Special Agent Dale Cooper meets Truman at the hospital and examines Ronette. Cooper meets Laura's psychiatrist, Dr. Lawrence Jacoby. In the morgue, Cooper examines Laura's fingers and finds a small piece of paper, imprinted with the letter "R," under her nail.

Act 4: Cooper examines Laura's diary. The police find the murder site— an abandoned train car in the woods. Cooper interrogates Bobby and tells him he knows Laura was seeing someone else. Bobby tells Mike Nelson they need to find "a biker." Cooper questions Donna but she has little to say. Cooper and Truman investigate the murder site and find a mound of dirt, a necklace with a gold half-heart pendant, and a note with the words, "FIRE WALK WITH ME" written in blood. Cooper says they need to find the person with other half of the gold heart. Just outside of town, a despondent James looks down at the other half of the heart necklace.

Act 5: Cooper and Truman search Laura's safe deposit box and find a bag of white powder, $10,000, and a copy of *Fleshworld* magazine featuring a picture of Ronette Pulaski. Leo threatens Shelly after finding a different brand of cigarettes in the ashtray. Cooper calls a town meeting and says that Laura may have been the victim of a serial killer who killed another young woman a year earlier.

Act 6: Bobby and Mike arrive at the Hayward home looking for Donna. Doc Hayward learns she's sneaked out. At the Roadhouse, Norma Jennings tells Big Ed she is going to leave her husband, Hank. Mike and Bobby arrive, followed by Donna. Mike accosts Donna, and Ed tries to protect her. Donna escapes to rendezvous with James. Donna comforts James and they kiss. They bury his half of the heart necklace in the woods and drive away. Cooper and Truman arrest James and lock him up next to Bobby and Mike. Mike and Bobby "bark" at James. Sarah has a vision of a gloved hand digging up the half-heart necklace.

Note: The above summary reflects the original broadcast version of the *Twin Peaks* pilot, which had limited commercial interruptions and therefore fewer act breaks.

Duality and opposition are fundamental themes in *Twin Peaks*. Right from the start, these ideas are evident in the show's hypnotic opening credits, as images of industrial machines alternate with those of peaceful forests and mountain streams. The sequence sets the stage for the story to come, one in which viewers enter a world of lingering scenes, captivating characters, potent settings. There is a dreamy allure to the work, despite its pervasive sense of dread. The *Twin Peaks* pilot might be David Lynch's most elegant film. It is seductive and engrossing—a work of visual poetry.

Much of the pilot's appeal is a result of the exquisitely structured script, co-written by Lynch and Mark Frost. Lynch's visuals might sometime meander, but Frost's tempering presence keeps the pilot from drifting too far. There is a focus to the piece, and, despite its lack of resolution, it is a whole and satisfying work.

The *Twin Peaks* pilot is designed in such a way as to inexorably draw the viewer into the story. A narrative momentum builds through each act; scenes flow one to another like slowly falling dominoes. Take act 1, for example: A body is found, and the police are called. They arrive and identify the body—Laura Palmer. They are stunned, and one of the officers begins to cry. The death has meaning. The story shifts to Laura's mother (we, the audience, now know what she does not). Sarah Palmer is distressed and desperate; she knows something is wrong (now the audience is attentive, wondering when and how she will learn the truth). There is a shift to Laura's father, Leland Palmer, at work. He gets a call from a very worried Sarah. He is troubled by her distress but tries to reassure her (and the dramatic irony builds because the audience knows he is wrong). Tension has been steadily mounting and a climax is imminent. Sheriff Truman arrives looking for Leland. Leland seems to grasp the truth—he knows Laura is dead before he is even told.

Audience expectation is subverted—we never hear the police speak of what has happened. The weight of the tragedy has broken through on its own. And once the facts are out, the emotions of the characters are unleashed. Sarah Palmer's anguished wails overwhelm the final moments of the act, and the audience is left absorbing a moment of raw despair. As the act ends, the viewer has been masterfully and unknowingly hooked. The story is only beginning but it already resonates. What else will happen? How will the other characters react? And, of course, *who killed Laura Palmer?*

The rest of the pilot continues the slow build of mystery and tension punctured by occasional release (Cooper's examination of Laura's body, the fight at the roadhouse, the arrest and jailing of James). The pilot ends with a simple, perfect line of dialogue, spoken by Josie when she is with Truman: "I'm afraid." But the episode does not end there. The story cuts to the Palmer house. Sarah is awakened, terrified from a dream or vision of a gloved hand pulling Laura's necklace from the dirt. We hear another scream of release, and the mystery only deepens.

If such a thing can exist, the pilot is, quite possibly, a perfect work. While there is a strong surface narrative featuring the investigation into Laura Palmer's murder, underneath is a powerful subtext—a theme of innocence lost, implicit in almost every scene and character. From the opening shots there is a mood of foreboding and concealment as the camera moves along Josie's vanity table to pause on a close-up of her face; she turns—beautiful, but worried. It foreshadows the events to come and instantly represents a central theme of the show: Secrets are buried beneath beautiful surfaces. The people of Twin Peaks fear that their secrets will be exposed and that their darker sides will be revealed to the world.

The story begins after a "big event" has occurred (Laura's death). Most of the characters are stunned and deeply saddened, but they also feel something more profound than the loss of a loved one, they respond as if the world has changed in ways they cannot quite identify. They grasp for understanding but are overwhelmed: Andy cries, as does Sarah Palmer, Donna, and the school principal. James is numb and Bobby is perplexed.

An unidentified woman screams in the school courtyard. The mill shuts down. The FBI arrives in town. The day dawns with the news of Laura's death and ushers in a world much different than the one of yesterday.

Lynch masterfully conveys a feeling of confusion in the characters; they all seem to ask, "Is this the true nature of the world? Have I been naïve to a darker universe?" Of course, there are no easy answers. Each character must learn to deal with his or her lost innocence, and must now face a reality they once chose to ignore. These themes give the pilot its power. The murderer may not be identified by the end of the show, but the characters have started to awaken.

The town of Twin Peaks is a throwback to simpler times, yet news travels fast. There is a tantalizing psychic connection between many of the people in town—a connection forged from the "free-floating guilt" (as defined by *Twin Peaks* screen-writer, Robert Engels) that pervades the area. Laura's mother realizes what has happened to her daughter before the words are spoken. Donna also realizes the truth about Laura—it only takes the appearance of a police officer at school and a glance at Laura's empty desk.

This undercurrent of guilt and tension bursts open when Laura's body is discovered. Emotions cannot be contained—in the first half-hour of the show just about everyone starts crying: Andy, Leland, Sarah, Donna, and the school principal all sob uncontrollably. These outbursts not only define character but also form a "wordless dialogue." Sobbing and shrieks create an aural landscape that propels the story as much as actual conversations. Perhaps the best example of this is when the girl screams as she runs through the school courtyard. Viewers are never told who the girl is or why she's wailing. (It may not even have anything to do with Laura's murder.) But the sound of the scream is important in the dynamic of the scene: it is the beginning of emotional release. At that moment, Donna begins to cry. Most television shows would arrive at this moment through dialogue or music. But not here. Lynch uses the scream as a sound-effect. It is sharp and startling and conveys in two seconds a mood of fear and despair that no music or dialogue could. Here at Twin Peaks High School, a high-pitched scream better represents the feelings of the students than anything else.

As themes of duality and doubling dominate the series, Lynch and Frost intertwine the gloom of Laura's death with doses of humor, thereby denying the audience any clear cue of how to react. When Truman instructs Andy to photograph Laura's body, and Andy begins to cry, it's both horrific and humorous—especially when we learn that this happens almost every time Andy encounters such a situation. When Cooper arrives in town, his unique way of looking at things adds a natural humor to the proceedings, particularly in the way his mind darts from the commonplace to the macabre, as if it's all the same to him. As he drives and records a tape for Diane he jumbles together notes and observations about what he had for lunch, the murder he's about to investigate, and the magnificent trees. When he meets Truman, he continues along these same lines. Later, after going through some of Laura's things and recording some observations, he says, "Diane, I'm holding in my hand a small box of chocolate bunnies." To contrast the absurdity of this comment, the scene jumps to the murder site where Andy is crying uncontrollably and telling Lucy, "It's horrible."

It becomes clear that Twin Peaks is place of contrasts and the inexplicable. A near-deaf, potentially senile old man is the mayor. Laura's psychiatrist, Dr. Jacoby, seems almost gleeful at Laura's death. And at the Roadhouse, a group of bikers sit quietly and listen to mellow, hypnotic music by Julee Cruise.

With *Twin Peaks*, the viewer is never sure of the importance (or lack of importance) of what appears on screen. Scenes are dense with cryptic or contradictory information that is never completely explained (flickering lights in the morgue, barking teenagers in the jail). The visuals stand on their own, and viewers are left to process what they see. What's more, the series' moody, haunting soundtrack provides *Twin Peaks* with a sense of strangeness and uncertainty. Music doesn't merely complement the images or punctuate the narrative with specific meaning; the music, like the visuals, becomes an element of mood and texture. This specific dynamic is established in the pilot, and is a style that will continue through the series.

Additional Notes

The *Twin Peaks* pilot was shot in February, 1989 in the Seattle, Washington area, specifically North Bend, Issaquah, and Bainbridge Island, Washington. Some notable, real-world locales include the Salish Lodge (used for the exterior of the Great Northern Hotel), the Mar T Café (the Double R Diner), the Weyerhaeuser Mill (Packard Saw Mill), the office of the Weyerhaeuser Mill (Twin Peaks Sheriff's Station), and the Kiana Lodge (exterior for the Blue Pine Lodge and interior for the Great Northern Hotel).

Some of the character names are based on real-life people or other fictional characters. Harry S. Truman is obviously a reference to the U.S. President of the same name. Laura Palmer's name comes from the 1944 film *Laura* (a film that will provide other names later in the series). Norma Jennings is a name derived from Norma Jean—the real-life name of famed actress, Marilyn Monroe.

The identity of the man Bobby killed will not be revealed until the film, *Fire Walk With Me*. (It was Deputy Howard from Deer Meadow.)

The song Bobby plays on the diner jukebox is titled "I'm Hurt Bad" and is from David Lynch's musical play, *Industrial Symphony #1*. Singer Julee Cruise performs two songs, "Falling," and "Into the Night," both written by David Lynch and Angelo Badalamenti. These songs appear on Cruise's first album, *Falling into the Night*.

The end credits list Father Clarence Hutchinson, although he does not appear in the pilot. (He does appear in the original script, however, where he is comforting Sarah in act 2.)

The Log Lady introduction to the pilot contains some important observations about the episode and about Laura Palmer. The Log Lady says the story "encompasses the all—it is beyond the fire, though few would know that meaning. It is a story of many, but begins with one—and I knew her. The one leading to the many is Laura Palmer. Laura is the one." The observation that the story is "beyond the fire" is cryptic. It could simply mean that the story takes place after the "fiery" events of Laura's final days (as depicted in *Fire Walk With Me*), but this seems too obvious, especially for Lynch. There could be many ways to read this comment, but one strong interpretation is to equate Laura with "fire." In the film, Laura Palmer is arguably depicted as a burning flame that was snuffed out. As the pilot begins, Laura is dead and the story is therefore "beyond the fire." What's more, the death of one person—Laura Palmer—is the event that will lead to a story of many; it functions as the transition point between film (the one) and series (the many).

Cast and Crew Comments

Sheryl Lee (*Laura Palmer*): This is the only time this has ever happened to me and it may be the only time it ever happens again. I went into the room with no knowledge of the character at all, with no script, with no scenes to read, nothing! I sat in a chair across from David and Mark and Johanna Ray. I was so nervous that I sat on my hands for the entire forty-five minute meeting. I knew if I took them out that I would be shaking! David just talked to me about where I was from and what I did. We laughed, and he talked to me about the freezing cold water.

I had no idea what the man, himself, would be like. I remember just being completely surprised when I saw him. He's a very nice looking man. He doesn't look dark, or evil, or anything like that at all! [*laughs*] He's very, very kind and he has a heart of gold. It was just wonderful to meet him! In terms of the show, it was so secretive that they really didn't tell us anything. He just talked to me about playing a dead girl, and could I stand the freezing cold water that I was going to have to be in.

Finally, at the end, he said, "So, do you want to do this?" And I said, "Yes, I'd love to do this!" So he said, "OK, let's do it!" I remember time stopped at that moment and I kept thinking, "Did I just get a job?" I looked up and all three were smiling at me, and I just kept smiling back at them. I couldn't figure out how to say, "So, umm, did you just hire me!?" I couldn't figure it out! So I didn't really say anything, I just smiled and giggled.

As I walked out of the room the casting director said, "Don't tell anyone." I said, "Don't tell anyone what?" And she said, "Don't tell anyone that you just got this job." I very calmly said, "I won't." I walked out of the office, through the room with all the other people, and then I cried the whole way home! I was so poor I couldn't get a cab. I had to walk, like fifty blocks home, and I was just in ecstasy, just crying out of gratefulness.

David Lynch (*series co-creator and executive producer*): If you start making actors read [for auditions], they come in with a preconceived thing. They read the thing [and] it's totally wrong ninety-nine percent of the time, even though they're good. It's so tormenting to actors to come in and do a cold reading. It's absurd. The person's got to fit into the part in a different way than just a cold reading. They've got to really be able to be that person. It's not just one. There could be ten or twenty, but you've got to find a person that can live in that character and make it real.

It's like building something. And you're asking everybody to get on the same track you're on. And so in the beginning—I've said this a million times—but in the beginning it's talking until you see that light bulb click. You know, that thing in their eye where they're getting the drift of the same track. And that goes for crew and cast. *Everybody.* Then we're all on the same track, and we're going along, and we're building something. An actor, I always say, has to go out on a limb where I think it's very frightening. They say goodbye to themselves, and they take on this other thing, and they gotta make it real.

Phoebe Augustine (*Ronette Pulaski*): It was my understanding that all of the big parts were cast already and they had some extra parts to cast up in Seattle. We just went in to audition and read for him. I don't know how he decided who would get which parts. I do remember being asked, when there were a few of us there, me and Sheryl Lee, "Do either of you have a problem with nudity?" And I said, "Um, I think I might." And she said, "I have no problems." [*laughs*] I think that's how I got Ronette, although today I couldn't imagine anybody else being Laura Palmer, so it worked out great.

Grace Zabriskie (*Sarah Palmer*): I think they asked me to look at the role of the receptionist [Lucy Moran]. Can you believe it? But when I walked in it was never mentioned. Never. David and I just talked. Somehow in the process, I got into a funny story that I told in a Cajun accent that had to do with a play I had done in New Orleans when I was a teenager. It came up because he had seen *The Big Easy* and I had done a Cajun accent in that. Apparently, that was when he began thinking about writing me the part for *Wild At Heart*.

Dana Ashbrook (*Bobby Briggs*): I remember walking into the audition and seeing Eric Da Re, whom I knew because he was Johanna [Ray's] son. Johanna had had me in for a few other projects. She was just always calling me in for stuff. God bless her, Johanna was really the one who "found" me. So Eric was there and it was great to see him there.

The interview with Mark and David was great. We just talked. They usually give you scenes and stuff but there was nothing like that. We had the script and I had read the script. Actually, right before I went in to the meeting I was talking to Eric about the script and saying, "Geez! All these things! The woman with the patch and the drapes and the craziness." We were just talking and laughing about it! So that was the tag I went in with. I said, "God, I love the script! I love all these things." I started talking about it. And they were laughing, too. When I started talking about the scene with the patch and the drapes they just looked at one another and giggled to themselves because they had written this funny thing.

I also talked about this theater company I was trying to start at the time. I was just being me; I wasn't trying to be the character at all. Then David said, "You know, Bobby doesn't smile a whole lot. Could you do that?" I said, "Yeah, no problem." And that was it!

Then we had this meeting with me and David and another actress, I can't remember her name, where we read a scene from the pilot—the one in the car where I talk about "happy hour in France." We pretended we were driving and I pretended I was steering. I asked David if I was supposed to do that and he said, "Yeah. Pretend like you're really there." I just did it. I don't know what happened to the girl. But the next thing I know I was testing and they only tested one person for every part. So that was it.

Everett McGill (*Big Ed Hurley*): I think David created the part for me because his nickname for me is "Big E." He's called me that from day one. I think he always envisioned the character in *Twin Peaks*. We shared an interest in hot cars. I'm a bit of a mechanic. And David was anxious to talk about all kinds of performance modifications you can do. There was a vehicle he was thinking about buying, a Studebaker Hawk, and we developed a common interest that was fun to explore. He'd always show up on the set with a question about the car, which he did buy later, and he was interested in some performance modifications. So, he'd show up on the set and say, "Big E, what about this?"

19

Catherine Coulson (*Margaret Lanterman—The Log Lady*): When [David] first got this idea and said, "You know, Catherine, someday you're going to play this girl with a log," he really had an image. And when we started the TV pilot (which he kind of sneaked me into because he didn't really think ABC would understand) he just sort of put me in on the sly, and of course she captured people's imagination.

Jack Nance (*Pete Martell*): A lot of directors have tried to form some kind of ensemble. Kyle was going to school up here [in Washington State] and he came down to Mexico City to work on *Dune*. Many directors have worked with the same people over and over. I've been in theater companies in which, over the years, you work with the same people. By the time *Twin Peaks* came along, a lot of us from in front and behind the camera—Frank Byers and some of the directors—had already worked together and knew each other. It was a dynamite thing to do.

James Marshall (*James Hurley*): I auditioned just with David. It was neat. You wished everyone auditioned that way. Just because it was the way his instincts go—as though it was like a feel. He had a feel for you. He had enough confidence as an artist that he thought, "We'll figure this out." I think he just gets a sense of people. That's what he was doing. Some people need to read you fifty-million times. I think [David's approach] has to do with the fact that he seems to know himself.

Nobody had to tell anybody anything. I think that was one of the reasons they cast that way—"We don't want to have to tell you what this guy's like." David wanted each car to race the race. He didn't want to get behind it and fix it all the time. He wanted it all up and running by itself. So that's what we did. I just felt very grateful to be cast in it. It was my favorite pilot.

Johanna [Ray] kept insisting, over and over again, that he should see me. She just would not stop. He kept refusing. He said that my head-shot was really, really, really bad. Which it was—he was totally right. It looked like "Wannabe *Teen Beat Magazine*." It was horrible. At the last minute he couldn't cast the James character and he said, "All right, fine, Johanna." She said, "Let me bring him in. You'll just see." I think he was almost angry with her: "Fine! I'll do it. I'll see him." I think he was unhappy with the people she had brought him so far and she said, "Those are the people closest to the whole character. You're asking for an off-beat type." So then she brought me in and it was all very cool. It was a very funny meeting. He was laughing and saying "You're nothing like your picture. You've got to change these head shots, they're horrible." And the way he said it was like he had made an instant decision: "Well, I want to cast you in this." I was like, "Wh- Wha?!" I was like twenty at the time.

We just hung out in a room for a half-hour. Afterwards, he said, "We've still got to bring you in for the network. We've got some stars on the show—like Mike Ontkean—he's got to read for the network. Everybody does. But I want you." I was so jazzed because I had grown up on *Eraserhead*. And that was an obscure thing because all of my friends never watched *Eraserhead*—only I did. Nobody knew what it was.

Al Strobel (*Phillip Gerard, Mike: The One Armed Man*): My agent sent a picture—just my photograph—to David. He looked at my picture and said, "OK, I want him." David has, I believe, some substantial psychic abilities. I have no idea what process went through his mind, but I never auditioned or interviewed or anything. I just showed up on the set.

David has the ability to see things almost immediately. He really has this ability to see deeper than what appears to be on the surface. That includes not only myself, as someone who has been fortunate enough to work with him, but I think he sees deeper in the larger world, also.

Kimmy Robertson (*Lucy Moran*): When I came in to read they had me look at the Shelley role, Audrey role, and Donna role. They had me look at those parts, and then also at Lucy and something else. I just went in and I never read or anything. It was just a conversation where I asked questions. I was asking David about all these specifics regarding his movies—all the coincidences, and all the names of people. He looked over at Mark and, looking back on it, I think he was flattered that someone took the time to know all this stuff. I basically interviewed him. I had this whole list of questions, not only from me, but from all my friends. No one was going to miss the opportunity where one of us was finally going to talk to Lynch live. It was so cool because we were at this tiny round table and there was one light in the ceiling right above us. It was really weird lighting. It was like I was interrogating him. [*laughs*]

Don Davis (*Major Garland Briggs*): [Getting the part] was fairly unorthodox! When they came up to do the pilot for *Twin Peaks*, my agent got me an audition for Major Briggs. I was actually filming that day on something else so my audition was at eight o'clock at night. I got there and they said, "Well, we're going to get you some sides, but David will just talk to you first." He wound up recognizing my accent and asked me where I was from. We started talking about trout fishing, because the Ozarks are known for fishing—bass and crappie and trout. We spent most of the time talking about that. There was only one real question about performance that came up. I mentioned that I had been a captain in the army and he asked if I could cry on camera. It happened that I had just done a thing called, *Beyond the Stars*, in which I played Martin Sheen's partner—it was an astronaut story. I had to cry in it because my partner was dying. So I told him,

"Yeah." And that was about it! It was the only question about acting that occurred in the interview.

My role, at least for the pilot, was really just a day-player role. We had a couple of scenes, one of which was cut. There's only about two seconds of the pilot that I'm even in. But [David] did ask at that time—on my last day of shooting—"Would you be interested in coming down to LA if we're picked up—if I made you a recurring character?" I said, "Sure!" So that's what happened.

Everett McGill: I do know that ABC approved David's cast—to a man—with the exception of me. They thought that because I had played so many heavies that I had no place on network television. In fact, that was a direct quote. And, of course, I was living in Arizona and it was almost unheard of that a cast member of a television series would be living in another state, especially when the network had to pick up the tab for the travel. I'd have to come in every week to do a role. But David fought for me. He said he wouldn't do it unless I was in it. Yeah, it was a crazy stand, but I love him for it.

Charlotte Stewart (*Betty Briggs*): David invited us to dinner. It was his birthday. It was Kyle MacLachlan, Laura Dern, Mark Frost, David, and myself. He told us that he was doing this series and he had plans for parts for us and that I would be playing this certain character. I didn't really know what it was going to be but it sounded like a lot of fun and I was excited about it.

At the time, Isabella Rossellini was supposed to play the Joan Chen part. It was written for her. Then we heard all these rumors and, all of a sudden, Isabella was out. We were all thinking, "Oh my God! Is it off?" But it was so great when everybody came together. I knew Richard Beymer from years before. I knew Russ Tamblyn; Russ and I had done a movie together with Dean Stockwell and Neil Young called *Human Highway*.

Julee Cruise (*Roadhouse Singer*): David never described any role to me. We wrote the music first. We were working on the music, mixing the music for the album [*Floating Into the Night*], and at that particular time it was so engrained in his head. That's when he was writing *Twin Peaks* with Mark Frost over the phone. So the music just naturally bled across into *Twin Peaks*. I just carried that across. It's not like he sat me down and said "OK, Julee, this is it." In fact, he didn't say anything. I think that's why David is a good director. Sometimes he doesn't say anything. You can go too far with an actor or a singer. And David sometimes doesn't say anything! He just lets someone do their own thing, or just to be confused, and it comes across.

We're all perfectionists in a way. But David oversees the whole thing. Without his vision, it doesn't matter how great a musician we are, how great my voice is, how great a musician Angelo is; without David's input I feel the music would lack. His vision catapults it into another world.

Everett McGill: I would say that generally a lot of the scenes from the pilot were shot from the hip. There was a lot of improvisation. So we might go into one scene with expectations we had from the script, and David would change the format and change the intent of the scene. And, of course, he was influenced by the powerful setting up there. The weather was changing by the minute. So sometimes we'd have to move the scene in under a shelter because it was lightly snowing, and that would change the mood. It was a wonderful experience, shooting that.

Kimmy Robertson: I was sitting there in my spot with my headphone thing on. David said, "Lucy, I want you to tell the sheriff that he's got a phone call—a very important phone call." He told me what the call was, that Jack [Nance] is calling. He said, "Be really clear. You just re-decorated; you just rearranged the furniture. Everything was taken out, cleaned, and put back. You've got to make sure he knows just which phone it is." [*laughs*] He told me which phone it was. He said, "I want you to take your time. Be clear. Be specific." He set up the whole thing for me. That was it. And Harry [Michael Ontkean] does that "move-it-along" thing with his hands! And then he has that great line, "Holy smokes!" That's my favorite.

I'm honored to be in that scene. David explained to me that Lucy is not stupid, she's just extra thorough. "She's got her finger on the pulse of this town." He always told me that, but that scene was the first time he told me.

That scene is me doing drama. When Truman says, "Don't tell anybody about the call," you can see all over my face that I was going to tell everyone. I just thought that that was drama. They say that nothing is funnier than the truth. They say that drama is when you hide the truth and comedy is when you tell the truth.

Dana Ashbrook: Here's how [the barking scene] happened: We were shooting upstairs in some sort of warehouse where they had built a jail cell. They also had a car up there and they were doing a scene between Donna Hayward and her father. It was snowing outside and cold as hell. David took me out on this little side roof and said he wanted to work with me on the end of the scene. He wanted something that I could do that was intimidating. I remember we were out there in the snow on this little roof and I said, "Well, you know, in high school at football games these guys would always bark, [*barking noise*], like that." I did a version of it. Of course, at the end he wanted me to hold it out, to make it bigger. I just went with it. I didn't think about it; I just said, "Yeah, sure." So we were out on the roof and the guy who owned the building told us, "Get the hell off the roof!" That's how it came about. Gary Hershberger jumped on board. I remember walking off of the set after doing it and Lara Flynn Boyle said, "What in the hell were you guys doing?"

James Marshall: It turned into this dog fight. That was the vibe of the thing. I played it up. We started getting creative on the pilot, with David. He started getting more and more "out there." He would do things and he wouldn't use them. I don't go over the top a lot but I thought, 'Let's just go over the top." I said, "Do you mind if I do this and we can just cut it?" We did takes that were pretty straight and pretty fine. And David could have done the whole scene on Bobby and just given me a reaction shot. Instead, I thought, "Let's go for it." We did this over-the-top, cartoony thing as though we were pit bulls glaring at each other. I didn't want it to seem that James was this little fluttery, sensitive guy. If these guys were gonna torment him and scare the hell out of him he wasn't just going to sit there and look tormented. And I did it like, "You want to play, boys? I can play." That strength, as if he was in battle.

Grace Zabriskie: His direction [for the telephone scream] was, "More! More! More! You got another one? No, you're not over the top—I'll tell you when you're over the top. More! More! More!" [*laughs*] He was determined to get something which was terrifying me. It was so over the top. And yet I knew it had to be kept real. It went so far beyond the conventions of cinematic grief that I was afraid. But I trusted him so completely.

James Marshall: [Lara Flynn Boyle and I] reshot some scenes in this little studio, this little place that was in the middle of Snoqualmie. It was upstairs, I remember. It was right outside the jail [set]. We did the jail sequence in there, too. Right outside that we had a branch with a motorcycle [for an exterior shot]. That's how simple shooting is, sometimes. In the end, what you end up with is a few faces and you can almost paint the background in—especially if the writing is really good. That's what [David] wanted. He used to talk about that: "I just want your faces."

Phoebe Augustine: During the filming of the scene on the railroad bridge there were a lot of people at the end of that track. I had to walk down the track a few times and I remember when we were taking a break I asked for David to come over so I could ask him a question, because one of the people on the crew was really freaking me out. And it was a huge crowd of people. David came over and I asked him, "That guy over there—he's really freaking me out. He's scaring me. Who is it? Does he have to be there?" It was Frank [Silva]! David said to me, "Shhh! He's the bad guy. But don't tell anyone!" [*laughs*]

Kimmy Robertson: Frank was on the set when we did the thing [for the European ending] where Harry [Goaz] was playing the trumpet, and I was playing paddleball. That was the first time I saw him. Totally freaked me out. And Little Mike [Anderson] did kinda' freak me out, too. [*laughs*] They were all walking around talking backwards. I was like, "Wow, what a cool job! So much better than my Bob's Big Boy commercial!" [*laughs*]

Frank Silva (*Killer Bob*): The day we were doing the town hall scene was actually the last day of filming on the mainland. The following day we were going to Bainbridge to the Kiana Lodge to do the Great Northern stuff. So we were doing the town hall scene and I was standing next to David and Debbie Trutnik, his secretary. David leans over and he goes, "Debbie, did you give Frank his scene yet?" And I said, "Scene? What do you mean 'scene?'" David said, "You better give it to him. We're shooting it after lunch." And I thought it's probably like one word, or one line. So then Debbie comes and brings me this huge scene in a boiler room with Kyle [MacLachlan], Michael Ontkean, and Al [Strobel] as the One Armed Man!

Kimmy Robertson: I was hired for the pilot as a guest, and they said, 'possible recurring,' which they always say to anybody who's a guest and they don't really know what they're going to do with the character. What happened was, we did the pilot, I rambled on, they liked it, and it just worked. I think that's how my part got bigger. When they screened the pilot at the Director's Guild everybody laughed after I did the phone thing. Then, when I came on again, everybody cheered. Nobody else in the pilot got the same boisterous response as I did. I was completely shocked. I couldn't shut my mouth. I have witnesses; they were there with me. Afterwards, David and Mark came up and said, "We've got plans for you."

Dana Ashbrook: I remember when we had the screening of the pilot at DGA. It was the first time where everyone came as a group and [we] really loved it. Everyone wanted to know who killed [Laura]. I told David that night, "Wow! I've never seen anything like this." He said, "Yeah, enjoy it, because it's not always this way!" It was a landmark moment for me in my career.

David Lynch: It's very interesting. In the theater, a film goes slower. The more people you have in the room, the slower the film goes. The audience—the group—their intelligence goes up. A group will get something quicker than one person, it seems to me. Also, in a group, there's a portion of the reaction that's guarded. People do not want to be [seen as] foolish. It's an interesting experience in a group. People will not cry because they will be guarded. Certain things people will laugh at, in a group. A single viewer does not have that group feel around him. There is a hair of loneliness but you see the film differently. You don't have to be guarded.

Sometimes certain things you will feel deeper or you'll have a different experience. It's tricky. You are more forgiving on your own, I think.

Sheryl Lee: So, we had shot the pilot and then it aired. And I remember that night as if it were yesterday. We had a big party at our house and lot of the cast members and crew were there. It was airing on television and the phone started ringing. People on the East Coast had just finished watching it. There was this wave of people across the United States calling as soon as it finished airing in their time zone. It never occurred to me that it was going to air on other people's televisions! I thought it was only on mine! Very surreal!

Kimmy Robertson: The pilot aired on Sunday night. On Monday morning I got three phone calls. One was Hanna-Barbera; they wanted me to audition for a cartoon show. And I had been trying to do voice-overs forever. I had thought, all I need to do is get a series and someone will hire me for cartoons. So they called. Then a publicist called. Then someone else called and told me that David Letterman had asked if David Lynch could come on his show. He couldn't, so he asked for Kyle, but he couldn't go. So he said, "I want Kimmy Robertson then." I was his third choice. And I screamed so loud! I jumped around my living room forever! My neighbor, who lived like three houses away, came over. She was a writer for *TV Guide* and she came over with her hat and glasses on and a pen and paper. She said, "I know something wonderful happened and I want to write it down!"

Robert Engels (*series screenwriter and season two co-producer*): I think that was a landmark. When people say, "Boy, that was a good pilot," I always say, "I'll tell you what a good pilot is—measure it up against [*Twin Peaks*]." Still, to this day, people say, "*Twin Peaks* was the best pilot I've ever seen." I mean, from people who were not fans of the show! They can tell you when they saw it. Lots of people felt it was one of the five best *movies* of the year. The simple thing about pilots is that you don't have to end the story. Sometimes they get demeaned by that because you leave everything hanging. But you can turn around and say, "Leave the ending out and the *Twin Peaks* pilot is still pretty cool."

Charlotte Stewart: We had absolutely no idea *Twin Peaks* was going to take off like it did. We were all just stunned. Within three weeks after it hit the air, it was everywhere. I really was hoping it would be something. David was pretty well-known by that time. I felt it was going to do something interesting because it was so unusual. Of course, we didn't know any of the style of it. Until you saw it on the air it was hard to say. There was that wonderful music and Julee Cruise. It was all so dark and weird. But you didn't necessarily get that sense while filming it. It came later.

David Lynch: I'm always learning. But each thing is different. So what I think you're doing—you could say it like this—you're *remembering* different things. It's like the thing is out there already and you are remembering it. It seems like that, because how else does it come together?

Episode 1 (Script number: 1001; First televised April 12, 1990)

Featuring: Alan Ogle (Janek Pulaski), Michele Milantoni (Suburbis Pulaski), Jill Rogosheske (Trudy), and Frank Silva (Killer Bob)

Written by Mark Frost and David Lynch; Directed by Duwayne Dunham; Edited by Jonathan P. Shaw

Saturday, February 25, 1989:

Act 1: Audrey Horne flirts with Cooper at breakfast. Doc Hayward delivers the preliminary autopsy report: Laura's cause of death was loss of blood due to numerous shallow wounds. Within the last twelve hours she had had sexual relations with at least three men. Hayward believes Ronette was attacked by the same perpetrator. Shelly finds a bloody shirt in Leo's laundry bag and hides it. Cooper interrogates James, who denies having the other half of the heart necklace. Leo searches for his shirt.

Act 2: Mike is worried because he and Bobby cannot pay Leo the money they owe him. Donna tells her mother that she loves James. Ed tells Truman that he believes he was drugged by the Roadhouse bartender, Jacques Renault. Nadine Hurley tells Norma that she is inventing a completely silent drape-runner. James asks Ed for help from the "Bookhouse Boys." Cooper warns Bobby and Mike to stay away from James.

Act 3: Cooper recognizes that Truman and Josie are romantically involved. Catherine Martell confers with Ben Horne about their "next step" to get the sawmill land. Ben suggests arson. Sarah has a nightmarish vision of a man at the foot of Laura's bed. Hawk learns that Ronette worked at the perfume counter at Horne's Department Store.

Act 4: Ben is angry that Audrey told the Norwegians Laura was murdered. Major Briggs lectures Bobby and slaps a cigarette out of Bobby's mouth. The Log Lady tells Cooper that her log saw something on the night of the murder. Leo beats Shelly because his shirt is missing. Dr. Jacoby listens to a tape Laura made for him. She mentions a mystery man. As Jacoby listens, he removes the other half of the heart necklace from its hiding place in a hollow coconut.

Episode 1 suffers from being positioned between two of the most captivating episodes in the series (the pilot and episode 2, of course). Still, there is a strength to the episode, evident in the show's distinct, well-drawn characters, all of whom gain better definition as the story progresses. In the first scene, Cooper mentions to Diane his keen interest in the deaths of Marilyn Monroe and John F. Kennedy. Cooper is established as a real-world character (i.e., someone from outside Twin Peaks) even though he remains somewhat eccentric. The episode also provides more information about Truman's relationship with Josie, explores Donna's emotions about James and Laura, and clarifies the dysfunctional relationship between Ben and Audrey. Many of the scenes barely move the plot forward; rather, they better establish the characters in the narrative and make them an organic part of the *Twin Peaks* universe.

Audrey becomes more complex and interesting in this episode. Here, and in other first season-episodes, she exhibits some possible emotional and psychological issues—issues that could help explain her manipulative behavior. In the pilot, she pokes a pencil into the bottom of concierge Judy's Styrofoam coffee cup, then pulls it out, spilling coffee all over the desk and papers. When she hears that the Norwegians should not be disturbed, she immediately tells them about Laura's death (thus ending their interest in the Ghostwood development deal). In episode 1, she joins Cooper for breakfast and delivers this memorable and telling line: "Johnny's twenty-seven and he's in the third grade. He's got emotional problems; it runs in the family." She doesn't understand the possible self-referential nature of the comment. Sherilyn Fenn's performance is quite good; she plays Audrey as a character who's a little bit removed from the everyday— and also as someone who seeks attention. The theme within the character will continue in episode 2, where her beguiling solo dance at the Double R Diner calls attention to her eccentricities.

A number of important events occur in the episode such as the introduction of Leo's bloody shirt, the re-introduction of the One Armed Man, and the suggestion to commit arson by Ben Horne. Still, this is a relatively sedate episode. The investigation into Laura's murder is just getting started and the narrative will continue to gain momentum as the season progresses.

Leo's attack on Shelly with the soap-filled sock is chilling. Part of this goes to Eric Da Re's sharp performance. (Da Re is highly underrated in the show; his Leo is uniformly menacing and creepy.) But the scene is effective for other reasons: sound effects and music provide a terrifying atmosphere, and the absence of graphic violence forces the viewer to imagine the horror of the scene. It's an unnerving way to convey Leo's abusive actions.

Leo's other behaviors raise some questions: If Jacques used Leo's shirt to stop his bleeding after Leo hit him at the cabin the night Laura died, how does Leo end up with the shirt? Did he take it with him? If so, why would it end up in his truck? After all, he drove his red Corvette to the cabin. (This brings up a whole other problem: It is established that he was already out in the truck, but somehow he came back to the house to drive the Corvette to the cabin—all without Shelly noticing.) Why move the shirt to the truck? Perhaps he wanted Shelly to wash it with the rest of his clothes, so he put it in the bag. But if he took all those deliberate precautions, why would he look for the shirt in the truck after handing Shelly the bag? It's a minor issue, but it stands out from the intricate plotting of the rest of the story.

Director Duwayne Dunham was a logical and appropriate choice to direct the first hour-long episode. As editor of the pilot, he had an intimate knowledge of the world and its characters. Dunham has commented that because time had passed between shooting the pilot and filming the following seven episodes he was able to help the actors "re-find their characters."

Dunham brought an editorial sensibility to the directing of the episode. He framed scenes so that all the action could be conveyed in a single shot, thereby easing the need to cut to close-ups or to rely on action/reaction shots. When commenting on the episode for the Artisan DVD, Dunham discussed the Bobby and Mike jail scene (act 2) and the Audrey and Ben scene (act 4) and how the action in each was choreographed so as to require a single shot. Note that at some point in both scenes the characters are positioned so that they both face the camera—this practice is sometimes referred to as a "two-shot west," a classic soap opera technique.

Additional Notes

This episode marks the first appearance of Killer Bob in the *Twin Peaks* narrative.

Cooper opens the episode with comments about Marilyn Monroe. Before working on *Twin Peaks*, Lynch and Frost were preparing to make *Goddess*—a film about the life and death of Marilyn Monroe, based on the book of the same title. Cooper's comment undoubtedly stems from their research into this project.

There is a Sherlock Holmes reference when Truman says, "I'm beginning to feel a bit like Dr. Watson." Mark Frost is an admirer of the Holmes stories and further explored the character's origins in his novels, *The List of 7* and *The 6 Messiahs*.

When Hawk delivers James to Ed he makes the Bookhouse Boys signal—a finger moved vertically along the cheek, just below the eye. Although the Bookhouse Boys are first mentioned in this episode, the signal will not be explicitly used in connection with them until episode 3.

When Cooper enters the sheriff's station at the beginning of the episode, some men are remodeling the interior. It looks as if they are removing the glass foyer that is visible in the pilot. The episode was shot on a set that was structurally different from the real location used in the pilot. To reconcile these differences, the producers made an effort to show why the interior has changed.

Many viewers once noticed a curious image that appears in James' flashback about Laura in act 1. According to the script, James and Laura are supposed to be at a "wishing well." When the camera shows the close-up of Laura's hands breaking the heart necklace, a face appears reflected in the water. It is visible in the upper left corner. For some time, (due to the poor quality of the existing home video versions) fans speculated that the face looked like Leland laughing. The improved quality of DVD and Blu-ray versions, however, shows that the face belongs to James Marshall (i.e., James) who was likely present when close-up "coverage" was being shot of the necklace. This is another instance of unintended reflections making their way into the show. (The most famous, of course, is the reflection of Frank Silva appearing in a mirror behind Grace Zabriskie when she screams at the end of the European version of the pilot.)

The "fish-in-the-percolator" scene was inspired by a real-life incident that happened to Duwayne Dunham: his kids put raw hotdogs in a thermos of hot coffee.

In this episode, different actors portray Maria and Suburbis Pulaski (Ronette's parents) from those who appeared in the pilot.

The first draft of episode 1 was completed on July 12, 1989; it was later revised on August 10 & 18, 1989.

Notable Deleted Scenes

Act 1: Several scenes from early in the first act were cut from the final version. Truman is shown at his "rustic log house" feeding the chickens in the chicken coop. Andy and Lucy are making a donut run at "Wagon Wheel Do-nuts," where banners read, "Go ahead; make my donut" and "Square deals on round donuts." Truman drives by and sees Andy "carrying a stack of donut boxes up to his neck." These scenes were likely cut for time reasons. While they help to better establish the characters and their routines, they did little to advance the plot.

During Cooper's breakfast conversation with Audrey, a few pieces of dialogue about Ben Horne were cut. At one point, Audrey says, "My father was crazy about Laura. He bought her a pony when she was nine, but he let her father say it was from him. Its name was Troy." This idea was later used in Jennifer Lynch's *Secret Diary of Laura Palmer* (although there, Troy was a gift for Laura's twelfth birthday, not ninth).

Act 2: In Donna's heart-to-heart conversation with her mother, she reveals that she and Laura made a pact to get away from Mike and Bobby. "I think Bobby's dangerous, I think he's capable of almost anything." This dialogue reinforces the menacing nature of Bobby (as revealed in James' dialogue the night before). As the series progressed, of course, Bobby's threatening nature was tempered and he became more of a misguided youth rather than a hoodlum. Deleting these lines here may have been the first steps in softening the character.

The next scene shows Leland in his office at the Great Northern Hotel making funeral arrangements. He becomes frustrated while talking on the phone, then "gets up, crosses to a cabinet stereo, turns on the sound of a modern jazz quartet record, 9/4 time, about as loud as it can go." Benjamin Horne catches the whole affair and tells Leland's secretary to "take him to the lounge and call Dr. Jacoby." She leads Leland away and Ben finishes the conversation on the phone with the funeral director, warning "Mr. Formaldehyde" not to take advantage of the tragedy. This scene presents the first evidence of Leland's mental imbalance—something that does not occur until late in the second episode of the series.

Act 3: Sarah Palmer has a frightening vision of Bob. But the script does not describe Bob crouching at the end of Laura's bed. Instead, as Sarah is "looking down a long [hospital] corridor, a frightening looking man we haven't seen before comes racing towards us at full speed. We hear a monstrous sound. Just as he's about to reach us we cut to Sarah." (This scene was likely shot—Frank Silva discussed shooting something similar to what is described in the script. See Appendix 2.)

Act 4: Dr. Jacoby listens to a tape Laura made in which she describes part of the dream Cooper will have in the next episode: "You're always bugging me to tell you what my dreams are—let me tell you about this one I had last night; it was a doozy . . . I was in this strange room and there was this little man and this other older man I'd never seen before either, but they both seemed to know me . . . there was music . . . and I was telling all my secrets to the older man." These lines were likely cut so as not to reveal details about the actual dream sequence that would be shown in the next episode.

Cast and Crew Comments

Don Davis: Dana [Ashbrook] and I hit it off right from the first. Charlotte Stewart—the woman who played my wife [Betty Briggs]—is one of the nicest people I've ever met in my life. We just really hit it off. Dana and I always got along well. And we're total opposites. It was one of those things where you start out assuring each other that it's only acting! There's that one scene at the dinner table where I knock the cigarette out of his mouth. Because I spent a life being an athlete and then a military man, and then doing the stunt stuff, I was worried about hurting him. And the opposite was true. He kept saying, "C'mon, Don, hit me!" [laughs]

Charlotte Stewart: I don't think I did a very good job in [that scene]. Because of the technicality of the way the cigarette had to be in the meatloaf, I wish we had done it again. I had other ideas on it. But more people mention that scene because it is really odd.

Dana Ashbrook: I maybe didn't understand the whole picture of what was going on—or unaware of some of the things that were probably going on in David's mind. I could sometimes fall into trying to be weird for the sake of being weird. I didn't want to do that. But you know what? It was all about trying to make this character "different-but-the-same" as everyone I've ever met: The kind of guys I would have grown up with, a conglomeration of all those types of people—people that I maybe would want to be and [also] people I didn't want to hang out with. I think a lot of the characters had the personality of the actor, or grew from the personality of the actor.

Episode 2 (Script number: 1002; First televised April 19, 1990)

Guest Starring: Miguel Ferrer (Albert Rosenfield) and Victoria Catlin (Blackie O'Reilly)

Featuring: Michael J. Anderson (Man From Another Place), Frank Silva (Killer Bob), Kim Lentz (One Eyed Jack's bartender), Charlie Spradling (Swabbie)

Written by Mark Frost and David Lynch; Directed by David Lynch; (Dream Sequence Director of Photography Ron Garcia); Edited by Jonathan P. Shaw

The events in this episode begin on Saturday night, February 25 (continuing from the previous episode), then, beginning with act 2, move to the morning of Sunday February 26, 1989:

> Act 1: Jerry Horne interrupts the Horne family dinner. Ben tells Jerry that Laura Palmer has been killed and that the Norwegians left. Ben and Jerry meet Blackie O'Reilly, the "proprietor" of One Eyed Jack's, a brothel/casino just over the Canadian border. Bobby and Mike meet Leo in the woods. Someone hides behind a tree in the distance. Leo gives them half of the drugs and wants the rest of his money. Leo threatens Bobby and Mike.

> Act 2: Nadine becomes angry at Ed because he spilled grease on her drape runners. Bobby promises to kill Leo if he hurts Shelly again. Cooper tells Truman, Andy, Hawk, and Lucy about a dream that gave him an unusual "deductive technique." He will use this technique to discover who the "J" in Laura's diary might be. As Truman reads from a list of names, Cooper throws a rock at a bottle. At Dr. Jacoby's name, Cooper strikes—but does not break—the bottle. At Shelly's name, Cooper accidentally strikes Andy. At Leo's name, Cooper breaks the bottle.

> Act 3: At the Double R, Donna watches Audrey slowly dance to the "dreamy" music on the jukebox. Albert Rosenfield arrives and is rude to everyone. A jubilant Nadine tells Ed that his spilled oil made her drape-runner completely silent. Josie opens a safe and finds two ledgers for the mill. Leland dances with Laura's picture. Sarah tries to stop him, but the glass on the picture breaks and cuts her hand.

> Act 4: Cooper has a dream. He is older and sitting in a chair in a red room. A "Little Man From Another Place" shakes nearby. The One Armed Man says, "Through the darkness of futures past/The magician longs to see/One chance (chants) out between two worlds/Fire Walk With Me." His name is Mike, and the other man's name is Bob. Bob promises to kill again. Cooper sees a woman sitting across from him. The little man has good news: "That gum you like is going to come back in

style." He says the woman is his cousin and she, "looks almost exactly like Laura Palmer." Cooper insists that she *is* Laura Palmer. The woman says, "I feel like I know her but sometimes my arms bend back." The little man says, "She's filled with secrets." Laura kisses Cooper and whispers in his ear. Cooper awakes. He calls Truman and says he knows who killed Laura Palmer.

David Lynch's episodes of *Twin Peaks* have a sharper, more dangerous feel to them than those by other directors. There is a pervasive threat of violence throughout. Bobby, Mike, and especially Leo are presented as menacing characters, and even Catherine and Nadine come across as threatening. When these characters are angry, they have no subtlety.

It may be cliché to describe Lynch's work as "dreamy," but this episode has a more otherworldly feel than most. Audrey's dance at the Double R is a great example. Lynch lingers on the slow-moving Audrey as she moves to the music. Audrey is lost in the experience, detached from the physical world. It is a beautiful sequence but also sad. When Audrey loses herself to the dance she exposes some of her inner self. She is not happy, nor is she at peace; rather, she seems lost and confused. In her preceding conversation with Donna there is a searching quality to the character, as if she is looking for a way out of some trap. (This sad, longing aspect to Audrey's character will fade as the series progresses; she becomes less melancholy and more impulsive, particularly in the second season.)

If Lynch is adept at conveying anger and sadness, he is equally good at depicting humor. Episode 2 is filled with little moments that make the characters rich and endearing. Ben and Jerry Horne gorge themselves on French baguettes; Andy is hit by one of Cooper's rocks but bravely soldiers on; Truman takes Cooper aside to confirm that his rock-throwing idea came from a dream (to which Cooper simply smiles and replies, "Yes"); Cooper inexplicably tweaks Truman's nose before they go to meet Albert. All these incidents show the playful side to Lynch, a director who is willing to step away from the narrative to dwell on curious or unusual behavior. Lynch revels in the "quirky" moments, and the story is enriched because of it.

Episode 2 will always be known as the "dream episode." No television series had ever devoted so much time to abstract, surreal imagery like that depicted in act 4. Cooper's dream is positioned as a crucial piece of the narrative—a puzzle whose solution will lead to the murderer's identity. But the dream sequence is arguably nothing but visual poetry by Lynch, an ad-libbed sequence developed to provide an ending to the pilot for its overseas release. Originally, this "European ending" had little connection with the *Twin Peaks* story; it was something Lynch had created at the last minute of filming in an attempt to make the pilot a stand-alone work. When describing the creation of the ending, Lynch said he was "just winging stuff for the ending we had to do," and that "nothing was really that thought out."[2] The rest of the *Twin Peaks* narrative—both on TV and film—will be driven by this unscripted, spontaneous piece of filmmaking. The result will be an astonishing and revolutionary (and sometimes convoluted) television series.

Lynch makes an unusual creative comment about the sequence in the Log Lady introduction for the episode. There, the Log Lady says, "Sometime ideas, like men, jump up and say 'hello'. They introduce themselves, these ideas, with words. Are they words? These ideas speak so strangely." These observations seem to describe how Lynch happened upon the idea of the Red Room; it was an idea that quite likely jumped up and said, "Hello."

Additional Notes:

The ending of the European release of the pilot is not depicted as a dream, but as a series of real events. In that alternate ending, Cooper meets the One Armed Man in a hospital, and Cooper and Truman confront Bob in the basement. The One Armed Man shoots and kills Bob, before dying himself. The story jumps ahead twenty-five years where Cooper, in the Red Room, meets the Little Man and Laura. The sequence contains one of the most debated pieces of dialogue in the *Twin Peaks* narrative: When the One Armed Man delivers his poem, he either says, "One *chance* out" or "One *chants* out." Syntactically, "chance" makes more sense in the sentence: The magician sees one chance to escape. Others argue that the magician "chants" the words, "Fire walk with me" in order to get "out" from between worlds. Still others argue that the sentence means the magician is chanting "out loud," even if it is redundant (if you are chanting, you are already speaking out loud). Al Strobel, who played the One Armed Man, has said that the original scripted words for the poem contained the word "chance" but that Lynch crossed it out and wrote "chants" before filming the scene. What's more, Lynch's 1994 book of photography, *Images*, reproduces the poem with the word "chants." The scripts for *Twin Peaks*, however, use the word "chance." It appears, then, as if both words were intended at different times.

Episode 2 marks the first appearance of the soap opera, *Invitation to Love*, although its appearance here in the story is curious. This episode of *Twin Peaks* takes place during a Sunday and it is unlikely a soap opera would air on that day. (There are two possible explanations: Shelly may be watching a video recording of the show, or, since she sees only the soap logo, she may be watching a commercial for *Invitation to Love*.)

There is a mistake in the show that may have resulted during the editing of the episode. In act 4, Catherine asks Pete about Cooper's visit. She asks,

"What did that FBI man want today?" However, Cooper visited Josie and Pete the day before. Episode 2 begins on Saturday night—the night of the previous episode—and this scene may have been intended for act 1 rather than act 4.

When Albert and his team arrive, Lucy is sitting at her desk reading a book titled, "Tibet." Earlier in the episode, Cooper gave Truman, Hawk, and Andy a lesson about Tibet and how a related "deductive technique involving mind-hand coordination operating hand-in-hand with the deepest levels of intuition" could help him solve the Laura Palmer murder.

Singing and music play important roles in this episode. Audrey tells Donna that Ben used to sing to Laura. Later, Leland dances with Laura's picture. And in Cooper's dream, the Little Man From Another Place dances as his "cousin" (Laura) walks over and whispers into Cooper's ear.

There are many other interesting items to note from this episode: Nadine's super-strength is exhibited for the first time (this will become more prominent in the next season); the identity of the mysterious person in the woods with Leo (in act 1) will not be revealed in either the first or second season; the Horne brothers are named Ben and Jerry, which is probably a reference to the ice cream brand; One Eyed Jack's is also the name of a Marlon Brando Western (as Donna acknowledges in episode 4); and, finally, Ben Horne's sonnet to Blackie is Shakespeare, Sonnet #18.

The red motif at One Eyed Jack's parallels the Red Room. In commentary about this episode, series production designer, Richard Hoover, revealed that the red drapes seen at One Eyed Jacks are the same drapes used in the Red Room scenes. This resulted in a circular structure to the episode: the story begins and ends with "red room" scenes, both "across borders." Ben and Jerry cross a geographical border (into Canada to visit One Eyed Jacks) and Cooper passes through a mental border (as he dreams himself into the Red Room).

In his commentary for the Artisan DVD release, cinematographer Frank Byers, the director of photography for the entire series (except the pilot), discusses the look of the series as a whole, and this episode in particular: Byers explained how he strove to provide a warm look to the interiors, emphasizing red, orange, and brown tones. Exteriors were more difficult, because he had to make the bright sunny environs of southern California look like the Pacific Northwest. In particular, Byers mentions the rock-throwing scene, which contains a lot of bright sunshine in the background. (Note, however, the final, wide shot; the sky has become overcast.) Byers described how he used wide-angle lenses to provide a more cinematic look to the show, even during close-ups. Lynch preferred the show to look this way, and Byers used a *noir* film—Orson Welles's *Touch of Evil*—as a template for composing these kinds of shots.

A number of new characters are introduced in this episode, including Jerry Horne, Albert Rosenfield, Blackie O'Reilly and The Little Man From Another Place.

The first draft of episode 2 was completed on August 2, 1989; it was later revised on August 10 & 11, 1989.

Notable Deleted Scenes

Episode 2 begins in the residence wing of the Great Northern. The family is gathered around the dinner table, but Audrey, Sylvia, and Johnny are mostly just staring at their food. Ben finishes his steak and excuses himself so that he and Jerry can have a meeting. Jerry dances around the table, addressing each family member with a silly rhyme, and concludes by saying, "And here goes Jerry with Brother Horne, long-gone like turkeys through the corn!" (This line is identical to the one Laura tells James early in *Fire Walk With Me*: "I'm gone . . . long gone like a turkey through the corn." The lines likely originate from an old American folk song sometimes titled, *Lost John* or *Long Gone*.)

Later, Catherine talks with Pete about Cooper's visit. She wants to know if Cooper asked about her brother, Andrew. Pete says that he overheard mention of the accident: "You know, the usual, how no one found his body. Mostly they talked about Laura." Andrew is a much more dominant figure in the scripts, but virtually absent from the earlier episodes of *Twin Peaks*. Perhaps Frost and Lynch deleted the explicit references to the missing body, realizing that these might telegraph Andrew's possible reappearance later in the series.

Act 3: Truman and Cooper engage in some inconsequential small-talk as the sheriff drops him off at the Great Northern. Cooper enters the hotel bar, where Ben and Jerry are tossing cashews into the air and catching them with their mouths. Introductions are exchanged (Cooper asks, "Is that Jerry with a 'J?'"). Cooper mentions that he's already met Audrey, "a charming and attractive girl. You must be very proud." Ben is surprised at this description for Audrey, but tells Cooper to sleep well. "I will," he responds. "The bed is almost exactly the right degree of firmness."

Act 4: The fourth act features Cooper's "dream sequence." The script follows almost exactly the final nineteen-plus minutes of the "European ending" produced for the overseas version of the pilot. There were a few new scripted scenes, however, that did not make the final cut of episode 2.

Cooper records one final message to Diane before going to bed: "Run a check for me on a Jerry Horne, Twin Peaks businessman, Jerry with a j . . . . Nothing specific. Call it an instinct. Check that; intuition. An instinct is when you get hungry." He also requests checks on Dr. Jacoby and Leo, then says, "The air here is as fresh and crisp as a cracker; you don't sleep, you slumber. Good night, Diane." This scene shows that Cooper has some strong suspicions regarding Jerry Horne. This line of inquiry is not pursued in the televised version of *Twin Peaks*. Jerry Horne was never a strong suspect in Laura's murder, primarily because he had such a good alibi: he had been out of town.

At the Palmer home, Leland talks to Madeleine on the phone. (Madeleine's name was spelled differently in many places: the script for episode 2 spells it Madelaine, later scripts and the Star Pics collector cards spelled it Madeleine; *The Secret Diary of Laura Palmer* spelled it Madeline.) This scene follows Cooper's message to Diane. Cooper made his recording as 1:18 a.m.; why does Leland—or Maddy—call so late? Leland tells Sarah that Madeleine ("Donald's girl") will be driving in for Laura's funeral. We never find out who Donald is (other than Maddy's father), though we do learn in the second season that Maddy's mother is named Beth.

Cast and Crew Comments

Miguel Ferrer (*FBI Agent Albert Rosenfield*): Lynch contacted my representatives after he saw *Robocop*, and said he wanted to use me in his next picture called, *One Saliva Bubble*, which was lost in that whole break-up with De Laurentiis. Years later, a call came from Lynch-Frost and they said, "He's doing a TV series and would you do this recurring role? We'll send you a script." I said, "You don't even need to send me a script, anything to do with David Lynch—if he wants me to carry a spear—the answer is yes!" They said, "No, no, we'll send you a couple of scripts." So they sent me episodes one and two, and no pilot—and no copy of the pilot. So, I'm reading episodes one and two thinking, "What the hell is going on?!" I read it four times, and I was lost! [*laughs*] I had a meeting with Mark Frost, and I went in and I'm sitting there, and, he's sitting there, and he says, "So, man, we're really glad you're on board." I said, "Hmm. Me, too." He said, "Is there anything you want to talk about?" I said, "No, it's great. This is going to be . . . great." He looks at me, and I must have had this look on my face, and he said, "Have you seen the pilot?" And I said, "No." He said, "OK, that explains everything. Trudy! Get a copy of the pilot! Go watch this. Call me on Monday."

I remember my dear, dear friend, Brandon Lee was over, and I said, "Watch this Lynch thing with me. They want me to do this TV show. Let's sit back and watch this." So we opened up a couple of beers and watched the pilot of *Twin Peaks*. And it was unbelievable! We didn't say a word to each other the whole two hours! It was just incredible. It was the kind of TV I had never seen. I'll never forget that endless shot of the telephone cord. Oh, man! It affected me as much as any movie I had ever seen. The two of us just sat there and said, "Let's watch it again!" And we did! I couldn't wait to call Mark Frost and just say, "God bless you. It's phenomenal!"

Kimmy Robertson: [The rock-throwing scene] was fabulous. We were out there in Malibu Lake and David set it all up. And he doesn't ever tell anybody things like why we're sitting in a row, or why I'm writing on the chalkboard. And why Andy is way over there. He said, "You just have to hit the bottle, Kale"—he always called Kyle, Kale—I guess he reminded him of cabbage. [*laughs*] He said, "Just try to hit the bottle." When he got to a certain one, he said, "OK, this time I want you to hit the bottle." You could almost hear humming in the air; he had worked the energy up so much. It was a real scene that was happening. He wanted to shoot the whole thing from beginning to end. He said, "So on this one you're going to hit it, Kale." So he hit it. And I jumped up and screamed! I wasn't supposed to! That was unbelievable! It was so incredible—it was David who did that. He put so much energy into scenes. That scene, for me, is one of the best proofs of his magic. I think we thought we were ad-libbing but it was just David's direction. Maybe he's got all these alternate personalities in there and he just hires people he knows he can "inhabit."

And then he said to Andy [Harry Goaz], "OK, you're going to pretend you got hit by a rock." And Harry had put a rock in his hand and he put his hand to his head and threw the rock out—if you look at it really slowly, it doesn't work. But the scene works; it looks like the rock "*pee-yonged*" off his head! [*laughs*] He doesn't quite hit the ground—"I'm OK, Lucy!" I was about peeing my pants! That was so funny!

Grace Zabriskie: Something happened during that scene where Leland and I dance and we fight over the picture. It is one of the things I will never forget about David Lynch. We were fighting over the picture and the glass actually broke. I cut myself. David didn't realize it, no one said, "Cut!" and so I kept going. At the end of the take, David saw that I was wounded and he came and got me, sat me down on the couch, sent for ice, and—I swear to God—he sat there for twenty minutes holding my hand above my head.

Everett McGill: I do remember that David had a very specific set of actions that he carefully set up, such as the noise of that exercise machine that [Nadine] was on. I remember that he was very concerned that the sound guys be able to pick up that noise. He felt that it was a vital element to the scene—an irritating, clacking sort of thing. And the grease—he personally attended to putting the grease on my hands. He wanted it to be on in such a way that it was a real disaster waiting to happen. He set the parameters up so that the action would spring from that kind of foundation. It's such a clever way of making the situation just right so that it's a launching pad for the performance. And you might not think that those things make a difference, but they really do.

Richard Beymer (*Benjamin Horne*): I didn't have a handle on the part yet, nor did I know about David. David has his own secret. He isn't the kind of guy who shares his vision with everyone. He just asks you to do something. He doesn't sit down and say, "The reason I think he's doing this is because of this and this and this." You know—talking to an actor about motivation and all that. He'll just say, "I think it would be great in this scene if you stood on your head." [*laughs*] And, I mean, that's all there is! And you say, "OK."

In the case [of the baguettes], we were ready to shoot and he said, "Really devour that baguette. Really chew into it." And we did a take. I remember I didn't go for it; I was new to the character and I thought, "Well, he's a sophisticated guy and he's at the table with his family. How would this guy, all of a sudden, act like a guy who is just chowing down?" So I went for it, but not enough. David said, "No, no, no. I really want you to devour it." So I still wasn't getting it! My head was still saying, "Sophisticated guy, Armani suit—it doesn't go together." So we did it again and he said, "No, no, no." We had to do about four or five takes, until I just abandoned my thoughts. David said, "I want you to stuff your mouth so much that I don't even understand what your words are." At a certain point I gave up the reasoning behind it and did it. And later on, as the months went by and I thought about that scene again, I realized I could have gone far more than I did. I later knew more about what David wanted and the more fun I could have had. So that was my own little lesson. But, finally, I just went for it as much as I did. But my head was caught somewhere else, in characterization, and it took me a little time to catch on to what it was all about.

Kimmy Robertson: I had been talking to the art department to please get me a book on Tibet. I was supposed to be just sitting there in that scene. I said, "No, I've got to be reading a book on Tibet." Because if Cooper has explained all this, I've got to be up on it. Well, nobody in the art department would get the book for me. I didn't explain in earnest that it has to be done because David would want it. So we're there in the office and before we're about to shoot, I said, "David, I need to be reading a book on Tibet. Wouldn't Lucy be reading about Tibet?" He said, "Oh my God! Yes! Quick! Get a book on Tibet down here right now! I need it in two minutes!" So the art department left and they came back with this big book. I enjoy when people notice that. To me, that was what David's stuff was all about—matching details.

Grace Zabriskie: [When Donna comes to visit] I start screaming and Leland runs in to hold me. I'm screaming, but there's an extra scream in there—and that's where it turns funny. There's an extra scream after what should have been the beginning of quieting down. If you watch it again I know you'll understand exactly what I'm talking about. Suddenly, if you're open, it's funny. That extra scream was an example of understanding what David was doing and being able to give it to him.

Everett McGill: We would always sit down at the beginning of a rehearsal session and talk about our characters: what we would like to see the characters do, where we would like to see the characters go. And David just liked to generally talk about those things and get some ideas. Get our feelings for them and our displeasure, or happiness, or delight, or whatever—just get a feel for us. It was a good way of opening up in preparation for rehearsal of the scene. He's smart. I think we were all pretty happy with where the characters were.

Michael J. Anderson (*The Little Man From Another Place*): In this business you shoot a lot of things. I've done a lot of films that never even emerged. That particular thing with the talking backwards, and the Red Room, and the shadows, and all that—nobody had any idea what it meant at the time we were shooting it. And I didn't expect that I'd ever see it again!

I think when Agent Cooper first arrived, his primary experience was that he was learning about Laura Palmer, but the truth of it was, he was falling in love with her. So when he went into the waiting room—which is like your subconscious—there was the Little Man [saying] there's always music in the air and pretty songs, because Cooper was falling in love with Laura Palmer.

Al Strobel: I did my little cameo bit for the pilot and David asked me if I would stay beyond my time on the set. And of course I said, "Sure!" The next day I went back to the old VA hospital in Seattle where this particular scene was being shot. It was a kind of a spooky place in itself—it was an old, old, old VA hospital. I sat around while they were doing stuff. I didn't know what was going on. David was talking to various people and he said, "My little black book! Go get my little black book!" So they got that—and I'm just sitting in this drab green hallway—and all of a sudden this hastily typed three-or-four page scene is presented to me. And he says, "OK, that's your scene." I looked at it and it's not just a simple scene, it's mostly written in poetry.

In normal film dialogue, if you can get the gist of it you can kind of paraphrase it and make it work. But if you're dealing with poetry you have to be letter perfect. And much of this was poetry: "Through the darkness of future past/The magician longs to see/One chants (and that's chant with a "t") out/Fire walk with me." That's the verse part of Mike's speech, but the rest of it is written in a very loose verse, so that if any of the words are changed, or paraphrased, it doesn't have the same impact. So David showed this thing to me and said to look at it, and ten minutes later they were saying, "OK, we're ready!" [*laughs*] It was probably the thirty years of training I had before, and the empathetic sense I have with David, that allowed me to be able to do all that cold.

Frank Silva: There's this monologue that Bob has to do. And David's saying, "See this? We do this scene. And see these four lines here? Well, that's a song, Frank. Those are lyrics. Make up a tune. Just make something up." So I was totally flipping out. They're running around looking for a location—they didn't even have the location for this scene yet. We're running late. It's now probably 11:00 at night. We have to catch the last ferry to Bainbridge at 1:30. We're still trying to shoot this stupid scene. So I didn't know what I was doing. I thought, "Here I am, I'm a crew member. If I'm horrible, everybody's going to laugh at me. I'm going to be this big joke doing this scene." So every ounce of energy, every ounce of everything, was drawn up. I don't know how I did it.

David Lynch: Any idea conjures up a world. It doesn't matter what [medium] it is—it can be a short thing but it has a certain feel. It has its own thing and you can feel it. When you start working there it just comes up stronger and stronger.

Episode 3 (script number 1003; First televised April 26, 1990)

Guest Starring: Miguel Ferrer (Albert Rosenfield), Royce D. Applegate (Father Clarence), and Jed Mills (Wilson Mooney)

Featuring: Jill Rogosheske (Trudy), Brett Vadset (Joey Paulson), Clay Wilcox (Bernard Renault), Erika Anderson (Selina Swift: "Emerald/Jade" on Invitation to Love), *Lance Davis (Martin Hadley: "Chet" on* Invitation to Love), *and Peter Michael Goetz (Evan St. Vincent: "Jared" on* Invitation to Love)

Written by Harley Peyton; Directed by Tina Rathborne; Edited by Toni Morgan

Monday, February 27, 1989:

> Act 1: Audrey tells Cooper about One Eyed Jack's. Cooper tells Truman and Lucy that he cannot remember the identity of the murderer. At the morgue, Doc Hayward and Albert argue about further autopsy tests on Laura's body. Truman punches Albert after being insulted. Leland is surprised to see Madeleine Ferguson, Laura's cousin, arrive.

> Act 2: Norma learns that her jailed husband, Hank, could be paroled soon. Cooper and Truman question Leo about the night Laura was murdered. Cooper tells Hawk to keep looking for the One Armed Man. Albert reports to Cooper and Truman: Cocaine was in the diary envelope; Laura was bound with two different kinds of twine; wounds on her neck were claw marks from an animal. Albert also found a small plastic fragment in Laura's stomach that depicted the letter J. Cooper refuses to sign Albert's official complaint against Truman.

> Act 3: James announces he won't be going to the funeral. Audrey spies on Dr. Jacoby as he works with her brother, Johnny. At the funeral, Father Clarence says some words, and Johnny Horne provides a loud "Amen!" James watches from a distance. Bobby blames everyone for Laura's death. Bobby and James begin to fight. A distraught Leland jumps on Laura's casket, which rises and falls as the hydraulics strain to compensate for the added weight.

> Act 4: Truman, Ed, and Hawk tell Cooper about the Bookhouse Boys, a secret society to protect Twin Peaks from "the evil in the woods." The Bookhouse Boys have captured Bernard Renault, a possible drug-runner. Cooper questions Bernard about his brother, Jacques. Josie wonders if somebody killed Andrew Packard, her husband. She suspects that Ben and Catherine want the mill land and worries they might kill her to get it. Later, Hawk and Cooper help a distraught Leland Palmer leave The Great Northern.

In her Artisan DVD commentary, Tina Rathborne said that directing *Twin Peaks* "felt like making a feature film on a very tight budget" with grueling time constraints. What fascinated her most was exploring the mysteries of the characters. Cooper is learning about both his innocent side (the idyllic life in the secluded town) and his dark side (he's willing to be seduced by Audrey, to a degree).

A Cooper/Audrey romance was already being plotted—an early draft of episode 6 hints that a relationship between the two may have already begun. The story was shelved for the first season but still planned for the second. Because Kyle MacLachlan objected to a romantic relationship between Cooper and Audrey, however, the storyline was abandoned before it could even start in season 2.

Episode 3 is the only episode of *Twin Peaks* to be nominated for an Emmy nomination in the "best writing" category. The nomination went to screenwriter, Harley Peyton. The episode is dominated by one major event—Laura Palmer's funeral. All the story elements either lead up to, or away from, this significant story point. Credit is due to Peyton, and director Tina Rathborne, for recognizing the narrative weight of the funeral and for skillfully constructing an episode around it.

Laura's funeral is a looming presence through Acts 1 and 2 and part of act 3. At the morgue, Albert's callousness about the body conflicts with Hayward's obligation to prepare Laura for the service; Leland is sedated in preparation for the funeral as Maddy arrives; Major Briggs attempts to talk to Bobby about death, but Bobby has other things on his mind; James is emotionally overwhelmed by the thought of the finality of the funeral. All these scenes lay the groundwork for the critical scene that will dominate act 3. There, Bobby will implicate all the townsfolk in Laura's murder; the emotions of both James and Bobby will boil over into conflict; and Leland's grief will overcome his sedation to result in one of the most shocking (and damning) sequences in the story: Leland leaping onto the casket. (Leland damages the mechanism holding Laura's casket, causing it to move up and down repeatedly. It's a scene both funny and horrific, and—in light of later revelations—symbolic.) Act 4 reverberates with the events of the funeral— Shelly and some diner patrons will mock Leland's behavior; Dr. Jacoby will pay a nighttime visit to Laura's grave and then tell Cooper about the importance Laura had on his life; and Cooper and Hawk will contemplate the afterlife before helping a grief-stricken Leland home.

Few other episodes of *Twin Peaks* will be so elegantly structured, though few other episodes will have one dominant event in which to involve all the characters.

If there is a flaw in the episode, it is in the first scene in which Cooper describes his dream to Truman and Lucy, a description that matches the European ending of the pilot rather than with the actual dream shown at the end of episode 2. The previous episode's cliffhanger had Cooper calling Truman to say he knew who killed Laura. Peyton is saddled with the unenviable task of relating—and then carefully sidelining—Cooper's dream. The story cannot move forward until (and unless) the writers can find a believable way to postpone the revelation. After describing his dream to Truman and Lucy, Cooper says that he "forgot" who the dream-Laura said was the killer. While this kind of thing certainly happens in real life—a dream can be clear immediately after one wakes and then the details fade quickly—it is hard to believe that Cooper, of all people, would forget the name of the killer.

Undoubtedly, Mark Frost had some say in creating the "Cooper forgot" scenario and it is unfortunate that he did not develop a more daring excuse for why Cooper could not remember the killer's name. A different scenario could have Cooper surmising that his knowledge was being blocked by some enigmatic force. Frost and the other writers may have been hesitant to introduce any potential supernatural element at this point, however, and so chose a more simplistic explanation. Whatever the case, it is to Peyton's credit that he softens the blow of the forgetful Cooper by portraying Cooper as confident—even eager—to "crack the code" of his dream. Peyton deftly uses Cooper's enthusiasm to keep the story moving and to further engage the audience with the mystery.

Additional Notes

Tina Rathborne had previously directed David Lynch in the 1988 film, *Zelly and Me* (co-starring Isabella Rossellini).

Madeleine Ferguson is a name that originates from the Alfred Hitchcock film, *Vertigo*. In that film, Judy (Kim Novak) posed as a dead character named Madeleine. Scottie Ferguson (Jimmy Stewart) makes Judy dye her hair blonde to look like Madeleine. (James and Donna will convince Maddy to change her hair to blonde in episode 6.)

Leo is shown cleaning his boots when he receives a call from Jacques. This may have been part of a running joke throughout the series regarding Leo and his footwear. Previously (episode 2), Leo meets Bobby and Mike in the woods and demands his $10,000 and then exclaims, "Leo needs a new pair of shoes!" In the second season, Leo keeps repeating, "New shoes. New shoes."

Walter Olkewicz's name is misspelled in the opening credits—it is spelled as Oklewicz.

The interior reconstruction of the sheriff's station is still underway. This is visible when Cooper and Truman walk down the hall and speak with Hawk (act 2).

This episode features the first appearances of Madeleine Ferguson, Jacques Renault, Bernard Renault, and, technically, Hank Jennings (in a photo only).

The first draft of episode 3 was completed on September 26, 1989; it was later revised on October 3, 1989.

Notable Deleted Scenes

Act 1: At the Double R Diner, Parole Officer Mooney meets with Norma about Hank. Some dialogue was removed from this scene. In the script we learn that Norma has been married to Hank "since high school" but they have no children because Norma "can't have any." This extra bit of character information may have been intended for a later storyline but was probably removed to focus the scene on Norma's uneasiness about Hank's return. In the televised version the scene ends as Mooney leaves. In the script the scene continues as Shelly arrives for work. Norma sees a gun in Shelly's purse and reacts with mild alarm. Shelly explains that she bought it for protection because of what happened to Laura. This additional material was probably cut because it merely let viewers know that Shelly had a gun, a fact that is established later when Shelly hides the gun at home.

Act 2: Cooper and Truman arrive at Leo Johnson's house. The script contains some dialogue deleted from the televised version. Truman worries about having hit Albert: "I can't believe I decked him. It was out of line, it was unprofessional, it was probably illegal." Cooper responds with understanding, but Truman is worried that the FBI will take some legal action. Cooper calmly explains, "Albert's been hit before. He will be hit again." He then assures Harry he will protect him. Although much of this scene is quite funny it was probably cut from the televised version because of time constraints. (The scene was ultimately redundant—a later scene in both the script and televised version shows Cooper refusing to submit Albert's written complaint against Truman.)

At the Palmer house a sedated Leland watches *Invitation to Love* on TV. The script contains an additional *Invitation to Love* scene, not shown in the televised version. In it, Emerald welcomes Montana back from his "year in the rain forest" while Chet watches. Montana says he is going to stay long enough to visit Jade, his ex-wife. The *Invitation to Love* music swells and the scene cuts to Jared writing a suicide note.

Leland watches and Madeleine Ferguson arrives. As Leland and Maddy embrace, the script contains some additional *Invitation to Love* dialogue from Jade, who says, "Oh Daddy. I was so afraid. I love you Daddy." These lines clearly hint at a potential *Twin Peaks* scenario—that Laura Palmer has returned in the guise of Maddy Ferguson. At the time of the show's airing, many viewers believed such a scenario was possible and that Laura has faked her own death. This was a credible theory given that the name, Madeleine Ferguson, came from the film, *Vertigo* where it was the alias of a supposedly dead character.

Act 3: The scripted version of act 3 describes a lengthier and more complicated funeral than was depicted in the televised version. The script takes great pains to show the various residents arriving at the service, taking their places at the grave site, acknowledging each other and sharing meaningful glances throughout the service. All of this was probably too ambitious for such a short act and would likely have taken too long to film (and to show). Much of what was scripted in act 3 had to be sacrificed in order to achieve a more focused sequence.

The act opens at Black Lake Cemetery where workers are testing the hydraulic mechanism that will lower Laura's casket into the grave. A mortician supervises the unloading of Laura's casket from the recently arrived hearse. These scenes establish the setting for Laura's funeral and, more importantly, the machinery used to lower Laura's coffin—machinery that Leland will strain with his weight at the end of the act. Scriptwriter Harley Peyton probably felt obligated to introduce the hydraulic lift so as not to confuse audiences later when Leland jumps on the coffin. It is unknown whether these establishing scenes were shot but, in the end, they were unnecessary—the televised version uses camera angles and sound effects to clearly define Leland's actions.

Mourners arrive. The Log Lady is prominent among the attendees and is described as "wearing a surprisingly appropriate funeral dress." Fortunately, this attire was abandoned for the televised version. The Log Lady was an important and enigmatic character in the *Twin Peaks* narrative and part of what made her unique was her earthy, backwoods clothes. To see the Log Lady in anything other than her woodsy attire would have diminished the character. (This very thing happened in the second season when Agent Cooper abandoned his black suit for the plaid look of a lumberjack. Cooper's character was weakened, his authority and eccentricity diluted by a mundane appearance.)

As more mourners take their places, Mike and Donna have an exchange. Mike tries to apologize for his behavior but Donna flinches at his touch. She tells him she does not want to see him anymore. Mike is described as "shell-shocked." This scene provides some closure to the Mike/Donna relationship and was probably written to establish tension between Donna and Mike as they glance at one another during the funeral.

Ed and Nadine arrive. Ed sees Donna hurrying away from Mike. He intercepts her and tells her James is not coming. Again, this scene was written to create tension in Donna and ratchet up the emotions of the funeral scene.

Tension is developed among other characters: Norma speaks with Ed and tells him Hank is due out of prison at any time. Ben escorts Sarah and Leland Palmer to the grave, sees Catherine and shares a few words. She tells him she shut the mill again for the funeral and expects it will go out of business soon. Ben mentally processes the information and moves on.

The funeral begins, resulting in a much longer service than what aired. In the televised version, Father Clarence gives a brief oration which is ultimately interrupted by Johnny Horne and then Bobby's speech. In the script, Johnny interrupts four times with a loud, "Amen!" His interruptions punctuate the silently growing tension among the attendees, described in the script as a "chain of glances."

Donna sees James arrive; Bobby sees him too and is furious. Donna looks to Truman for help. Truman is looking at Josie, who meets his gaze and turns away. Josie looks at Pete, who nods politely. Pete looks to Catherine, but she is "leering" at Ben Horne. Ben returns her gaze but is jostled by Bobby who moves forward next to the grave. Shelly notices the movement, follows Bobby's gaze toward James. James is looking at Donna, "seeking comfort, approval." Donna turns to Big Ed for help but he doesn't notice, he's trying to get Norma's attention. But Norma is looking at Nadine. Oblivious to all, Nadine is "gazing intently at Leland and Sarah." Nadine wipes a tear from her eye. Maddy sees Nadine, but looks away to Audrey who notices Maddy's resemblance to Laura and reacts. Audrey seeks Cooper, wondering if he, too, sees the resemblance. Cooper stands apart watching all the glances, "fascinated by all the connections and the clues they offer him." Then Cooper sees Bobby and knows there's about to be trouble.

The intricate exchange of glances would have been difficult to shoot—each "glance" would have meant separate camera and lighting set-ups. Due to the time-consuming complexity of shooting the scene as written, the production staff may have decided to abandon most of the various interactions. On the other hand, if these exchanges were shot they may have been removed from the final cut because they detracted from the somber mood of the funeral. As televised, most of the characters appear introspective, sad, and deeply moved by the service. This is more in keeping with the grief displayed by the characters in earlier episodes. (It is hard to imagine, as the script would suggest, Ed trying to get Norma's attention or Truman enrapt with Josie during this solemn ceremony.)

Act 4: At the Blue Pine Lodge, Truman visits Josie in an extended scene that was shortened significantly for the televised version. Josie explains in greater detail her fear of Ben and Catherine and her suspicion that Andrew's death was not an accident. As Josie seeks comfort in Truman's arms she recites a lengthy meditative poem from the *Tao Te Ching* by Lao Tzu, which ends with the lines: "To be without prejudice is to be kingly/To be kingly is to be of heaven/To be of heaven is to be of Tao/Tao is forever and he that possesses it,/Though his body ceases, is not destroyed." As written, this is a powerful scene, one that shows a deep bond between Josie and Truman and a strength-of-character in Josie. But it contradicts Josie's soon-to-be revealed duplicity (a subplot that begins in the next episode) and was likely cut so as not to interfere with that unfolding story.

The script ends at the cemetery where Cooper observes Laura's grave. A caretaker approaches and asks Cooper if he can hear the coffins. The caretaker explains: "It's the metal and the wood, I guess. Some caskets, you stick 'em in the ground, and the wood starts to expand, starts to rub against that metal. And if it rubs just so you get a strange sort of sound. . . . well, it's like music. You can almost hear the caskets singing." Cooper finds this fascinating and presses his ear to the ground. He sees someone approaching. Dr. Jacoby appears. The rest of the scene, in which Jacoby explains why he did not come to the funeral, is the same as what aired. The written scene with the caretaker's dialogue is more powerful and strange—a fitting and haunting end to the episode. The caretaker's lines about music also recall Cooper's dream and the cryptic comment, "There's always music in the air."

Cast and Crew Comments

Harley Peyton (*series screenwriter and season two producer*): I knew Mark Frost from a kind of baseball pool. He invited me to go to a screening of the *Twin Peaks* pilot. I saw it and I said, "I've never written television before, but if you ever need someone to write a script, I'd love to." He said, "Sure!" Then I ended up writing two of the first seven and then more after that. It was just like that. It was just out of friendship. It was really funny.

For the first season in particular, Mark would do very detailed scene outlines and then you'd sit down and go through a scene outline and you'd write the stuff. Mark might also make a pass, or change things because succeeding episodes were going to alter the plot content. It would depend on who the writer was. We worked from real good outlines that first year. In the second year it got a little wackier, but the first year the outlines were complete—in every act we had certain things we had to do and we'd just go ahead and write them. But you had a lot of freedom to do the things you wanted within those outlines.

Sheryl Lee (*Madeleine Ferguson*): David told me that he wanted me to come back on the show, but he didn't know what he wanted me to do! He'd figure something out. So I sort of came, not knowing who I was going to be playing! [*laughs*] Then, when he started talking to me about the idea [of Laura's brunette cousin], I thought it would be great. In fact there was a time when, if the series would have continued, I would have come back again as the red-headed, long-lost *something*!

Harley Peyton: People assume there's some incredible plan. You get credit for something you didn't even think of. It's like naming Maddy, "Maddy" after the character in *Vertigo*. Howard Rosenberg, who's a TV critic in L.A., wrote this long thing about it: "Well, they named her Maddy because of this-and-that." Well, no. We named her Maddy because we liked the movie.

Walter Olkewicz (*Jacques Renault*): I couldn't spend a lot of time working on the Canadian accent. I went in and they auditioned me for that scene with "Bite the bullet." I got it. I was very happy to learn they were hiring me. I called about three days before the first day I was supposed to work and I said, "Can I get with a dialect coach, because I really want to work on this Canadian accent." They said, "Oh, no, what you did in the audition was fine, just do that again." I said, "Wait a minute, what I did in the audition was Pepe Le Pew! It was the only French accent I could think of, going in there. That's not Canadian at all! I got to get a coach!"

Don Davis: I went into the army in 1965 and stayed in until almost 1968. I served under many people who seemed to be Jekyll-and-Hyde. Partly, I think, because of what was happening both at home and on military locations. You'd serve under somebody who, during office hours, would be by-the-book and the most rigid and seemingly unreasonable person you'd ever met. You'd meet the same person off-hours and discover that they were a poet, or they painted, or grew Bonsai trees. There was this one guy who, until I got to know him, I would have told anyone was a Neanderthal madman. But he was a freak for Bonsai trees! He had a very poetic soul. I just drew Briggs from people I had served with.

Charlotte Stewart: I went to David and Mark in the very beginning and I said, "You know, with Major Briggs being this straight military guy, and Bobby is obviously screwed up, I think it would be interesting if Betty is really Catholic." What could screw a kid up more than strict Catholicism and a military background? He's got to rebel in every way. And the next scene we had was with Bobby and this huge crucifix with palm fronds on the wall. That all came out of that conversation.

Dana Ashbrook: I came with lots of suggestions to David that he shot down. But he was totally open to them. I remember asking him about the scene in the house before the funeral—the one with the cross where I put my arms out. I'm 22 years old, I'm thinking this is cool and this is deep. I remember talking to David about that many episodes later; I asked him, "Did you see that? What did you think about it?" He was like, "Yeah, it was alright." I felt like I was definitely dabbling in someone else's forte. I thought, "Oh, maybe I'm being weird for the sake of being weird."

Miguel Ferrer: I remember one of the first shows I did, the one where I landed on top of Sheryl Lee after Sheriff Truman slugs me; I kept saying, "OK, Sheryl, listen, I'm not going to land on you hard." She said, "Hey, do whatever you have to do. I'm just here." You know when I did that bit with the drill? I had said, "OK, what do you guys have here that I can play with?" I saw this drill. "OK, it's going to make this sound, Sheryl, but don't worry I'm not going to put it anywhere near you." She said, "I don't care, I trust you." She was so sweet.

Robert Engels: Miguel would like to change stuff. [*laughs*] Someone like Miguel has such great instincts you would usually let him make the change. You would pretend you were thinking about it: "Well, I don't know, Miguel." But then you'd let him do it. [*laughs*]

Harley Peyton: Albert was the character I liked writing the most because he was mean and sarcastic. He was really fun to write. We had much in common. I loved writing him. I think Mark wrote the first Albert episode, but he got nastier when I did him. Miguel was great at it. He was a pleasure to write for. I don't think there was a single person in there who you'd say, "Oh great, I've got to write a scene for so-and-so." Some have gone on to more success than others. But they were really, really good. That was the best part of it.

Miguel Ferrer: I suppose there's something in my sensibilities—the way that I approach a character—for some reason I'm able to make a pretty despicable guy likable on some level. It's not even something I think about. Although I do acknowledge that it is something I am able to do. I don't know why that is. It's nothing that I consciously do, to say, "How can I warm this character up so that all the guys in the audience would want to have a beer with me?" It's just something innate that I'm able to do.

We would always try to crack each other up off camera. During [Kyle MacLachlan's] close-up, I would sit there and do some really weird stuff and I never got him, never once! [*laughs*] For my close-up he would get me back. He would read all his dialogue as Captain Kirk! [*laughs*] He always got me. He always nailed me!

I remember one time, the two of us, we went to Dana Ashbrook and we said, "Hey, we figured out what your acting style is! It's so cool!" He said, "What are you talking about?" We said, "You're doing Captain Kirk. You're the Captain Kirk of the nineties!" He said, "What do you mean?" I said, "It's perfect! You know, when you say things like, 'No! I! Loved! Her!'" I said, "C'mon! That's Captain Kirk!" He stood there with this look on his face, like, "Oh my God! Is that what I'm really doing?" It freaked him out for like two weeks! [*laughs*] I think we totally messed with his mind. It was hysterical. Then after, we said, "C'mon, man, we're just kidding."

Dana Ashbrook: [The funeral] was tough to shoot. They didn't get all the coverage they needed because it took so long. I, as an actor, don't think I hit that one out of the park. It was a dream when I got that script. It always seemed that Harley wrote the coolest lines for me to say. I thought, "Oh, my God. This is the greatest thing ever. I get to scream at the funeral!" When I got there, every cast member was there. It was tough. I was thinking, "I'm here with all my peers and I have to do this scene." So I ended up just going with it. I think, in retrospect, it was an OK performance. But that's just me.

Grace Zabriskie: When we shot my walk through the cemetery with Ray and Richard on each side of me I remembered being hit with absolute certainty that, in all her vulnerable grief, [Sarah] should still be trying to smoke a cigarette. I remember saying to Tina, whom I adored, "I think she should be smoking." Her face just animated, but before the animation was complete, it fell, and she said, "Oh, you know, that might be a bit much." And I think to myself, "Fifty or sixty more of those 'a bit much's'—that's what happened to the series."

Episode 4 (Script number 1004; First televised May 3, 1990)

Guest Starring: Jed Mills (Wilson Mooney)

Featuring: Mary Bond Davis (Female Parole Board Member #1), Mary Chalon (Female Parole Board Member #2), James Craven (Male Parole Board Officer), Adele Gilbert (Midge Loomer), Kevin Young (Toad), Erika Anderson (Selina Swift: "Emerald/Jade" on Invitation to Love*), Lance Davis (Martin Hadley: "Chet" on* Invitation to Love*)*

Written by Robert Engels; Directed by Tim Hunter; Edited by Paul Trejo

Tuesday, February 28, 1989:

Act 1: Andy sketches the man in Sarah Palmer's vision (Bob). Cooper questions Jacoby: The night Laura died, Jacoby followed a man in a red Corvette—a man Laura had spoken about. Cooper knows Leo Johnson drives a red Corvette. Cooper's supervisor, Gordon Cole, calls to report Albert's test results: Laura was bound with Finley's Fine Twine, and the marks on Laura's shoulder were bird bites. Cooper recognizes Andy's sketch of Bob as the man from his dream. Hawk has found the One Armed Man (Phillip Gerard) at the Timber Falls Motel. Cooper and Truman burst in and find Gerard.

Act 2: Cooper and Truman interrogate Gerard: His best friend, veterinarian Bob Lydecker, is at the hospital in a coma. Audrey tells Donna that Laura was seeing Dr. Jacoby. She also suspects that Laura was working at One Eyed Jack's and plans to investigate. Hank has his parole hearing. Cooper and Truman arrive at the Lydecker clinic. Cooper suspects the bird that attacked Laura was a patient at the clinic and he confiscates all the office files.

Act 3: Bobby tells Shelly that Leo and Jacques may have supplied Laura with drugs. Bobby takes Leo's bloody shirt. Andy explains that Lucy won't speak to him. Cooper reminisces about a woman who was once special to him. Shelly tells Norma that she is scared of Leo. James sees Madeleine. She looks like Laura. Norma learns that Hank has been given parole.

Act 4: Ben talks to Icelandic investors on the phone. Audrey convinces Ben to give her a job at the department store. Cooper learns that the plastic fragment in Laura's stomach was a piece of a One Eyed Jack's poker chip. Andy finds a file on Waldo, a mynah bird owned by Jacques Renault. Cooper and the police raid Jacques' apartment where Bobby has hidden Leo's shirt. Cooper finds the shirt and sees Leo's initials. Ben hires Leo to burn the Packard Mill. Donna and James and discover that the buried necklace is gone. Josie finds a letter from Hank—a sketch of a white domino. Hank calls and asks if Josie got his message.

This episode moves all the existing stories into new territory while introducing new subplots. Cooper receives information about Leo's Corvette, One Eyed Jack's, and Sarah's vision of Bob. Josie spies Catherine and Ben at the Timber Falls Motel; at the same location Cooper, Truman, and Andy are questioning Phillip Gerard, the One Armed Man. This leads them to Lydecker's Veterinary Clinic, where Cooper "conveniently" finds the type of twine in which Laura was bound. He also confiscates the patient files that will lead to Waldo the mynah bird. Hank Jennings' parole hearing begins; Leo's bloody shirt ends up in Jacques's apartment; Leo kills Bernard Renault; Ben hires Leo to set the mill on fire.

Despite this whirlwind of plot development the episode doesn't feel rushed. Director Tim Hunter maintains the pace and texture of previous shows. He also allows himself time to play: The great dialogue during the shooting-range sequence has all the men opining about women (and Cooper revealing some of his painful past); a passionate Bobby spits out his gum in response to Shelly's erotic play with a gun; Josie has time to make Pete a sandwich with "plenty of mayo;" a llama stares Cooper in the face; and a pair of winter-clad tennis players face-off as Cooper and the police prepare to raid Jacques' apartment. These are fascinating touches that bring the characters and the narrative vibrantly to life. For a series only five hours into its run, there is a confidence in the ways the show is written, directed and performed.

Robert Engels and Tim Hunter explained why this episode worked so well in their commentary for the Artisan DVD release. Engels described how *Twin Peaks* was written with a soap-opera-like structure which gave the writers freedom to explore and introduce abnormal ideas and themes. Even though *Twin Peaks* was filled with clichés (such as Maddy, Laura's twin cousin), these were accepted by the audience because the clichés were *so* obvious. Although Engels does not say so explicitly, he seems to acknowledge the postmodern nature of the show—that is, the writers and the viewers are both in on the joke; each knows the other party is aware of the fictional nature of the show and so neither rejects clichés as part of the narrative.

Engels says this episode might have been a little too busy—too many things are going on, such as the odd extras in the background. Engels specifically noted the bizarre tennis players who are visible just before Cooper and the police raid Jacques' apartment.

Tim Hunter provides many fascinating details about shooting the episode. Although confined to a specific script and strict schedule, Hunter found working in television liberating. Many of the decisions about character and plot were beyond his control and so he had more time to think about the composition and framing of shots. Hunter talked about how he used camera movement to underscore the emotions (or changing emotions) of characters. For example, in act 3, he moves from a close-up of James (who is in an important, but intimate, conversation with Donna) to a wide shot of Maddy arriving at the diner (thereby visually emphasizing a major change in James's world).

Hunter provided valuable insight as to why the show was so intriguing: while there was a lot of plot, "it mattered little, because the subtext of the scenes is almost everything in *Twin Peaks*." As a result, surface emotions could be exaggerated because "there was so much stuff going on underneath . . . . Characters are thinking things different from what they're saying." (He points to the Audrey/Ben scene in act 4 as a great example.)

Hunter credited the invaluable contribution of music editor Lori Eschler. Angelo Badalamenti had provided pre-recorded music cues for the series and Eschler had a deep knowledge of the show's music library. When a director needed a "new" or specific cue, Eschler would find it. Much of the unique musical sound of *Twin Peaks* can be attributed to Eschler's good work.

Hunter related a humorous anecdote about shooting episode 4. Apparently, he had driven by a llama farm on the way to work and thought it would be fun to have a llama in the veterinary clinic. Kyle MacLachlan was deliberately chewing gum so that the llama would smell it and therefore stop and look at him in the scene. The llama scene took only one take. (Watch Michael Ontkean in the scene. Oddly, he looks down when the llama stares at MacLachlan and then looks up with a slightly strange expression. It appears as if Ontkean is trying not to laugh at the bizarre scenario that just transpired.)

Additional Notes

This episode finally reveals that the scene at the end of the pilot does, indeed, mean that Sarah Palmer has seen a vision of a hand digging up Laura's necklace buried in the woods. Jacoby, of course, has that necklace, and he had been counselling Laura for six months before her death.

As Jacoby talks to Cooper in the conference room of the sheriff's station, a large map of Tibet is displayed on the chalkboard behind him.

The name Gordon Cole originates from the film, *Sunset Boulevard*, reportedly a favorite film of David Lynch's. The names Waldo and Lydecker originate from the film, *Laura*, which featured a character named Waldo Lydecker. The name Phillip Gerard originates from the television series, *The Fugitive* (which featured a one armed man).

An interesting visual mistake occurs about 21 minutes into the episode—a cameraman is clearly reflected on the side of the police cruiser as Cooper and Truman pull into the Lydecker clinic. (The cameraman is also reflected in the glass of the gas pumps.)

For the first time on the show, an owl will become an important part of a scene. When Donna and James look for the buried heart necklace in act 4, they hear an owl. They look up, and the bird is perched on a branch above them, as if looking down and spying on them. In the second season, the presence of the owls will become more enigmatic; in episode 8 Cooper learns that "the owls are not what they seem."

Various sets were apparently being repurposed during the shoot. Note how the wallpaper at Jacques Renault's apartment is the same wallpaper in the Double R Diner.

This episode marked the first appearance of Hank Jennings, Toad (frequent Double R patron), and Gordon Cole (via speaker phone).

Before joining the production staff on *Twin Peaks*, Robert Engels had worked as a writer on the CBS TV series, *Wiseguy*. Shortly before the *Twin Peaks* pilot aired, *Wiseguy* began a storyline set in a small town in Washington State called Lynchboro. The town had its share of eccentric characters, including a police officer who cried when he found murdered bodies; a tough teenager named Bobby; and a serial killer on the loose. There was also a notorious brothel/gambling parlor called the Corvette Club. Because the *Twin Peaks* pilot was shot long before it aired, the producers of *Wiseguy* probably heard about the show and created an *homage*/parody for their series. Robert Engels has stated that the *Wiseguy*-*Twin Peaks* storyline was in the works before he joined the staff at *Wiseguy*.

The first draft of episode 4 was completed on September 26, 1989; it was later revised October 23, 27 & 31, 1989.

Notable Deleted Scenes

Act 1: At Big Ed's house, Ed and his assistant, Sparky, tiptoe into the living room. Sparky is eager to see Nadine's bent rowing machine. He's amazed: "That's tempered steel, Edsker." Ed makes a call to the Double R looking for Norma. Shelly tells him Norma has already left for Hank's parole hearing. Nadine enters and Ed pretends to be talking to a customer. Nadine is unperturbed; she tells Ed she's getting a patent lawyer for her drape runners. Although this scene does little to further either the Nadine/drape-runner subplot or the Ed/Norma subplot, Sparky's comment reminds viewers of Nadine's unusual strength. Nadine's super-strength does not become a story element until the next season, when she recovers from her drug overdose. But the strength element was already present early in the first season. What, if anything, the writers were intending with this plot point is unknown.

Act 3: At the Great Northern, Ben speaks with Jerry by phone. Jerry gives Ben an update about the Icelanders. Ben is interrupted by his secretary who says they have "a situation in the dining room." Ben finds a distraught Leland dancing with another secretary. Leland dances over to Ben and show's him a photo of Laura and Audrey. Excited, he exclaims, "This was on your desk! Our daughters, together!" Ben grabs Leland by the shoulders, tells him, "You gave me that picture, remember?" Leland, still distraught and distracted, cries, "She loved dancing. She loved to dance . . . she'd stand on my shoes . . . I taught her . . . ."

These scenes were probably cut due to time constraints; the first scene (with Ben on the phone) is essentially the same as a later scene in which Ben talks to Jerry and prepares for the Icelanders' arrival. The second scene is more significant. This is Leland's only major appearance in the episode. (He had a cameo in the first scene.) It cements Leland's growing irrationality and his obsession with dancing. It also introduces the photo of Audrey and Laura—the same photo that Audrey will see later in the episode. While none of this information is vital to the episode (the likely reason it was cut) it does remind viewers of Leland's grief and mental collapse.

The shooting-range sequence contains some intriguing dialogue that was cut from the final version: When Andy complains that he can't understand Lucy, Cooper tells him, "There are a number of old sayings which might pertain to this discussion. Suffice it to say you're up against the oldest unsolvable mystery known to man." Truman agrees: "The mystery's what I like the most . . . and the less I know the more interested I get." Cooper looks at Truman and knows he's thinking of Josie. A few moments later Cooper clarifies his position on women: "Harry, the way I look at it a mystery's just a solution waiting for the right set of facts. Here, we're dealing with an area that's closer to a paradox or an enigma." Although these lines are ostensibly written about women, they have far greater meaning if put in a slightly different context. These few deleted lines sum up the entirety of the *Twin Peaks* series, whether they were knowingly written that way or not. The characters (and the audience) were attempting to "solve" the mystery of Laura's murder, when, in fact, the "mystery" was essentially unsolvable. Cooper's search for meaning ultimately led him to confront the "paradox" or "enigma" that was Laura Palmer.

The "mystery" and "enigma" approaches to Laura (and her murder/fate) may serve as useful labels for the different ways Mark Frost and David Lynch imagined the series. Frost was determined to resolve the mystery of Laura's murder using the "facts" of Cooper's dream. These facts would pave a way to the solution ("break the code, solve the crime"). In contrast, Lynch was satisfied to revel in the paradox that was the character of Laura Palmer. It was the enigma he wanted to explore, whether there was solution or not. Cooper's superb and succinct lines about the differences between mysteries and enigmas perfectly define the contrasting approaches of the show's two creators.

Cast and Crew Comments

Robert Engels: I knew Mark since I was seventeen. His dad was my college advisor at the University of Minnesota. When I moved to California, Mark was working with David on *Goddess*—the Marilyn Monroe project. That's when I met David. Later, when they were working on *Twin Peaks*, I remember Mark saying, "This show is really screwy. You'd be really good on it." [*laughs*] So I wrote my script for *Twin Peaks* and right at that time I went over to meet with the guys at *Wiseguy*. It was literally within a week from one to the other. I went to *Wiseguy* one day to write a script and I was there at, like, eleven o'clock and then they gave me an office at three. Someone quit or someone got fired and I just started there.

Everybody always thinks I took the [*Twin Peaks* story] to the other. But when I got to *Wiseguy* they were already planning that arc. That was just complete coincidence. There were plenty of coincidences. *Wiseguy* was filmed in Vancouver—a stone's throw from Snoqualmie—so it looked the same. We were using the same non-descript cop uniforms. All these "television" accidents happened that really made it look like one had ripped-off the other, but both were started earlier. *Wiseguy* had always planned to do a small-town arc. That had started before I got there but I think the fact that I had done *Twin Peaks* made it more alluring to them. Yeah, there are lots of similarities. And I realized, "Oh man, when Mark and David see this, I'm done!" [*laughs*]

Chris Mulkey (*Hank Jennings*): I noticed when I arrived on the set of *Twin Peaks* that I felt like I had just fallen into a mosaic. I felt like it was just perfect. I felt immediately at home, immediately empowered by the character, and just incredibly immersed in the story. And that was very strange. When I got there, I felt like I'd been doing it for a long time—that I had really lived it, or something. I don't know. It was very strange.

At first, I think they just left [the character] alone and let me find it. After that, we talked about his history and what he had done and what he had been through. He's the "guy who thought great things were going to happen but he's just stepped in shit." I think that is the thumbnail sketch of Hank.

Robert Engels: The first seven were well plotted-out. David and Mark knew where they were going. Mark and Harley and I would do the episodes in-depth: We would plot out what was happening. Then, when you wrote your episode, you would work more with Mark. David would come in and

Mark and David would go through what the rest of us had worked up. Then you would go ahead and write it. It was a pretty simple process. It was outlined. Everybody says, "Well, you didn't have a plan." But, to the contrary, everything was pretty well planned-out.

Mark Frost (*series co-creator and executive producer*): What would generally happen—I pretty much did all the stories, with some assistance from Harley occasionally. We'd bang out the stories in a story conference, and when we were under pressure to finish things we would divide things up, usually just by act. I'd give somebody a first act to write, give somebody else a second, and so on. And then I did the final rewriting on every episode to smooth things over at that point and bring it into line. It was a lot of work.

Robert Engels: Writing-wise, the two coolest things I did were when Dr. Jacoby was talking about the healing rhizome of Hawaii and all of that—it's right off a shampoo bottle! [*laughs*] It was great, because people see it on television and think it's cool; but if you just looked at a Breck bottle, you'd get it! And then the poem that Michael Horse says at the shooting gallery—all that stuff's a highlight.

Episode 5 (Script number 1005; First televised May 10, 1990)

Guest Starring: Don Amendolia (Emory Battis)

Featuring: Jill Rogosheske (Trudy), Brian Straub (Einar Thorson), Mary Stavin (Heba), Lance Davis (Martin Hadley: "Chet" on Invitation to Love*), Rick Giolito (Jason Denbo: "Montana" on* Invitation to Love*), and Peter Michael Goetz (Evan St. Vincent: "Jared" on* Invitation to Love*)*

Written by Mark Frost; Directed by Lesli Linka Glatter; Edited by Jonathan P. Shaw

Wednesday, March 1, 1989:

Act 1: The Icelanders arrive and awaken Cooper. Truman and his men search Jacques' apartment. The blood on Leo's shirt is Jacques' (AB Negative). Cooper finds a copy of *Fleshworld*. Leo's truck is pictured in the magazine. Shelly tells Andy that Leo and Jacques argued about Laura. At Big Ed's, Norma tells tell Ed that Hank has been paroled. She says not to call for a while, but that she loves him.

Act 2: Audrey insists on working at the perfume counter. At Jacques', Cooper finds a photo of a cabin in the woods, and then finds Laura's ad in *Fleshworld*. Maddy agrees to help James and Donna solve Laura's murder. Norma and Shelly return from the beauty shop and find Hank at the restaurant. Shelly watches a few minutes of *Invitation To Love*— Montana punches Chet.

Act 3: The Briggs meet with Jacoby. Bobby says that Laura wanted to die. Jacoby says that "Laura wanted to corrupt people, because that's how she felt about herself." Cooper, Truman, Hawk, and Doc Hayward find the Log Lady's cabin. Cooper asks that log what it saw the night Laura died: "Two men. Two girls. Flashlights pass by in the woods. Later, footsteps. One man passes by. Screams far away. Terrible." Truman wonders who the third man was. The group continues to Jacques' cabin and find Waldo, twine, a camera, blood, and a One Eyed Jack's poker chip with a missing piece.

Act 4: The Great Northern hosts a reception for the Icelanders. Audrey spies Ben and Catherine together talking about the mill. Music starts and Leland begins to dance erratically. Catherine dances with Leland to defuse the situation. Maddy finds one of Laura's hidden tapes. Josie gives Ben the ledger she stole from Catherine. Hank beats up Leo for "opening up his own franchise." Leo stumbles home and Shelly shoots him. Cooper returns to his room and finds Audrey waiting for him in bed.

Episode 5 reveals certain characters to be more emotionally complicated than they have appeared so far. Dr. Jacoby's intense psychological deconstruction of Bobby shows Bobby to be a weaker, more naïve character than his previous behavior would have indicated. The scene also gets to the core of a significant aspect of Laura's identity. This is one of many scenes that demonstrate why the characters in *Twin Peaks* were so engaging. They are complex and nuanced; each may exhibit the characteristics of a particular stereotype (Cooper, the infallible detective; Audrey, the romantic flirt; Bobby, the misguided youth, etc.), but all soon defy expectation, becoming more rounded and flawed as the show progresses.

Nowhere is that more apparent than in a later sequence involving Audrey as she spies upon others at the Great Northern. In just a few simple scenes Audrey is depicted as someone with deep and perplexing emotional distress. She laughs when she sees her father conspire with Catherine to burn the mill and she cries when she sees a distraught Leland being inadvertently mocked and ignored by the celebratory crowd in the ballroom. These few scenes show Audrey to be flawed and unpredictable. She, like others in the story, is alluring and mysterious, provoking a desire to know more about her. This is one of the great strengths of *Twin Peaks*.

In her commentary for the Artisan DVD, Lesli Linka Glatter noted that most of the directors on *Twin Peaks* were present during the first-season shooting. So, while she was preparing for her episode, Tina Rathborne and Tim Hunter were still around. This was unusual; on most network productions, directors are like hired-hands, directing their episodes and absent from the rest of the production. Many dramatic series have an uneven feel from episode-to-episode because of this manner of production. Not so with *Twin Peaks*, which benefitted from a close creative collaboration between writers and directors.

Piper Laurie delivers a strong performance in two memorable scenes—one in which she confronts Ben about the One Eyed Jack's poker chip, and a second in which she tries to dance with Leland as the music in the Timber Room starts. As Leland writhes, holding his hands to his head, Catherine quickly glances at Ben, wondering what to do, then creates her own solution—she joins Leland on the dance floor, holding her hands to her own head and waving them, as if it's part of the dance move. Ben then follows, as do the other guests, and a potentially disastrous situation is averted. Laurie manages to keep a potentially farcical scene grounded and realistic.

The opening scene, in which Cooper (and most of the other guests, we soon learn) are awakened by loud singing recalls the scene in episode 1 where Ben reprimands Audrey for disturbing the guests with "that racket."

The memorable meeting with the Log Lady—she expected them to arrive two days ago, on Monday—provides a clue as to the meaning of the ambiguous phrase, "Fire, walk with me." Margaret says, "Fire is the devil hiding like a coward in the smoke." "Fire, walk with me," then, could essentially mean making a pact with the devil, entering into a partnership in order to kill.

The Log Lady scene will turn out to be one of the most important scenes in the narrative—it defines the events that happened the night of Laura's murder. These events will be referenced again in the series (for example, in the second-season premiere) and then actually depicted in the film, *Fire Walk With Me*.

Additional Notes:

In this episode, viewers learn that Jacques' blood is on Leo's shirt and is AB Negative. This will cause significant continuity problems later. (See episode 8.)

As Cooper flips through the copy of *Fleshworld* in Jacques' apartment, there appear to be only three different pages in the magazine, repeated over and over.

The book next to Cooper's bed is *Great Expectations* by Charles Dickens.

As in the season finale (also written by Frost), this episode loads up the cliffhangers—Maddy finding Laura's tape, Ben and Josie's secret deal, Shelly shooting Leo, and Cooper finding Audrey in his bed.

The first draft of episode 5 was completed on September 26, 1989; it was later revised November 1, 7, & 8, 1989.

Notable Deleted Scenes

Act 1: At Big Ed's, James tells Ed that his mother came home. The dialogue indicates that Colleen Hurley has been getting more and more drunk and her physical and psychological condition is degrading. James expects she might end up dead someday. He is also ashamed of her. Ed encourages James not to give up, that they both need to help his mother. James responds, "What's left to do? Talk about it some more? She won't get help, she won't listen to either of us." James goes further, "She's killing herself... if she won't let us help her sometimes I think it'd be better if she'd just get it over with." These lines are clearly setting up a new subplot, one in which the fate of Colleen Hurley is uncertain. Will she kill herself? Can Ed and James help her? The storyline was yet another minor melodrama in a narrative already burdened with soap opera subplots. Given that another storyline would soon deal with attempted suicide (Nadine's overdose) and that James was already part of other complicated stories, the writers of *Twin*

Peaks (most likely Mark Frost) wisely decided to excise this rather bland subplot.

Act 3: The Briggs family attends family counseling at Doctor Jacoby's. The televised version ends with a strong sense of sadness; Bobby starts to cry as "Laura Palmer's Theme" swells. (Dr. Jacoby has touched upon the essence of Laura.) In striking contrast, the script ends with a moment of quirky humor: Bobby cries, Jacoby seems moved, but . . . suddenly offers Bobby a malted milk ball. He pops one into his own mouth and thinks about what Bobby's just told him. The televised version is more effective; it illustrates the power Laura Palmer still has over people, even after death. The script was trying too hard for another example of quirky humor.

In a clearing at the edge of the woods, Cooper, Truman, Hawk and Doc Hayward prepare to search for Jacques' cabin. Andy arrives and tells Truman about what Shelly said. He also says that he noticed extra dishes on Shelly's table and surmised that someone else was in the house. Truman tells Andy to stay by the car. The men begin their trek. This scene functioned primarily as transition—the hikers leave Twin Peaks and enter the woods. It also showed that the police may have had some suspicions regarding Shelly Johnson. This aspect of the plot was never developed.

The hikers arrive at the Log Lady's cabin. The scripted scene is essentially the same as the one aired with a few minor (though intriguing) lines of dialogue deleted. When the Log Lady directs the men to come into her cabin she tells them, "My log does not judge." The script contains an extra line—the Log Lady explains, "It only records." The men sit at the table as the Log Lady prepares tea. Cooper and the Log Lady have a fascinating exchange. Cooper asks, "Do you use fire for cooking?" The Log Lady responds with ambiguity: "I go to great lengths to keep it under control." This intriguing line foreshadows the Log Lady's advice to Laura in *Fire Walk With Me* ("When this kind of fire starts, it is very hard to put out"). In all of her dialogue the Log Lady shows she is aware of forces beyond the natural. Her references to fire and smoke are fascinating and in this deleted line she implies the idea of fire as an autonomous entity—a force that one must struggle to control. This idea is central to *Twin Peaks* and the characters of Leland and Laura Palmer. The "dark side"—the dark impulses—must be kept in check or they will consume you.

Act 4: Catherine and Pete Martell arrive at the Great Northern for the Icelander reception. Major Briggs is already chatting with one of the visitors about Icelandic folklore. In the televised version, Briggs makes only a brief comment, but in the script, Briggs goes into greater detail about his knowledge and his beliefs. Some amazing lines reveal characteristics of Major Briggs that will not be revealed until the second season. Briggs explains, "I find these last remnants of connection to a natural, more primitive, almost pagan way of life, endlessly fascinating; locally, for instance, we have the Sasquatch mythos, or Bigfoot, a large, evil-smelling forest-dweller, which I suppose would correspond to your 'huldufolk' or hidden people." The Icelanders listen as Briggs continues, "I also happen to be a firm believer in the UFO. I've seen some high-level classified data that would curl your hair." Here, in these deleted lines, we have the first evidence of Briggs's connection with UFOs (and by extension, Project Bluebook), a connection that is not established in the televised narrative until episode 9 in season 2.

Cast and Crew Comments

Catherine Coulson: David knew how the Log Lady would look, very specifically, and exactly what kind of log she would have, and then we both developed her background story. He would give me ideas, and then I would ask questions, like, "What do you think her husband was like, the love of her life, this fabulous woodsman that she was married to for such a short time?" So he's always been able to give me the specifics. And then I, of course, have to take that information and make it into my own truth, as an actor, to come back out again. I feel like I know the Log Lady extremely well.

Robert Engels: There probably was a misunderstanding as to what *Invitation to Love* was. It had actors in it who were funny guys—Peter Goetz and Lance Davis, two of my favorites that I've used a lot—so suddenly you've got a chemistry going that got out of control. Part of it also is TV production. All of those [scenes] were shot in a day. As my memory serves, it was really a case of going so fast and it seemed funny to Mark. I don't think David wanted it to be so funny. He felt like it was commenting on the real people—by having a funny soap opera it made everything else seem less real. When David's work is very funny it is also deadly serious. He's not a *farceur* whereas that was kind of farcical. And lots of times with television shows you start [going] one way and about halfway through it's too late and you say, "Oh no, this isn't going to work. But maybe we can make something out of it."

Everett McGill: We were always delighted in one another's scenes. If I was doing a scene with Wendy, then Peggy would be around to watch. If I was doing a scene with Peggy, then Wendy would come around to watch. In terms of working with the two of them, I would say that they're both wonderful gals and a delight to be around. They had a good sense of humor and were always upbeat. And of course, Peggy had done an awful lot of television work, and Wendy had done none. But they both were sweet as they could be. You know, I miss them. It was certainly pleasurable for me to work with them.

Catherine Coulson: The Log Lady speaks in a mysterious way, and certainly the world of *Twin Peaks* is a mysterious world. I don't know if I'd go so far as to say she personifies the world of *Twin Peaks*; I don't know what Dale Cooper would say about that. But I do think she knows all the elements of Twin Peaks; she knows the underbelly.

Episode 6 (Script number 1006; First televised May 17, 1990)

Guest Starring: Walter Olkewicz (Jacques Renault), Don Amendolia (Emory Battis), Victoria Catlin (Blackie O'Reilly), Mark Lowenthal (Walter Neff)

Featuring: Eve Brent (Theodora Ridgely), Lisa Ann Cabasa (Jenny), Mary Stavin (Heba), Brian Straub (Einar Thorson), Erika Anderson (Selina Swift: "Emerald/Jade" on Invitation to Love*), Lance Davis (Martin Hadley: "Chet" on* Invitation to Love*), Rick Giolito (Jason Denbo: "Montana" on* Invitation to Love*)*

Written by Harley Peyton; Directed by Caleb Deschanel; Edited by Toni Morgan

Thursday, March 2, 1989:

Act 1: Cooper tells Audrey that she needs to get dressed. Lucy gets a call from her doctor. Truman and Doc Hayward look at a picture of Waldo on Laura's shoulder. Cooper leaves a voice-activated recorder near Waldo's cage. Leo spies Bobby visiting Shelly. She tells Bobby that she shot Leo. Maddy, James, and Donna listen to Laura's tape.

Act 2: Audrey hides in Emory Battis's closet as he talks to Jenny about opportunities at "the club." Audrey finds Ronette's name in Battis's notebook. Truman and Cooper warn Hank not to miss an appointment with his parole officer. Ed finds a depressed Nadine—a patent attorney rejected her silent drape runner idea. Josie tells Truman she was at the Timber Falls Motel taking pictures of Ben and Catherine. She's worried they're planning to burn the mill.

Act 3: Cooper, Truman, and Ed prepare for their trip to One Eyed Jack's. Catherine's insurance agent, Mr. Neff, needs a signature on her new life insurance policy. She finds that her ledger is missing. Audrey slips a note under Cooper's door. Waldo begins talking; Leo shoots the bird and speeds away. Cooper plays the tape: "Laura, don't go there. Hurting me. Hurting me. Stop it. Stop it. Leo, no. Leo, no."

Act 4: Cooper and Ed (as Barney and Fred) meet Blackie at One Eyed Jacks. Maddy sneaks out of the house; Leland sees her. Ben tells Josie to get Catherine to the mill tonight. Blackie hires Audrey ("Hester Prynne") after Audrey ties a cherry stem with her tongue. Jacoby gets a call from "Maddy-as-Laura." Maddy tells him to meet her at the corner of Sparkwood and 21. Bobby spies Maddy. Someone is spying on Bobby. James and Donna sneak into Jacoby's office. Bobby hides drugs in James's motorcycle.

Episode 6 can be viewed as "part one" of a two-part *Twin Peaks* episode. The episode serves to move all the plotlines forward and to set them up for the cliffhangers that will take place in episode 7. As such, this installment is structured as a straight-line narrative; little time is spent on diversionary or tangential material.

There are some wonderful moments in the episode, especially involving Audrey. Her scene in the closet as she eavesdrops on Battis is particularly good. Boldly smoking a cigarette as she spies on the hapless Battis, Audrey exudes confidence and fearlessness. Harley Peyton described Audrey as someone who is always at play, which is evident here. But there is a dangerous recklessness to Audrey as well. She behaves as if she is in control of every situation and that nothing will go wrong (of if something does, she will be able to fix it). When she meets Blackie for the first time, her amateurish attempt at disguising herself as Hester Prynne from *The Scarlet Letter* immediately backfires. Audrey remains unfazed. Here, of course, she performs the famous cherry stem trick to prove her experience and "sophistication" to Blackie. Audrey inserts herself into a dangerous situation, unmindful of the consequences.

There is a curious psychology to Audrey and the character has been fascinating to watch as the season progresses. Sadly, it is with this episode that the series abandons further examination of Audrey's psyche. She will soon become a "damsel in distress" awaiting rescue by Cooper. Those eccentric attributes that made her dance at the Double R or made her cry at the Icelander reception will never be satisfactorily examined. Although Audrey will remain vibrant and engaging into the second season, a certain mysterious nature to her character will be lost.

The Ben/Josie/Catherine dealings, which became more interesting in episode 5 when it was revealed that Ben and Josie were in league against Catherine, continue here. Mr. Neff (the insurance agent) informs Catherine of a change in her life insurance policy—one made by Ben and Josie. Catherine is now wise to the deception, although Ben and Josie don't know she's learned of it. Ben is capitalizing on Josie and Catherine's animosity toward each other by playing both sides, though in the end he wants Catherine to die in the mill fire. Meanwhile, Josie is working to entrap Ben and Catherine, even planting hints in Truman's mind about her fear that Ben and Catherine are planning to start the fire. Catherine is in the most precarious position because she doesn't have an ally outside of Neff, who is essentially a bystander.

Episode 6 is beautifully directed and contains some memorable images. Caleb Deschanel creates an eerie sequence when Waldo the mynah bird is shot. With rain and thunder pounding outside, Cooper and the other characters hear a gunshot and cautiously enter the conference room. They find a dead Waldo, whose blood drips onto the donuts. Outside, Leo flees. The scene ends on a haunting and blackly-comic note as Cooper replays the audio tape and we hear Waldo mimicking some of Laura's last words: "Leo, no!" The whole sequence has a *noir* feel (the rain, the blood, the dying girl's cries), and yet this *noir* quality is twisted by the surreal nature of *Twin Peaks* (the dead bird, the donuts, the squeaky whine of Waldo's voice). It is a wonderful scene and incorporates all the elements that made *Twin Peaks* special.

In another mesmerizing scene, "Maddy-as-Laura" emerges from a car to meet James. It is exquisitely directed (and lit), showing Maddy walk from darkness into light (reminiscent of Sandy's introduction in *Blue Velvet*). As James greets her, there's an interesting look from Donna, hinting that she's worried about losing her boyfriend to this new incarnation of Laura. All of this is preceded, of course, by Maddy's sneaking out of the house, which includes the chilling (especially in retrospect) shot of Leland sitting in the living room in the dark, turning to watch Maddy leave, then turning back, the front of his face in shadow.

In his Artisan DVD commentary, Caleb Deschanel describes some of his directorial decisions and editorial considerations for the episode. He shot some scenes to imply someone else was secretly watching and listening to the characters. In the middle of the conversation between Donna, James, and Maddy (in act 1), Deschanel cuts to a distant wide shot to convey the sense of another person watching. This approach perfectly fits with concept of "evil in the woods" (as Truman explained in episode 3) and with the eventual direction of the storyline (the idea of the demonic Bob being a presence in and around Twin Peaks). But, more importantly, this shot foreshadows the scene in act 4 in which "someone else" really will be watching them at the park.

Deschanel also talks about the subversive nature of the show. There was an implied "sexiness" to *Twin Peaks*, and although the network did censor a few things they often did not perceive the subtext of the show. Deschanel explains that the implication of certain ideas and themes (including sexuality) was a strength to *Twin Peaks* because it allowed the audience to use their imaginations. Often television programs are more blatant; the audience sees and hears everything that happens. With *Twin Peaks*, the audience "had the pleasure of discovering for themselves" the hidden nature of the series.

In the same commentary, Harley Peyton talks about the exaggerated nature of the show and how the writers were able to "push" the humor and the melodrama. He describes how the slow pace of the show was made up for in rich detail. (Peyton contrasts the deliberate, "languid" pace of *Twin Peaks* with other TV dramas, which he says are edited based on Attention Deficit Disorder.) Not surprisingly, Peyton regards *Twin Peaks* as "revolutionary TV"—a show that was "as good as it gets."

Peyton also talks about writing in the voices of the characters: "hearing" their voices and trying to capture the appropriate cadence for their delivery. Cooper was the hardest character for him to write and it was rewarding when he came up with a good Cooper line (Peyton cites Cooper's "give yourself a present" line as an example). Audrey was a character he liked to write. He describes her as someone to whom "the world is a chessboard."

Additional Notes:

The name of Mr. Neff (Catherine Martell's insurance agent) originates from the film, *Double Indemnity*, which featured an insurance salesman named Walter Neff.

When Cooper and Big Ed go undercover, they use the names Barney and Fred, an obvious reference to the cartoon series, *The Flintstones*.

The episode begins with a shot of a half-moon, which must be a mistake since the last episode (i.e., the previous night) showed a full moon.

Notice the 52 Pick-Up Girl who escorts Audrey in to see Blackie (at time 39:33)—she can be seen smiling and looking off screen (presumably at someone else).

The first draft of episode 6 was completed on November 3, 1989; it was later revised November 8, 16, 17 & 18, 1989.

Notable Deleted Scenes

Act 1: The episode opens as Cooper and Audrey are having breakfast in the Great Northern dining room. The script indicates that Cooper is focused on his breakfast; he "never looks up from his food" and his conversation with Audrey is limited to simple questions and one-word replies. Audrey is described as "loving the moment" and having a "loving smile." As they eat, they talk about Laura and her secrets. Audrey then tells Cooper she has a job but won't say where.

The breakfast scene is deliberately ambiguous; it is impossible to tell what happened between Cooper and Audrey the previous night. Did they sleep together? Audrey's behavior indicates they did. And so does Cooper's—he seems distant and preoccupied, as if whatever happened between them is giving him pause. But the scene can be read another way, that only the promise of a relationship exists between Cooper and Audrey. Audrey is clearly in love, and Cooper, who finally "sees the adoring expression on [Audrey's] face," does little to dissuade her. In effect, the scene is a tease. It is designed to leave viewers wondering about what happened. The televised version dramatically altered the dynamic of the relationship: A tactful but certain Cooper tells Audrey that a relationship between him and Audrey is impossible.

Why was the scene changed? Kyle MacLachlan had expressed reservations about a love story featuring Cooper and Audrey but it has always been assumed that the storyline was designed for the second season.

According to Harley Peyton, the Cooper-Audrey romance was supposed to happen after the Laura Palmer mystery was resolved: "It seemed like a great thing to do next—to have that love affair carry the show for about six episodes. We had planned it, but unfortunately Kyle refused to do it."[3]

Did MacLachlan balk at the storyline as early as the first season? Possibly. Or maybe the writers decided to shelve the romance for later. The final scene of episode 5 is tantalizing—but the opening scene of the televised episode 6 is definitive (Cooper is not interested in pursuing a relationship with Audrey). Something happened to cause the producers of *Twin Peaks* to re-write the scene and to effectively close doors on a storyline they had introduced so early in the narrative.

Act 2: At the Great Northern, Catherine Martell sits on Ben Horne's desk. She complains about the Icelanders, calling them "heathens." Einer Thorson, the lead Icelandic delegate, enters and Ben introduces him to Catherine. Jerry Horne interrupts; he's about to take the Icelanders on a tour of the Ghostwood development site. He leaves with Einer. Catherine and Ben discuss Josie and the burning of the mill. Ben assures her the mill will burn soon. All of this material was cut from the televised version; it did little to move the plot forward and functioned primarily to remind viewers of Ben and Catherine's plan to burn the mill (and to remind viewers of Ben's double-dealing with Josie). This is one of many Ben-and-Catherine scenes that was deleted or shortened. Almost all these deleted scenes feature Ben and Catherine talking about burning the mill. Perhaps the writers of *Twin Peaks* thought it necessary to regularly remind viewers of this unfolding story but during the filming and editing of the series realized such scenes were redundant.

At the Hurley house, a forlorn Nadine watches *Invitation to Love*. Nadine tells Ed her drape-runner patent was rejected. The script contains some additional lines of dialogue, cut from the televised version. Nadine describes the life she wanted to lead with Ed: "Long peaceful Sundays on the water, just the two of us, a whole new world. That's what I was gonna buy. A new love." Nadine then tells Ed, "If you want to leave me, I'll understand. I won't blame you and I won't get mad." Then, "I want to leave me too. I want to climb right out of my skin." These deleted lines reveal much more about the psychology of Nadine. Despairing (and aware of her unhappy domestic life), Nadine was hoping to fix things between herself and Ed. She wanted their life to be happy. These lines humanize the character—Nadine is shown as a loving person, despite her skewed psyche. (In contrast, the televised version diminishes Nadine and relegates her to a quirky supporting character.) This scene also foreshadows Nadine's "memory regression" in the second season. Nadine explicitly states, "I want to leave me too." That, coupled with her desire to regain a loving relationship with Ed may explain why Nadine later "wakes up" as teenager, newly in love with Big Ed Hurley.

At the Great Northern, Audrey hears voices from her father's office and ducks into her hiding place to investigate. She sees her mother, Sylvia, with Dr. Jacoby and Johnny. Jacoby is trying to explain to Johnny that Laura is not coming back, that she has gone to "someplace safe and warm." Jacoby tells Johnny that Laura has gone to a place, "where every stranger is a friend. And every friend greets you with a smile. All those smiling faces make a kind of music. . . . Laura's hearing it now. She's singing for you and me." These lines (like those of the cemetery caretaker's lines in episode 4) recall Cooper's dream and the place "where there's always music in the air."

Jacoby and Sylvia Horne step away from Johnny and move only inches from Audrey's peephole. She's sees their lips as they talk. Sylvia tells Jacoby a secret about Johnny and Audrey: "When Johnny fell. Johnny was nine. Audrey was just a baby, crawling then. We were standing at the top of the stairs, talking, Johnny and I. Audrey tried to stand up and pushed against Johnny's leg. He took a step back onto one of her toys and slipped and the next thing I knew . . . Johnny was falling down the stairs . . . all the way down . . . he didn't just fall. Audrey pushed him." Upon hearing this, Audrey is devastated. She quietly flees from her hiding place and does not hear the rest of the conversation. Jacoby explains, "Johnny's condition is not the result of a fall or physical injury of any kind. His faculties are intact. He has simply retreated to a world of his own devising, a place where he feels safe. . . . His fall had nothing to do with his current condition and neither does Audrey." Sylvia Horne is confused. Why would Johnny retreat into his mind? Jacoby theorizes, "He made this choice in order to escape some emotional psychological trauma from early childhood, or perhaps infancy. And if I can unearth his secret, I know I can bring Johnny back to us again."

All of this plot and backstory was dropped, probably because it over-complicated the already complicated storyline. Had the plot been introduced it would have burdened Audrey with tremendous guilt, something with which she'd have to cope while investigating Laura's murder. Still, the guilt factor does help explain Audrey's motivation for boldly applying to One Eyed Jacks as a prostitute instead of simply informing the authorities of the perfume-counter connection (something she was trying to do before the Jacoby/Johnny scene). Audrey's potential feeling of low self-worth may have propelled her into the dangerous course of action she pursued at One Eyed Jacks.

The Johnny plot opened some interesting possibilities. It would have allowed Dr. Jacoby to do more in the series and it would have undoubtedly led to another secret of the Horne family. But the *Twin Peaks* narrative was sprouting a variety of story branches and this subplot was likely pruned to keep the tangled narrative more manageable.

Later, Audrey slips a note under Cooper's door and notices the "Asian Man" checking in. The script describes Audrey as having "eyes red from crying," an obvious reaction to news she recently heard about how she pushed Johnny. The televised version does not depict a crying Audrey. (The earlier scene between Sylvia Horne and Dr. Jacoby was definitely shot. Jan D'Arcy, who played Sylvia Horne, commented on it during the 1993 *Twin Peaks* Fan Festival: "Around the sixth episode we did shoot material that never was played. I told Dr. Jacoby that Audrey had pushed Johnny down the stairs . . . . Of course, the story went another direction.") Audrey's departure scene may have been shot two ways (one with crying, one without) in order to give the editors the option of deleting the earlier scene yet still maintain continuity.

Cast and Crew Comments

Harley Peyton: Sherilyn's character was fun. It's funny, because typically my favorites were relatively minor characters. But it was always fun writing that Cooper stuff. Once you found that rhythm there was a lot of fun to be had. You know, where he's talking into the recorder, and all that. I always enjoyed that. That was one of the best parts of the show, particularly for me because we had these dialogue lines and I could focus on dialogue, which is what I like to do.

Sheryl Lee: Maddy didn't walk on the dark side like Laura did. With Laura that is so much a part of who she is. It was always present. Whereas with Maddy it wasn't there at all. She was completely naïve of any sort of a world like [Laura's].

Everett McGill: I think that David always had in his mind that in the first season I could be a potential suspect. And I think that as the viewers began to feel more comfortable and become more interested in the character that possibly he saw him less as a suspect. Or maybe David just thought of it as a sweetening of the character, but still wanted to keep Big Ed as a possible suspect. I think the natural evolution of the character sweetened it up. I'm not sure that it didn't take some of the bite out of Big Ed. Because he was always somewhat mysterious. He was comfortable in the community and he had a good relationship with the kids. And he was tolerant. I think that made him something special to the community.

We also had the involvement of Mark Frost on *Twin Peaks*. And the relationship between Mark and David is something I never inquired about. But I suspect that there might have been some kind of small conflicts there, which could have gotten in the way of some story ideas and character development. I don't know.

Harley Peyton: That first season of *Twin Peaks*—we could do whatever we wanted. I've never seen anything like that before. The network barely looked at scripts. We never got a script note from them. I've been pounded by networks since—and that's their job—but on *Twin Peaks*, not at all! They had no idea what to tell us.

Episode 7 (Script number 1007; First televised May 23, 1990)

Guest Starring: Walter Olkewicz (Jacques Renault), Victoria Catlin (Blackie O'Reilly)

Featuring: Charles Hoyes (Decker), Brian Straub (Einar Thorson), Lance Davis (Martin Hadley: "Chet" on Invitation to Love*), Rick Giolito (Jason Denbo: "Montana" on* Invitation to Love*), Peter Michael Goetz (Evan St. Vincent: "Jared" on* Invitation to Love*)*

Written and Directed by Mark Frost; Edited by Paul Trejo

The events in this episode take place on the night of Thursday, March 2, 1989—one week after the death of Laura Palmer:

Act 1: James and Donna find Laura's necklace and some audio tapes. Jacoby is beaten by a masked assailant. Cooper gives Jacques the poker chip with the piece missing. In Blackie's office, Audrey sees Cooper on a monitor. Hawk and Ed listen as Cooper talks with Jacques and offers him a job "across the border." Jacques tells Cooper about the poker chip.

Act 2: Leo assaults Shelly. Truman and Andy arrest Jacques. Andy shoots Jacques when he pulls a gun. James, Donna, and Maddy listen to Laura's February 23 tape. She talks about a "mystery man" with a red Corvette who has tried to kill her. Leo has Shelly tied up in the mill and is about to set it on fire. Nadine prepares to commit suicide by overdose. Hank collects his $90,000 from Josie; Hank wonders if it was worth spending eighteen months in jail to avoid implication in a murder (presumably Andrew Packard's boating "accident"). Hank says he and Josie are in business "for life." He slices their thumbs and mixes their blood.

Act 3: Catherine searches for the missing account ledger. Lucy tells Andy she's pregnant. Cooper learns that Jacques and Leo fought at the cabin; Jacques was bleeding and used Leo's shirt to stop it. Jacques says he doesn't know anything about the train car. Hank calls Catherine and tells her the ledger is at the mill. Hank asks Norma to give him a chance to make her proud. Ed finds Nadine passed out.

Act 4: James gives Laura's February 23 tape to Cooper. Truman finds the drugs in James's gas tank. Bobby is attacked by Leo who is then shot by Hank. Catherine finds Shelly as the fire begins. Leland smothers Jacques with a pillow. Pete enters the burning mill looking for Catherine. To celebrate the development deal, Ben decides to see "the new girl" (Audrey) at One Eyed Jacks. Cooper believes Leo is responsible for Laura's death. Returning to his room, he finds Audrey's note (left in episode 6), and gets a phone call from Andy (they've found Leo). He answers a knock on the door, expecting it to be room service. Someone shoots him in the chest three times.

The first season comes to a satisfying and exhilarating conclusion in an episode written and directed by series co-creator, Mark Frost. All the subplots reach critical mass. Episode 7 is easily *Twin Peaks'* most action-packed episode.

Almost every scene in every act has an urgency to it. Tension and action increase as the episode hurdles toward a series of major cliff-hangers. While these cliffhangers introduce new questions and uncertainty, many of the story's existing questions get resolved. Episode 7 explains what happened in the cabin the night Laura Palmer died; how Jacques' blood got on Leo's shirt; and the relationship between Hank and Josie. Other, minor arcs are resolved—Andy is redeemed by saving Truman's life; the mill fire is finally set (by Leo, under Ben's employment); and the Ghostwood development deal, which Audrey sabotaged in the pilot, gets finalized with the Icelanders. Even *Invitation To Love* reaches a conclusion, of sorts, with the shooting of Montana (though, like *Twin Peaks*, the shooter is not revealed; it could be Chet, Jared, or even someone else). The close-up of the gloved hand foreshadows the attack on Cooper at the end of the episode.

Naturally, given the serial nature of the show, many of the dramatic developments—Audrey's arrival at One Eyed Jack's, the burning of the mill, Nadine's physical condition, Leland's mental stability—are not given closure. Instead, they create new directions for the storyline to travel in season 2. While episode 7 is intensely satisfying because it supplies so many dramatic shifts it is also tantalizingly incomplete because it leaves all the stories open.

The major storyline is, of course, the mystery of Laura Palmer's murder, and it's clear that had the series ended with the first season (its renewal was unconfirmed until just before the final episode aired), Leo would have been considered the killer. Obviously, he is capable of murder, and his alibi—that he was on the road—is false, since he was at Jacques' cabin. Leo was the last person to be seen with Laura and Ronette. On her February 23 tape, Laura mentioned a man with a red Corvette who had tried to kill her several times; and her final diary entry stated that she was nervous about meeting "J" that night, which could have been a reference to Leo Johnson (if it did not refer to James). Even Cooper's Tibetan deductive technique, described in episode 2, suggests that Leo is the killer. Under this scenario, the blood on the rag near the train car would have to be Leo's blood.

So, if the series ended with Leo as the killer how would one explain the "third man" mentioned in episode 5 (who is revealed to be the killer in the second season)? This could easily have been another red herring, such as the man hiding behind the tree in episode 2. Remember, there is nothing in the investigation so far that proves a third man was necessarily at the scene.

The Log Lady's account in episode 5 is vague; the other man need not be connected to Laura's murder—it could have been Jacques, who told Cooper that he had to walk home fifteen miles.

If the show had not been renewed, all of the subplots would have been left unresolved. Mark Frost has explained that there were no plans to change the ending if the show did not get picked up for a second season. Still, the primary question: "Who killed Laura Palmer?" could be said to have been resolved.

Additional Notes:

The construction of episode 7 is different from the others because it does not depict a full day in Twin Peaks, but is a continuation of the day started in episode 6. Everything takes place on the night of Thursday, March 2, one week after the party in the cabin that led to Laura's death.

The lines Ben Horne speaks near the end of act 4 are from Shakespeare's *The Tempest*.

Look closely at the bottom of Cooper's door when he enters his room at the end of act 4—two feet can clearly be seen stepping into place. These are the feet of Cooper's assailant.

According to production designer, Richard Hoover, the hunchback fixing Audrey's dress at One Eyed Jack's was inspired by Grimm's Fairy Tales.

The first draft of episode 7 was completed on November 25, 1989; it was later revised on December 4 & 11, 1989.

Notable Deleted Scenes

Act 1: At the park, Jacoby sees Maddy dressed as Laura. He is attacked by the mysterious assailant and suffers a heart attack. He watches as Donna and James arrive to pick up Maddy. The script contains an additional sequence that was cut from the televised version. According to the script, "Jacoby fumbles in his pocket for a vial of medication. He finally pries the lid off the vial, spills the small pills on the ground, desperately scrabbles for one, manages a tenuous grip and pops it into his mouth. He lies on his back trying to breath, staring up at the night sky." This scene, though not essential, helps explain how Jacoby survived his heart attack.

Act 3: At Calhoun Memorial Hospital, Cooper interrogates Jacques Renault. The script contains some substantial dialogue that was cut from the televised version. Cooper asks about the *Fleshworld* connection and the ads Laura and Ronette placed. Jacques explains, "It was a scam. Takin' these horny old guys, sending money in for dirty pictures, underwear." Jacques confirms Cooper's theory that the pictures were taken at the cabin. These brief lines help explain a number of small, unresolved elements of the Laura storyline (the kinky pictures addressed to Laura and Ronette and sent to Jacques' P.O. box, the pictures of Laura and Ronette, the camera found in Jacques' cabin). The televised version never properly resolves the *Fleshworld* connection. In contrast, the script efficiently resolves the subplot by revealing all the preceding *Fleshworld* "clues" as mere red herrings (i.e., a "scam"). Jacques' *Fleshworld* information may have been deliberately deleted by Mark Frost so that he could continue to use the *Fleshworld* element in the second season. (In episode 8, Cooper and Truman find a copy of *Fleshworld* at Leo's. Cooper theorizes that Teresa Banks may have also had a connection to *Fleshworld,* and he assigns Andy and Lucy to scour back issues for her picture.)

Back at the Blue Pine Lodge, Pete and Catherine continue to search for the ledger. Catherine gets a call from a stranger (Hank) who tells her she'll find "what she's looking for" at the mill. Catherine grabs a gun and prepares to leave. The televised version cuts away at this point but the script contains more material. Pete wants to know where Catherine is going, but she won't say. Pete wants to help, but Catherine is insistent: "You can help me by staying here, that way if I need you I won't have to go looking for you." Pete is not happy with the situation. Meanwhile, Josie, listening from another room, checks her watch. This scene was not necessary and was probably cut for time constraints. Still, the scene establishes Pete's frame-of-mind and provides clearer motivation for his later action of entering the burning mill in search of Catherine.

Act 4: Ben and Einer complete their deal. Ben asks Blackie about the new girl. The script cuts to Audrey's room where the "bell goes off." Audrey looks at herself in the mirror, and then turns to the sound of the door opening. This sequence was changed for the televised version. There, a strange old woman sews a playing card to Audrey's corset and leaves. Audrey retreats to her bed. Ben Horne opens the door and walks down a short hall leading into the room. The script contains no mention of the strange old seamstress (an ad-libbed moment that showed Mark Frost at his most Lynchian.) The script also did not explicitly show Ben entering the room. As written, Ben's presence is only implied.

At Calhoun Memorial Hospital, Leland smothers Jacques Renault with a pillow. The televised version cuts away after this scene but the script has more. Leland leaves Jacques' room and heads towards Dr. Jacoby's. Jacoby is awake with, according to the script, "one eye open." He closes it when Leland enters. Leland advances on Jacoby but he hears voices in the hall and he hastily leaves. This scene clearly indicates that Jacoby had seen Leland in the hospital. It also strongly implies that Leland was going to kill Jacoby. The scene may have been cut to allow the writers more story options for the second season. (Recall that Jacoby only remembers Leland's presence after hypnosis.)

At the Hayward house, Donna and Maddy "huddle on the sofa in front of the fire." Eileen Hayward brings cookies and milk. An unidentified figure is watching them through the window. The figure moves to another window then reaches up with gloved hands and attempts to open it. The script cuts away, leaving the fates of Donna, Maddy and Eileen uncertain.

Who was this unidentified figure? The script only provides a point-of-view description (that is, the audience only sees what the figure sees) so we might assume this is the same person who stalked Maddy at the beginning of the episode (and who attacked Jacoby). Later events (from the second season) revealed Jacoby's assailant to be Bob (inhabiting Leland). Was the mysterious voyeur at the Hayward's also supposed to be Bob? If so, that would mean Bob followed Maddy, attacked Jacoby, "withdrew" from Leland (who then killed Jacques), then re-possessed Leland and continued his pursuit of Maddy—a confusing and complicated sequence of events.

It may be that Mark Frost had not worked out the identity of the mysterious person at the time he was writing the script, the stalker was just a malevolent figure to whom an identity would later be assigned. By the time of shooting and editing the episode, Frost may have realized this cliffhanger introduced too much complexity to the narrative and so deleted the scene.

The writing (and subsequent deletion) of this scene implies that the *Twin Peaks* narrative was not as fully developed as viewers might have thought. At one point Frost clearly intended an extra cliffhanger. Did he know how that cliffhanger might resolve? Or was it purposely left open and undefined? If so, were all the cliffhangers open to different outcomes? Frost may have scripted the first season finale with a multitude of resolutions in mind. That way, when (or if) *Twin Peaks* was renewed he and Lynch could choose the best direction for the narrative.

Cast and Crew Comments

Walter Olkewicz: I only did three episodes and in two of them I didn't do anything. But for one, Mark Frost did that wonderful thing with just my lips: that scene in front of the fish tank. "Bite the bullet, baby."

[In the hospital scene] Kyle MacLachlan had a practical joke going. He was trying to make me laugh the whole time. I was all tied up, I couldn't really reach him. He was putting jelly beans in my mouth. He was saying, "You want this, don't you? You want this." I would tell him, "Cut it out, I'm trying to get in character here." That's almost my favorite scene I did in the show or the movie. There was a physical state there [that] I worked on for a really long time. Just the in-and-outness of being drugged from painkillers. I liked where it all went. There were a couple of times I just drifted off totally and then I came back and my eyes came back into focus. When I saw all of that put together I was most pleased with it.

Chris Mulkey: I always liked Joan Chen. She's one of the people that I really hooked with. I thought she was a wonderful actress. We got huge mail from [the blood scene]. The AIDS epidemic is certainly more understood now but, as raging as it was then, there was a huge amount of paranoia about it: "How could Chris and Joan Chen drink each other's blood and how could they share that? It's disgusting." People were writing into the LA *Times* about it. But it was a great wrap. Mark Frost directed that episode. It was the end of the first set of shows before we came back. He said, "This is great!" Actually, he didn't tell us to lick the blood, but we just kind of did it. Good stuff. That's what good bad guys do. Drink their blood and eat their heart.

Mark Frost: I was not very responsive to ABC's notes all the way through, particularly that first season. David wasn't even around. He was off making *Wild at Heart*. And I'd fought plenty of wars with networks in the past. So we just really stuck by our guns and did exactly what we wanted to do. I was always planning to leave them stuck with a cliffhanger—in fact a massive cliffhanger. I wanted to [involve] everybody—sort of do a number on that usual, stupid, season-ending thing that those shows did. So I put *everybody* into jeopardy.

Catherine Coulson: I think [David] really thought *Twin Peaks* was going to be a miniseries. I think he always intended it as a short-term project, but because of its popularity, everyone kind of got seduced into making it longer. It captured people's imagination, and it kept going, and the network played with the timeslot, and it lost that initial fire of what they call the water-cooler effect, you know?

Charlotte Stewart: I remember we were at Dana Ashbrook's house for the last episode of the first season. He had us all over for dinner. We all sat down to watch the show. And the last shot came and Kyle got shot. We all just went, "What? Oh my God! We've just been fired!" We didn't know of it was going to get picked up. We were all just looking at each other saying, "Is that it? Are we over?"

Sheryl Lee: We were all trying to figure out what was going to happen because we wouldn't get our scripts very far in advance. [Cooper] was so interested in the case, and so present there. But you just never knew which way these writers were going to go.

Charlotte Stewart: Every episode was different; we never knew where it was going; we couldn't wait to watch the show every week. There was so much going on about it and there were so many young people starting out! I remember when we were shooting the pilot; Sheryl [Lee] thought that all she was going to do was be the body. And she was OK with that. But I think they fell madly in love with her. She was an interesting girl and did such a good job. The story unfolded as they got to know the cast.

Chris Mulkey: In that particular cast it seemed like a lot of the actors were musicians or artists or poets. And they were kind of multifaceted artists. It was extraordinary in that way. I don't know why that was. It was a very "rock-and-roll" cast—a pretty wild cast. This whole group of people had all kinds of passions flying in every different way. I think that was maybe a common theme through it and what made it so great a group of actors— they all had these incredible passions going in every different way and it made them all individual and unique.

Dana Ashbrook: Richard [Beymer] and Catherine [Coulson] and Russ [Tamblyn] and the rest of us went to New York to do *Donahue*. We ended up hanging out one night and Richard took us to his favorite Indian restaurant. I was not familiar with New York City at that point. Richard was in *West Side Story*! That was always a huge movie around our house. My dad was a musical director. We just loved that movie. And it was just bizarre to be there with him and Russ and Catherine. It was trippy, man. It was cool! I was just soaking it up. I really enjoyed it. They were really great to me and they are really sweet people.

Kimmy Robertson: The whole experience, even though it was hard in some ways, was so phenomenally wonderful. It was a dream-come-true. A lot of people miss their dreams. I was really lucky to have every one of them come true. It was a magical and spiritual experience for me.

Miguel Ferrer: It was such a joy. You know, between Kyle [MacLachlan] and Mike [Ontkean], everybody just got along so great. We were all just thrilled to be at work. Everybody showed up with a big smile. The crew was great! Nobody was making any money, except for Kyle and Mike. But it was really a special time.

Catherine Coulson: [Viewers] felt personally involved with what was going on in *Twin Peaks*. We were in their living room and there was a real connection, which may also be why the fans have stayed so loyal. There's this real personal connection that they have with the stories and with the people who played those characters.

THE SUMMER OF 1990:

SECRET DIARIES AND SATURDAY NIGHT LIVE

Four months passed between the end of *Twin Peaks* season one and the beginning of season two. For fans of the show, the summer of 1990 was a time of intense speculation and heightened anticipation. The identity of Laura Palmer's killer remained unknown, and fans of the series had many theories about whom the killer might be. It was, in fact, a fun party game, with many followers of the show trading guesses about likely suspects. What's more, the question, "Who killed Laura Palmer?" became a pop-culture sensation (much like, "Who shot J.R.?" from the TV series, *Dallas*, years earlier). It was not uncommon to see the mystery referenced in such places as *The New Yorker* magazine or in political cartoons in national newspapers.

To build on the excitement for the second season, ABC television started re-broadcasting the first season in August. This not only allowed new viewers to see what all the hype was about, it also provided a kind of "review" for the regular audience as they prepared for the new season. At one point, there was even a rumor of a recap (or "bridge") episode—an original production designed to fit between the first and second seasons and one that would review all the critical season-one events. Such a program never came about.

But merchandise did. The *Diane* audio tape *("Diane . . ." The* Twin Peaks *Tapes of Agent Cooper)* was released, giving listeners a recap of all Cooper's messages to Diane during the first season, plus original material recorded by Kyle MacLachlan and written by Scott Frost. The tape provided a tantalizing glimpse into the upcoming season: it included Cooper's season-two dialogue about seeing "a giant" while he lay wounded on the floor of his room in the Great Northern. This cassette teased fans with cryptic clues about what the upcoming season premiere would actually show. (In 1991, the *Diane* tape earned MacLachlan a Grammy nomination for best spoken word performance.)

That summer also saw print of an unauthorized book, *Welcome to Twin Peaks: A Complete Guide to Who's Who and What's What* by Scott Knicklebine. The book contained an overview of the *Twin Peaks* phenomenon, profiles of all the main characters, and a concise summary of each episode. It also featured information on Lynch, Mark Frost and other behind-the-scenes personalities. But the book was a rushed and simple affair; Knicklebine culled quotes from various newspaper or magazine articles about *Twin Peaks* to fill-out his chapters. He also lapsed into easy and simplistic descriptions of the main characters and their stories ("James must avoid the wrath of Laura's former two-timing boyfriend, Bobby Briggs"). So, the book did little to meet the needs of eager *Twin Peaks* fans. Still, years later, the book's questions and theories about the upcoming season 2 recapture the mood of those four summer months of frenzied discussion, debate, and expectation.

Kyle MacLachlan on Saturday Night Live

Kyle MacLachlan was the guest host on *Saturday Night Live* on September 29, 1990—the night before the second-season premiere of *Twin Peaks*. MacLachlan appeared in a number of skits with the regular *SNL* cast—a group that may have been one of the most talented assemblages of comedic talent in the history of *Saturday Night Live*. Regulars on *SNL* during the 1990-1991 season included (among others) Dana Carvey, Mike Meyers, Phil Hartman, Chris Rock, Dennis Miller and Chris Farley. Writers (and featured players on the show) included such talents as Conan O'Brien and Al Franken. It is not surprising, then, that the MacLachlan episode of *SNL* was funny from beginning to end.

MacLachlan first appears in the opening monologue. He introduces himself and mentions his work on *Blue Velvet* and *Twin Peaks*. Then he asks the audience if they have any questions for him. He receives a few basic questions about himself until an audience member asks, "Who killed Laura Palmer?" MacLachlan fields the question as if it was any other and casually answers, "It's Shelly-the-waitress, and we reveal it in the last episode." There are no other questions and MacLachlan is about to start the show when a voice from the control room tells him he has a phone call. MacLachlan makes his way to the control room where he learns that the call is from "David Lynch." MacLachlan innocently says, "Hello" and asks David if he is watching the show and what he thinks. Suddenly, he hears Lynch "yelling" at him (the voice is not really Lynch, but another actor). Lynch is furious that MacLachlan would reveal the identity of the killer. At first, MacLachlan tries to excuse his remarks, "He asked me—what was I supposed to do? Lie? They're gonna find out anyway." Lynch (shown in a photo) browbeats MacLachlan who starts to respond, "Yes, sir." MacLachlan, mortified, hangs up the phone and returns to the stage. He tells the audience he was "just making a joke" and that he would never reveal the killer: "Only a real idiot, who never wanted to work in

Hollywood—and who deserves a real big spanking—would do something like that!" MacLachlan then introduces the musical guest and begins the show.

The opening monologue is funny for many obvious reasons: MacLachlan matter-of-factly reveals the killer, as if unaware of the magnitude of the secret. The identity of the killer is rather unlikely (although, sure, it *could* have been Shelly; at this point just about everyone was a suspect). Then Lynch, who in reality has a reputation as a gentle and kind person, *screams* at MacLachlan! (Some may not have fully appreciated this part of the skit, but the idea that Lynch would get so furious is funny, even without the murderer's identity being an issue.)

MacLachlan later appears in the funniest skit on the show: The *Twin Peaks* parody. The skit (running 8 minutes, 45 seconds) succeeds on a number of levels: It works as a stand-alone sketch, a hilarious parody of the first season of *Twin Peaks*, and also as a precise satire of the series.

The *Twin Peaks* skit is well-written and nicely structured. Unlike many *SNL* skits, the *Twin Peaks* parody tells a complete story (one with a beginning, middle and end). Often, sketches on *SNL* lose their way either by becoming repetitive or by ending too abruptly. Not so here.

Cooper (MacLachlan) opens the sketch in his room at the Great Northern. In a monologue to Diane, Cooper provides all the minute details of his day, from his shower routine to the number of donuts he's consumed. Sheriff Truman (Kevin Nealon) bursts in to announce they have caught Laura Palmer's killer: "It was Leo. He just confessed." Cooper ignores him and this sets up the main premise of the skit: Cooper prefers to follow his own unusual methods of investigation—he does not want to accept the simple facts before him. He tells Truman, "Harry, in the FBI we are trained in one very important thing—to look beyond the obvious. Last night I had a dream [in which] I saw a hairless mouse holding a pitch-fork and singing a song about caves."

Deputy Andy (Conan O'Brien) arrives escorting a handcuffed Leo (Chris Farley). Leo is surly but admits to the murder: "I guess you heard I did it. I'm ready to do my time. Get me a beer!" Cooper refuses to accept the confession ("This certainly puts him high on the list of suspects!") but everyone else does. Leland (Phil Hartman) arrives to thank Cooper for catching the killer: "Now that it's over—I'm going to miss you!" Cooper tells Leland that Laura's killer is still at large. Leland breaks down and "dances" from the room in grief. Audrey (Victoria Jackson) comes in. She heard that they caught Leo and wants to say good-bye to Cooper. She has brought him a gift but hasn't finished wrapping it. She gobbles up some red ribbon she spits out a perfectly-tied bow!

Leo says he has pictures of the murder: "Here's me—about to kill her. Here's me—killing her. Here's me—wrapping her in plastic." To rid himself of Leo, Cooper has an idea to throw a rock through the window: "If it breaks, Leo is innocent." Cooper throws the rock and (of course) the window shatters. Cooper quickly announces, "Leo, you're free to go." Leo repeats his confession then asks if Cooper received the notes he sent. Truman sees them on the desk and reads: "Dear Agent Cooper, why no response about me killing Laura Palmer? Are you still on the case? If not, please forward to proper authorities. Yours truly, Leo 'the killer-of-Laura-Palmer' Johnson."

Nadine (Jan Hooks) interrupts. She knows the case is over and wants Cooper to bring her silent drape runner to the patent office when he returns to Washington, D.C. Nadine exits and Truman is ready to go—but Cooper still wants to hear from the Log Lady. Kevin Nealon "breaks out" of the skit to announce that a visit from the Log Lady is impossible because, "There are only two women left on *Saturday Night Live* and we've already used them both up." (In fact, Nealon is referring to the absence of former *SNL* cast member, Nora Dunn, who was not asked to return to the show for the new season. Dunn had boycotted the final episode of *SNL* the previous season because she objected to the crude comedy of guest host, Andrew Dice Clay. The Andrew Dice Clay controversy caused the musical guest for that same show—Sinead O'Connor—to also back out. As a result, Julee Cruise appeared as one of the musical guests on Clay's show. Sinead O'Connor ended up as musical guest on the MacLachlan show.) Suddenly, the Log Lady appears (played again by Hooks, who is "out of breath" from the quick costume change). The Log Lady tells Cooper, "My log says Leo did it."

Truman starts to leave. Cooper, desperate, admits that Leo is the killer but tells Truman, "We still haven't figured out who shot me." In a perfect punchline, Leo says, "I did! Geez! You saw me!"

Cooper is left alone. He reports to Diane, "I guess I'm going to be heading home several months earlier than I planned." Then the door opens and the Little Man from Another Place (Mike Meyers) enters. In "backwards talk" (complete with subtitles) he consoles Cooper about the case: "Heard about Leo confessing. Tough break." Cooper, dejected, goes to bed. The skit ends as the Little Man dances to "Dance of the Dream Man."

Obviously, the *Twin Peaks* sketch pokes fun at a number of the unusual and memorable elements from the first season of *Twin Peaks*: Cooper tells Diane details about everything he's done during his day (including the kind of towel he used after his shower); Leo demands a beer (even though he is under arrest); Leland dances with grief (to which Cooper remarks, "His dancing is actually getting quite good"); Audrey ties the ribbon with her tongue (a delightful parody of her cherry-stem trick from the series); Cooper throws a rock (a mockery of Cooper's unusual rock-throwing detective work). These, and other parts of the sketch, acknowledge the already exaggerated nature of *Twin Peaks*, a show that was laced with idiosyncratic humor (tongue-tied cherry-stems and investigative rock-throwing) and over-the-top black comedy (a menacing Leo and a wailing Leland).

But the sketch also cleverly satirizes *Twin Peaks*. During the first season, viewers and critics acknowledged the drawn-out nature of the show. Many viewers wondered if the show had a plan, if the murderer would be revealed before too long. By positioning Cooper as an agent who refuses to solve the case, the sketch reminds the audience of a potentially frustrating aspect of the series—that the murder has not yet been resolved. What's more, once it does get resolved, what will happen to Cooper? The *SNL* skit addresses these concerns and in so doing functions as a legitimate critique of the series.

Ironically, the *SNL* skit inadvertently works as a metaphor for a real situation. In the skit, Cooper doesn't want to leave Twin Peaks. He knows who the killer is but he doesn't ever want to tell anyone. The same could be said for David Lynch who, when asked about the structure of the series, said, "The murder mystery was eventually to become the background story. We [were] not going to solve the murder for a long time. The progress toward it, but never getting there, was what made us know all the people in Twin Peaks."[1] In effect, the Cooper in the skit is a surrogate David Lynch. He wants to stay in Twin Peaks, keep the murderer's identity a secret, and get to know all the people from the town.

The *SNL Twin Peaks* sketch is brilliant piece of comedy. It deftly incorporates many of the wonderful aspects of *Twin Peaks* while commenting on the nature of serial storytelling. Of course, the writers at *SNL* had a rich mine from which to draw material; no other show was as complex and astounding as *Twin Peaks*. It deserved to be "made-fun-of" well. And it was.

The Secret Diary of Laura Palmer

The most important development between season one and two of *Twin Peaks* was the release of *The Secret Diary of Laura Palmer* by Jennifer Lynch (Pocket Books. 1990, 184pp), a powerful and informative work that enhances the filmic world of both series and film. The book covers the final five years of Laura's life, beginning with her twelfth birthday.

At the beginning of the Diary, Laura is an almost happy and innocent child. But hidden between the lines, barely perceptible both to the reader and to Laura, is a looming threat of terrible magnitude. Laura writes of being a bad person and describes her guilt over that conviction. She also describes a preoccupation with death, her disturbing dreams, and an obsession with sex. Obviously, something serious has transpired in her life before she started her diary.

From the beginning, there is a strong suggestion that Laura has been sexually molested, perhaps for many years. In her inability to deal with that reality she has apparently imagined the figure of BOB, a long-haired, bearded man who climbs through her window and attacks her in her own room, destroying all sense of security. Her powerlessness to escape the attacks leads her to a hellish world of promiscuity, drug abuse, and depression.

BOB's attacks upon Laura are emotionally draining to read, and, as Laura battles against the demons in her life, her struggle reaches almost epic proportions. Although the book stands on its own, it meshes well with the series and *Fire Walk With Me*. In fact, Sheryl Lee, who played Laura Palmer, described using the book to get additional insight into her character:

> "The book was with me night and day [during the filming of *Fire Walk With Me*]. I carried it everywhere and would constantly refer back to it. It was such a blessing to have. I think that Jennifer's amazing—she's so talented and writes from a place of truth. It's funny, when I see people hold the diary I almost feel like they shouldn't be reading it. I feel like it's personal. It's a very strange thing; we get very close to our characters. So I did carry the book everywhere and use it."[2]

Jennifer Lynch Discusses The Secret Diary of Laura Palmer

Jennifer Lynch: The idea started years before *Twin Peaks* did. I would be in the car with my father. I told him that I had long had this fantasy of walking home from school and finding another girl's diary at the edge of the sidewalk by a gutter, of tucking it under my jacket and running home to read it to see if other girls dreamt and felt and feared the same things I did. That stayed with him. When *Twin Peaks* was born, the idea of the diary inevitably came up as a way to tell [more of] the story. He called me right away and said, "Would you write Laura's diary?" "Of course," I said, "Are you kidding me?!" [*laughs*]

We had worked together on ideas and projects and I had assisted him in the office for years, but this was a new step—a new level—of working with him. It was also the seed-to-fruition of a childhood fantasy.

He and Mark Frost took me into the office one day and told me who Laura's killer was and said, "You are one of the three air-breathing mammals who know." And then they said, "Go write the diary." They gave me full reign.

Did you think the title—The Secret Diary of Laura Palmer—*was a bit of a joke since diaries are supposed to be secret?*

My take was that the title was a very male way of seeing diaries. Of course, the assumption is that they are secret. For a while, in the seventies and eighties, there were diaries that were sold in stationary stores that said, "My Secret Diary." That, somehow, became ingrained in the brains of both David and Mark. And it made it all the more tantalizing because both of them are men who are particularly fond of secrets, and, hence, "The Secret Diary of Laura Palmer." (As opposed to the newspaper she wrote every day telling everybody everything! [*laughs*])

Here is the funny and tragic story of *The Secret Diary*: It was written in nine days and it was lost four times. There was a weird thing going on—they first thought it was my computer but it was ultimately blamed on my heart murmur sending out electrical pulses. And then an X-ray machine at the airport supposedly deleted the disk. Ultimately, it was written four times, beginning to end, with some things being retrieved and others not. This was over a two-and-a-half or three-week period. It was quite a thing.

Trust me, when you have little sleep and everything keeps vanishing, you think, "Maybe Bob is involved somehow." But the final product was something like what would have come out of Laura's mindset—something that was sleep-deprived and fearful and anxiety-ridden, but always with a frank belief that there is goodness in humanity.

It was a blast. I could write epistolary novels over and over again. Because I think there is something about the voice of someone writing things [that] they think no one will ever read. It really lends itself to being brutally honest and without judgment.

Did you see an immediacy to it that you could not get with a third-person narrator?

Exactly. Who doesn't want to read or hear other people's confessions? There was an exercise I did with one my favorite teachers when I was at Interlochen Arts Academy—it was writing letters to a dead person. And the beauty of them was you could write to them about anything and no one was ever forced to read them, and you were safe in assuming you wouldn't get a response from the dead person. [*laughs*] So it was an interesting exercise and I really grew attached to that one-way communication, because if there could be any response it would be in an ethereal sort of way.

It was what I always hoped it would be. There were only two pages that ended up being, indeed, "pages ripped out." In other words, there were things that some people were concerned might be too revealing and had to be removed. I had Laura in some really dark situations and some really light

88

situations—all of those surprisingly stayed. It was only at two different points that Mark and David were concerned that it was too much of a give-away about Leland. Simon and Schuster agreed that it would be best to allow this to be an episodic treatment rather than a reveal.

I was really proud of it. I did feel, strangely, that part of me had nothing to do with writing it—that I really got into that space of being someone else, which is always a gift.

Did you envision the diary as a stand-alone work or did you assume and hope that people had a working knowledge of Twin Peaks?

I wanted to make sure that if you didn't have a working knowledge you were at least introduced to these characters enough so that you could understand the area in which Laura was living. It has a different relevance if you know the series, obviously. I wanted to make sure that if people hadn't seen the series they could at least still read it, that you weren't excluded from the adventures.

Given the constraints of the format, you did provide Laura with some closure—she knows who Bob is and is about to take some decisive action. She also seems to ask for a kind of forgiveness. Would you have liked to do more?

I feel like I had gotten Laura to the place she needed to be—in the sense that it is very hard to write, in a hopeful way, for someone you know will die tragically. So what I wanted to give her, at least, were eyes that were open enough to see that, before she died, she was going to, as you say, take these steps to emancipate herself from the situation. I didn't want her to just die as someone who didn't know—which would have been more tragic. To me, the purity of Laura was still intact because she did want forgiveness for these things that humans do. That's the sort of beauty of her—as dark and as sexual and as crazed and as victimized and as victimizing as she could get—she was human. She was still the prom queen. That's a beautiful thing. I wouldn't have given her anymore because I think we would have been less sad that she dies. I wanted to give her enough so that she went away with some of her last thoughts being, "I know who I am and I know what is being done to me. Whatever the other side is, I have done as much as I can with this life."

Were you given an end-point for the story by either Mark or David?

That was left up to me. I knew that the last entries had to be some sort of realization. I talked to them about it as I was finishing. I knew we were going to be seeing her in the Red Room and I wanted to give her some sense of ownership of that life. There was no real decisive move to say,

"Here is where it happens," but I knew that a few days later [after the end of the book] her body would be found. I wanted her last words to be as hopeful and strong in her fear as they could be. I also knew they should lead into something that Leland would tear out. Whatever was removed had to be something that had affected his ego. When I pictured him reading it, I really felt for her. And I felt him choose what to leave in as an attempt to almost embarrass her. I think in his wickedness—and in his love for her—there would be that decision to allow her to assign blame to herself, somehow, as well. You know, her naughtiness. But when she pointed a finger at him, [those pages] would have to go.

You mentioned that were some things that you wrote that David and Mark felt had to be removed. But the diary is also designed to deliberately include "missing pages." Did you actually write these missing pages or, at the very least, envision their content?

Yeah, I kind of had it in my mind. And in a lot of the pages following a missing page Laura would know that somebody had looked at her diary. Whether he tore them out at the time he read them, or at the time he killed her, I tried to leave open as much as possible. I had a sense of what those pages would be—that there would be a real calling out of him. I also think a lot of them would contain things in which her mom was also starting to know. He really needed to keep that perfect family picture alive. And Mom could not know.

The second season was being shot as I was writing it. Things were changing. Everything I wrote had happened before the season opened so I had this great freedom as long as I didn't kill anybody who needed to be alive! [*laughs*] Then I was in good shape!

TWIN PEAKS SECOND SEASON CREDITS

Kyle MacLachlan - *FBI Special Agent Dale Cooper*
Michael Ontkean - *Sheriff Harry S. Truman*
Sheryl Lee - *Madeleine Ferguson*
Joan Chen - *Josie Packard*
Sherilyn Fenn - Audrey Horne
Richard Beymer - *Benjamin Horne*
Ray Wise - *Leland Palmer*
Dana Ashbrook - *Bobby Briggs*
Mädchen Amick - *Shelly Johnson*
Peggy Lipton - *Norma Jennings*
Lara Flynn Boyle - *Donna Hayward*
James Marshall - *James Hurley*
Michael Horse - *Deputy Tommy "Hawk" Hill*
Everett McGill - *Big Ed Hurley*
Wendy Robie - *Nadine Hurley*
Russ Tamblyn - *Doctor Lawrence Jacoby*
Jack Nance - *Pete Martell*
Piper Laurie - *Catherine Martell/Tojamura*
Kimmy Robertson - *Lucy Moran*
Harry Goaz - *Deputy Andy Brennan*
Warren Frost - *Doctor Will Hayward*
Grace Zabriskie - *Sarah Palmer*
Charlotte Stewart - *Betty Briggs*
Don Davis - *Garland Briggs*
Gary Hershberger - *Mike Nelson*
Eric Da Re - *Leo Johnson*
Mary Jo Deschanel - *Eileen Hayward*
David Patrick Kelly - *Jerry Horne*
Chris Mulkey - *Hank Jennings*
Miguel Ferrer - *Albert Rosenfield*
Catherine Coulson - *Margaret Lanterman, The Log Lady*
Al Strobel - *Phillip Gerard/Mike, the One Armed Man*
Kenneth Welsh — *Windom Earle*
Ian Buchanan — *Richard (Dick) Tremayne*

Created by Mark Frost & David Lynch
Music Composed & Conducted by Angelo Badalamenti
Produced by Harley Peyton
Supervising Producer: Gregg Fienberg
Co-Producers: Robert Engels (episodes 13-29) and Robert D. Simon
Director of Photography: Frank Byers
Production Designer: Richard Hoover
Casting by Johanna Ray
Art Directors: Okowita and Daniel Proett
Costume Designer: Sara Markowitz

SEASON TWO (AND THE SUPERNATURAL):

EPISODES 8-16

The second-season premiere of *Twin Peaks* was broadcast on a Sunday night (before settling in on its regular Saturday night schedule, six days later) and was an important episode in the series. The program had the difficult task of resolving the half-dozen or so cliffhangers left by the first-season finale, as well as recapping most of the program's story for both regular and new viewers.

In this one episode, the storyline of *Twin Peaks* "bridged" the first season to the second, altering both the direction and tone of the series. This episode was responsible for redefining *Twin Peaks* from the eerie, "mystery-dominant" plot of the show's first few episodes to the supernatural element of the new season.

David Lynch, the series' signature director, was behind the camera once again for the two-hour premiere, working from a script written by both Lynch and *Twin Peaks* co-creator, Mark Frost.

Episode 8 (Script number 2001; First televised September 30, 1990)

Guest Starring: Victoria Catlin (Blackie O'Reilly)

Featuring: Galyn Görg (Nancy), Phoebe Augustine (Ronette Pulaski), Stephen C. MacLaughlin (pie eater), Charles Miller (doctor), Mak Takano (Jonathan), Jessica Wallenfels (Harriet Hayward), Sandra Kaye Wetzel (nurse), Alicia Witt (Gersten Hayward), and Hank Worden (room service waiter)

Written by Mark Frost and David Lynch; Directed by David Lynch; Edited by Duwayne Dunham

Thursday, March 2, through Friday, March 3, 1989:

Act1: At the Great Northern Hotel, Cooper lies bleeding on the floor. An old room-service waiter delivers warm milk. The Giant appears and offers more clues. The Giant takes Cooper's ring. Ben approaches Audrey but she hides behind a mask. Jerry calls Ben away. Truman, Hawk and Andy burst into Cooper's room. Later, at the hospital, Cooper tells Truman his assailant was wearing a mask. Shelly watches a news report about the mill fire. Cooper sees the dead Jacques in a bag on a stretcher.

Act2: Leland's hair has turned white. Maddy has a vision of a distorted carpet, as if a body has been dragged across it. [*Note: this scene on the Japanese laserdisc shows a distorted image of Bob superimposed over the carpet.*] A singing Leland arrives at the Great Northern while Ben and Jerry dance. At Leo's, Hawk finds a copy of *Fleshworld* and a gas-soaked jacket while Cooper and Truman find a pair of Circle Brand boots and "a lot of cocaine." Donna and Maddy worry that Dr. Jacoby was attacked because they lured him out. Norma gives Donna a note that says, "Look into the Meals on Wheels."

Act 3: Andy tells Cooper that Leo has an alibi. James tells Truman that one night Laura started reciting a scary poem and then said, "Would you like to play with fire, little boy? Would you like to play with Bob?" Cooper demands that James give him the other half of Laura's heart necklace. James said he got it from Jacoby's.

Act 4: Cooper directs Lucy and Andy to search back issues of *Fleshworld* for pictures of Teresa Banks. Jacoby tells Cooper he saw James and Donna bury the necklace. He says that Laura was leading a double life, that she was two people. He felt that Laura had decided to end her life, that maybe she allowed herself to be killed. Jacoby says he remembers the smell of scorched engine oil at the time Jacques was killed. Shelly tells Bobby that Leo tried to kill her. Ed tells Cooper that Nadine is in a coma. He recounts the story of how he accidentally shot out Nadine's

eye. Cooper tells Truman he is ready to "lay the whole thing out."
Norma spies Ed sitting by Nadine's bedside.

Act 5: Major Briggs tells Bobby about his vision; Bobby is moved to
tears. Cooper and Albert summarize the Laura Palmer case and conclude
that Jacques and Leo are innocent and that only a "third man" could
have been the killer.

Act 6: Pete tells Truman that Josie went to Seattle on business. Truman
answers a call from the Asian man who is asking for Josie. Ben realizes
Audrey is missing. Hank tells Ben and Jerry about how he shot Leo and
lured Catherine to the mill. At One Eyed Jacks, Blackie threatens Audrey.

Act 7: Donna asks Norma if she can take over Laura's Meals on Wheels
route. Leland, Sarah and Maddy visit the Haywards for dinner. Leland
collapses. Audrey "prays" to a sleeping Cooper about the note she left.
(The camera pans across Cooper's bed to show the note under the bed.)
The Giant reappears to Cooper. He says "One person saw the third
man." At the hospital, Ronette awakens, she remembers Bob killing
Laura: Bob screams in pain and rage.

The opening sequence of episode 8 seems interminably slow at first viewing
but is, in fact, a perfectly-paced piece of comedy (not the sort of thing eager
viewers were expecting the night of the premiere). The old room service
waiter's lack of awareness at Cooper's situation, his absent-minded hanging-
up of the phone, and Cooper's worry that the bill includes a gratuity, all
represent Lynch's off-kilter sense of humor.

This episode is filled with such humor—often featuring Andy (including
the bizarre scene in which a loose floorboard at Leo's house hits him in the
head) and Albert, who is relentless in his ridicule of the town (in general)
and the sheriff's department (in particular). In another strangely humorous
scene, Albert quietly chuckles as Ed recounts, in melodramatic fashion, the
story of how Nadine lost her eye.

There is little humor in Audrey's situation. Considering the incest theme
that will become an important part of the Laura Palmer story, the
Ben/Audrey scene at One Eyed Jacks is alarming and unsettling. Audrey
slightly disguises her voice to try to avoid detection, but only Jerry's last-
minute intervention prevents the mutual discovery. As is, Audrey knows
Ben's secret, but he doesn't know hers.

A clue is given early in the episode that a person named "Bob" will
become an important character. When Truman is questioning James about
a "mystery man" that Laura mentions in her tape to Jacoby, James says he
doesn't think the man is Leo, but someone named Bob whom Laura once
mentioned to him cryptically.

The increased emphasis of Bob in this episode marks a significant shift in tone of *Twin Peaks*. Until now, the series (despite its quirky and unusual elements) was arguably grounded in an objective reality. With Bob, however, episode 8 emphasizes a supernatural element and, as noted by essayist, Marc Dolan, shifts the plot "out of the forensic, terrestrial territory in which it had been pretty much grounded in the first season and reorients it toward the extraterrestrial dimension."[1]

Dolan continues: "The murder of Laura Palmer is thus reinvented as a spiritual crime as well as a physical one, and the viewer is essentially set up for the revelation of the Black Lodge as well as its denizen Bob as the origin point of the previously peripheral mention of 'the evil in these woods.'"[2] When the Giant tells Cooper that "Three have seen [the third man—i.e., Bob], *but not his body*," he explicitly signals that the mystery is no longer confined to the physical act of murder, but now involves a set of unearthly circumstances. Cooper learns that Bob is more—or other—than human. If the mystery of the first season was summarized by the question, "Who killed Laura Palmer?" the mystery at the start of the second season became, "Who is Bob?"

The final few moments of this episode feature the first significant appearance of Bob (if you dismiss the "European ending" of the pilot) and contain some of the most chilling images yet to appear on the series. By using a strobe-light effect as Bob murders Laura, Lynch essentially creates still-shots of the action, depicting the characters frozen in their own private hells. Viewers are not shown everything in the murder scene, allowing them to imagine even greater terror and atrocities than what appears on the screen.

Episode 8 is important because it begins to redefine some of the characters. Bobby, who is essentially a bad-boy jock in the first season, starts to develop nuance and depth. This is effectively depicted in a powerful scene with Major Briggs, who recounts a vision he had of Bobby's future. His father's optimistic outlook resonates with Bobby and drives much of Bobby's storyline for the remainder of the season. Donna, on the other hand, begins to turn from a prim-and-proper best friend to a more sensual, *femme fatale*-like schemer. Donna's change in character is striking and seems abrupt. But it makes sense in a larger context. The night before the events of this episode, Donna saw how James reacted when he saw Maddy dressed as Laura (episode 6). It would be understandable, then, for her to also imitate Laura. In fact, her behavior makes more sense as the storyline progresses. In episode 10, Donna visits Laura's grave and admits she wanted to be like Laura, to have her strength and courage.

Leland's change is perhaps the most peculiar—his hair inexplicably turned white overnight. Leland interprets this as a sign that he has "turned a corner" and that a sadness has been lifted from his heart.

In addition to redefining some characters, this episode expands the plot concerning the investigation into Laura Palmer's murder. During the first season, suspicion lay primarily on two individuals who were believed to have been the last people to have seen Laura alive: Jacques Renault and Leo Johnson. In the first season finale, Cooper is convinced that Jacques did not kill Laura, leaving Leo as the prime suspect. He even leaves a message on his recorder for Diane stating his belief that Leo is responsible for Laura's death.

With the renewal of the program, however, the writers needed a way to keep the investigation from being solved too quickly. Thus the introduction of the "third man" who was hiding outside Jacques' cabin and later took Laura and Ronette to the train car where the murder took place. It was this "third man" who wrote a note in AB Negative blood, "Fire walk with me." The blood type didn't match any of the known participants of the evening (Laura, Ronette, Leo, or Jacques), so an entirely new investigation had to begin for this suspect.

This new information results in one of greatest errors in the *Twin Peaks* narrative. In Episode 5, Cooper, Truman, Andy, and Dr. Hayward are searching Jacques' apartment. As soon as Cooper arrives, Hayward reports to him that the blood on Leo's shirt was not Laura's—it was AB Negative. Cooper says, "So it *was* Jacques Renault's blood on Leo Johnson's shirt!" as Hayward and Truman look at each other in amazement. Hayward gets a phone call and then confirms to Cooper, "Jacques Renault's blood type is AB Negative."

This fact contradicts Albert's claim in episode 8. If Jacques' blood type *is* AB Negative, then that essentially pinpoints Jacques as the killer. It also makes the basis for suspicion of the "third man" moot. When Mark Frost was asked about this mistake at the Florence Gould Hall *Twin Peaks* Seminar on November 17, 1990, he claimed no knowledge of the mix-up and dismissed the issue. It seems as if the *Twin Peaks* narrative dismissed the issue, too.

Additional Notes:

Cooper's line about fear in act 1 has greater significance knowing how the series ends. In this episode, Cooper emphasizes the importance of keeping fear from your mind. But it is fear (or, as Hawk might say, "imperfect courage") that arguably leads to Cooper's downfall in the last episode of *Twin Peaks*.

The first of the Giant's clues comes true in this episode when Cooper sees Jacques Renault's body-bag hanging on a wall suspended from each end, almost forming a giant smile ("a man in a smiling bag").

Mark Frost makes a cameo appearance as a television news reporter at the scene of the Packard Mill fire.

Josie does not appear in this episode—Hank made sure she was out of town when the mill fire started. (Pete thinks she's in Seattle shopping.) She will not appear again until episode 11.

As noted above, the scene in which Maddy reacts with horror when looking at the carpet was changed for the Japanese laserdisc version. There, a distorted image of Bob is superimposed on the carpet.

Although the script contains eight acts (normal for a two-hour episode), when aired this episode essentially ended up with seven. The first act is 23 minutes long (twice the usual length) and comprises most of the scenes of the first two acts of the script.

The episode ends with a note: "Dedicated to the memory of Kevin Young Jr." Kevin Young Sr. is the actor who plays frequent Double R Diner patron, Toad.

Episode 8 features the first appearances of the Giant, Donna's sister, Gersten Hayward, and Jonathan.

Ratings throughout the first season of *Twin Peaks* had fallen gradually but they rose again for the season finale. Anticipation was high for the series return on September 30 1990, and while it was quickly established that Agent Cooper survived being shot, Lynch and Frost still confounded expectations by presenting a measured and slow-paced first act. Reportedly, viewership dropped significantly during the first half-hour, as impatient viewers tuned-out once they learned that Cooper had not died.

Notable Deleted Scenes

Act 3: At One Eyed Jack's, Audrey plays solitaire on her bed. A Fifty-Two Pick-Up Girl enters, and Audrey asks why she can't leave her room. The girl tells her it's because of security reasons, and that Audrey better not ask many more questions. Despite these warnings the two become friendly, and Audrey learns the girl's name is Nancy—Blackie's sister, who appears later in the series. Nancy was featured in the *Secret Diary of Laura Palmer* as a fairly benign character (as she was in this scene). These early portrayals indicate that Lynch and Frost may have had a different role in mind for her as the second season got underway. Later, Nancy became a scheming associate of Jean Renault.

Act 4: Phil Gerard enters the station followed by Tom the mailman (described as "a small, chatty fellow"). While Gerard asks for the sheriff, Tom interrupts, telling Lucy about the box he is delivering. Tom, who is "a snoop," mentions that the box is addressed to Cooper and wonders what it could contain. As Lucy attempts to help Gerard, Tom continues to pester her with details about the package: "Return address Washington D.C., our nation's capitol. I don't think it's fragile, least ways it's not marked as fragile." Finally, Lucy is able to get rid of him. Tom was completely cut from the televised version which featured only Gerard and Lucy.

Act 5: Cooper and Truman ask Jacoby some questions. A deleted scene offers some dramatically different dialogue in which Jacoby discusses what he knew (and what he suspected) about Laura. Jacoby first came to treat Laura nine months earlier, after she picked his name out of the phone book. As in the televised version, Jacoby believes Laura was "leading a double life." But in the script, he elaborates: "Laura was, in essence, leading a double life; two people, self-divided, and those two selves were literally at war. A war of attrition. And the part of her that was good and loving was gradually losing ground." Jacoby says that the last time he saw Laura, "she had reached a kind of peace with herself...where her 'good self' believed that death was the only way to prevent the other side from complete domination. Death, in this sense, represented a kind of victory." This interpretation of Laura's death will strongly influence the scripting of *Fire Walk With Me*. It will also present a significant narrative obstacle for Lynch to resolve while making the film. (See Chapter 11.)

Act 7: At the Palmer house, Leland and Sarah are "dressed for an evening out." Leland is shown "deftly spinning Sarah around the room with a few light dance steps," and Sarah is "smiling and enjoying it in spite of herself." Maddy and Donna are watching from a doorway. Leland explains that both he and Sarah have always enjoyed dancing and that they "used to win all the dance contests down at the Grange Hall." They both leave to go to the Hayward's and Donna remarks, "I half expected them to start dancing up the walls like Fred Astaire." This scene recalls Donna and Laura's brief conversation in *Fire Walk With Me* in which Donna asks about "Fred and Ginger." The scene seems unusual, at least as written. It has only been a week since Laura was found dead and Leland and Sarah have apparently moved past their grief rather quickly.

Later, Donna studies the map of the Meals on Wheels route and Maddy "feels an odd, disquieting feeling come over her." Looking into the living room she sees Bob, "standing there, stock still." Maddy is "frozen in fear" and starts to tremble. Donna finally notices Maddy's distress, and Maddy snaps out of her fugue. When she looks back into the living room, Bob is gone, and Act 7 ends. This would be Maddy's first glimpse of Bob. The televised version deleted this scene in favor of Maddy's "carpet vision." A scene similar to the one scripted here, however, occurs in the following episode in which Maddy, after singing with James and Donna, sees Bob approaching her in the Palmer's living room.

Cast and Crew Comments

Harley Peyton: Mark and I met with Steven Spielberg and discussed the possibility that he might direct the first episode of the second season. Steven agreed, and his only request was that we make it as challenging and surreal as possible. Mark told David about this particular coup, and David suddenly changed his mind and decided that he would direct the episode himself. I have always had a great deal of sympathy for David, and feel that he wanted to contribute in a more dynamic fashion to the show—he'd just been on the cover of *Time* magazine—and I completely understand why he became a more vivid presence during the second season.

Mark Frost: Most of the strange things in the series were joint ideas. The exception was the Giant. One day, David rushed in and said, "MARK! THERE's A GIANT IN COOPER's ROOM!"‘ [*laughs*]

Carel Struycken *(the Giant):* I wasn't on the set as much as the rest of the cast, but what came across to me very strongly—and something I hadn't experienced before—was that as a director, Lynch created an atmosphere more than anything else. The whole set, including everybody behind the camera, was in a kind of trance. That was how he operated. So, [the only] instruction I got was to talk a little bit slower, down-to-earth stuff like that. At the same time, you were very aware of this strong atmosphere.

The second thing I was very aware of while we were shooting [the opening scene], was I thought, "This is going to be the season opener, and I'm afraid people are going to turn the TV off before he [Hank Worden] has crossed the room!" That all went through my head while that scene was being filmed. Then David Lynch said, "Cut!" and I thought, "Oh, OK, he's going to tell him to speed it up, to go a little bit faster." He walked over to him and said, "I want you to play the scene as if you are one hundred and twenty years old!" He wanted him to do it *much* slower! [*laughs*]

Robert Engels: I recall that the second-season opener was pretty wacky. And the Giant appearing—that scene redefined pace! [*laughs*] But I liked all that. Somewhere in there was the beginning of the discussion of: "You guys are gonna finish this thing, aren't you?" And David said, "No, we're not." And ABC would say, "You have to!"

Don Davis: The acting training I had has helped me on monologues because I actually studied under a student of Stanislavski. A lot of emphasis was put on "interiorizing"—the thought that most conversation that is important to the speaker reflects his thoughts about his own life and path. A speaker who is not simply trying to sell you something spends a great deal of his time in conversation with you looking back into himself. That's a lot of what I was doing throughout the palazzo monologue. That's what the looks downward were—it was mostly me trying to picture my childhood, and the past, and the scene that I was describing.

Dana Ashbrook: I think there was a little conflict between Mark and David [about Bobby]. There is one instance I can give. It was where Don Davis is describing his dream. I had asked Mark about the scene. I asked, "How am I taking this dream? Am I into it? Am I put off by it?" He said, "You don't want to give him the time of day. Bobby doesn't really take it to heart." And then, of course, I get out on the set and David was there, and I asked him. He said, "No, no, no." It was the total opposite! It was like I was supposed to be hearing him for the first time. So the turn, there, threw me a little bit.

And Don, God bless him. David took Don aside and talked to him. So on my coverage—during Don's off-camera lines to me—he starts to break down and cry. And it made me cry. That's how that whole thing happened. It was pretty cool.

Mark Frost: There was always a scene I loved—it was the scene where Major Briggs told his son about the dream that he'd had. That scene always resonated for me in some way that I really liked. I like that moment.

Everett McGill: I think that scene [where Ed explains to Cooper how he shot out Nadine's eye] represents a quality that David has. He doesn't want any one thing to make the scene run away in a particular direction. He always brings you back. It's a real delicate touch. And, although I was very much aware that Miguel [Ferrer] was doing his routine over there, when David was on my dialogue he gave it all the attention of something serious and important. And even the stuff that sounds funny or odd in how I behaved with Nadine when I shot her eye out—he never treated that as quaint. It was of grand importance. And of course when we were shooting with Miguel, it was as if all the stuff that I'd done was not important. I could have been in another room! [*laughs*] Yeah, it was a marvelous scene. In fact, I get a lot of comments from people who remember that scene.

Miguel Ferrer: So much of my stuff was just expository: "OK, if you haven't watched the show for the last four episodes, let me catch you up in the next six minutes!" It was all this exposition. Just columns of dialogue and names and dates, with nothing to hang your hat on.

The most awful words in the English language are, "OK, let's get this in one!" [*laughs*] Kyle and I would sit there with sometimes literally five, six, or seven pages where I would have to talk for 30 seconds, and he would talk for a minute, then I'd talk for minute-and-a-half—if one of us blew it, we're back to square one! We're sitting there at the table thinking, "Get through it. Get through it! OK, my turn!" At one point we were holding hands underneath the table, squeezing each other, "Go! Go! We're almost there!

Two pages left to go!" So when they'd come in and do these sweeping re-writes, it was really hard! [*laughs*]

Chris Mulkey: David always wanted the razor part of Hank. He always liked the danger part of him, the unrelenting criminal. He liked that better. Instead of playing the soft side—the manipulating side—of Hank, he liked Hank more as a kind of criminal freight-train. I just knew what he wanted. It was all about that feeling of empowering the character. When David would tell me what the scene was about, I just knew what to do. It was kind of an intuitive deal. That was what was spooky about that series, too. People just knew stuff.

It was so great to work with Richard Beymer. He's become a great friend of mine. I remember how that scene [at the fireplace] was really fun to do. We had great glee in laying that down. I think it was the chemistry between the actors. You just kinda' kick it off. Also, remember what that episode was about, it was about bad guys trying to stay to the plan. And clearly, both of them wanted to do the other one in while swearing that they were trying to make it right by them. It was just a scene about total lies. A celebration of lying. I like that. Everyone postures and lies and then walks out of the room. One of the true moments in human behavior.

[*In a deleted scene from episode 8, Hank sniffs ammonia to appear as if he were crying, so as to fool Norma.*]

It was a real popper. I was doing it and I took this huge hit off of it and David said, "Chris! God! You really took a lot." And I said, "Yeah. It worked for you?" And he said, "Yeah, it worked great. But if we were doing a scene about heroin would you just take the heroin?" [*laughs*] I said, "I don't know, dude. Probably not!"

Catherine Coulson: She [The Log Lady] has a slight sense of humor, but she also knows more about worlds that people don't even know they want to know about. She's got a real insight to human behavior and her particular point-of-view is "the right one" as far as she's concerned. I don't think that she's aware that she is amusing, but certainly she likes to tease. She and Norma had a whole thing about the pitch gum and that's probably as far as her teasing would go. But she's a pretty serious woman. I mean, she's had a tremendous amount of pain in her life.

Dana Ashbrook: If David was there, he would always have us add stuff. The whole thing with Shelly in the hospital where I go in there and we pull each other's hair and we do that thing—that was all just David telling us what to do and coming up with that whole groove. It was a kick, man.

Frank Silva: A lot of times David doesn't know, at the time he's making something, where it's really going until he sees something happen and that starts to make it different. It starts to twist it a little bit. When we were actually doing the murder scene [in the second season premiere] I didn't know who Bob was. None of us did. So I didn't know really how to play him. When we were doing the killing scene I was playing him as if, after the killing, or during the killing, it was almost erotic to Bob. He felt sad about what he did. So there were points when, after it was over, some of the screams turned into sobs and crying. And I think David picked up on that and went into another direction where it was actually *Leland* feeling remorseful after he had done this horrible act. Like, "Oh, wait a minute, what have I just done here?" Whereas, Bob would have never done that.

Episode 9 (Script number 2002; First televised October 6, 1990)

Guest Starring: Victoria Catlin (Blackie O'Reilly), Don Amendolia (Emory Battis), Francis Bay (Mrs. Tremond)

Featuring: Phoebe Augustine (Ronette Pulaski), Austin Lynch (Little Boy), Jill Pierce (Ice-Bucket Girl), and Mak Takano (Jonathan)

Written by Harley Peyton; Directed by David Lynch; Edited by Jonathan P. Shaw

Saturday, March 4, 1989:

> Act 1: Albert informs Cooper that Windom Earle has escaped. Donna delivers a meal to Mrs. Tremond and her grandson. Donna is unnerved by their behavior. Donna slips a note under Harold Smith's door. Cooper and Truman show Ronette the sketch of Bob. She reacts violently and tries to say, "Train." Ben and Jerry can't decide which of the two mill ledgers to burn.

> Act 2: The Log Lady informs Major Briggs to "deliver the message." Andy tells Lucy that he is sterile. Hank makes a parole visit to Truman. Truman tells Cooper that Hank used to be a Bookhouse Boy. Ben Horne calls to say that Audrey is missing.

> Act 3: Jerry delivers Catherine's unsigned insurance policy to Ben. Leland recognizes the sketch of Bob. Jerry wonders, "Is this real, Ben, or some strange and twisted dream?" Doc Hayward tells Shelly that Leo may never recover. Emory Battis tells Audrey that Laura knew Ben owned One Eyed Jacks.

> Act 4: Bobby hatches a plan to get Leo's insurance money. Major Briggs delivers the message to Cooper: "The owls are not what they seem." Donna plans to meet with Harold Smith. Maddy has a horrifying vision of Bob. Cooper dreams: He sees Ronette thrash. He hears the Giant and Major Briggs say, "The Owls are not what they seem." He sees an image of Bob that turns into an owl. Audrey calls and says she is in trouble. Blackie hangs up the phone before Audrey can say more.

The second episode of *Twin Peaks* season 2 was, in many ways, more crucial than the season premiere. The season opener served to re-familiarize viewers with the show's many plotlines as well as redirect the series toward a more supernatural tone. But the second episode decisively moved *Twin Peaks* into new territory. The script for episode 9 was written by Harley Peyton and was completed on July 18, 1990. David Lynch served as director as he had with the season premiere. Like the two-hour premiere, the televised version of episode 9 deviated only slightly from the original script. Lynch is often credited with adding his own unique touches to a script in order to add that "Lynchian" quality. While some of this did happen in episode 9, much of what we see on the screen—and might inadvertently credit to Lynch—originated with Peyton.

Peyton's first-rate dialogue for Albert, aided by Miguel Ferrer's impeccable delivery results in some of the most memorable lines of the series: "I'm thrilled to pieces that the Dharma came to King Ho-Ho-Ho;" "Color me amazed;" "I like to think of myself as one of the Happy Generations." All these lines (and many more quotable ones) are delivered in the first scene where Albert meets Cooper for breakfast. In a typical (for *Twin Peaks*) oddball touch, a barbershop quartet sings at the table behind them.

This last bit was probably Lynch's doing, as there is no mention of it in the original script. Another unscripted bit occurred when Truman and Cooper visit Ronette at the hospital. Lynch adds a lengthy and somewhat nonsensical sequence in which the two men struggle with two metal stools. They attempt to unobtrusively adjust the height of the stools after Truman quietly reads the instructions. None of this material is present in the script and likely exists because of Lynch's on-the-spot improvisation. (One can imagine Lynch deciding to incorporate such a scene into the show after observing someone actually struggling with these stools.) Another funny bit happens as Ben and Jerry try to decide which mill ledger to burn (the real one or the fake) and Ben pulls out some marshmallows to roast.

Although Cooper was shot less than two days before, he is already showing no ill effects of the nasty injury. (He hobbled around a bit in the previous episode.) Whether this represents a failure on MacLachlan's part to maintain the continuity of the character, or whether the producers did not want a wounded agent for the entire second season, it does bring up one of the drawbacks of airing a weekly series that is supposed to take place on successive days.

Albert brings news that Cooper's former partner, Windom Earle, has escaped from a mental institution and the FBI cannot locate him. This concerns Cooper. While Earle himself will not appear until episode 21, the show temporarily creates suspense by suggesting that the Asian man (Jonathan) currently spying on Cooper might have some connection to Earle.

Donna takes over Laura's Meals-on-Wheels route and meets Mrs. Tremond and her grandson, who is studying magic (and makes creamed corn disappear). These characters (and the corn) will return in *Fire Walk With Me*. In these scenes, Lynch effectively builds suspense by carefully pacing what is ostensibly a straightforward scene. Lynch added the element of the magic trick and the disappearing corn, which was not in the original script.

Maddy's vision of Bob is terrifying, especially because of the way Bob crawls across the couch and directly into the camera (i.e., Maddy's point-of-view.) Lynch's decision to have Bob approach Maddy in this way reinforces the menacing, overpowering nature of the character. In effect, the presence of Bob is inescapable.

The second of the giant's clues came true in this episode when Major. Briggs "delivers the message" to Cooper: "The owls are not what they seem."

Notable Deleted Scenes

Act 1: In the "Get Acquainted Room" at One Eyed Jack's, Audrey sits next to Nancy, who is reading the morning paper. Nancy tells Audrey about the fire at the Packard Mill. Audrey continues to chat with Nancy, and then asks about Ronette and Laura. Before Nancy can provide any information, Audrey hears Emory Battis coming down the hall. She quickly leaves, and Nancy watches her go with "a cold look in her eyes." Nancy acknowledges Battis as he walks through the door and identifies Audrey to him.

Act 2: At the Blue Pine Lodge, "Cooper, Truman, and Albert gather around Pete Martell at the dining room table." Pete tells the group about how fearful Catherine had been during the night of the fire. Albert rolls his eyes and Cooper gives him a "stern glance." Pete produces an account ledger and explains that it is the false ledger. Pete is distracted by thoughts of Midge Jones, his high school sweetheart. Albert responds, "Pete let's make a heroic attempt to keep our minds, and what's left of yours, on the night in question." Pete looks hard at Albert says "I don't like you." Cooper gently interjects, "No one does, Pete." This is another wonderful scene featuring Albert and his cutting disdain for the residents of Twin Peaks. It helps establish a certain dynamic between Cooper and Albert and also sets up a potential conflict between Albert and Pete.

As Deputy Andy struggles to tape a poster of Bob to the door of the Double R Diner, Maddy Ferguson and Leland Palmer enter. Leland brags about the Double R's great chocolate malts and orders two. He and Maddy talk, and Leland explains that he "is coming through the pain." Meanwhile Norma talks with Hank, who seems happy. Hank tells Norma he is buying her a car. She is skeptical of his motives, but seems pleased none-the-less. Leland and Maddy drink their malts. Maddy talks about the death of her father while Leland tries to convince her stay in Twin Peaks. This scene provides further insight into Maddy, and hints at her unique relationship with Leland. Did Leland view her as a surrogate Laura? Did Maddy see Leland as a father-figure? This tantalizing scene could have added more complexity to the relationship between the two characters (and, in retrospect, foreshadowed Maddy's fate).

Act 4: In the Great Northern Hotel, Cooper is playing his "handmade wooden flute" while he watches television. He activates his tape recorder and leaves a lengthy message to Diane about Audrey. (Only part of this message was heard on the televised version.) Cooper tells Diane that Windom Earle's disappearance matters less to him than Audrey's. He then describes Audrey in ways that hint at deeper feelings. According to Cooper, Audrey's smile "gives lie to her delinquent posing, the hardened exterior which I suspect is more a matter of self-preservation than a heart that is cold. Audrey's heart is warm." These fascinating lines are not only beautifully written, they give insight into both Cooper and Audrey's characters. It is shame they were removed from the televised version but, given that the Audrey/Cooper romance was already a chancy proposition (see episode 6), it is no surprise they were cut.

Cast and Crew Comments

Harley Peyton: David was making *Wild At Heart* during the first seven episodes. So he really wasn't there. Then, suddenly David was on the cover of *Time* magazine, and there are all these stories that he was like Rain Man and Mark is the Tom Cruise character. I think David really felt bad that he wasn't earning all the credit he was getting. That was very much like David. He was really going to get in there and do work.

James Marshall: There was a thing where David heard me playing guitar on the set, or someplace, and he asked, "Do you want to play the guitar in a scene?" I was like, "Yeah! That would be so cool!" He said, "What do you want to do?" I thought, "His thing is the Fifties and I love the Fifties." So I said, "Let's do a doo-wop thing like, 'Only You.'" I thought that was so cool. We practiced on a piano, and Angelo Badalmenti and David wrote something. They were kidding around and playing around and they wrote it. David said, "Next week I'll set up a date at the recording studio and you can come in." I said, "Maybe I can lay the guitar track down, too." David said, "Fine."

And then when I got there, it was all recorded already—everything was already down. They said, "Alright we're gonna lay the singing track down." I was a little bit bummed that I didn't get to play the guitar but I was perfectly happy to be there. I thought, "This will still be cool; this will be fun." And it turns out the tracks were in the key of C. I can't sing in C. By that time they had already put the money into it and they didn't have time to re-record it. David said, "Why didn't you tell me you couldn't sing in C?" I said, "That's an obscure thing to have to tell you!" [*laughs*] He was trying not to be pissed and he didn't know who to be pissed at! So I'm all off-key and desperately trying to sound like I'm in key—and that's what goes across to the entire world. But, I think it may have been cheesy if James, all of a sudden, broke into this incredible falsetto doo-wop and sounded great. That almost would have been more cheesy. The fact that James was struggling to sing to this girl was maybe sweeter.

Don Davis: I don't remember there being much tension on the set. In fact, one of the things I tell to everyone about David Lynch is that, in two-and-a-half years of association, I never, ever saw him evidence any anger or raise his voice. Even to the extent that on one scene, when the Giant and I are in Cooper's bedroom, somebody came running in from the editors to report that the processing lab had done something—the chemical mix was wrong, and the scene came out with a strange tint to it. David just laughed and said, "Well, don't panic. Let me look at it." He went up and looked at it and he came back and told us it was fine: "It looked kind of weird, and it'll work for the scene." [*laughs*] He's a very calm person.

Frank Silva: Sometimes David wouldn't say that much. It would be general. Like the scene with Maddy, Donna, and James. David said, "Well ... I think I want Frank to walk into the room, and maybe *leap* over the sofa!" That was it. And he'd tell the camera man, and so they'd light it. Then they'd call the first team—that's first team on the set. I was standing there and David walked up to me in the dining room of the Hayward house and he said, "Frank, just walk in, blah, blah, blah . . . you know what to do!" [*laughs*] I turned and said, "I know what to do?!" "Yeah, you know what to do." Then he said, "Action!"

Instead of leaping—I just didn't feel comfortable leaping—I just crawled over it. As I started crawling over it, and got over the sofa, David said, "Keep crawling." So I kept crawling and he didn't say anything. He didn't say, "Stop." He didn't say, "Cut." I kept crawling, and I kept crawling, but I was always taught that you're not supposed to look at the camera, or look at the lens of the camera. So I crawled to the side of the camera, just alongside of the camera. And David said, "Cut! That was great, Frank! Do it again, and crawl right into the camera!" And so we did it in two takes. I crawled right into the camera.

Don Davis: The owls were, in some sense, a representation of a greater power. It was through the owls in those woods that these entities—be they forces for good or ill—communicated with us and affected our lives. Not that they themselves were the beings, but that they were the tools of these forces.

Episode 10 (Script number 2003; First televised October 13, 1990)

Guest Starring: Lenny Von Dohlen (Harold Smith), Don Amendolia (Emory Battis), Victoria Catlin (Blackie O'Reilly), and Michael Parks (Jean Renault)

Featuring: Galyn Görg (Nancy), Phoebe Augustine (Ronette Pulaski), and Mak Takano (Jonathan)

Written by Robert Engels; Directed by Lesli Linka Glatter; Edited by Paul Trejo

Sunday, March 5, 1989:

> Act 1: Cooper removes a "B" from under Ronette's fingernail. Harold Smith tells Donna that Laura wanted him to contact her. Harold says he can't go outside. Albert tells Truman that he rejects revenge, aggression and retaliation. Cooper releases James. Richard Tremayne arrives to take Lucy to lunch. Leland tells Cooper that Bob used to live in a house on Pearl Lakes. His name was Robertson and he used to flick matches at Leland.

> Act 2: Lucy tells Dick she is pregnant. Donna sees James and Maddy holding hands. Blackie and Battis drug Audrey. Gerard sees the Bob sketch and nearly faints. Cooper suspects Shelly's insurance scam. Phil Gerard fails to take his medication and becomes Mike. He senses Bob and says, "I'm after you now."

> Act 3: Ben advises Cooper to keep some distance from Audrey. Jean Renault gives Audrey more drugs. Renault wants to get revenge on Cooper for the death of his brothers, Jacques and Bernard. Cooper and Truman find Gerard's unused syringe. Cooper deciphers the Giant's third clue: "Without chemicals he points." Nadine wakes and thinks she's 18 years old.

> Act 4: Cooper hypnotizes Jacoby who says he remembers who killed Jacques. Donna watches as James and Maddy kiss. Leland comforts Maddy. Cooper and Truman arrest Leland for the murder of Jacques Renault. Donna notices Laura's secret diary on Harold's table.

The first draft of the script for episode 10 was completed on July 17, 1990. The script subsequently went through six revisions—indicating that the show's producers (including Mark Frost and David Lynch, as well as Harley Peyton and Robert Engels) were fine-tuning the various plot lines. The script's final revision was completed on August 3, 1990, and the episode began shooting on August 8.

Ian Buchanan, a mainstay of daytime soap operas, represents another bit of perfect casting for *Twin Peaks*. Richard Tremayne's high-brow demeanor in the small-town community makes him appear either hopelessly out of place (with an inability to see that) or a ridiculous fraud (depending on whether one sees him as authentic or not). While this portrayal will later get pushed to unbearable limits, the introduction—notably his conversation with Hawk, who looks at him and calls him a robot—is a lot of fun.

The reclusive, agoraphobic Harold Smith was another major character to enter the *Twin Peaks* narrative. His appearance in the story added an extra dimension to the mystery surrounding Laura Palmer's life (and death). Unfortunately, Harold represented a mystery that—like so much in *Twin Peaks*—never got fully explained. Harold's character could have been explored more satisfactorily, especially since he had a crucial connection to Laura. Their relationship is briefly revisited in *Fire Walk With Me*, but even there, Harold remains an enigmatic figure in the life of Laura Palmer.

James refers to his drunken mother but does not mention her again in this episode or any other. The "Colleen Hurley" scene was originally shot by Tim Hunter for a season-one episode. In 1990, Harley Peyton explained more about the scene in Mark Altman's book, *Twin Peaks: Behind the Scenes*: "It was a scene Tim Hunter shot and Bob Engels wrote that was cut twice since we've tried to use it."

Nadine comes out of her coma with super-strength and a belief that she's 18 years old. While this makes for an amusing one-shot joke, its continued presence in the storyline—especially after the resolution of the Laura Palmer murder—contributes to the dip in quality of the middle second season episodes.

Ben's scene with Cooper regarding the missing Audrey is peculiar. In the previous episode, Ben reported her disappearance to Truman, yet now, when Cooper asks for an update and tells him about the phone call he received, Ben seems completely unconcerned about his daughter.

Albert again becomes a highlight of the episode with a surprising speech about how, despite his cynicism, he is a man of non-violence who chooses to live "in the company of Gandhi and King."

Additional Notes:

The third of the giant's clues (without chemicals, he points) comes true in this episode when shoe salesman Phil Gerard is unable to take his medication in the sheriff's station restroom and deduces that Bob is near.

Co-creator Mark Frost's interest in golf is well-known and there are many references to golfing in the series. This episode contains a less obvious reference: Cooper hypnotizes Jacoby by reading the doctor's previously-prepared hypnotism-script which describes putting a ball on a golf course.

Blackie's line, "She's ready for her close-up now" is probably a nod to the film, *Sunset Boulevard*, in which Gloria Swanson says, "I'm ready for my close-up now." (Recall that the name, Gordon Cole, also originates in *Sunset Boulevard*.)

This episode features the first appearances of Richard Tremayne, Harold Smith, and Jean Renault.

Notable Deleted Scenes

Act 3: A lengthy scene at "James Hurley's home" was entirely cut from the televised version. James lives in "a house trailer on a lonely lot." He pulls up on his motorcycle as a "late model car pulls up with a man driving. Colleen Hurley gets out. She is fortyish and gave James his good looks." James watches as his drunken mother walks unsteadily toward him. She asks where he was and he explains he was at school. Colleen, says, "God bless the public indoctrination system. Keeps the kids off the street, keeps the streets safe for the street sweepers. In San Francisco, the street sweepers have an epic quality."

James worries that his mother has been gone for a week, to which she replies, "When the muse calls out we're helpless to resist. She explains, "I learned early on. Write it down, escape the humdrum that life has dealt you. Play with marked cards." She proceeds to read a poem she has written, but James interrupts. He grabs her vodka bottle and pours the rest on the ground. Colleen seems to ignore the action and says to James, "I know girl trouble when I see it. Some little logtown siren's cut you up. I recognize the wound pattern." James says that it was Laura. Colleen continues, "Forget her . . . . The danger for you, my darling boy, is that you'll never know if she's an angel or a harpy sent from hell to rend your heart, and believe me, she'll be one or the other." James replies, "She was both." Colleen responds, "Ah, but that's the secret, Jimmy boy. They all are."

This interesting scene never made it into the televised version. In a later televised scene, however, James refers to the fact that his mother is back and is "loaded." The cut scene explains more of why James was later distraught. The televised version implies that he was upset because his mother was drunk. But the dialogue in the scene hints at further reasons for James' trauma—his frank discussion about Laura with his mother.

Cast and Crew Comments

Harley Peyton: Harold Smith was based on an actual person—Arthur Crew Inman. Inman spent his life writing a diary from 1919 to the time of his eventual suicide in 1963. In that time, he lived confined to a dark room in Boston and, through newspaper ads, hired "talkers" to tell him the stories of their lives. He then wove these histories into his own diary. Young women were a particular fascination. According to his brief bio, he bought them clothes, studied their moods, "fondled them," and gave them romantic advice. Inman's edited diaries were published in 1985 by the Harvard University Press in two volumes. That's where I first heard of him and his strange life's work. And that was the basis for the character I later created . . . Harold Smith.

Lenny Von Dohlen (*Harold Smith*): [I got the part because] I changed a line. Which is probably sacrosanct. It's in the show. At the end of the scene where Donna comes to see Harold for the first time, he gives her an orchid for Laura's grave. At the end she says, "I'll be back," and he was supposed to say something like, "I'll look forward to it." But I said, "I'll be here." It amused me. I audition so horribly. I hate it with all my heart; so if you can find one or two ways to amuse yourself then it is not quite so hideous.

I was part of the ignorant masses [regarding *Twin Peaks*]. I had not seen any David Lynch movies. They sent the tapes [of the series] up to the house after I got the part so I could go into that world. That's what I like to do, feel the world I am in, completely, and then enter it as authentically as possible. I thought, "This reminds me of some acid trip I had a long time ago! I can't believe this is happening on TV! Yeah, count me in!"

I approached it with that kind of naked, genuine need to be real. I talked to a lot of homebound people all across this country. They were very sweet and helpful. I found out that people who have one phobia generally have more than one. I thought that maybe [Harold] would be a clean freak and an order freak. That's, I think, where all that came from.

I had a great relationship with Frank Byers, the director of photography. He was behind the camera and he shot it as well as lit it. I needed him and I trusted him. I would look to him after every take. We had a relationship going into *Twin Peaks*. I knew his crew and they were good guys. There was a family there.

Phoebe Augustine: I remember [Lesli Linka Glatter] leaving the lighting and everything to the people whose job it is to handle that. I remember David knowing exactly how everything should look, and being involved with the lighting and all of that. She just left that part to them.

Miguel Ferrer: It was such an honor to be part of that show. Everybody says, "Oh, you were so great!" But the fact of the matter is anybody could have scored with that part because it was all on the page. They gave me the most wonderful things to say. I still remember when I opened up that script with the "I love you Sheriff Truman" line. I was on set and they passed out scripts. I'm scanning through it, and I see this speech, and I said, "Do we have a few minutes before we're ready to shoot?" I went up to Mark Frost's office and I almost broke into tears! I said, "Thank you, man. This is so awesome!"

Episode 11 (Script number 2004; First televised October 20, 1990)

Guest Starring: Lenny Von Dohlen (Harold Smith), Royal Dano (Judge Clinton Sternwood), Don Amendolia (Emory Battis), Fumio Yamaguchi (Tojamura), Ritch Brinkley (Daryl Lodwick), and Michael Parks (Jean Renault)

Featuring: Bellina Logan (Desk Clerk), Claire Stansfield (Sid), Mak Takano (Jonathan), and Michael Allen Lerner (Stunt Double)

Written by Jerry Stahl, Mark Frost, Harley Peyton, and Robert Engels; Directed by Todd Holland; Edited by Toni Morgan

Monday, March 6, 1989:

> Act 1: Leland admits to killing Jacques. Hayward tells Andy to get him a sperm sample. Hawk's report says no one by the name of Robertson lived on Pearl Lakes. Cooper notices Andy's Circle Brand boots. Andy says he got them from Phil Gerard. Jean Renault shows Ben the tape of Audrey. He says that Ben must pay a large sum of money for Audrey and he wants Cooper to bring the ransom.

> Act 2: Norma tells Hank that food critic, M.T. Wentz, is coming to town. Harold shows Donna Laura's diary. He says Laura gave it to him for safe keeping. Harold says he writes the stories of others. Ben asks Cooper to deliver the ransom. Pete tells Josie that Catherine is dead. Audrey tells Renault that Battis hit her. Renault shoots and kills Battis.

> Act 3: Lucy tells Cooper about Dick Tremayne. Cooper tells Truman he needs the help of the Bookhouse Boys. Hank learns that district attorney Daryl Lodwick is in town. Donna tells Maddy that Harold has Laura's diary and that she is going to try to get it. Truman wants to know why Josie left. They embrace as the Asian man watches through a window.

> Act 4: Judge Sternwood greets Truman, Lucy and Cooper. Dick Tremayne offers to pay for Lucy to have an abortion. Ben meets Mr. Tojamura, who is checking-in. Josie introduces Pete to her "cousin," Jonathan (the Asian man). Jonathan and Josie scheme about selling the mill. Truman meets Cooper at the Roadhouse and says that he will help Cooper. Jonathan beats up Hank and says he will kill him next time.

The opening scene featuring Leland's confession to the murder of Jacques shows some bravura acting by Ray Wise. His ability to portray the various aspects of Leland's personality has been noted by many fans of the series. Here, he portrays a broken character stricken with grief, intent on revenge, and unapologetic about either. It's quite an extraordinary performance.

Leland's agency in the murder of Jacques will always be murky. And it raises interesting questions that the series will never satisfactorily answer (questions that will pop up again in episode 17). How much did Leland know about Bob? Was he aware of Bob but completely powerless to stop him? Was he aware of Bob yet partially complicit in the awful crimes he committed? In the specific case of Jacques' murder, did Leland truly act alone (i.e., without Bob's control) because he was seeking revenge for Laura's murder?

It is tempting to think that Leland sought one of the few options available to stop Bob: to commit a willful murder so that he might be arrested and jailed, thereby keeping Bob contained. But it is hard to believe Bob would ever allow such defiance; the more likely scenario has Bob reveling in the death of Jacques and then doing everything possible to keep Leland from getting caught. This explains why Leland covered his tracks as carefully as did.

Harold Smith's reading of Laura's diary is a fascinating way to bring the spirit of Laura Palmer back into the show (and the scene is particularly haunting if one has already seen *Fire Walk With Me*). Lenny Von Dohlen does a superb job of channeling Laura, but Donna's mild surprise to the reading is curious. After all, she knew many of Laura's secrets and was quite aware of her double life, even if she didn't know the specifics.

Meanwhile Audrey is being held under torturous circumstances. She is being drugged and forced to witness murder at point-blank range. Such terrible agonies would surely break most people, but Audrey will emerge from the ordeal a stronger person. This might explain why she will later challenge her father and assert greater power in their relationship. Even so, Audrey will fail to achieve any lasting independence. As later plots develop, she will fall into the orbit of other characters, specifically Ben Horne during his mental collapse (which she tries to cure), and John Justice Wheeler (with whom she becomes infatuated).

The Lucy/Andy/Dick subplot was likely designed to provide comedic counterbalance to the heavy material found elsewhere in the episode, but the story is already showing signs of camp and silliness. This is evident in the scene between Lucy and Cooper at the beginning of act 3. Lucy and Andy are becoming one-note characters, their personalities flattening to accommodate the thin material they're given.

Additional Notes:

The primary writing credit to episode 11 is given to Jerry Stahl, but it is unlikely he contributed anything of substance to the story. Stahl admitted in his memoir, *Permanent Midnight*, that he was high on drugs when given the *Twin Peaks* scripting duties, and that he missed deadlines and produced little material of use. In his book, Stahl attempts to make light of his experience, assigning a flip nick-name to Frost and portraying the whole *Twin Peaks* production as smug and uptight. This still doesn't disguise the fact that Stahl failed to meet his obligations to the production. Because of Stahl's failure, the primary writing team (Frost, Peyton and Engels) had to save the script and keep the story on track (hence their names on the credits). Stahl ended up with a "mercy credit" on an episode that succeeds only because of the work of others.

Tod Holland, who will later go on to great acclaim directing sitcoms (notably *Malcolm in the Middle*) does a fine job of building tension in an episode that does not have many overly dramatic scenes. Occasionally he resorts to clichés (the thunderstorm in a couple of scenes is used to artificially punctuate lines of dialogue), but overall it's a commendable work.

The Great Northern is apparently hosting a beauty pageant: signs touting the "Tri-County Lumber Queen Semifinals" appear in the background of a few scenes, as do some pageant contestants. It seems odd that such an event would be held only weeks before the upcoming Miss Twi`n Peaks pageant.

Cooper's ordered mind and interest in patterns is evident in the way he arranges the peanuts on the roadhouse bar: a perfect triangle.

Fumio Yamagushi, listed in the opening credits, is actually Piper Laurie. The producers wanted to keep Catherine's return to the story a secret.

Josie makes her first appearance during the second season. She introduces Jonathan as her cousin. It turns out that they are both employees of Thomas Eckhardt, and they are expected back in Hong Kong soon.

Judge Sternwood and Daryl Lodwick make their first appearances in this episode. Their names likely have origins in film *noir* (as did insurance agent Neff in episode 6). "Sternwood" may be a reference to General Sternwood, the client who hires Philip Marlowe in *The Big Sleep*. "Lodwick" may originate from name Mitchell Lodwick, the prosecutor in *Anatomy of a Murder*.

The first draft of the script for episode 11 was completed on August 8, 1990. The script's first and only official revision was completed on August 13, 1990.

Notable Deleted Scenes

Act 2: The scripted scene in which Donna visits Harold Smith is much longer than what was televised. The televised version opens half-way into the scene when Harold and Donna drink a toast to Laura. In the script, Donna arrives and Harold takes the tray of food from her. He shows her his place: "He's turned his living room into an indoor picnic, silverware and plates, he's even produced a wicker basket." Donna is impressed.

They sit, and Harold compliments the food. Donna says she wanted this to be special. In reaction, Harold jumps up to fetch wine. He asks her if she has any requests. Donna is further impressed and says, "All the boys I know drink beer." Smith offers to select something appropriate, a German wine. He "opens the wine with subtle ceremony and pours a little into a glass for Donna to sample." Donna gives him a wondering look and he prompts her to sip, which she does. At first she says, "Wow." Then, in a "more adult" tone, she says it's very good. At this point the televised version begins.

The material that was cut from this scene clearly establishes differences between Donna and Harold. Donna is portrayed as a young, somewhat naïve girl. She knows little about wine, and refers to her male friends as "boys." Harold is a little more worldly-wise and clearly more experienced than Donna. While there is little essential information in the edited material, it sheds more light on Donna's fascination with Harold, an "older" man. These plot points were downplayed in the televised episodes in which Donna's attraction to Harold seemed secondary to her true purpose of obtaining Laura's diary.

Act 3: Dr. Hayward is on the phone with Big Ed. He tells him that he's been talking with the "Saeger Swenson Clinic in Seattle. Nadine's problem might be related to something called pheochromocytoma; affects the adrenal gland, it could account for her strength and erratic behavior."

After Hayward hangs up, Donna "makes a defiant descent of the stairs, hoping her father will notice her. She takes out a cigarette and lights it." Hayward says he wants to talk to Donna but she flippantly refuses. He tells her to sit and asks why she missed two days of school last week. She explains that she was busy. Hayward senses that Donna is troubled. He asks her to talk to him, to share her feelings. When Donna says there is nothing going on, Hayward says, "I have to reluctantly admit I don't believe you." He presses her to say what's troubling her. Donna admits that since Laura died everything has been different, but she doesn't want to talk about it. She tells her father that it doesn't have anything to do with him. Hayward pleads with her, "Donna don't shut us out of your life." To which she responds, "I have to, I'm sorry." She then leaves.

The first part of this scene is interesting in that it reveals for the first and only time why Nadine has become so strong. The televised episodes never provide an answer. The remainder of the scene serves to show Donna as a young girl coping with adult problems. With this scene cut (as well as the earlier exchange with Harold Smith), the entire subplot of Donna-as-confused-teenager is effectively excised. The televised version of this and subsequent episodes portray Donna as a more mature young woman, determined to find the truth about Laura. It is interesting to note, however, that a subplot later in the season (Donna learning about her true father) again portrays Donna as young and confused.

This cut scene also contains a rather significant error. Dr. Hayward mentions that Donna missed two days of school a week earlier. The scene implies that Donna's troubles and reason for missing school stem from her relationship with James and Harold. According to *Twin Peaks* time, however, this episode took place on March 6—Donna had met Harold for the first time only the day before.

Cast and Crew Comments

Chris Mulkey: I went in the tank for Mr. Lee. I hated that. I mean, I didn't want to do that. I said, "No way! You're doing this? It's a racial stereotype! You have a Chinese guy come in and he does-in the Anglo bad guy? Come on!" He'd do some Kung Fu and Hank would pull out a meat cleaver and cut off his right hand and stick it in his mouth. With some pie. And then the hand in the mouth. And then throw him out.

The only thing I didn't do [in the fight] is the tumble over the counter. The director said, "Oh, you don't want to do that, Chris." And Bruce [Bauer, the stunt double] was there and Bruce said, "Well, I'll do it." I always have the stunt guy do it because why should I do it and take money away from him? He works. And because I don't wanna get hurt! [*laughs*] I've never really gotten hurt, but this particular time Mr. Lee and Bruce tumbled over the counter and Bruce caught his back on the napkin holder and it just tore him. Bam! He missed the pad and fell on the floor. And, oh, it was just bad! It was just one of those things. It was ugly. I mean, it was a little thing—it was a three-foot fall off the counter—but the metal caught his back and cut it.

Lenny Von Dohlen: I thought, "What can I bring to this?" Anybody who lives in Los Angeles with any sense at all and who has to get on the freeway, contemplates agoraphobia. I am not an agoraphobic but I have those tendencies. I could easily go there. I think someone hurt [Harold], damaged him in a way that left him almost legless. It is a horrible thing.

Robert Engels: We pretty much followed a soap opera structure. I don't know if anyone else has called it that. It's four scenes in each act and we knew which characters had to be serviced and what had to happen. [The writing] went awfully fast because Mark, Harley and I had done so much together. There was a master plan that was worked out roughly by Mark and David and a little more by the three of us. Actually, we would do the "beat sheet"—the beats for each episode—in an afternoon. It was nice because you just knew it; you go back to that soap opera structure: Bobby had to get from here-to-here in that episode and you had four scenes to do it. That part of it was not complicated because we were shooting inside so much and the [setting] was a small town. How people would get together was predestined. Mark and Harley can [write] fast! They're speedballs!

Episode 12 (Script number 2005; First televised October 27, 1990)

Guest Starring: Lenny Von Dohlen (Harold Smith), Royal Dano (Judge Clinton Sternwood), David L. Lander (Tim Pinkle), Victoria Catlin (Blackie O'Reilly), Van Dyke Parks (Jack Racine), Ritch Brinkley (Daryl Lodwick), Fumio Yamaguchi (Tojamura), and Michael Parks (Jean Renault)

Featuring: Galyn Görg (Nancy), Claire Stansfield (Sid), Mike Vendrell (outside bodyguard), and Bob Apisa (bodyguard on stairs)

Written by Barry Pullman; Directed by Graeme Clifford; Edited by Jonathan P. Shaw

Tuesday, March 7, 1989:

Act 1: Cooper finds Audrey's note under the bed and learns she is at One Eyed Jacks. Mr. Pinkle shows Bobby and Shelly a device to raise and lower Leo into bed. Sternwood releases Leland and sets a date for trial. Donna offers to tell her story to Harold if he will let her read Laura's diary. He agrees to read it to her as long as the diary does not leave the room. Donna snatches the diary and lures Harold to the door. He attempts to exit but has a seizure and collapses. Donna apologizes.

Act 2: Sternwood rules that Leo is not competent to stand trial and may be returned home. Ed brings Nadine home. Nadine pulls the door off the refrigerator. Tojamura offers Ben a "superior" offer (five million dollars) for the Ghostwood project. Ben gives Cooper the ransom and then tells Hank to follow Cooper and bring Audrey back.

Act 3: Renault plots how he will kill Cooper. Andy learns he is no longer sterile. Cooper and Truman plan their approach to One Eyed Jacks. Hawk reports that he has found where the One Armed Man is staying. Andy thinks he is calling Lucy but gets an abortion clinic. James sees Maddy at the Double R and follows her.

Act 4: Donna tells more of her story to Harold. Cooper and Truman overpower a guard and enter One Eyed Jacks. They spy Blackie and Renault. Harold and Donna kiss. Donna sneaks away to signal Maddy. Nancy tries to stab Cooper but he punches her and rescues Audrey. Renault kills Blackie and shoots at Truman. Cooper and Truman are trapped but Hawk rescues them. Donna distracts Harold while Maddy tries to get the diary. Harold hears her and threatens them both with a garden trowel.

The episode is well-constructed and the surprise appearances by Hawk and James (Hawk at the end of this episode; James at the beginning of the next) are set up beforehand so as not to seem forced. (Hawk finds Cooper and Truman planning the mission to One Eyed Jacks, and James bumps into

Maddy at the Double R.) The construction of the episode moves the plot incrementally forward. Nothing of great significance happens, other than the obvious rescue of Audrey from One Eyed Jacks. The investigation into Laura's murder merely inches along; the real work is being done by Donna as she makes every effort to secure the diary. But even that task is left unresolved until the next episode.

The scenes with Donna and Harold are quite effective in capturing the "*Twin Peaks* atmosphere." The pacing is leisurely and camera work unobtrusive; the lighting and music create an other-worldly mood. What's more, Donna recounts a story that foreshadows (or "recalls") the scene in *Fire Walk With Me* in which Donna and Laura go to the Roadhouse and leave with Chuck and Buck. Boyle's and Von Dohlen's performances are especially good. In particular, Von Dohlen gives Harold a quirky intonation, suggesting a character who has spent most of his life isolated from others and doesn't quite know how to say things normally.

Harold is a curious character who is never fully developed (see the deleted scenes notes below). He claims to have written the stories of other people ("friends, lovers") but we never learn more about these people, or how such a reclusive person could come into contact with them.

The humor in this episode veers toward the slapstick at times, such as Tim Pinkle's contraption for Leo, and Andy's excessive reliance on sticky notes. Plus, the ongoing Nadine storyline is a bit silly. Clearly, the writers have to service a great number of actors, and a number of marginal subplots have been introduced so everyone has something to do. The large cast of *Twin Peaks* is beginning to weigh down the production. Once the Laura Palmer story is resolved, some of these subplots will sag beyond repair.

One other element of the episode verges on parody: The scenes at the Roadhouse have a deliberate "Western" motif. The "courtroom" is a saloon (complete with peanut shells littering the floor) presided over by Judge Sternwood, a travelling magistrate with a hearty accent and who, according to the script, is adorned in "Western wear." The lawyers in the room (both Lodwick and Racine) sport Western-style bowties as they debate the cases before Sternwood. It's as if Twin Peaks is supposed to be a kind of frontier town, too far removed the world to be part of the standard legal system. (Did Leland regularly argue cases at the Roadhouse?) But this reliance on exaggerated Western cliché calls attention to itself and effectively dilutes the mystery and "otherworldliness" of the series. What made *Twin Peaks* so appealing was its intangible quality, its resistance to labels and definition. "*Twin Peaks*-as-Western" was a misstep.

Additional Notes:

This episode features the first appearances of Tim Pinkle and Jack Racine.

The first draft of the script for episode 12 was completed on August 17, 1990. The script's first and only revision was completed on August 21, 1990.

Harold explicitly states the date of March 7, 1989 when he begins an entry for Donna into his journal in act 4.

Notable Deleted Scenes

Act 1: At the Roadhouse hearing, Andy escorts Leland past Sarah and Maddy. Leland takes Sarah's hand for a moment. Judge Sternwood arrives and notices that Daryl Lodwick is not present. Sternwood takes time to describe his morning: "Took a long constitutional this morning. The path leading down to the waterfall. A fine, invigorating mist in the air. There was a twelve-point buck drinking from the pool, he saw me but didn't bolt. Time stood still. In the presence of the eternal I suppose that's as it should be."

Ben Horne enters and greets the Judge. Sternwood compliments Horne on the good food at the Great Northern and tells Cooper he has spent many years living and eating at the hotel—he "hammered his way through law school there." Ben explains that Sternwood helped build the Great Northern with Ben's father. Cooper describes a wooden door near his room, "it's like nothing I've ever seen. Two panel oak, all joined with tongues, tenons, and dowels. Not a nail or screw in it." Sternwood says he remembers the door, "dryclamped and lying in the sun. Beautiful piece of work." At this point Daryl Lodwick arrives and apologizes for being late.

This scene provides much more detail about the history and personality of Judge Sternwood and clearly establishes him as wise elder in the community—and a potential mentor to Cooper. Although the scene does not further any plotline (which is probably the reason it was cut), it provides interesting interaction between Cooper and Sternwood.

The scripted scene in which Donna attempts to lure Harold outside contains a few fascinating lines of dialogue that were cut from the televised version. As Harold timidly steps beyond his door, "a trembling ignites in his fingers." He collapses and says, "I just . . . I just got too close." Donna asks, "To what?" But Harold doesn't answer. After he recovers, Harold kisses Donna tenderly.

Harold's intriguing comment hints that he knows of some force in the outside world, beyond his tiny apartment. The trembling in his fingers, (which in the televised version extended to his arm) is eerily reminiscent of the many trembling arms that will plague residents of Twin Peaks in episode 27. These small incidents indicate that the writers may have intended a more significant role for Harold—one in which he was aware of the mysterious forces surrounding the town. Finally, Harold and Donna's kiss makes clear that their relationship was growing stronger. With this part of the scene cut (as well as other scenes between Harold and Donna in the previous episode) the relationship between Donna and Harold never goes further than friendship in the televised versions.

Act 4: At the Double R, Norma tells Hank she thinks Tojamura is M.T. Wentz. Hank looks him over, and believes Tojamura is the same man who attacked him the night before (Jonathan, the Asian Man). He says, "I think he's been here already. . . . Let me handle this." Hank takes a plate of sliced turkey and mashed potatoes from Norma as she looks on anxiously. Hank places the food in front of Tojamura and "shoves the back of the Asian's head forward, ramming his face into the gravy mountain of mashed potatoes." Hank "slaps his palms clean in self-satisfaction and looks back at a stunned Norma." A moment passes as Tojamura raises his face out of the food. Hank looks down and realizes he attacked the wrong Asian. Norma looks on with a "face of death."

This slapstick and somewhat silly scene serves little purpose other than comic relief—Hank makes a fool of himself and suffers Norma's wrath. The scene illustrates how the Hank character was poorly conceived by the show's writers. In the previous episode (and then later in this episode), Hank is involved in dangerous and serious schemes. This scene, however, shows us Hank's foolhardy side, making it hard to believe he may have killed Andrew Packard or is working for Ben Horne. What's more, the scene adds nothing to the mystery of Tojamura and may be why it was cut.

Cast and Crew Comments

Lenny Von Dohlen: That image with the trowel going down my face—I hated doing that. I didn't think that was right for [Harold]. It seemed out of character. But you try to make it work if somebody wants it. I remember arguing strongly about it. He was not capable of doing harm to others. It was not something he could do; he was a nurturer, he was an arbiter of secrets. He had plenty of his own, but he wouldn't do it. It comes back to me now—we compromised. They said he had to do something and so it was, "He'll do it to himself." I could make that work.

Chris Mulkey: I never did [the mashed potatoes scene.] I'll tell you why. It's probably because Piper Laurie said, "You're not going to have Mulkey do that to me. He'll really hurt me." Piper Laurie is great.

In that particular cast, it seemed like a lot of the actors were musicians or artists or poets. They were kind of multifaceted artists. It was extraordinary in that way. I don't know why that was. It was a very "rock-and-roll" cast. This whole group of people had all kinds of passions flying in every different way. I think that was a common theme and what made it such a great group of actors—they all had these incredible passions going in every different way and it made them all individual and unique.

Episode 13 (Script number 2006; First televised November 3, 1990)

Guest Starring: Lenny Von Dohlen (Harold Smith), Ian Abercrombie (Tom Brockman), David Lynch (Gordon Cole), Fumio Yamaguchi (Tojamura)

Featuring: Jill Engels (Trudy), Ron Kirk (Cappy), Leonard Ray (Lounge local), Mak Takano (Jonathan), and Brett Vadset (Joey Paulsen)

Written by Harley Peyton and Robert Engels; Directed by Lesli Linka Glatter; Edited by Paul Trejo

The evening of Tuesday, March 7 through March 8, 1989:

Act 1: James saves Donna and Maddy from Harold, who howls in agony at the betrayal. Truman identifies Jean Renault in a suspect photo book. He and Cooper realize that Renault was after Cooper. Cooper tells Ben that Audrey is free and explains what happened to Blackie. Cooper says that Audrey is recovering from a drug overdose.

Act 2: Bobby and Shelly's insurance scam starts to backfire. Agent Cole delivers Albert's report: the fibers from Cooper's shooting came from a Vicuna coat; the drugs in the One Armed Man's syringe were a combination that Albert has never seen; the papers found near the murder site were from a diary. Audrey tell Ben says she has learned "a lot of new things." Nadine shows her affection for Ed. Jonathan gives Josie a ticket to Hong Kong. Jonathan says "Mr. Eckhardt" will make it worth her while.

Act 3: Maddy announces that she is going home tomorrow. Ben gives Josie the five million dollars he got from Tojamura. Shelly is spooked when she sees Leo move. Cole is worried about Cooper's involvement in the case and how it reminds him of the shooting in Pittsburgh. Cole also gives a note Cooper from Windom Earle: an opening chess move (P to K-4).

Act 4: Leland removes some fur from one of Ben's stuffed animals. Truman pleads with Josie to stay, then tells her he loves her. Tojamura wants Ben to close the Ghostwood deal, but Ben puts him off. Leland starts to sing, "Getting to Know You." Pete strikes up conversation with Tojamura. Gerard becomes Mike, and Cooper interrogates him. Mike says he is an inhabiting spirit and Gerard is his host. Bob was Mike's familiar. Mike says Bob is like a parasite and requires a human host. Bob feeds on fear and the pleasures. Few can see Bob's true face—the gifted and the damned. Mike and Bob were once partners. Bob has been in Twin Peaks for nearly forty years. Cooper believes Bob is in the Great Northern Hotel.

This episode is sharper than the previous two; there seems to be extra energy in every scene. Perhaps this is because of Glatter's fine directing (she also directed the strong episode 10). Another possible explanation for the improvement is that David Lynch was on-set. He makes an appearance as Gordon Cole (previously only heard via speakerphone) and may have contributed some creative input to the various scenes. In any event, a number of sequences stand out: Cooper's return of the ransom money to Ben (who seems more pleased to see the money than to learn the status of his daughter); Josie's meeting with Ben and her insistence to be paid before she hands over the contract signed by Pete; Bobby and Shelly's birthday party for Leo that takes an ominous turn; and, of course, Cooper's interrogation of Mike.

The Windom Earle storyline—not mentioned since episode 9—is reintroduced when Cole delivers a chess move from Earle. Cole is concerned about Cooper, particularly because Cooper was shot, and he does not want a repeat of a situation that happened in Pittsburgh (no details are provided about this situation, but the suggestion is that Cooper was attacked). Cooper says the current case bears few similarities.

Cole delivers the chess move to Cooper in an unmarked envelope. Since Earle has made the first move he plays the white pieces, according to the rules of chess. Even though in most popular mythos—including *Twin Peaks*—white represents good, and black represents evil, Earle must play white if he is to make the first move. This particular use of symbolic opposites, however, fits with other opposing themes found in *Twin Peaks* (i.e., doppelgängers and Laura's dual nature). Earle's first move is considered aggressive by some chess experts, and is exactly what one would expect from a foe that Cooper describes as "cold, hard, and brilliant." Earle may be aware that this opening move is well-known; in his first taped message to Cooper, Earle refers to it as an "emphatically traditional opening."

David Lynch provides a superb dose of comic relief with his performance of the near-deaf Gordon Cole. Although the "misheard-question-and-incorrect-reply" can be tiring *shtick*, Cole, with his loud voice and "can-do" personality, comes across as a fresh and delightful character. Lynch has a great sense of comedic timing and a definite understanding of his character. Although he has acted in other films (bit parts in his own work and as a lead role in Tina Rathborne's film, *Zelly and Me*), Cole may be Lynch's most memorable performance. When asked about his acting, Lynch said, "*Twin Peaks* was my best work. It was really fun. And also the mood on the set of *Twin Peaks* was . . . so fantastic. There was a lot of experimenting, and a lot of just goodwill, and just a great working atmosphere."[3]

One of the Giant's clues, "Without chemicals he points," is fully explained in this episode. While some information is provided back in episode 10, here Cooper learns that when Phil Gerard does not receive his injection, his "inhabiting spirit," Mike, comes to the fore and is able to provide information that will point the way to Bob.

The first draft of the script was completed on August 28, 1990. The script went through three revisions, and the final revision was completed on September 17, 1990.

Notable Deleted Scenes

Act 3: When Maddy and James talk at the lake, she has one intriguing line of dialogue that was cut. She tells James that she and Laura were so close it was like their brains were connected. She also says, "Our mothers were the same way." Maddy's fascinating revelation about both her mother and aunt hints at a possibility that they were both psychic. Sarah Palmer exhibits many signs of psychic prowess in the series but, up to this point, the series has only made one brief mention of Maddy's mother, Beth. (Maddy mentions Beth to Sarah in episode 8.) The writers may have intended to introduce a subplot involving Beth and Sarah and then decided to abandon it, possibly explaining why this comment was cut from episode 13.

Act 4: While Ben and Mr. Tojamura talk in the Great Northern dining room, Leland starts singing a show tune. In the televised version Leland sings a song from *The King and I*. In the script, he sings a song from *Pal Joey* (which Pete readily identifies.) The song's lyrics are significant, given Leland's other identity. Leland sings, "I'm wild again. Beguiled again. A simpering, whimpering child again. Bewitched, bothered, and bewildered am I." This song was likely replaced because the lyrics strongly hint that Leland could be Bob.

At the sheriff's station, Cooper, Cole, Truman, and Hawk question Phil Gerard. One critical line of dialogue was deleted. Cooper asks Mike where he and the others like him come from. In the televised version, Mike replies, "That cannot be revealed." But in the script, Mike says, "There are indications that we come from another world." This is the only time where the show addresses where Mike and Bob originate. The line may have been cut because the producers did not want to commit themselves to anything regarding the origin of Mike and Bob, hence Mike's vague line. While Mike's comment in the scripted version of episode 13 about "another world" does not reveal any specific detail, it may indicate that Engels, Peyton and the other writers had discussed a place of origin for Bob and Mike. (Remember, the Black and White Lodges had not been introduced into the narrative at this point.)

Cast and Crew Comments

Grace Zabriskie: I had talked to Harley [Peyton], and we had a long conversation in which I was asking for more psychic background for Sarah. I was asking for two aunts who had looked preternaturally alike, just as the cousins did. The aunts would have been Sarah Palmer and her sister. I was asking for untold generations of, well, basically witches. I was asking for there to be generation-after-generation of women who, during one period or several periods of our history, would have been called witches, because of their knowledge and their powers. Also, in terms of backstory, this family history had been forgotten—or that it had, in fact, been denied out of shame, for a number of generations. So Sarah is in complete denial of this background, what little she's ever heard of it. Whereas her sister, Maddy's mother, wants it.

Sarah and Maddy are not closer because Sarah has not encouraged it. Sarah is afraid of what would happen if they get together. The line about the aunt came out of that, but then it didn't go any further. You can imagine how excited I was when they did script that.

I was so excited when they seemed to be developing the story. Harley seemed interested in it and was buying it and wanted to go there. It seems to me there might have been three little snippets of things that hinted at the story. That always struck me as an interesting way to proceed with the character once Laura's killer was known.

Lenny Von Dohlen: It's a world where you're apt to howl. [*laughs*] I mean every character in [*Twin Peaks*], given the chance, might throw their head back and howl! It's not a bad thing to do! In most shows you'd call that, "Chewin' up the scenery," but [here] that was just, "Getting by in 'lynchville!'"

Dana Ashbrook: I think the show got "spread out" a little too much. There was almost too much going on all the time for people to focus on. I don't really know. When we did the first seven and the pilot no one knew who we were. No one knew anything about the show. We were free. Then all of a sudden we got to the second season and it was a whole different thing. We had security. You had to approve people coming to the set. It was a different vibe. But I had a great time, all the time. It was the best time. I was working all the time and I had the best job. It left me wanting to do more.

Episode 14 (Script number 2007; First televised November 10, 1990)

Guest Starring: David Lynch (Gordon Cole), Fumio Yamaguchi (Tojamura)

Featuring: Julee Cruise (Roadhouse singer), Carel Struycken (the Giant), and Hank Worden (the room service waiter)

Written by Mark Frost; Directed by David Lynch; Edited by Mary Sweeney

Thursday, March 9, 1989:

> Act 1: Cole says farewell to Cooper and the police. Cooper and Truman bring Mike, the One Armed Man, to the Great Northern. Ben Horne approaches and Mike collapses. Hawk finds Harold Smith has hanged himself. At the Palmer's, Maddy tells Leland and Sarah that she is leaving. Cooper and the police search Harold's. Hawk finds Laura's diary.

> Act 2: Bobby thinks Leo had some hidden money. Leo makes a noise then says, "New shoes." Shelly says she took some of Leo's boots in for repair. Bobby thinks it is important. Audrey tells Ben she knows about One Eyed Jacks and Laura and Ronette. She tells him she was the girl behind the mask. Ben tells Audrey that he knew Laura worked at One Eyed Jacks. Ben says he slept with Laura and that he loved her.

> Act 3: At the Double R, Shelly tells Norma she has to quit. Ed is worried about Nadine. Mike and Bobby break the heel off Leo's boot and find an audio tape. Cooper believes Laura's diary implicates Ben Horne. Audrey tells Cooper about Ben and Laura and One Eyed Jacks. Cooper tells Truman they need to arrest Ben.

> Act 4: Cooper and police arrest Ben but he tries to flee. At the Palmer's, Sarah, seemingly drugged, crawls down the stairs. The Log Lady tells Cooper that there are "owls in the Roadhouse." Tojamura reveals "himself" to be Catherine to Pete. Sarah Palmer sees a vision of a white horse and collapses. At the Roadhouse, Donna and James discuss the death of Harold. Cooper, Truman and the Log Lady arrive. The old waiter and Bobby sit at the bar. Cooper watches the singer. Suddenly the giant appears and says, "It is happening again." At the Palmer's, Leland sees Bob in the mirror. Maddy smells something burning. She sees Bob. Bob/Leland attacks and brutally murders Maddy. Cooper senses that something has happened. The old waiter tells Cooper, "I'm so sorry." Bobby looks sad and lost. Donna starts to cry and James comforts her. Cooper looks up, searchingly.

David Lynch returns to direct one of the finest hours of television ever made. Contradicting the critics who maintain the stronger episodes were in the first season, this one resolves many of the plots that have been simmering for weeks (such as the identity of Tojamura), and does so with a style rarely seen on network television, certainly to that point in time.

Lynch succeeds at doing what he does best—establishing a mood and atmosphere, and weaving incidents into that mood so seamlessly that the effect upon the viewer is as much emotional as intellectual: scenes connect with each other in more than just a logical, plot-oriented way but also in a kind of intuitive, almost subconscious manner. As Maddy dies, a sadness pervades the Roadhouse even though none of the characters understand what has happened. The look on Bobby's face exhibits the uneasy confusion they all feel. There is a sense of pent-up emotion waiting for release and it finally does when Donna breaks down and sobs.

David Lynch has talked about this scene in some detail. In the book, *Lynch on Lynch*, he told interviewer Chris Rodley:

> "Suddenly these emotions came, and everyone was just overcome with sadness. Something was going on. You could feel it, like, 100 percent. It was everywhere in the room and it was overwhelmingly sad.
>
> "And then Donna starts crying. And Cooper sees this— he's the only one seeing the whole story. Maybe the Log Lady, too. And then Bobby breaks. And you could see Donna feeling it—being moved by this abstract thing. But when Bobby gets sad and feels it, that was what did it for me. It was one of the coolest things because when certain people get moved, knowing their character, then something is really happening."[4]

Set against the emotional anguish of the teenagers, Cooper, the Log Lady and the Giant attempt to communicate. The Giant calmly relates (in his own cryptic way) information to Cooper, who sits passively though attentively, straining to understand, yet ultimately failing to get the facts he needs.

And then, positioned between the emotions of Donna and the calm of Cooper, is the elderly waiter from the Great Northern. He has the dignity of old age as he comes to comfort Cooper, yet his words reflect the anguish present in Donna that Cooper cannot yet express: "I'm so sorry."

The scenes in the Roadhouse bracket the brutal scene of Maddy's murder, which may be the most violent sequence ever to air on network television. The scene depicts the entire murder of an innocent victim, from the time she sees her assailant to the time she finally dies. Lynch unflinchingly shows Bob's terrifying pursuit of Maddy, his violent assault, and his final, savage blows. Maddy—and the viewer—are not spared any of the gruesome details. Though difficult to watch, Mark Frost explained why such a scene was necessary: "We wanted that to be a very violent scene because we were suddenly seeing the consequences of everything that led up to it. In a way, you are kind of seeing Laura's death."[5] Frost is right about how this scene effectively shows the death of Laura. It is the most explicit murder scene in the whole *Twin Peaks* storyline. Laura's murder in the R-rated, *Fire Walk With Me* is depicted within shadows and strobe lights, hiding much of the visceral details. Not so with the death of Maddy, a scene where Bob is explicitly shown killing his victim. Here, for the first time, we see the full brutality and depravity of Bob.

The first Great Northern scene cheats just a bit when Gerard goes into convulsions during Ben's entrance. Later, it will be implicit that Leland was nearby, but at this point he is nowhere to be seen. For a while, the writers were trying to convince viewers that Ben was Laura's killer. (Even original scripts were altered, giving Leland's lines to Ben, so that word wouldn't leak out from the cast or crew about Bob's true identity. In addition, the attack on Maddy was filmed with both Richard Beymer and Ray Wise as the aggressors.) Cooper, himself, becomes convinced of Ben's possible guilt.

Despite the intensity of this episode, Lynch's sense of humor is still present. During the Great Northern scene, the background is filled with sailors bouncing balls on the floor (creating an aural discomfort that adds to the stress and urgency of the moment). Later, just after Hawk discovers that Harold has hanged himself, Lynch cuts to the Palmer household where Louis Armstrong's "It's a Wonderful World" is playing. While Bobby and Shelly are wading through her bills, Leo grunts, and a terrified Shelly jumps back and screams, "He's alive!" (A notable allusion to the *Frankenstein* films, especially in light of Bobby's reference to Leo later in the season as "Leostein.")

This episode, though an artistic triumph, still represents a significant victory of commercial network demands over creator desires. ABC Television, along with many viewers, was becoming impatient with what they considered the prolonged plot of the Laura Palmer mystery. The network insisted that the producers deliver *some* sort of resolution. Lynch and Frost had long fought such a decision, believing that the mystery was the main hook that kept viewers watching. When Leland was revealed as the killer, and interest in *Twin Peaks* quickly fell, Lynch and Frost were arguably proven right.

Still, ratings *had* started to decline, in part because the audience was beginning to suspect there might never be resolution. Lynch and Frost were trying to keep the identity of the murderer secret for as long as possible. But, while this episode shows that Leland is the killer, the mystery is redefined: Leland is positioned as a "human host" for another entity and Cooper must now deploy an entirely different set of techniques to locate and stop Bob. (Unfortunately, the investigation into Bob never gathers momentum; Lynch and Frost sacrifice what could have been a very compelling plotline.)

Additional Notes:

The bodies behind Donna's independent investigations are piling up. Jacoby was attacked at the gazebo in part because of her plan to send him the videotape of Maddy dressed as Laura (in the first season finale), and now Harold has committed suicide because of her betrayal of his trust.

Lynch's fascination with flashing lights is on display during the search of Harold's apartment. A photographer documents the scene and bright flashes punctuate the proceedings. The scene ends with Hawk, Truman, and Cooper gathered around Laura's "secret" diary—which they are now seeing for the first time—as a flash fades the screen to white.

In this episode, the power relationship between Audrey and Ben changes dramatically. She reveals that she knows about Ben's ownership of One Eyed Jacks and about Blackie and Battis' recruitment of girls from the perfume counter at Horne's Department Store. And she admits that she was Prudence, the new girl Ben tried to sleep with in the season premiere. Under pressing questioning from Audrey, Ben admits that he slept with Laura.

There is a slight continuity error within the episode. When the police struggle to arrest Ben, his glasses come off and fall to the floor (Andy briefly turns his head as he watches them come off). Everyone (but Tojamura and his assistant) leaves the room. Later, when the police bring Ben into the station, he is wearing his glasses again.

Julee Cruise returns to perform a couple of songs at the Roadhouse. The songs, "Rockin' Back Inside My Heart" and "The World Spins," are from her first album (produced by David Lynch), *Floating Into the Night.*

Like many episodes directed by David Lynch, episode 14 varied widely from what was originally scripted. Whole scenes were cut, and many scenes were rearranged within the episode. Also, because the commercial breaks in episode 14 did not follow their standard pattern (i.e., one about every 10 to 12 minutes), act 2 was shortened, and the final act of the episode was substantially longer than usual.

The script for episode 14 went through two drafts. The first draft was completed on September 5, 1990, and the second was finished on September 12. The script was then revised once on September 13, the day shooting began on the episode.

Notable Deleted Scenes

Act 1: At Harold Smith's apartment, Cooper, Truman, and Hawk "pour into the room, weapons drawn." They soon see Harold's hanging body, and Cooper finds Harold's last note: "*Je suis une a me solitaire.*" Later, paramedics remove Harold's body as Cooper brings in Phil Gerard (now Mike). "Cooper raises a hand, stops the gurney, gestures to Gerard. Gerard puts his hand on the bag, closes his eyes." Cooper asks if Bob was here and Mike shakes his head. Truman rolls his eyes and takes Cooper quietly aside. Truman wonders if such actions are a good idea, especially in front of other officers. Cooper replies, "Harry, we're at the chicken-soup stage in this crime. . . . It couldn't hurt." Truman produces Smith's wallet and tells Cooper that Harold was a patient of Dr. Jacoby. Cooper is curious about Harold's blood type, but must wait for test results. As Cooper offers Mike a cup of coffee, Hawk finds something among Harold's papers—Laura's diary. This last part of the scene is the only part to survive to the televised version, and is the closing scene of act 1.

This scene contains a number of interesting story points. First, it reveals that Smith was a patient of Dr. Jacoby, who, if the plotline were allowed to develop, could have explained why Harold refused to leave his apartment. (Again, earlier scripts hint that Harold was afraid of something.) Second, Cooper suspects that Bob may have been in the room. It's not clear whether Cooper suspects that Bob killed Harold, or if Harold was acting as Bob's host. Either way, he relies on Mike's senses to tell him if Bob had been there. Finally, we see the beginning of Truman's exasperation at Cooper's methods. Truman will not show these feelings for another two episodes, when, in episode 16, he tells Cooper he's had enough of Cooper's mysterious methods.

Later, at the sheriff's station, Cooper examines the diary found at Harold's. He confirms that the handwriting is Laura's, and Truman hopes the answers to the murder are inside. Cooper agrees, but comments, "It's a shame that Mr. Smith saw fit to mutilate about 45% of the contents." Hawk enters with the scraps of paper he found by the railroad tracks. Cooper matches them to the new diary, then makes another observation about the ripped pages: "Look at the way the pages are torn, clean, ripped out at the roots. Smith ripped and slashed his way through, like the others we found in his apartment." He looks closer at the pages Hawk brought in, "Nine pages. They were taken some time ago. . . . By the killer. The day she died." Cooper concludes that Harold is not the killer as Dr. Hayward enters to report on Harold's blood type. It was "O." Truman reads from the diary and is shocked; Laura has written, "Beware of Bob." Cooper is "galvanized." He orders Hawk to get a cruiser, tells Harry to get the diary, and moves to get Mike. He wants to go to the Great Northern.

This lengthy scene lays to rest any suspicions that Harold may have been Laura's killer, especially once his blood type is revealed. The scene also reveals the shocking content of Laura's true diary. Her entries are enough to make Truman mutter, "Oh my Lord . . . oh my Lord . . . ." This is the only time where any of the characters really react to what Laura's written (although Cooper does describe some of the diary contents in a later scene).

Because many previous episodes had spent time focusing on the whereabouts and contents of the diary, this lengthy scene served as a climax to the diary subplot (and also allowed Act 1 to end in a moment of dramatic tension). The diary is the focal point of the scene, and much time is spent discussing it. Many aspects of this scene are similar to Cooper's later scene in which he narrates his findings to Diane. The show's producers may have felt that the diary could be dismissed in the shorter scene, and, hence, opted to use only the one involving Cooper.

Act 2: At the Great Northern Hotel, "deputies are shepherding an interesting mix of hotel guests, one by one, past Gerard." He starts to hyperventilate, and loosens his collar. Cooper is concerned and instructs Hayward to stay close. Behind them, the elevator doors open and Ben Horne steps out. As he does, Gerard screams, "My arm!" and passes out. Dr. Hayward is upset. He tells Cooper, "This has gone on long enough." The crowd is watching, and Ben speaks for them. He demands answers from Truman, asking, "Why are my guests being hounded like this?" Truman agrees to leave, and Ben turns to the crowd reassuring them that all is well. Hayward is still concerned; he says they must get Gerard to a bed. Truman asks Ben for a room, but Ben stalls, asking if Gerard wants to check in. Cooper gives him a look, and Ben complies, offering them a room down the hall. Truman and Hayward take a limp Gerard down the corridor. After they're gone Cooper turns to Ben and asks how Audrey is feeling. Ben's almost hostile response is, "tip-top."

This scene contains some extraneous material, and it's easy to see why and how it could have been trimmed down for the televised version. It does, however, explain why Phil Gerard is in the Great Northern in episode 15.

Act 4: At the Palmer house, a drugged Sarah Palmer crawls into the living room and has a vision of the "pale horse." The scene dissolves to sometime later as Maddy enters the living room carrying a couple of packed suitcases which she sets down. She calls back to someone, "I'm going to leave these down here tonight. I'll be ready to get an early start." Behind Maddy, Ben Horne comes down the stairs. He looks at himself in the mirror and sees Bob staring back. He puts on surgical gloves and approaches Maddy. Sarah Palmer is still lying on the floor and Maddy has noticed her. She rushes to her side as Ben moves in behind, raising his hands.

Obviously the Ben Horne character in this scene is supposed to be Leland, (why would Ben be upstairs, anyway?). The name Ben Horne was substituted in the script so as to keep the identity of Bob a secret. (Had there been leaks from the set as to who killed Laura Palmer, the information getting out would have been false.)

The scene is also much milder than what Lynch shot. Ben (re: Leland) is revealed to be Bob, he then stalks up to an unsuspecting Maddy as the scene fades to black. Maddy's death happens off-screen. Lynch, of course, showed the entire, brutal death of Maddy at the hands of Bob/Leland.

Mark Frost was the writer of this episode, and it appears that he introduced the vision of the pale horse in the script. Many have debated the horse's meaning (did it mean death, or drugs, or something else?). It may be safe to assume that the pale horse (as described in the script) meant death. Frost even substantiated this interpretation while attending a *Twin Peaks* Seminar at the Florence Gould Hall on November 17, 1990 (one week after this episode aired). Because Frost was the author and originator of the idea, this interpretation is probably correct.

Cast and Crew Comments

Mark Frost: We knew it was him from the start. One day writing, David and I looked at each other and both said "Leland!" But nobody else knew who it was until the episode where it was revealed, not even the actors. Neither of our ex-wives even knew!

Lenny Von Dohlen: I knew [Harold] would meet his demise. I just didn't know exactly how. I suggested something at a very late hour. It came to me that he should not hang, but gas the orchids and himself, and have [the orchids] all laying over him. It was kind of exotic and bizarre. I ran it by David and he said, "Lenny! Never come to me with a great idea twelve hours before shooting. The beam is already up there!" [*laughs*] So he hanged himself.

I may be giving away a secret; I might be screwing with people's heads so use your own judgment. But, no, those were not my legs [on the hanging body]. I have better legs!

Al Strobel: There was a lot of stuff I would have liked to see. One of the scenes I think David was most creative with, was the scene in the Great Northern Hotel lobby, with a convention of Navy WAVES all bouncing tennis balls. At the same time, I'm brought into this incredible scene to try to identify who Bob was. They brought Piper Laurie, dressed up as [Tojamura], in front of me. There was a lot more of that scene shot than what actually aired. The whole "bizarreness" of that thing was incredible. But the reason that it got bumped was for [time], because later in that episode was the murder of Maddy, which obviously was more important.

131

It's a pity that David's incredible vision in that bouncing ball scene couldn't have been carried on farther, and Madeleine's murder postponed to another episode.

Dana Ashbrook: I just came by the set to hang out. I liked to come and watch him. I think he just threw me in [the Roadhouse scene]. I was like, "OK." It was just me trusting [David] so much. That's one thing I haven't found since then—just being able to trust the director so much that you would do whatever for him!

It was probably one of those ethereal, supernatural things that was going down outside of Bobby. David was saying, "Do this and I'll plug it in later."

Grace Zabriskie: I remember that the crawl was "rug-burn city" for me. [*laughs*] Once I got down to the floor my positioning became critical. So it meant that I had to try to stay there between takes. I discovered—not for the first time, and God knows, not for the last—that as far as the crew is concerned, when an actor is lying on the floor the actor is like a piece of carpet, [or] something else on the floor. You really start to become aware that it is marginally dangerous. You sort of talk every once in a while, "OK, I'm here. I'm alive. I want all my toes. Take it easy!"

Frank Silva: It took us all day to film the scene where Maddy was killed. First of all, nobody knew who the killer was. When we did that scene there were three people killing Maddy, so that even the crew wouldn't know. There was Bob, there was Ray Wise, and there was Benjamin Horne. Everything was choreographed, and all of us did the same thing. And Sheryl Lee had to get killed by all three of us. She was meat by the end of the day, a rag doll.

Richard Beymer: David called us up to the room that morning and told us who the murderer was, and that Ray wasn't going to be in the show [anymore]. But he was going to work something where he was going to come back. And he told us we were going to do this scam. He didn't want anyone to know who the killer was and we were going to shoot the same scene three times. I went first and blocked the scene and then Ray did it next.

It was OK. It didn't bother me at all. This was the way he wanted to do it? Fine. I had more problems with doing the particular scene. I found it incredibly brutal and not needed. Just to do it was . . . not fun. Sheryl Lee was not having fun.

Since I was the first one to do the scene, I had the advantage of trying different things, and blocking it with David. It was kind of tailored that way the first time. When Ray did it he had certain blockings he had to follow, although he added his own things to it. But he did have blocking—finding out how to hit her head against the picture. [That was] a bit much.

Frank Silva: There was a lot of sexual stuff going on between Bob and [Maddy]. Part of that killing scene is dancing with her, the slow dancing with her in the super slow motion. When we were doing that, David's only direction was, "Dreamy. I want it dreamy. Make it dreamy." That was what he wanted in that scene. He wanted it dreamy and sexual and really slow—and almost, as I take it, animalistic. That's how I sense Bob anyway. He's more animal than anything. So I played him more like an animal. I wanted that feeling for him. But that was like the big thing for the dance, he kept saying, "Dreamy." For all of us, for when Leland did it, for when I did it, for when Ben Horne did it.

That scene was so horrific to do. I remember when we did the master of me doing it; I was so exhausted towards the end of the scene because we had shot it all in one sequence. At the end, where I shove her head into the painting of Missoula, Montana—I fucked up the line too, I kept saying Missouri—we were both so exhausted. She falls to the floor and I was so exhausted and so into it, I fell to the floor with her, over her body. It ended with me animalistic, over the body, kind of licking the body and hovering over the body. It was such an intense thing to do.

Sheryl Lee: The feeling was very eerie, as it is when you do scenes like that. It was very intense. It also required so much focus and concentration from the actors so that no one got hurt. Because accidents happen all the time in scenes like that. Inevitably if you're the one being hit you do get hurt at some point. At least bruised or sore. It was a very, very intense day and I was sure glad when it was over! The next day I woke up in bed and I tried to sit up and I couldn't! I absolutely could not sit up. I had to roll over and kind of fall off the bed! [*laughs*]

Mark Frost: You can't keep tap-dancing forever. And that was sort of David's inclination: "Why do we ever have to tell anybody who killed Laura?" I said, "Because, David, they're going to hate you if you don't!" [*laughs*]

Episode 15 (Script number 2008; First televised on November 17, 1990)

Guest Starring: James Booth (Ernie Niles), Kathleen Wilhoite (Gwen), and Jane Greer (Vivian Smythe)

Co-Starring: Emily Fincher (Louise Dombrowski)

Written by Scott Frost; Directed by Caleb Deschanel; Edited by Jonathan P. Shaw

Friday, March 10, 1989:

Act 1: At the Palmer home, Leland putts golf balls. Leland puts his golf club into a bag that contains Maddy's body. Ben tells Jerry he was with Catherine the night of Laura's murder. Ben and Jerry recall when they were boys and their babysitter, Louise Drombowski, would dance on the hook rug with her flashlight. Truman tells Leland they arrested Ben. Leland excuses himself and begins to cry and then laugh.

Act 2: Doc Hayward takes a blood sample from Ben. Cooper shows Laura's diary to Ben and explains that he knows about One Eyed Jacks. Cooper implies that Ben killed Laura to keep her quiet. Bobby listens to Leo's tape: It is a recording of Ben talking to Leo about burning the mill. Norma's mother, Vivian, arrives at the Double R. She has a new husband, Ernie Niles. The One Armed Man overpowers his guard and escapes from the Great Northern.

Act 3: Hank returns and says he was hiding from people who want to see him fail. Truman and Pete have serious suspicions about Jonathan. Catherine says she will provide Ben with an alibi in exchange for the Ghostwood Estates and the mill. Truman pulls Leland over. Leland says he remembers Ben making a call the night Laura was killed and that his voice was raised. Leland wants to show Cooper his golf clubs. Before he can, Cooper is called away by Truman.

Act 4: Andy believes he is the father of Lucy's baby. Mike examines Ben and says that Bob is not there. Truman charges Ben with the murder, anyway. Cooper says Ben should be released. Truman is frustrated and refuses. Norma suspects something about Hank and Ernie. Audrey visits Cooper. He gets a call and tells Audrey to go to her room and lock the door. At the bottom of the falls, the police have discovered the body of Maddy, wrapped in plastic.

This episode feels like a brief pause in the *Twin Peaks* narrative, a chance for viewers to catch their collective breath after the shocking events of the previous installment. Leland has been revealed as the killer; Cooper and Truman close-in, but Leland will not be arrested until the next episode.

This episode marks one of the rare instances in the narrative when the audience knows more than the characters do. Until now, viewers have been attempting to solve the mystery along with Cooper. Here, Cooper is in the dark about Leland, but the audience knows just how dangerous Leland can be. This creates a different kind of tension, particularly in scenes like the one where Leland wants to show Cooper his golf clubs. Is Leland going to harm Cooper? Will Cooper discover Maddy's body? The confrontation is cut short and these questions are forever left open.

It is unclear whether Bob or Leland is in control when he meets Cooper on the road. Why would Leland/Bob bother to invite Cooper to look in the trunk, unless he expected to be discovered? Perhaps Leland was struggling against Bob and trying to reveal his misdeeds to the authorities. After all, it is unlikely Bob would be so careless about confronting Cooper. Leland could have been exerting control, however, hoping to end the nightmare he is enduring. We will never know the reason, however; the story does not address this curious scene again. (And, in all likelihood, it was written simply for the dramatic irony and tension it brings.)

Ray Wise continues to provide and outstanding performance as Leland. In the first act, Leland dances around the Great Northern with golf club in hand until he hears the news from Truman that Ben has been arrested for Laura's murder. He feigns distress then becomes even more gleeful as soon as the sheriff and Cooper leave. With each murder he is becoming increasingly unhinged. Wise must convincingly portray all the facets of this complex character, and he does so with great skill.

Maintaining interesting storylines for all of the characters, however, is not easy. The introduction of Gwen and Vivian give Lucy and Norma something to do, but neither of the new characters are all that intriguing, nor are their stories.

The quality of the episode comes both in the performances (especially Wise, noted above, but also James Patrick Kelly) and the writing, which makes virtually every scene interesting. Jerry provides a couple of humorous moments as his inept lawyering continues to complicate matters for Ben (at one point he even recommends that Ben get himself a better lawyer). Pete has an uncharacteristic moment in which he gleefully taunts Ben with a tape of Catherine offering to exchange an alibi for Ben for ownership of the mill. Pete Martell will continue to be a curiously-defined character, alternating between avuncular good-neighbor and scheming side-kick. He had the potential for greater depth but will remain a marginal character for the rest of the series.

Ben is being hit from all sides in this episode, though he doesn't know it yet. While Truman pursues a murder arrest, and Catherine works at regaining the mill, Bobby is preparing to blackmail Ben by sending him a tape found in Leo's boots. The tape contains a recording of Ben hiring Leo to burn the mill. It is little wonder that, later in the season, Ben will suffer a kind of mental breakdown and retreat into the past (both his own past and, ultimately, the country's, in a re-enactment of the Civil War).

This episode contains one of the most memorable scenes of the second season: Ben and Jerry's reminiscence of Louise Dombrowski's flashlight dance on the hook-rug. So popular was this scene, that the musical piece, "Hook Rug Dance" was included on the *Twin Peaks - Season Two Music & More* soundtrack. The origin of the Louise Dombrowski dance seems to have numerous sources. Richard Beymer recalls introducing the idea of the dance to director Caleb Deschanel, who then envisioned a captivating short sequence. The scene represents one of the few instances where a director other than Lynch "ad-libbed" a piece of visual poetry.

The first draft of episode 15 was completed on September 12, 1990. It was revised again on September 14, 20, and 26, 1990.

Notable Deleted Scenes

Act 4: Jerry's visit to Ben in jail varies slightly between script and televised version. Louise Dombrowski's "flashlight dance" does not appear in the script. (It is only mentioned by Jerry.) Instead, the script has Ben asking, "What is that smell?" Jerry responds, "Ginger root. I'm supposed to take a bath in it when I get home. Cures jet lag. Little trick I picked up from a Geisha named Meko. Wish you'd been there, Ben; she had the cutest little feet." While this scene undoubtedly contained great comedic delivery by David Patrick Kelly, the flashlight dance was certainly the better choice.

Audrey's visit to Cooper contains some interesting (if minor) changes in light of the abandoned Cooper/Audrey romance and Kyle MacLachlan's refusal to participate. When Audrey knocks, Cooper is shirtless. In the televised version he grabs his shirt and eventually buttons it (after Audrey sees where he's been shot), whereas the script has him shirtless for the entire scene.

After Audrey looks at Cooper's wound, "She wants to reach out and touch it, but doesn't. Then embarrassed, turns around and looks out the window." Later, after beginning to tell Cooper that nothing happened to her at One Eyed Jacks, "She looks at him longingly. Starts to reach out to touch him." After Cooper answers the call in which he learns about Maddy's death, he tells Audrey to go to her room and lock the door. On the televised version he says, "No questions. Do what I say." But the original script has, "No questions. Do this for me." In the former, his instructions come from a position of authority, whereas the latter emphasizes a possible personal bond. It is, of course, a minor change but it hints at major plot alterations that were going on behind-the-scenes.

Cast and Crew Comments

Scott Frost (*screenwriter, episode 15*): I don't remember how [I ended up writing episode 15] but the timing turned out to be really good. Those three episodes were as good as the show got, except for maybe the very beginning. I remember watching the episode that David directed and just being stunned at the power of that television. I mean, it was horrifying. It was exciting to be part of that little arc. Mine was a little odder in the sense that there was a certain lightness to it. But, at that point in the series, it still had a quality of a creepy realness to it. That was maybe lost toward the end of the series.

I still have very fond memories of the Horne brothers in jail reminiscing about Louise Dombrowski doing the flashlight dance on the rug. [Caleb Deschanel] came up with the flashback idea. And when Caleb came up with visual ideas, you don't argue, because he is one of the great cinematographers alive. He did a great job. He shot it, as you would expect, perfectly. It was just that one little shot of these two little kids sitting on the bed watching this flashlight dance. I still don't have any clue as to where I came up with the idea for a flashlight dance. It was just one of those moments of poetry in *Twin Peaks* that somehow endures.

Richard Beymer: I mentioned that scene to the director. The girl came into the scene with her own flashlight—she had control of the flashlight—which I didn't understand. Because when I explained the scene, the idea was that he and I would be sitting on the bed with flashlights. We would be roaming our flashlights over the girl. That way, we were in control of the vision, so to speak. When she came in with a flashlight, that, to me, didn't work.

The idea was that we were sneaking a look with our flashlights on this young woman. If she comes in with a flashlight, it's a whole other statement. It's not as voyeuristic. She's tantalizing us. But I knew it was going to be in because the director said he was going to shoot it.

Mark Frost: I think the only time we saw [Leland] playing golf was the time he was dragging Maddy's body to the trunk! Leland was definitely the golfer in *Twin Peaks*. But that had nothing to do with the fact that he was a demonic killer. [*laughs*]

Episode 16 (Script number 2009; First televised December 1, 1990)

Guest Starring: James Booth (Ernie Niles), and Jane Greer (Vivian Smythe)

Co-Starring: Michael J. Anderson (Man From Another Place), Clive Rosengren (Mr. Zipper, the plumber), Frank Silva (Killer Bob), Carel Struycken (the Giant), Mae Williams (Mrs. Tremond), and Hank Worden (the room service waiter)

Written by Mark Frost, Harley Peyton, and Robert Engels; Directed by Tim Hunter; Edited by Paul Trejo

Saturday, March 11, 1989:

Act 1: Cooper asks Truman to give him twenty-four hours to solve the murders. Donna takes Cooper to Mrs. Tremond, but a much younger woman is at the home. She gives an envelope to Donna, left for her by Harold. It's a page from Laura's diary describing a dream on the night of February 21—the exact same dream Cooper later had. Laura also remarks that she will die on the night of February 23 to escape from Bob.

Act 2: Cooper questions Gerard, who channels Mike: Mike and Bob had a "perfect relationship" of appetite and satisfaction. The police search Ben's apartment; Truman is convinced Ben is the killer. Tojamura visits Ben and reveals herself to be Catherine. He signs the Ghostwood contract over to her in exchange for her testimony. Donna tells Leland about Laura's secret diary. Beth calls Leland to tell him Maddy hasn't come home.

Act 3: Leland dances with Donna, making her uncomfortable. Bob begins to take control, but Donna is unaware. Truman shows up and asks for Leland's help. Donna meets James and tells him about Maddy's death. Distraught, he rides away. Cooper convenes a meeting at the Roadhouse with Truman, Ben, Albert, Leland, Ed, Hawk, Bobby, Leo, Major Briggs, and the waiter. Cooper believes the killer is in the room and says that he will employ a new tool—magic. Cooper remembers Laura telling him in his dream that her father killed her. The Giant appears and returns Cooper's ring.

Act 4: Cooper pretends to arrest Ben but instead lures Leland into a cell. Leland/Bob confesses to the murders. Cooper explains to Truman and Albert how the dream and the other clues revealed Leland to be the killer. Leland recites the "fire walk with me" poem and smashes his head against the door. Leland finally realizes that he killed Laura. He explains how as a boy he "invited" Bob inside of him; when Bob was in control, Leland didn't know what was happening. Laura refused to be taken over by Bob, so Bob used Leland to kill her. Cooper comforts Leland as he dies. The next morning, Truman, Albert, and Major Briggs try to comprehend what has happened and whether Bob was real. Truman wonders where Bob is now. An owl flies through the forest.

The Laura Palmer storyline comes to an extraordinary close in an episode directed by Tim Hunter. Here, Hunter does a superb job of capturing the mood of the series, sometimes with overt dream-like imagery (such as the Roadhouse scene in which the Giant returns Cooper's ring), but also with less showy scenes, such as those featuring Donna and James. In one distinct scene, James and Donna meet at the Double R Diner and he gives her a ring. It's a subdued moment, given power by the cinematography and Badalamenti score. Later, Donna meets James on the road and tells him of Maddy's death. In both scenes there is deep emotion, something that *Twin Peaks* always portrayed well.

The more dramatic moments, however, are from the aforementioned Roadhouse scene and Leland's arrest. In Ray Wise's final regular appearance on the show, he gives an unforgettable performance, presenting Leland as confident killer, then as someone possessed by Bob (who is in total control), and, finally—tragically—as a remorseful father. Al Strobel, perhaps the most overlooked actor on the series and someone who provided uniformly superior performances, has a riveting scene in which he describes to Cooper the perfect relationship of appetite and satisfaction, a "golden circle."

The writers are careful to let Cooper explain to Truman the reasons he believes Leland is guilty, thus reminding viewers of the clues that have been accumulating during the series: the dancing dwarf, the killer's gray hair, the letters under the fingernails, etc. Some connections seem a bit murky (what exactly is the relationship between the dancing dwarf and dancing Leland?) but recounted at Cooper's breakneck pace, they seem to make sense.

Still, this episode contains a curious and quickly-dismissed line that requires some examination. At the roadhouse, Cooper declares that he will employ magic to solve the murder. This statement is met with some smirks and skepticism, but mostly by silence. Granted, the events in Twin Peaks have taken a definitive supernatural turn; and Cooper has always been an instinctual character, open to unusual, possibly paranormal crime-solving techniques. But this overt statement about magic seems peculiar, even for Cooper (though he admits this, himself). None of the other characters seemed shocked or dismayed. Yes, Truman has been growing more exasperated but he, like the others, is always willing to defer to proven tactics of Agent Cooper. Here, Cooper is asking all involved to suspend their forensic senses and make a leap into the fantastic. No one questions this request.

The scene is critical, for it is positioned as turning point in Cooper's journey. He has seemingly embraced the supernatural, accepting it as a reliable and useful method of getting to the truth. Cooper has already accepted that there is more to world than his five senses can show him, but he has always been a grounded character who realizes that human agency is most often to blame for tragedy. Here, Cooper is fully committed to the supernatural. This helps explain the redemptive tone he takes with a dying Leland, and it also informs the conversation in the final scene with Truman, Cooper, Albert and Major Briggs. These characters are all trying to make sense of a world far less stable than they believed it to be. If Laura's death was the first real challenge to their world-view, the possible existence of Bob (and the proven, heinous acts of Leland) shakes many of the characters to their core. (Truman is particularly affected—he can't even stand up during the conversation.)

But the series will now shy away from fully exploring these profound ideas. Albert will leave the narrative for a while, Truman will turn his attention toward Josie, and only Major Briggs and Hawk will hint at the possible deeper forces at work in and around Twin Peaks.

Additional Notes:

Leland's actions toward Donna are quite odd and it appears that he is considering killing her, too. He starts playing a record and begins to dance with her—not unlike the scene with Maddy in episode 14—but Truman arrives and asks for Leland's assistance before anything else can transpire. At this point Donna does not know that Leland is the killer, yet she is clearly shaken by Leland's actions. What was Leland/Bob's motive here? Apparently, he was willing to take another victim. Bob seems to be growing much stronger as Leland shows signs of a growing instability.

In this episode, Ben finally learns that Tojamura was Catherine all along. She gets him to sign over the mill and the Ghostwood development but doesn't promise anything in return.

The sheriff's station sprinkler system is set off by a couple of smokers inside the building. Tremayne lights up while talking to Lucy. At the holding cell, Albert listens to Cooper and also lights a cigarette. Apparently, neither character notices the "No Smoking" signs hanging everywhere in the building.

This episode marks the last appearance of Phillip Gerard/Mike, the One Armed Man in the series.

Notable Deleted Scenes

Act 1: Hank and Ernie talk at the Double R. Hank says he's "got a piece of something north of the border; little gambling, some female company. Full service kind of place. I want this operation to grow. I'll need your help. And a good-sized chunk of Vivian's do-re-me." Ernie isn't interested but Hank makes a not-so-veiled threat and Ernie is "chilled" by it. Meanwhile, Norma has been watching (but not hearing) this conversation. She tells Vivian she thinks the two men are up to something. Vivian dismisses Norma's suspicion: "The men you and I fall for are boys. The men we love spend their life in the dark. Our job is to keep them there."

Act 3: Donna arrives home and talks with her father. Under Donna's demands, Hayward admits that Maddy is, indeed, dead and was killed the same way Laura was. Donna says, "NO! I am sick and tired of all this pain. Sick in my heart. Everything good turns to bad. No matter what we say or do. No matter how hard we try. Someone has to stop it. Someone has to...." Hayward interrupts, "I love you, Donna." But she doesn't want to talk about love and runs off.

Act 4: When, Cooper, Truman, Albert, and Major Briggs meet in the woods, some critical (and ultimately deleted) lines of dialogue are spoken: Truman says of Leland, "He was insane. Schizophrenic. Gerard too." Cooper expresses doubt but Truman presses: "What's the alternative? Ghosts and goblins?" Albert suggests that perhaps Bob was an elemental spirit. Briggs quotes Shakespeare: "Gentlemen, there is more in heaven and earth than is dreamt of in our philosophy." Cooper readily agrees. Albert continues to ponder the nature of Bob: "People saw him. People saw Bob. Laura, Maddy, Sarah Palmer." Then he wonders how Cooper was also able to see him. Briggs answers for Cooper: "That question may require a bit more self-examination." These interesting lines of dialogue not only show how the characters are struggling to define the nature of Bob, but also how the writers were struggling to convey the complicated nature of the resolution to the murder storyline. Was Leland ultimately responsible for the death of Laura Palmer? Or was another force involved—one that frees Leland of culpability? The series and the film never firmly settle on a definitive answer. That, of course, is part of the story's enduring fascination.

Cast and Crew Comments

Mark Frost: I love that scene—that whole episode, in fact—where Leland died. I thought that was one of the best in the whole series.

Al Strobel: I certainly didn't know anything. And from conversations with other actors, some became quite upset that they didn't really have an idea of what they were supposed to be, or do, or think. One of David's favorite sayings was, "Loose lips sink ships." And he was dealing with a serial, not some kind of episodic piece. So if you got too far ahead of what was going on you'd give it all away and people wouldn't bother to tune in.

It became a procedure that I would be sent my sides which are, basically, my lines and those of the people I'm sharing the scene with. Usually it would be very short-term before we would do the actual filming. Then we'd go in and film that scene, usually with no rehearsal, sometimes with a very brief rehearsal if there was something complex that had to take place. But usually with no rehearsal. Then when we would finish filming and we were required to give in our sides—turn them back into the [Associate Director]. Then they'd shred them.

I think that for the most part a lot of people enjoyed working in that manner. I certainly did, but to do it that way you have to be on your toes and focus all the time, and just be right there and do it. A couple of people—and I'm not going to mention names—found that a difficult way to work. They wanted to know what their inner feelings were supposed to be. And they wanted to have it much more clearly defined as to where they were going.

Robert Engels: David didn't want to resolve it. Had we been allowed not to solve it, the show could have gone on forever, very successfully. I tend to agree with David on that. David loves *The Fugitive*, the series. The fun of writing *Twin Peaks* was [the show] was all about guilt. Every person felt bad Laura was dead, for one reason or another. And everything centered around that.

The pressure to solve it did come from ABC. And there was lots of pressure on us. I remember walking up the stairs, talking to David, and behind him I see that he is on the cover of *Time*! It was just sitting there. The pressure just sort of grew. My brother-in-law said, "I knew you guys had made it when there was a cartoon in *The New Yorker* about Laura Palmer."

Al Strobel: I never knew [what happened to my character on the series]. I never knew. I have my own speculations, but they're only that, my own speculations. I don't think the disappearance really had that much to do with Lynch/Frost productions. I think that had something to do with forces outside [the production company].

Carel Struycken: The beauty of *Twin Peaks* was this it came so totally out of left field. It was so completely unlike anything else that had ever been on TV. It had this wonderful subversiveness—it was just oozing with subversiveness. That's very much David Lynch.

The danger always is that you carry it a little too far. I think it would have been much more productive for the general psyche of the country if he were to have kept his subversive edge in the content of the show, as he did, and [then] if he would have been a little less subversive in the way the story was presented. If he had conformed more to the standard TV timing of things and kept the subversive edge to the content, then the show might have been even more successful than it already was.

Frank Silva: Most of the time Bob was never written in the scripts. It was something that David thought of at the last moment. Originally, when we did the pilot, he had shot me at the end of the bed and had also shot that scene with Grace Zabriskie on the sofa.

During the process of filming it, ABC kept saying, "David, David, you've got to have a killer in this. You've got to have an ending. You've got to have an ending." Because it just didn't have anything. It left people hanging. That's what made it so great, but ABC kept saying, "You've got to have a killer."

Mark Frost: [Laura's] father killed her. I think Leland was culpable. Ultimately, the human person has to take responsibility. And Bob may have just been a figment of his imagination.

SECOND SEASON SLUMP:

EPISODES 17-22

Twin Peaks took fewer chances with its narrative during the second half of the second season. In the wake of the Laura Palmer storyline, *Twin Peaks* introduced and developed new storylines, many of which were tepid and insubstantial. These were simple, short-term subplots that served as narrative "filler" while the next big plotline was building.

That plotline was the showdown between Agent Cooper and his former partner, Windom Earle—a story which took many episodes to truly get underway. The Earle story simmers in the background through four episodes (17-20), and not until episode 21 does the viewer actually get to see Windom Earle. *Twin Peaks* co-creator, Mark Frost has noted that both the Earle and Black Lodge stories were the next big plots he wanted to develop after the Laura Palmer story, but, he explained, "Laura was a very hard act to follow in terms of storytelling, and we probably should have come out of the gate a little quicker with the Windom Earle story."[1]

In the meantime, viewers had to suffer through *Twin Peaks'* lowest moments—the episodes which chronicled such stories as James Hurley's involvement with Evelyn Marsh, Andy and Dick's misadventures with Little Nicky; and Ben Horne's delusional return to the American Civil War. The strongest drama in these middle episodes concerns Cooper's suspension from the FBI and his confrontation with Jean Renault—a good story that could have used more screen time.

Episode 17 (Script number 2010; First televised December 8, 1990)

Guest Starring: James Booth (Ernie Niles), Jane Greer (Vivian Smythe), Clarence Williams III (Roger Hardy), Gavan O'Herlihy (Sergeant King), Tony Jay (Dougie Milford), Don Calfa (Vice Principal Greege), and Michael Parks (Jean Renault)

Co-Starring: John Boylan (Mayor Dwayne Milford), Lisa Cloud (P.E. Teacher), Tiffany Muxlow (Cheerleader), and Susan Sundholm (Samantha)

Written by Tricia Brock; Directed by Tina Rathborne; Edited by Toni Morgan

The events in this episode take place "Three Days Later" (as stated in the first scene) after the death of Leland in episode 16 (Saturday night/Sunday morning), making it Wednesday, March 15, 1989:

Act 1: Sarah refuses a sedative as she prepares for Leland's funeral. Cooper comforts her. He says that Leland fell victim to a "dark and heinous" thing long ago. Eileen, Sarah and Audrey reminisce about Laura. Donna talks with Ed about the missing James. Briggs invites Cooper to go fishing. Mayor Dwayne Milford and his brother, Dougie, argue. Ed and Truman break it up. Pete explains that Dougie and Dwayne have had a feud for years, but it has gotten worse since Dougie got engaged to a young woman.

Act 2: Ed and Dr. Jacoby convince the principal to admit Nadine to school. Cooper tells Audrey that he lost someone close to him once. She was a material witness that he (and his partner, Windom Earle) was supposed to protect. Catherine explains to Truman that she escaped from the fire and into the woods. Dick Tremayne says he has enlisted at the Happy Helping Hand program as a part-time big brother. Truman gives Cooper a fishing lure and a Bookhouse Boy patch. Cooper responds, "I am honored beyond my ability to express myself." Before Cooper departs, Special Agent Roger Hardy and Mountie King arrive to inform Cooper that he has been suspended.

Act 3: Hardy tells Cooper that Internal Affairs is suspicious of his conduct. Hardy and King suspect Cooper stole some drugs that King was using for a drug bust of Jean Renault. Hardy asks Cooper to surrender his gun and badge. Truman tells them they are wrong about Cooper. Nadine shows her amazing strength by throwing a student across a field. Leo begins to move.

Act 4: Vivian says the Double R is not a good restaurant and Norma tells her to get out of her life. Hank wants Ernie to steal money for Jean Renault. Renault introduces them to King. He has the drugs Cooper was supposed to have stolen and plans to plant drugs in Cooper's car to frame him. Truman is awoken by a badly beaten Josie. Cooper and

> Briggs roast marshmallows and talk about Bob. Briggs asks Cooper if he
> has ever heard of the White Lodge. An unseen force moves through the
> woods. A bright light flashes and a cloaked figure appears among the
> trees. Cooper rushes to Briggs as the light goes out.

Tina Rathborne delivers a well-directed episode with some clever angles
and careful framing. This kind of directorial attention won't be evident in
the series again until Diane Keaton directs episode 22.

This episode marks a major transition in the series as it bridges the
Laura Palmer story to the second half of the season. The opening act
masterfully assembles the entire cast at the Palmer home for the funeral's
reception, and while there is no major advancement of the plot, each
character gets a few lines to remind viewers where their various storylines
stand. The act almost serves as a pause in the series, a breather for everyone
(audience included) to get their bearings and prepare for a resumption in
the narrative.

There's a wonderful scene between Audrey and Cooper in act 2 as he
packs for his fly-fishing trip with Major Briggs. The chemistry between the
two characters is undeniable, and it's not surprising that the writers had
wanted to follow the Laura Palmer storyline with a Cooper/Audrey
romance. Here that door is essentially shut. But the scene is done well, with
Cooper bringing up the name of his former partner, Windom Earle (whom
Albert had reported missing from an asylum in episode 9). Cooper gives a
vague description of what happened, saying only that he was in love with a
woman and was unable to prevent an attempt on her life. Later, in episode
21, the missing pieces are revealed: the woman was Earle's wife, Caroline,
and it was Windom himself who made the attack.

With the Audrey/Cooper romance dead, the writers hint that there
might be something ahead for Audrey and Bobby but this story never goes
very far.

In the first scene, Cooper tries to partly absolve Leland of his horrible
crimes by saying that there are "things dark and heinous in this world," and
that Leland "fell victim to one of these long ago when he was innocent and
trusting. Leland did not do these things; not the Leland that you knew."
This roughly coincides with what Leland told Cooper before he died: "I was
just a little boy. I saw him in my dreams. He said he wanted to play. He
opened me, and I invited him in." Apparently Leland did not recognize the
evil with which he was aligning himself. It should be noted, however, that
when Bob is speaking through Leland, he says, "Leland's a babe in the
woods, with a large hole where his conscience used to be." This suggests
culpability on Leland's part—that either a moral failure allowed Bob to
possess him, or a moral failure allowed the possession to continue—
because if Leland truly had no free will about Bob's ongoing presence it
would make no sense to say he had no conscience.

Is Bob's interpretation reliable? Although he is the antagonist, the information he speaks is not proven wrong in the narrative. Indeed, Cooper also tells Sarah that before he died, Leland confronted the horror of what he had done to Laura and agonized over the pain he had caused his wife. Cooper also notes that he believes Laura forgave Leland. When all is said and done, Leland's responsibility for his crimes remains unclear. (In fact, Cooper's comments to Sarah contradict each other: He starts by saying that "Leland did not do these things" but ends by noting that he believes Laura forgave him. Both are intended to comfort Sarah but both can't be true. If Leland were completely innocent, he wouldn't require Laura's forgiveness. If she did, indeed, forgive him it must have been for some degree of culpability he had in the crime.)

Additional Notes:

There's a subtle visual joke at Leland's wake: despite the gloomy occasion the amount of food is copious, even Sarah's plate is piled high by Hank. Are all these grieving people *that* hungry? Meanwhile, the scene introduces Mayor Milford's brother Dougie, publisher of the local paper. The two brothers have been feuding for years and end up in a minor scuffle that Truman breaks up. (The mayor first appeared in the pilot episode.)

Catherine meets Truman in his office, and he asks where she's been the past "two weeks." Indeed, she was last seen on Thursday, March 2, when she found herself inside the burning Packard Mill with Shelly, and episode 17 takes place thirteen days later on March 15th.

Clarence Williams III was one of the three main stars of the 1970's action/crime series, *The Mod Squad*. Peggy Lipton was another of that show's main stars. Their presence together on *Twin Peaks* marked an on-screen reunion for the two actors.

The first draft for the script to episode 17 was completed on September 27, 1990. The script subsequently went through five revisions. The final revision was completed on October 22, 1990, almost a full month after the first.

Notable Deleted Scenes

Act 1: Cooper delivers some comforting and poetic lines to Sarah. He simply tells her that, "The experience we have of people doesn't leave when they do. If you close your eyes, you can see Laura blowing out the candle of her birthday cake, Leland mowing the yard, shaving at the sink. These moments are yours. Always." Cooper's original dialogue is more appropriate to the situation and more in keeping with his character. It's unfortunate that it was changed.

Act 2: At the Double R Diner, Vivian Niles and Norma Jennings are setting up the diner for the day. Vivian comments that Norma is suffering in her marriage. Norma does not want to talk about it. Hank Jennings and Ernie Niles enter the diner "decked out in hunting gear." Norma is surprised that Hank didn't tell her he was going hunting. Norma seems suspicious of Hank's familiarity with Ernie; it gives her a weird feeling. This scene served only to remind viewers of the relationships between these four characters and to create more dramatic tension between Hank and Norma. Norma's behavior indicates that she might uncover Hank's true connection to Ernie, but this plot was never pursued in the televised episodes.

At the high school, Big Ed and Dr. Jacoby meet with vice-principal Greege in order to enroll Nadine in high school. Much of their dialogue was cut from the televised version. Greege can't believe they want to enroll a thirty-five year old woman into the senior class. Jacoby explains that it is strictly for "medical reasons." Greege notes that Nadine never finished high school, but dropped out to marry Ed. Greege, however, is still unconvinced. Jacoby explains what is happening to Nadine: "A classic case of clinical regression. What's important here is that Nadine be allowed to maintain her own reality. Being eighteen is all she can manage. And it could be a lot worse. Be glad she's not napping in a crib." Greege agrees to admit Nadine, provided that she "performs like a regular student." He advises Ed to make sure Nadine does her homework. Ed nods and "grimaces." In addition to keeping Dr. Jacoby more prominent in the narrative, this scene clearly and satisfactorily established why Nadine was back in school. Because the Nadine subplot was minor and comical, however, the producers may have wished to devote less time to the story, and cut the scene.

Act 3: At the sheriff's station, Cooper says he believes Leland killed Jacques Renault because "he wanted to prevent Renault from ever testifying against him" for Laura's murder. This is a strange line, and indicates that Cooper at least believes Jacques actually saw Leland abduct Laura from Jacques' cabin. No evidence in the series has ever supported this theory. Leland's motive for killing Jacques was one of grief, believing that Jacques was actually Laura's killer. Luckily, this odd and confusing line was excised from the televised version.

Act 4: At the Double R Diner, Truman watches as Cooper prepares his next chess move against Windom Earle. Their talk turns to Cooper's legal troubles. Cooper explains that he is preparing his defense. He has been studying the works of William O. Douglas, and says, that "somewhere between William O. Douglas and the Dalai Lama lies the perfect man." This brief mention of the Dalai Lama recalls the characterization of Cooper from the first season, and is a reminder of what drives and inspires Cooper. Keeping the line—and the scene—would have helped cement familiar aspects of the Cooper character, who seems otherwise poorly defined in this and subsequent episodes.

Act 4 ends at Briggs's and Cooper's campsite. The script contains some extensive dialogue between Cooper and Briggs that was cut from the televised version. Cooper and Briggs are discussing love and fear. Briggs explains that "fear is the absence of love." This crucial line will influence many of Cooper's actions over the next few episodes. In fact, in the next episode, Cooper tells Agent Hardy that he is "seeing beyond fear" and "looking at the world with love." These lines take on more meaning after placed in context with Cooper's conversation with Briggs, whose observation about fear and love also reveals much about the philosophy and intellect of the character. Briggs will reiterate his philosophy to Windom Earle in episode 27 when he explains that his greatest fear is "the possibility that love is not enough."

Cooper and Briggs further discuss the topic of love and fear. Cooper comes to the understanding that "when I let fear into my life I am not loving myself." He then realizes that Leland Palmer didn't love himself. Cooper resolves to face his demons "without fear." Again, these lines foreshadow Hawk's description of the Black Lodge and the need for perfect courage. In effect, much of the cut dialogue between Cooper and Briggs establishes the Black Lodge plot that is to come. This scene may have been the best part of the episode, especially given the acting talents of Don Davis and Kyle MacLachlan. Although part of the scene survived to the televised version (Briggs's mention of the White Lodge and his eventual disappearance), the full, uncut, scene is more powerful than what aired. What's more, the complete scene essentially defines the second half of the second season. Although many mistakes can be attributed to a weak second half of *Twin Peaks*' second season, the gutting of this scene is one of the worst.

Cast and Crew Comments

Grace Zabriskie: I remember saying to people, "After all, it's not about who killed Laura Palmer. The series is about infinitely more than that." I later felt that that was true enough, but a dramatic convention was flouted. When the killer was named, something important and bad happened. I have no way to know if it could have been possible to name the killer and not lose the dramatic tension of the series. In fact, it did not happen that way.

I suspected there was no true closure to [my character]. Because it was not like having a fight and then you make up. It's a loss that doesn't stop. Closure is not something I would have been entirely comfortable with.

There was a period when it was looking as if they were interested in possibilities for Sarah. I suppose once Laura's killer was known I rather lost hope for everything—for the series.

James Marshall: Don Davis has always been one of my favorite actors and Briggs was a lot like James. He had this whole military thing on the surface yet he was this very thoughtful, sensitive, gentle person! That's what a great leader is; that's what a great father is. That, to me, is what honest strength is.

Episode 18 (Script number 2011; First televised December 15, 1990)

Guest Starring: Clarence Williams III (Roger Hardy), James Booth (Ernie Niles), David Duchovny (Dennis/Denise Bryson), Tony Jay (Dougie Milford), Robyn Lively (Lana Budding), Annette McCarthy (Evelyn Marsh), Royce D. Applegate (Father Clarence), Ron Taylor (Coach Wingate), and Dan O'Herlihy (Andrew Packard)

Co-Starring: John Boylan (Mayor Dwayne Milford), Jill Engels (Trudy), and Joshua Harris (Nicky)

Written by Barry Pullman; Directed by Duwayne Dunham; Edited by Jonathan P. Shaw

Thursday, March 16, 1989:

Act 1: James rides his cycle away from Twin Peaks. Betty Briggs discusses the disappearance of Major Briggs with Cooper and Truman. Gordon Cole calls to tell Cooper that the DEA is sending Dennis Bryson to investigate the missing drugs. Cooper says Bryson is a good man. Cooper says he is trying to see beyond fear. Hardy says he may recommend a full psychological work-up.

Act 2: Nadine wants to start seeing Mike. James meets Evelyn Marsh. She flirts with him and asks him if he can repair her husband's Jaguar. Dick Tremayne arrives at the sheriff's station with Little Nicky, his charge from Happy Helping Hands. Hawk knows of the White and Black Lodges: "It is said if you confront the Black Lodge with imperfect courage, it will utterly annihilate your soul." Agent "Denise" Bryson arrives dressed as a woman.

Act 3: Josie tells Truman that she used to work for a man named Thomas Eckhardt in Hong Kong. She says she thinks Eckhardt was responsible for Andrew's death. Evelyn offers to let James stay at the house while he works on the car. Ben Horne watches old home movies of the groundbreaking ceremony for the Great Northern. Hank tells Ben he is no longer owner of One Eyed Jacks. Ben realizes that Jean Renault is behind it. Cooper receives a note (a chess move: P to Q4) and taped message from Windom Earle: "The King must die."

Act 4: Mayor Milford interrupts Dougie's marriage and is escorted out. Bryson believes Cooper is being framed and offers to help. Josie tells Catherine that they are both in danger from Eckhardt. She begs for Catherine's mercy. Catherine says that Josie will work as her maid. Josie leaves and Andrew Packard enters. He says, "Everything is going exactly as we planned."

The second season begins to fall apart with this episode, specifically in act 2 at Wallies. The James/Evelyn scene doesn't work: flat performances, clichéd dialogue, inappropriate music and lighting. The scene is trying to be a *film noir* allusion, complete with *femme fatale* and conveniently available naïve male. Such an *homage* could work but the mood and the atmosphere are all wrong. It's as if these few minutes were written and shot for another show and accidentally got cut into an episode of *Twin Peaks*.

That scene is immediately followed by the introduction of Little Nicky, and the freefall continues (there is too much humor throughout the episode, though perhaps the producers thought it important to lighten the show following the dark intensity of the Laura/Maddy/Leland story). Fortunately, the scene following Little Nicky is one of the more interesting (and oft-referenced) scenes of the second season, and one that sets up the storyline that will dominate the final third of the season: Deputy Hawk's description of the White Lodge. Unlike the James/Evelyn scene, this one succeeds because of well-written dialogue, a perfect musical score, and Michael Horse's earnest performance. Hawk warns Cooper about confronting his shadow-self with imperfect courage, which recalls Cooper's earlier comment to Hardy about seeing the world without being hindered by fear. The scene ends on an amusing, lighthearted note as Agent Bryson arrives, resulting in a startled reaction from Hawk.

Whatever the aforementioned drawbacks of this episode, Richard Beymer shines in an extraordinary scene with Chris Mulkey. Reeling both from Catherine's success at manipulating him to relinquish Ghostwood and the Packard Mill, and having been arrested for the murder of Laura Palmer, Ben watches old home movies of the groundbreaking ceremony of the Great Northern Hotel. In an early reference to what would popularly become known as *feng shui*, he wonders if "the proper spatial relationship between all the objects in a given space . . . could create a resonance the benefits of which to the individual dwelling in that space could be extensive and far-reaching." Hank refuses to help Ben move a desk and instead informs him that Jean Renault has succeeded in procuring a "friendly take-over" of One Eyed Jack's. Ben becomes enraged, and Beymer successfully maneuvers his character through emotional twists and turns. It's an incredible piece of acting that makes this one of the stand-out scenes in the episode.

Josie returns seeking Catherine's protection from Thomas Eckhardt, for whom Josie worked in Japan. The surprise ending has Catherine's brother, Andrew, enter after Josie has left the room. Unbeknownst to her, he is not only still alive, but has faked his death and is in league with Catherine.

But what plan is Andrew referring to at the end of the episode? The faking of his death? The faking of Catherine's? In episode 21 Catherine explains to Pete that Andrew helped her wrest control of the mill and

Ghostwood from Ben, but the implication here, in episode 18, is that Andrew and Catherine coordinated Josie's return and her current position as maid. How could they have manipulated—or foreseen—such an unusual result? The details of this convoluted (and rather flat) subplot are never adequately explained in the series.

The chess game between Windom Earle and Cooper continues. Earle's opening move in episode 13 was P-K4 (e4). Sometime between episodes 14 and 17, Cooper responded with P-K4 (e5), which he printed in the personal columns of various national newspapers. Earle anticipates the move perfectly and responds to it a day before the move sees print with P-Q4 (d4). This continuing aggressiveness on the part of Earle clearly shakes Cooper; he confesses to Diane his fear that Earle is "toying with him."

According to experts, Earle's strategy seems sound and well-defined. Perhaps Earle is aware he's developing a Center Game strategy. In his message to Cooper, he claims his response is leading them both toward a "classical confrontation." So, either the writers of *Twin Peaks* were deliberately basing the game on a Center Game strategy, or (more likely) they were simply using these specific moves to hastily put a black pawn into potential danger.

Additional Notes:

Mark Frost, in an interview with *The Independent* (August 22, 1992) explained that Dion Fortune's, *Psychic Self-Defense*, was, "exactly where I got the Black Lodge from. The whole mythological side of *Twin Peaks* was really down to me, and I've always known about the Theosophical writers and that whole group around the Order of the Golden Dawn in the late nineteenth and early twentieth century—William Butler Yeats, Madame Blavatsky, and a woman called Alice Bailey, a very interesting writer."

David Lynch makes an "appearance" (so to speak) in this episode when Gordon Cole calls Cooper from Bend, Oregon, to give his support and to tell Cooper that the DEA is sending Dennis Bryson to investigate. Surprisingly, Lynch's dialogue remains essentially as scripted, with one addition at the end that may have been Lynch's idea: "Couple words of advice: Let a smile be your umbrella."

David Duchovny, who of course would later find fame playing FBI agent Fox Mulder on *The X-Files*, makes his first appearance here as DEA Agent Bryson.

This episode also features the first appearances of Andrew Packard, Evelyn Marsh and Little Nicky.

The first draft of episode 18 was completed on October 11, 1990. The script was subsequently revised October 18, & 23, 1990.

John Thorne

Notable Deleted Scenes

Act 2: In Truman's office, Cooper, Truman and Hawk discuss Major Briggs and the White and Black Lodges. Some crucial and telling lines of dialogue were cut from this scene in the televised version. The scene opens with Cooper discussing his reasons for joining the FBI and the liberating feelings he has after being suspended: "Nine years ago I joined the bureau because I felt it was the strongest statement I could make about the man I wanted to become and the world I wanted to live in. And now, suddenly, all that's brushed aside. I have absolutely no responsibilities. Nothing to do. And it feels . . . fantastic." Cooper's statement indicates that he is more than content with being away from the FBI. It surprises him. He acts as if he is reconsidering his purpose in life.

A few lines later, Cooper recounts his conversation with Briggs: "Major Briggs planted a seed in my mind. And it's been germinating. The idea that by focusing on our fears and desires about something, we give them tremendous power. Consider this Harry: perhaps by our best intentioned resistance of evil, we somehow unknowingly join hands with it. Perpetuate it." Truman is confused by Cooper's new philosophy, but Cooper is coming to a profound new way of looking at the world: "And now, by being suspended, I'm suddenly empowered to let go of my preoccupation with wrongdoing. I feel like I've been exiled back to the natural rhythms of life." Truman then assures Cooper that he will always have a job in Twin Peaks, if he decides to stay. And that's exactly what Cooper's deciding to do in these excised lines of dialogue. The Cooper character is carefully being positioned to become a lawman in Twin Peaks, to leave the FBI for good. This is even more evident in dialogue from act 4 that was also cut.

At the time these scripts were written, the *Twin Peaks* narrative was heading in a specific direction: Cooper was to leave the FBI, and settle down in Twin Peaks. If the series was to continue with its main character, Cooper had to remain in the town. But to do so he had to leave the FBI and become a sheriff's deputy. The narrative was unwaveringly headed in this direction. Somewhere between writing and filming, however, the scenario was put on hold. The producers probably wanted to leave their options open, to allow Cooper to return to the FBI if that proved to be a stronger narrative scenario (which it did). So, in the televised versions of episode 18 (and those following), we have indications that Cooper may be staying in Twin Peaks (most notably his attempt to find a home) but Cooper has not convinced himself that he wants to leave the FBI. Still, this mildly schizophrenic handling of the character contributed to the show's already obvious slump. Cooper was no longer the dependable lawman with a definitive goal. This, in a small way, reflected the meandering nature of the series as a whole.

Act 4: In his room, Cooper recites a long message to Diane. This entire scene was cut from the televised version. Most of Cooper's message is redundant dialogue designed to remind viewers of various plotlines. Cooper observes that the Milford wedding is taking place and that he is not enjoying the revelry. Cooper then wonders about where Major Briggs has gone and the significance of the White and Black Lodges: "Has the Major, clearly a man of no small spiritual advancement, perhaps been attempting to make contact with some element of these places in his top secret work?" Cooper provides a revealing and succinct description of the Major: "Briggs is a man of clear eye and deep thought; he sees right through the illusory texture of this world and fluently reads beneath it. You might meet a handful like him in a lifetime." Briggs was obviously being positioned as a major player in the upcoming Lodge storyline, but the excision of these lines diminishes his importance. Briggs probably knew more about what was happening in the town than anyone else (save, maybe, the Log Lady). Recall that he appeared to Cooper, Truman and Albert just after Leland died. His presence there indicates that he was aware, to some extent, of the existence of Bob.

But sometime after Cooper's descriptive lines were scripted, Briggs's role in the story was subtly altered from active participant to passive bystander. Briggs didn't do things (i.e., make contact with the Lodge) but had things done to him (i.e., be taken captive by the Lodge). There is some indication that Briggs would have become a more active player in the third season had there been one. But for the duration of the remaining episodes, Briggs was relegated to supporting player.

Cooper suspects that Major Briggs could be in terrible danger: "If what Hawk related to me about the Black Lodge is true, even a man of Briggs's considerable fortitude would be tested to his ultimate limits." Again, the removal of this line indicates that Briggs's active role against the Black Lodge (or with the White) was diminished.

Cooper turns his attention to Windom Earle which causes him to consider his own place in the world: "Diane, as a human being learns and matures, one's experiences grow proportionately more rich and mysterious. Perhaps the questions I now seek answers to lie beyond the old parameters. Beyond my life at the bureau." This is the clearest indication so far that Cooper is considering leaving the FBI, despite the outcome of his investigation. These lines mesh perfectly with those that were cut from earlier in the episode. Cooper would supposedly continue his spiritual journey, but as a civilian living in Twin Peaks.

Cast and Crew Comments

Mark Frost: [Dion Fortune's, *Psychic Self Defense*] and also some of the work of Alice Bailey influenced me as a young person and it became then the basis for my thinking about the duality of good and evil in the world. Is evil, in fact, made manifest anywhere in the world? And the Black Lodge was all about the idea that there was, in fact, a true manifestation of evil that needs to be actively and physically combatted. We never actually got a chance to [tell] all of it.

Charlotte Stewart: They were always receptive to any suggestions we had. There was a time when Cooper and Truman are talking to Betty about the disappearance of Major Briggs. It was written really odd. I just didn't think it was right. I made some suggestions and, of course, you had to clear everything with the writers. People came downstairs and we had to talk about it. But we all agreed on it. It didn't fit; it wasn't right. It was really nice that they were always open to suggestions.

Miguel Ferrer: *Twin Peaks* was the only time [for me], in a movie or a television show, that if you wanted to do something like move a comma—if you wanted to change anything—there were high-level phone calls made. They really worked on those scripts, and they didn't want you to change a word. And we all were pretty much held to that.

Don Davis: One thing that was not brought out during the filming period, but that had been told to me, was that Briggs was actually the best pilot the Air Force had. I was the kind of guy who would have been the test pilot for astronauts and things like that. But I had this spiritual side and that's why I had been shunted off into this job—which was still a critical job for the Air Force—to keep track of these supposed signals from beyond. In some way this business of me being such a great pilot would prove important. I don't know what that meant. Nothing ever happened, and the series got canceled. So there's an awful lot that I never really knew. `

James Marshall: Even if I didn't see the corny aspects of [James]—the way other people saw it—I still was able to close the show up, and get into and honor the character without laughing at him. Because there was such a truth in that. As long as you are not laughing at your character you can get into it.

I think what happened to characters like mine and the sheriff's [was that they] became a little bit more one-note. I thought it would have been cooler if the show had had more balance.

Richard Beymer: I remember the scene [watching the old movies] was the first time I ever felt like an actor. I have heard actors talk, all my life, about the part taking over, and really getting into it. I've always thought, "Yeah, yeah—to a certain degree." But I'd never had that total giving over to it. For some reason or other, that scene did it. I was having fun doing that.

It was supposed to end when I say, "Ben, you're through," and I walk out of the scene. The director just kept the film going, and I started saying, "You're out, Ben" and laughing at it all. Then I went back to the desk, sat on the desk with my legs crossed and played shadow games. All of that was just [improvisation]; no one had said, "Cut," yet, so I kept going.

There was just something about that scene where I felt totally comfortable. As an actor, and in my own mind, I didn't have any anticipation about what was going to happen the next second. Usually, in the back of my head there's a little voice that is the actor looking at the next mark to hit, where I'm supposed to go—all of that stuff which usually gets in the way of spontaneity. I just found myself taking time and letting it go. For me, that was the high point of the shooting.

Episode 19 (Script number 2012; First televised January 12, 1991)

Guest Starring: James Booth (Ernie Niles), David Duchovny (Dennis/Denise Bryson), Robyn Lively (Lana Budding), Tony Burton (Col. Reilly), Tony Jay (Dougie Milford), Annette McCarthy (Evelyn Marsh), Nicholas Love (Malcolm), and Ron Taylor (Coach Wingate)

Co-Starring: John Apicella (Jeffrey Marsh), John Boylan (Mayor Milford), Joshua Harris (Nicky), Geraldine Keams (Irene Littlehorse), Molly Shannon (Judy Swain), and John Epstein (Utility Stunt)

Written by Harley Peyton and Robert Engels; Directed by Caleb Deschanel; Edited by Paul Trejo

Friday, March 17, 1989:

Act 1: Bobby realizes that Ben is going crazy. Ben tells Bobby to follow Hank and take pictures. As Bobby leaves, Lana Milford races past him, screaming. Cooper meets with a real-estate agent about a place called Dead Dog Farm. Truman, Andy and Doc Hayward examine a dead Dougie Milford, who died in his wedding bed. Mayor Milford arrives and is saddened by his brother's death. Nadine and Mike wrestle. She floors him—literally—then asks him out.

Act 2: James meets Malcolm Sloane, Evelyn's brother. He tells James that Jeffrey beats Evelyn. Cooper discovers that drug dealers were recently at Dead Dog Farm. Air force Colonel Reilly is investigating the disappearance of Briggs. The Colonel admits that deep space monitors intercepted messages emanating from the woods surrounding Twin Peaks. He says Briggs is the best pilot he has ever known and that "his disappearance has implications that go so far beyond national security." James asks Evelyn if she is afraid of her husband.

Act 3: Audrey spies on Bobby and Ben as they meet. Ben is dressed as a Confederate soldier and he studies a model of Gettysburg. Bobby delivers pictures of Hank. Pete thinks Catherine is being too hard on Josie. Audrey shows Cooper photos of Hank and Ernie with Jean Renault and King at Dead Dog Farm. Cooper shows Bryson the pictures and tells him about the cocaine. Hank watches Ed and Norma talk.

Act 4: Dick wants to find out what happened to Nicky's parents. The Mayor thinks Lana killed his brother with sex. Denise shows Ernie the photos and tells him he needs to cooperate. James hears Marsh hitting Evelyn. Malcolm wants revenge. Bobby tells his mother about his father's dream. Major Briggs suddenly appears wearing an old aviator's outfit. Betty asks if everything is alright and he replies, "No dear, not exactly."

The Civil War storyline begins as Ben makes his first appearance in his Confederate jacket while he looks over a model of The Battle of Gettysburg, Day One. Echoing his fascination with home movies in the previous episode, Ben is consumed with past events, hoping to understand how they affect current situations. Despite the South's apparent advantage, it still lost the Civil War, just as Ben's apparent control over events in Twin Peaks turned out to be less solid than he had thought, resulting in Catherine's ability to wrest control of the mill and Ghostwood from him.

Undoubtedly, the Civil War plotline was inspired by the hit PBS documentary, *The Civil War*, by Ken Burns (see the comments for episode 21). This series aired on PBS in September of 1990 and the first draft of the script for episode 20 was completed on October 8, 1990.

Meanwhile, in the ongoing chess game between Cooper and Earle, Cooper's first opportunity to match Earle's aggressiveness is instead a defensive, more passive reply: N-QB3 (Nc6). Cooper chooses to defend his pawn with his knight, believing that Earle will not capture the pawn because of the Knight's threat. It appears that Cooper has a strong defensive strategy, but, as we see later, this strategy gives way to even more passive moves. Cooper's defensive strategy and passive replies foreshadow the "imperfect courage" he displays in the Black Lodge. (Cooper eventually capitulates to Earl's demand for his soul in exchange for Annie's life.) Cooper's refusal to play offensively at this point hints at the fear he will show later. (This is Cooper's last move before he seeks the help of Pete Martell. This move and the shift to Pete's strategy mark a noticeable turning point in the game.)

There is a greater reliance on slapstick comedy in this episode: Bobby drops Ben's expensive camera as Lana runs by; Hawk leans against a door that is opened by Andy, causing the deputy to lose his balance; Nadine manhandles Mike at wrestling practice; Tremayne attempts to change a tire (while he wears matching attire with Little Nicky); Andy's "thought balloon" of a devilish Nicky.

Malcolm attempts to create tension between James and Mr. Marsh by claiming Marsh beats Evelyn. It continues the *noir* storyline that probably sounded like a good idea in the story conference (*noir* and *Twin Peaks* seem like a perfect match) but exhibits the same problems as in the previous episode with a flatly-lit scene and uninspired performances (this time from Nicholas Love).

All in all, the episode is a near-total disaster, redeemed only by a fine concluding scene with Bobby, Betty, and Major Briggs, and individual performances by Richard Beymer, David Duchovny, and John Boylan. Virtually every scene has major problems, often descending into a sitcom mentality. This seems barely like a *Twin Peaks* episode at all: the characters appear under the correct names, but everything else has been changed. It is not the worst episode in the run (see episode 21), but it is close.

Additional Notes:

Molly Shannon, who would later come to fame as a regular on *Saturday Night Live*, appears as Judy Swain from the Happy Helping Hands Adoption Agency; she is Little Nicky's case manager.

Twin Peaks was always notable for its unique and stunning imagery, but the shot of Andy with the superimposed "Devil Nicky" is awful and marks a visual low for the series. It is, in fact, the worst single moment of the entire run.

This episode features the first appearances of Malcolm, Jeffrey Marsh, Judy Swain, Lana Budding and Colonel Reilly.

The first draft of episode 19 was completed on October 8, 1990. It subsequently went through four revisions and was completed on November 6, 1990.

Notable Deleted Scenes

Act 1: There is a fascinating tidbit regarding Major Briggs and his relationship to the top secret government project in Twin Peaks that did not make it to the televised version. Colonel Reilly explains that Briggs has "been walking point on this operation for three years, carrying a full pack." Briggs, therefore, has been involved with the project for some time, meaning he may know far more than the televised versions of *Twin Peaks* episodes ever show.

Act 4: Cooper and Denise hatch their plan with Ernie. The televised scene ends on a humorous note as a nervous Ernie realizes that Denise is a man. In the scripted version, however, Denise acknowledges the frame-up of Cooper. He says, "They almost had you, Coop." To which Cooper smiles and replies, "Almost. Now it's our turn." This ending builds more suspense for the next episode and shows Cooper's determination to win back his good name. Deleting the dialogue did nothing to alter the story but the scripted ending was more dramatic than the one that aired.

Cast and Crew Comments

John Boylan (*Mayor Milford*): I assumed that they had some reason in mind to embellish [my] role. It didn't matter to me, I was very busy in characterization and trying to do the best possible job that I could do for those scenes. I was very happy with it. It was a pleasure to me because I had very little chance to develop any kind of a character, but then when it kept recurring it gave me an opportunity, and I became a little benevolent and a little more understanding of things. It was a good role. I liked it.

I was rather pleased. An old actor [Tony Jay] who I knew, was cast as my brother. And I was elated, I thought we'd have a series of times together and meetings [but] the following episode he was bumped off and he was deader than a doornail. I had a scene with him on the deathbed.

Don Davis: [My character] had been taken to the Lodge and had had further information revealed to him that was then blocked from consciousness. It would enable me to provide spiritual guidance to Cooper. They said that I had come back wearing clothing from my journey. That, to me, meant that I had traveled in time.

We rented [the aviator outfit] from a film museum. It had been worn by Gary Cooper. I was warned that it was much more valuable than I was. It was four sizes too small, so I took great care not to breathe deeply. [*laughs*]

I never thought that much about it because, quite frankly, I'm simply a character actor. There are a thousand guys that can do any role I do just as well, if not better. For a character to get as hot as I was getting during the second year—I was just so thankful.

Charlotte Stewart: One of the [scenes] that I enjoyed is after Major Briggs has disappeared and Bobby comes in to console Betty. I said to the director, "As odd as this family is, Betty and Garland are very much in love and this is a real tragedy. She is really scared and really missing him." It is the first time you see Bobby understand this and try to help his mom. He becomes sympathetic. It is the only time—every other scene he's in, he is surly and a little brat. He came in and consoled. I really thought it would make it more interesting.

Kimmy Robertson: I felt they [the producers and writers] were less interested in Lucy and Andy. They were writing comedy. I hardly ever do sitcoms because I'm really not that funny. And that's what it became—an odd, "sit-comy" thing. I wasn't even allowed to use words that I knew Lucy would use. They would say, "No, you can't say this, you have to say that." It was awful! We had to just give up. Harry [Goaz] and I would talk on our car phones on the way to work about how we didn't know what to do.

Harley Peyton: We had this big problem—when we revealed who killed Laura Palmer, the show would be over! We needed to figure out something that would take the place of that. Mark and I figured the best thing would be to have Cooper become passionately involved with Audrey. To have a big affair. That was what all our mail was about, and that's where it all was headed. It seemed like a great thing to do next, to have that love affair carry the show for about six episodes. We had planned it, but unfortunately Kyle refused to do it. So we ended up with no second season! All we had were back stories. Every story that you saw for those five episodes was meant to be a secondary and really unimportant story. Suddenly, that was all we had. And we had nothing to replace it.

It was just a mess. And once Kyle was allowed to do that, all the actors felt that they should determine their storylines, too. Who can blame them? But that was less of a problem. As I said, everyone was great. Michael Ontkean was tremendous. All these guys were great because they loved it. It really was a fun job. You'd go to this place every day and you'd do the work and everyone got along pretty well. So that part of it was wonderful.

Richard Beymer: One storyline was stopped: Cooper with Audrey. I think, as the grapevine goes, that Kyle didn't want to do it. That was the obvious fun trip to take. Why be so conservative?

It was something about, "she's too young" and all this sort of stuff. I mean, *come on*. It would have been great if she was twelve! That's the fun of it, to take these extreme rides. Why he got so puritanical about that, I don't know. Why would someone?

And it had been such a set-up. You knew it had to happen. You were waiting for that. They were the two people you had to see together. I think that's where David wanted to go.

Episode 20 (Script number 2013; First televised January 19, 1991)

Guest Starring: James Booth (Ernie Niles), David Duchovny (Dennis/Denise Bryson), Gavan O'Herlihy (Sergeant King), Annette McCarthy (Evelyn Marsh), Nicholas Love (Malcolm), and Michael Parks (Jean Renault)

Co-Starring: J. Marvin Campbell (M.P. #1), Will Seltzer (Mr. Brunston), Craig MacLachlan (The Dead Man), and John Epstein (Utility Stunts)

Written by Harley Peyton; Directed by Todd Holland; Edited by Toni Morgan

Saturday, March 18, 1989:

> Act 1: Major Briggs says he remembers stepping from flames, a vague shape in the dark, then nothing. Doc Hayward says Briggs has three triangular scars on the base of is neck. Briggs reveals he is part of a project searching for the White Lodge. An army officer escorts Briggs away. Shelly is mad at Bobby. She slaps him and he walks out. Evelyn says she needs James to help. Nadine flirts with Mike at the Double R.

> Act 2: Truman confronts Josie. Norma tells Ed she wants to be with him. Truman deputizes Cooper so he can help with the sting operation. Andy and Dick break in to the Happy Helping Hands Agency and read Little Nicky's file. Donna offers to take money to James. As Norma leaves, Hank punches Ed. Nadine arrives and pummels Hank, knocking him out.

> Act 3: Ben lectures Bobby about the battle of Gettysburg. Bobby and Audrey plan a way to help Ben. Evelyn asks James not to leave. Ernie and Denise conduct the sting at Dead Dog Farm. Ernie's wire starts to smoke and Renault and King realize they are being set up. They pull guns on Ernie and Dennis and demand that Cooper let them go. Cooper trades himself for the hostages.

> Act 4: Evelyn meets with Malcolm. Cooper urges Renault to surrender. Renault blames Cooper for the death of Jacques and Bernard. He thinks Cooper brought a nightmare with him to Twin Peaks. Denise, dressed as a waitress, approaches with food. Cooper grabs a gun from Denise's leg and shoots and kills Renault. Shelly discovers Leo's empty wheelchair. He is standing and staring at her, menacingly. Cooper finds a dead body in the conference room, pointing at a chess game. He realizes this is Windom Earle's next move.

The opening scene sets the stage for a better episode than the previous, with a series of mysterious visions by Major Briggs. (Here he first mentions Project Blue Book, in which it will later be revealed Windom Earle played a part.) Unfortunately, the mysterious mood is broken when Dick Tremayne shows up dressed in a trench coat and ready for an investigation into Nicky's past. On the whole, however, while many of the misguided plotlines from the previous episode continue, episode 20 is an improvement: The writing is sharper, the performances stronger, and the reliance on slapstick comedy reduced. Even silly scenes are presented with an ominous tone, such as when Audrey sees the young woman fleeing Ben's office (interestingly, an unscripted scene) in act 2, or Nadine's fight with Hank.

After their showdown with Jean Renault at Dead Dog Farm, Cooper and Truman return to the sheriff's station to find the power out, and a dead vagrant at Truman's desk pointing at a chess board. Windom Earle has struck and taken Cooper's pawn with the move PxP (de). Cooper now realizes the deadly nature of the game and acknowledges Earle's "genius." Despite this grim conclusion, however, it will take him another two days, and another taped threat from Earle, before he enlists Pete's help and replies with another move.

Problems begin to creep into the continuity of the game at this point, however. The board in Truman's office bears virtually no relation to the chess match in progress. In fact, Cooper would not be able to determine Earle's move based on this board because of the number of pieces in different positions. The most egregious error is that the white king's pawn has somehow moved back to its original position, which, of course, is impermissible in chess. (Pawns may only move forward.)

In the following episode, a dazed Leo enters Earle's cabin. A chess board sits on the table, and Cooper has not yet responded to Earle's capture of the pawn. But this board matches neither the correct game nor the one in Truman's office.

Additional Notes:

This episode could easily be subtitled, "The Kissing Episode": Evelyn kisses James (twice), Nadine kisses Mike, Truman kisses Josie, Catherine kisses Ben, Evelyn kisses Malcolm. All this kissing wouldn't be so bad if it wasn't so obviously being used for dramatic effect. As a result, the series is starting to resemble the very nighttime soaps it was once parodying.

For the first time in many episodes, *Invitation to Love* makes a brief appearance in the background as Shelly attempts to feed Leo.

David Duchovny makes his first appearance as Dennis Bryson (rather than as Denise).

Windom's new victim, found in Truman's office, will be named in episode 22: Erik Powell, a transient. The dead vagrant was played by Craig MacLachlan, Kyle's brother (note the obvious resemblance).

The first draft for episode 20 was completed on October 18, 1990. It subsequently went through five revisions and was completed on November 16, 1990.

Notable Deleted Scenes

Act 4: Truman inexplicably tells Hawk to call in the Bookhouse Boys for the stand-off at Dead Dog Farm. The script makes no further mention of this scenario. Why would Truman want the Bookhouse Boys? Did he want to circumvent legitimate police forces? Did he believe the Bookhouse Boys could be more help than the state police? The script offers no clue. Perhaps Harley Peyton, who wrote the teleplay, originally envisioned a standoff between Renault and the local "militia" of Twin Peaks (i.e., the Bookhouse Boys). But such a scene would have diminished the seriousness of the hostage standoff. As televised, the showdown is more intense due to the numerous police vehicles shown surrounding Dead Dog Farm.

Cast and Crew Observations

Harley Peyton: The show was the easiest thing ever. It was great fun to do because it all took place in this one warehouse. All week long, we went out to this warehouse in the valley and it was like a *Twin Peaks* theme park. Every set was in this warehouse. Our writing offices were just above the sets. In seven days, we'd only shoot outside for maybe one day. We'd go to Lake Malibu and wrap pine bark around palm trees—to fake exteriors. In that sense, in terms of the production, it was a very easy shoot.

Robert Engels: We had that unfortunate excursion into *noir* where James goes off. That was a disaster! Part of it was [because] we had solved the [Laura Palmer] mystery and we could never live up to that again. But in the second season (of anything) you always have this reassessment from critics: "Maybe it isn't that good." Then out of nowhere people like Tony Hillerman—the mystery novelist—blast us! What the hell? Who asked you?! For a while we were going to have this character on *Twin Peaks* called "Hill-Man" and he was going to be the complete idiot wandering around town.

Episode 21 (Script number 2014; First televised February 2, 1991)

Guest Starring: Robyn Lively (Lana Budding), Annette McCarthy (Evelyn Marsh), David Warner (Thomas Eckhardt), and Dan O'Herlihy (Andrew Packard)

Co-Starring: Brenda Strong (Jones), John Apicella (Jeffrey Marsh), John Boylan (Mayor Dwayne Milford), Ron Blair (Great Northern receptionist Randy St. Croix), Craig MacLachlan (The Dead Man), Hannah Kozak (Utility Stunt), John Epstein (Utility Stunt)

Written by Scott Frost; Directed by Uli Edel; Edited by Jonathan P. Shaw

Sunday, March 19, 1989:

> Act 1: Cooper explains that Earle "has taken his first pawn in a very sick game." Audrey wants Bobby's help to cure Ben. Leo stalks Shelly in their darkened house. Leo grabs an axe and is about to hit her when Bobby interferes. Shelly stabs Leo in the leg. Leo flees the house into the woods.

> Act 2: Hawk reports that Hank is in the hospital and that Leo has run off into the woods. Jeffrey drives away in his Jaguar and crashes. Norma thinks Hank is going back to jail; she wants to get back together with Ed. James tells Evelyn that their relationship is wrong and he must leave. Cooper reveals some of his past—that he fell in love with Caroline Earle, Windom's wife. Cooper thinks Earle killed Caroline and feigned his madness. Donna meets Evelyn. James is in anguish over his current situation.

> Act 3: Jacoby explains Ben's mental state: "By reversing the South's defeat, he in turn will reverse his own emotional setbacks." Briggs believes he was taken to the White lodge and must now lay low. Mayor Milford brandishes a shotgun. Cooper suggests that Lana and the Mayor talk things over alone.

> Act 4: Milford and Lana resolve their fight. Catherine and Andrew tell Pete that Thomas Eckhardt is coming to Twin Peaks. Eckhardt and his assistant, Jones, arrive at the Great Northern. Truman wants Cooper to check Josie's story. Evelyn says she loves James as the police arrive. James realizes Evelyn killed Jeffrey and that he has been framed. James escapes with Donna. Leo finds Windom Earle waiting in a cabin.

Episode 21 is the weakest episode in the *Twin Peaks* series. It contains James Hurley's terrible and repetitive dialogue ("It's wrong!"), Dr. Jacoby and Ben Horne's rendition of "Dixie," Mayor Milford's tepid threats with a shotgun, and Andy and Dick's crying upon hearing of Little Nicky's history. These are the silliest and most embarrassing scenes in the series. (Only Andy's "thought balloon" of Little Nicky from episode 19 is worse.)

Watching it again is like visiting an old friend who isn't quite the same person you remember, even though he looks and sounds the same. Episode 21 marks the first—and only—time *Twin Peaks* became pedestrian television; and if the long, sometimes challenging Laura Palmer plot drove casual viewers away, this episode likely sent some longtime fans packing.

The Civil War story continues, and Dr. Jacoby explains to Jerry that if Ben's re-enactment allows a victory by the South, it will reverse Ben's own emotional setbacks. He believes there is a parallel between Ben's defeat by Catherine and the South's defeat by the Union. A victory in the re-enactment will somehow ripple through his psyche and allow him to break out of his psychosis.

The Civil War storyline has (rightly) received harsh criticism, and the reasons are obvious. Why, of all historical events, would Ben choose the Civil War, especially since he has shown no interest in it so far? The real reason is because Ken Burns's *The Civil War* documentary series was airing on PBS just before these scripts were written. The documentary was a huge hit and captured the imagination of much of the country. The writers of *Twin Peaks* were probably caught up in the excitement and wanted to find some way to incorporate that enthusiasm into *Twin Peaks*.

It's not an altogether ridiculous idea: a "civil war" being, in essence, a battle between opposing sides of a single entity. It's perfect thematic material for *Twin Peaks* (given the show's already existing themes of duality). Likewise, the idea of Ben's re-creating history to reverse his current misfortune is solid. The endeavor went wrong because the story got more ridiculous and exaggerated as it progressed. It turned into farce, going as far as having Ben's family and employees dressed in full Civil War costumes (where did they get those, anyway?). The more interesting psychological possibilities and parallels were lost in the silliness. To his credit, Beymer gives it his all, but it's not enough to rescue things when, for instance, everyone starts singing "Dixie."

Additional Notes:

The scene in act 1 with Shelly, Leo, and Bobby is well-directed and quite suspenseful. It conveys a *Twin Peaks* mood with its bizarre touches of humor (such as the giant clown on the wall at the end of the scene).

Cooper tells Truman about Caroline (and her death) in a nicely-performed scene. It moves the Windom Earle storyline dramatically forward by giving the Windom/Cooper conflict an intense backstory.

Mayor Milford comes to the police station ready to shoot Lana, blaming her for Dougie's death. Cooper suggests Milford and Lana talk things over and he lets them have a conference room alone. But why does he allow Milford to keep his gun?

Thomas Eckhardt, Andrew Packard's former business partner in Hong Kong, and Josie's employer, arrives in Twin Peaks. In one of the episode's memorable scenes, he stands in front of a Great Northern fireplace and the flames are reflected on his sunglasses.

This episode has a great concluding scene—an *homage* to the classic 1931 film, *Frankenstein*, with Leo wandering through the forest and finding Windom Earle's cabin.

There is a slight continuity error when Dr. Jacoby appears at the sheriff's station in act 3. In the previous scene he was at the Great Northern where he had been studying Ben. In the very next scene he says he has spent most of the last 24 hours with Lana. Jacoby may be good, but it is hard to reconcile just how he gave two patients simultaneous attention.

This episode marks the first appearances of Windom Earle, Thomas Eckhardt, Jones, and Randy St. Croix.

The opening credits were abbreviated when broadcast on ABC. The full credits appear on home video versions (DVD and Blu-Ray).

The first draft of episode 21 was completed on November 5, 1990. The script went through two drafts and was followed by four revisions. The final draft was dated November 8, 1990.

Notable Deleted Scenes

Act 1: In Sheriff Truman's office Dr. Hayward and Cooper examine the body of the vagrant. In the script, Cooper hands an evidence bag to Andy who is "standing inside the door with his eyes closed so he won't see the body and cry. Andy turns to leave and walks into the wall with a thud. Andy peeks, adjusts his trajectory and makes it." This extensive slapstick never made it to the screen. But look carefully at Andy in the televised version; he's clearly keeping his eyes closed as Cooper hands him the bag. Hawk reports that there are footprints outside. The script contains some dialogue that was cut as Truman suggests getting molds of the footprints before it rains. Cooper explains that Earle would "have been wearing the wrong size shoe, untraceable and already destroyed." These extra lines reinforce the clever and diabolical nature of Windom Earle.

Cast and Crew Comments

Scott Frost: [The writing] was all fairly loose. There were certain touchstones in the story that you had to hit on. As I remember it was people sitting around in the room talking about the general story and then you went off to see what you could do with it.

I think that the guys in the room got a little obsessed with that [*Civil War*] documentary. As any good investigator would tell you, "There is no such thing as coincidence." I am not at liberty to divulge much more than that. [*laughs*]

Harley Peyton: Windom Earle's name comes from two places: Windom from William Windom, a TV actor I remembered dimly (I believe he was the star of a show called, *The Farmer's Daughter*) and Earle from Mad Dog Roy Earle, the character Humphrey Bogart played in *High Sierra*.

Robert Engels: I'm a big fan of Sherlock Holmes, and Mark is, too. Windom Earle is Professor Moriarty. That's where the idea came from. Kenneth Welsh is a real good friend of mine and I got Ken to do it. I was involved to a great degree. But it did start slowly. Some of that was because, budget-wise, we had blown it. We couldn't do things we wanted to do.

Kenneth Welsh (*Windom Earle*): I met Mark Frost [in Minneapolis]. That's also where I met Bobby Engels. Bob, and the woman who turned out to be my second wife, Donna Haley, were both in an MFA program. Bob and I became great friends because he and Donna were great buddies. Mark was there, but I knew Mark's father, Warren Frost, before I knew Mark. He was teaching at the university and was working at the local theater quite a bit. So the Minneapolis connection was what brought about *Twin Peaks*.

Skipping ahead now: I was in Los Angeles shooting something and I called Bob Engels just to say hello. I called him up and said, "Bob how ya doin'? This is Ken." He said, "Ken, funny you should call! There's this part that's come on *Twin Peaks*. You gotta come in here and talk to us about it!" So I came in. David wasn't there, it was just Bob. I think I met Mark—he was coming and going. I met the costume person and some other people. The next thing I know, Bob says, "Well, when can you start?!" I said, "Oh my God! This is unbelievable! I've never gotten a job like this in my life!"

I read for nobody! It was handed to me on a plate. Bobby knew the kind of stuff I could do. He had seen me at the Guthrie. I played all these different kinds of parts all the time. I've always been a character actor. With Windom, Bob really had an opportunity to trip me up every week. He would try to throw something at me and say, "All right, what are you gonna do with this?" [*laughs*]

Robert Engels: Favorite moment: The one I think about every once in a while is Richard Beymer and Russ Tamblyn singing ["Dixie"] together. When they finished that scene, I think Russ said to Richard, "You know, I haven't sung with you since *West Side Story*." I didn't even think of that when I was writing it. I mean, I was always aware that those two were in *West Side Story*, but I didn't think of that. Never crossed my mind. (I had always heard that story about *The Odd Couple* by Neil Simon where Felix Unger leaves a note for Oscar, and he signs it "F.U." —you know, "Felix Unger." [*laughs*] And Simon said, "I never thought that was a joke until I heard it happen." I was always skeptical of that story until it happened with me and the singing scene. It never dawned on me. But that was a pretty funny moment.)

Kenneth Welsh: My first director, Uli Edel, directed an episode I was barely in. I came in at the very end. I can't remember much about him except that he was very precise about what he wanted. He was very interested in different and precise camera angles. We would go over and over it until he got *exactly* what he wanted.

Kimmy Robertson: Uli, or whatever his name was—his thing was to turn the camera upside down, and, this is my pet peeve, then do twenty-five takes. And Michael Ontkean and Kyle and Michael Horse got so mad they started cutting the cheese at around the eighteenth take. [*laughs*] So when I think of Uli, I think of farting. [*laughs*]

I don't know who wrote that stuff. If I did, I'd point the finger right at them, and you know which finger it would be. I know that we were powerless to do anything else. If we did say or try anything different, we would be told not to. You know: "I'm tired of you actors questioning every P and Q!" "Well, write us something besides P and Q!"

Whoever was in charge and writing the show wouldn't know the truth if it hit them in the face. David [Lynch] shoots in a certain way—it's not with a camera tilted to the side. It's got to affect some part of you, otherwise it's just sick. That's what happened on the second season: People who thought they could do it in a Lynch style were too stupid or too unevolved to see that the Lynch style is something spiritual and real—as real as you get. It's not TV! [*laughs*] It's so simple, and it sounds so profound that it sounds stupid. But it's not. I do all this other stuff now and you just can't ever expect it to be a spiritual experience. You just work for a living.

Robert Engels: Most of the time you couldn't make a change because you knew where the story was going. Someone might say something like, "Couldn't I say such-and-such?" And you would say, "No, you can't say that," because you knew where it was headed. That was the fun of a continuing story, you knew where it was going. Then, by accident, an actor would say something they thought would improve the line and you would think, "No, no. You can't say that." But you couldn't tell them why!

John Boylan: The way I attack a character: One uses imagination and develops a person[a]. One of the things I learned was to become as familiar as possible with a character who is a figment of my own imagination, and mine only. The director and the screenwriters—they can't supply me with the person, I have to find it myself. And one of the things I do, I write a biography of him: *The Mayor of Twin Peaks*—where he started, how big the family was, what his father did, what his mother was like, how happy he was as a young man, or how unhappy, his dreams that in many cases did not come to fruition.

The fact that he was the Mayor indicated that he was a man of some substance, although somewhat of a fixture. People just thought of him as the Mayor, and that's it; [they] had forgotten that he's a human being. I wrote what must have been a dozen pages, longhand. It was the biography of the mayor of Twin Peaks. Good, bad, or indifferent, it was mine. It can't be anybody else's.

He was born nearby on a farm. He was educated at the community school and later studied for law, and spent his time in the law library reading. He always had tucked away, in a little corner of his psyche, a desire for something exciting occurring to him. He led an uneventful existence as mayor of a small town. He was respected and elected, again and again.

The event with his brother made him absolutely, violently involved with this hussy [and] he suddenly realized this may be the opening to what he had always wanted for himself. And the thought he had was, "Oh my God, I hope I can make it physically." And the rest was in the laps of the Gods. Whether he'd (ultimately) make it, I don't know.

Episode 22 (Script number 2015; First televised February 9, 1991)

Guest Starring: Annette McCarthy (Evelyn Marsh), Nicholas Love (Malcolm), and David Warner (Thomas Eckhardt)

Co-Starring: Brenda Strong (Jones), Robert Bauer (Johnny Horne), Matt Battaglia (Cop), and Gerald L'Ecuyer (Bartender)

Written by Harley Peyton and Robert Engels; Directed by Diane Keaton; Edited by Paul Trejo

Monday, March 20, 1989:

> Act 1: Evelyn and Malcolm talk to the police. James tells Donna he's been framed. Cooper tells Truman that Hank shot Leo the night the mill burned. Albert says Windom Earle is making his move. Leo tries to flee but Earle fixes an electric collar to his neck.

> Act 2: Nadine apologizes to Norma about hitting Hank. Cooper and Truman talk to Josie. Cooper surreptitiously removes some fibers from Josie's coat. Eckhardt wants to meet with Josie. Audrey tells Jacoby to bring Ben back. Jacoby decides to implement the "Appomattox Scenario." Donna argues with Evelyn about James. Malcolm threatens to kill Donna if she doesn't leave.

> Act 3: Albert says Josie is a suspect in Jonathan's murder. Truman reports that Earle's murder victim was named Eric Powell. Cooper says that Powell was Caroline's maiden name. Cooper enlists chess expert, Pete, to stalemate his game with Earle. Norma agrees to give Shelly her job back. Catherine and Eckhardt barter for Josie. James confronts Evelyn about what she did. Malcolm knocks James out.

> Act 4: Jacoby pretends to be General Ulysses Grant, who surrenders to Ben's Lee. Ben collapses and reverts to his normal self. Earle plans to make Donna, Audrey or Shelly his queen. Malcolm is about to kill James when Donna arrives. Evelyn shoots and kills Malcolm. Cooper arrives at his room to find a death mask of Caroline on his bed. Earle left a taped message: "Dale, listen carefully. It's your move."

Episode 22 is notable for the stylistic touches brought to it by director Diane Keaton, who introduced a surreal tone to some scenes and a quirky, comedic tone to others. These touches are a welcome change from last episode's dismal offering; in fact, Keaton's contribution makes this episode stand in sharp contrast to many of the past few installments.

The episode is also notable because it marks a change in story direction. First, it closes two of the series weakest storylines (the James-Evelyn frame-up, and Ben Horne's Civil War delusion) and, second, it moves two almost-forgotten subplots forward (Josie is revealed as Cooper's shooter, Hank is revealed as Leo's).

This episode features one of the cleverest and memorable opening sequences: a point-of-view shot that moves past and around giant chess pieces. It perfectly symbolizes the major drama that will dominate the remainder of the series: The battle between Windom Earle and Cooper. Keaton's bravura directing continues: The very next shot, for instance, is a slow pan up the legs of a "grieving" Evelyn Marsh (a departure from the script, which originally opened with an establishing shot of the Marsh mansion). In fact, numerous changes were made after the script was finalized, and all were creative touches that embellished the episode. When the three cops leave after questioning Evelyn and Malcolm, the trio practically marches out, their arms swinging in unison and their footsteps hitting the ground simultaneously. At Wallies, mailmen sit at a bar in identical positions, all facing the same direction. As Donna and James attempt to have a conversation, a bartender keeps interrupting them; later a cop interrupts Donna as she talks to Ed on the phone. In the fourth act, Windom affixes a fake mustache to his face as part of his disguise. But it was filmed with one added touch: the glass of the mirror is cracked, creating a fractured image of Earle's face and thereby emphasizing his fractured mental state. None of these embellishments were in the script but each adds a sense of unease.

Episode 22 is an accomplished work, especially considering that this is one of Keaton's earliest directorial efforts. She shows an astonishing artistic eye that makes this one of the best-directed episodes of *Twin Peaks*.

Additional Notes:

There's a clever editing cut in which Cooper's chess instruction by Pete Martell at the Double R is followed by a shot of Shelly's walking across the floor of the diner with alternating red-and-yellow tiles—a visual allusion to a chess board.

Bobby refers to Leo as "Leostein" for the first time—another line that does not appear in the original script.

Albert makes a welcome return to *Twin Peaks*, his first appearance since episode 16.

This episode reveals the last name of the Asian man previously identified as Jonathan. Albert tells Cooper the name is "Jonathan Kumaguy." This episode also reveals the name of the transient killed by Windom Earl, Erik Powell. (Powell was Caroline's maiden name.)

Pete turns out to be a chess expert, and Cooper seeks his advice in his match against Windom Earle. He says he wants a stalemate game, losing as few pieces as possible. However, as pointed out by chess expert, John Jacobs, "In fact, he wants a draw or a tie. Stalemate is a somewhat rare form of a draw in chess which more commonly occurs by mutual agreement, perpetual check, or insufficient mating material left on the board."[2]

Strangely, Ed does not seem worried about James when in bed with Norma, even though he had earlier received a worried call from Donna.

This episode resolves several major storylines, allowing the Cooper/Earle conflict to dominate the end of the season.

The first draft of episode 22 was completed on November 20, 1990; and underwent six revisions. The final version was completed on December 11, 1990.

Notable Deleted Scenes

Act 4: At Windom Earle's cabin, Earle dons a disguise and Leo is forced to transcribe the poem. The televised version shows photos of Shelly, Audrey, and Donna on Leo's writing desk. These pictures are simple, black-and-white head shots (probably from the actual *Twin Peaks* publicity department). The script describes a more intriguing set of pictures—Leo is working on "three child-like Valentines. In the center of each heart is a picture: Shelly, Donna, Audrey. They are surveillance photos." While the photos are a minor set-piece in either version, their depiction in the script is far more chilling than what aired.

Cast and Crew Comments

Robert Engels: Diane [Keaton] had directed very little. I think she had directed a video. But you could tell she knew how to do everything and she was well-prepared.

It was really kind of a director's series. We tried to give them their way. I can remember that Diane had gone farther than we thought she was going to go. [*laughs*] I can remember the big chess pieces. And I know that on the first day she ran way long. She didn't stop until ten. I had to go down and explain, "OK, after ten hours, we stop. This isn't the film business. You're done." We had to stop because she was just so far behind, and it's always about money. Then, the next six days she did great—she picked up and caught up. All the movie directors are the same—no matter what series you're on, the first day scares the hell out of me because they think they're making a movie, and then you talk to them, and they pick up right away. It's only in the beginning it's a problem. Otherwise they'll go all night.

Sometimes [directors] expressed themselves in ways that weren't as obvious as the large chess pieces. But all the good ones did it their own way, which was always kind of fun about the show—it was always so different.

She probably wanted to do stuff differently and we wrote it down [in the script] that day. There's a lot of that that goes on! But it's been put back together so that it looks like we planned it that way. [*laughs*] "Oh, sure, that was always in the script!"

Everett McGill: Diane was just crazy about the show and she was tickled to be there. She just couldn't be happier. And I thought that what she brought to the series was a maturity and a feminine understanding of things. How I expected Nadine to respond catching us together in bed was probably a very male kind of response. And I was surprised that Diane decided on something much more nurturing and understanding than a male director would have pulled off. I do remember that.

Diane was a delight. She was so much fun. She was so up. And we just had a lot of off-camera fun.

James Marshall: She was cool. She really respected and liked David's work and was sort of enamored with it. I think a lot of people came in and were intimidated—"Why did I take this? Now I have to match David?" Diane came in and said, "This might be fun."

Richard Beymer: I had fun doing the Civil War stuff, but, to me, it looked like the art department was doing it and not Ben. If Ben had just taken the stuff in the room and the stuff available to him and played with that—and gone mad within that—I think it would have been much more interesting. And then Diane Keaton took it to a level which I thought was ridiculous. Silly. Not interesting, "David Lynch stuff" at all. There was the whole battle scene on the wall—that was the art department at work. I mentioned this at the time. I said, "This is ridiculous. This should be Ben's drawing of the battlefield. It should be a mess! It shouldn't look like someone came in and drew this beautiful wheat field."

And the other actors were wearing Little Bo Peep outfits! I kept asking, "Where did they get all these costumes? Why are they all so perfect?" I could understand someone coming in wearing a bonnet to appease him. And I could understand Ben finding part of a uniform. But the boots and the right pants? *No!* To take some old hat and make it a Confederate hat, and to let his beard grow, and to maybe have a sword with his Armani suit—to play it from that point of view—then I could see how the guy is losing it, and it's interesting. The model railroad, that whole thing, it looked like the prop department came and made it. We spent how many thousands of dollars on one of those train sets?!

Kenneth Welsh: I didn't actually meet David [Lynch] until the second episode I shot. Diane Keaton directed it. I was dressed up in this weird plaid suit and a mustache, pretending to be this Greek guy who went up to the hotel counter. David came on the set that day and Bob said, "David, I'd like you to meet Windom Earle—Kenneth Welsh." David looked me up and down and said, "Good deal!" Then off he went, and that was it! [*laughs*]

My major input to the episode directed by Diane Keaton [was] the shakuhachi flute. In the original script it was only a flute—Bob wrote it in because he knew I played the flute. I said to Bob, "Listen, I also play this thing called the shakuhachi flute, which is a Japanese flute made from bamboo." At a certain point in the history of Samurai fighting the warriors were not allowed to use their swords, for some reason. The Samurai then took up the use of the shakuhachi flute both as an instrument and as a weapon. If you remember, these flutes have a sharp, knobby end of bamboo that is as hard as hell! They made a rubber copy of my shakuhachi flute with which I practically beat poor Leo to death. There were more than a few near misses, I must say. But, that's where that came from, because I played it.

The only thing that I despair of is that they didn't use my actually playing that we recorded. I called Angelo [Badalamenti] on the phone. He said, "All right, how well do you play this thing?" I said, "OK, here's my notes," and I played it for him on the phone. He went to the piano on the spot and came back with the music that we used in that episode. We recorded it, but they didn't use [my version]! They used the melody but not my actual playing. They synthesized it. I don't know, the sound editor didn't think it was good enough. I thought it was just perfect. It might have been bad shakuhachi flute, but it wasn't totally bad. There is a recording somewhere of me actually playing it. Angelo may have it.

Jack Nance: The ambiguity [in Pete Martell] is probably my own. All I think about Pete Martell is that as things went along he began to remind me more and more of my old man. Pete was probably the only person in Twin Peaks—or the only person in the country—who didn't give a damn about who killed Laura Palmer. [*laughs*] It was just not something that was a big concern to him. Neither was anything else. As for Josie, she was adorable and there was a lot of affection. But as far as that business with Catherine went, his attitude was, "Hey, I'm going fishing." The next time he went out there, the only thing on his mind was the next big halibut he was going to land.

SECOND SEASON REBOUND:

EPISODES 23-28

The final seven episodes of *Twin Peaks* represent redirection, of a sort, for the series. After the previous half-dozen dismal episodes, *Twin Peaks* was finally getting back on track, though it wouldn't really find firm footing until episode 25; it is at that point that the distracting and frivolous subplots give way to a central narrative line: the growing conflict between Windom Earle and Dale Cooper. As this storyline developed, other intriguing events took place. Josie Packard died a mysterious death that was linked in some way to the reappearance of Bob. Gordon Cole returned to town and reinstated Cooper in the FBI (thereby ridding Cooper of his rustic, lumberjack garb and returning him his familiar black suit and overcoat). Finally, Cooper became involved with Annie Blackburne in a love story that had none of the melodrama of the James Hurley/Evelyn Marsh story or the saccharine-sweet romance of the developing Audrey/Jack Wheeler subplot.

But these episodes were not without low moments. While Ben Home's "Stop Ghostwood" storyline was a marked improvement over the recent Civil War story, it spawned a few ridiculous subplots featuring Dick Tremayne and Tim Pinkle (two nonsensical and distracting characters). A number of episodes contained slapstick comedy, including episode 24's fashion show and Pine Weasel attack, episode 26's wine-tasting party, and, of course episode 28's Miss Twin Peaks Pageant. While undoubtedly scripted to provide comic relief from the darker subplots, this material was outlandish and absurd. These sequences worked too hard to be comedy and provided anything but relief. What's more, the scenes paled in comparison to the surreal tone of the series' more significant storylines.

Episode 23 (Script number 2016; First televised February 16, 1991)

Special Guest Star: Billy Zane (John Justice Wheeler)

Guest-Starring: David Warner (Thomas Eckhardt), and Dan O'Herlihy (Andrew Packard)

Co-Starring: Michael J. Anderson (Man From Another Place), Ron Blair (Randy St. Croix), and Frank Silva (Bob)

Written by Tricia Brock; Directed by Lesli Linka Glatter; Edited by Toni Morgan

Tuesday, March 21, 1989:

Act 1: Cooper ponders Caroline's death mask and says that Caroline was the love of his life. Josie sees Andrew and faints. Truman charges Hank for attempted murder against Leo. Hank says he has info on the murder of Andrew—it was Josie. Albert concludes that Josie killed Jonathan Lee (the Asian man) and shot Cooper. John (Jack) "Justice" Wheeler introduces himself to Audrey. Audrey opens a note advising her to meet at the Roadhouse for a "gathering of angels."

Act 2: Nadine tells Ed she is in love with Mike. Cooper wants Josie to turn herself in. Josie asks Catherine for help and receives a gun. Ben wants to stop the Ghostwood development by starting the Pine Weasel Project, an environmental effort to protect the endangered Pine Weasel species. Norma learns that her sister, Annie, is coming home. A disguised Earle leaves a note for Shelly—it contains another third of the poem and the meeting message. Ed proposes to Norma.

Act 3: Norma visits Hank in jail and asks for a divorce. Pete provides a safe, stalemate move to Cooper. Albert tells Cooper he's got irrefutable evidence of Josie's guilt. Andrew wants Josie to go to Eckhardt. James says good-bye to Donna and tells her he will come back someday.

Act 4: Andrew reveals himself to Eckhardt. He says that Josie betrayed Eckhardt and that is why he is still alive. Donna, Shelly and Audrey meet and compare their notes. Earle watches from across the room. Cooper approaches Josie's door and hears her scream. He hears a gunshot and bursts in. Eckhardt has received a gunshot wound to the chest. Cooper wants to know why Josie shot him. She says she knew he would discover her secrets. Truman enters and Josie asks for forgiveness. She has a seizure and dies. Cooper suddenly has a vision of Bob, who crawls over the bed and says, "Coop! What happened to Josie?" Bob is replaced by an image of the Little Man from Another Place, who dances on the bed. Josie's face appears in a wooden drawer pull. She screams, and her face, contorted in the wood, freezes in agony.

Like the previous installment, episode 23 wraps up a few storylines and details the departure of some main characters, namely James Hurley, Hank Jennings, and Josie Packard (it is also the last episode to feature Jerry Horne). Events in both episodes 22 and 23 indicate that the producers are attempting to get *Twin Peaks* back to a more mysterious, darker tone. This is especially evident with the reappearance of Bob and the Little Man from Another Place at the end of this episode.

After Diane Keaton's stand-out episode, the show restarts to some degree, picking up momentum as it moves toward the year-end climax between Cooper and Windom Earle.

Still, this episode is rather lackluster, especially following Keaton's sharp contribution. Many plotlines are set in motion—the introductions of Jack Wheeler, and (by phone) Annie Blackburne; Earle's plan to target Audrey, Shelly, and Donna; Nadine's break-up with Ed, freeing him to be with Norma—but none is particularly interesting and the scenes play out predictably. Billy Zane is a perfectly acceptable actor but his scenes with Sherilyn Fenn seem pulled from a standard soap opera, lacking the offbeat sensibilities one expects from *Twin Peaks*.

But a few scenes do shine. Chris Mulkey is great when Hank is dragged into Truman's office and tries to make a deal by testifying against Josie. With a snap of his fingers, he envisions himself in a new identity: "Hank Jennings, witness [*snap!*] for the prosecution!" The always reliable Miguel Ferrer is effective as an increasingly frustrated Albert prodding Cooper to arrest Josie (even as he expresses sympathy for Truman). Piper Laurie and Joan Chen have a wonderfully tense scene as Catherine leads a distressed Josie to a gun she can use against Eckhardt. Laurie's ability to convey a cool manipulation and Chen's portrayal of Josie on the verge of a nervous breakdown, gives the scene the an off-kilter atmosphere missing in other parts of the episode. A more subtle scene occurs in the elevator as Eckhardt and Andrew meet and Andrew manipulates Eckhardt into thinking that Josie plans to kill him. Warner and O'Herlihy are fantastic in underplaying the action, which counters the urgency of the imminent confrontation (the scene includes Warner's great delivery of the line, "I'm always careful"). Overplayed, it would have devolved into melodrama, but here it works as a perfect *Twin Peaks* moment.

Josie learns that Andrew is alive in this episode, one day (one episode) after learning that Eckhardt is in town. It's all too much for her, and she faints. (A reminder of the full backstory puts some of the plot in perspective: In episode 7, Josie paid Hank $90,000 for having killed Andrew in a boating "accident," thus leaving her the Packard Saw Mill. In episode 21, Catherine and Andrew tell Pete that it was Eckhardt who tried to kill Andrew. Episode 23 confirms that Eckhardt persuaded Josie to carry out the assignment, claiming that Andrew never loved her, when, in fact, Eckhardt was seeking revenge on Andrew for stealing away Josie.)

Cooper asks Pete, a chess expert, for help in what he calls "a game of considerable importance." Cooper, however, does not explain to Pete the life-or-death stakes involved in playing against Windom Earle; he simply requests that Pete construct a stalemate strategy. Pete agrees, noting that he has learned to play chess by studying the great José Raúl Capablanca (World Chess Champion from 1921-1927). Pete studies the board for only a few minutes before providing the move P-QN3 (b6).

According to Pete, this brilliant move will give Earle "sleepless nights" and will prevent Earle from capturing any pieces for another four or five moves. According to experts, this move is not the best response to Earle's capture of the black pawn, and it shows that Pete is nowhere near the expert player he is supposed to be. It also proves that the show's writers had not given proper attention to the importance of the game, relegating it instead to a convenient symbolic cliché around which to play the whole Cooper-Earle/White Lodge-Black Lodge conflict.

A question arises as to what move Cooper would have made had he not sought Pete's help. The previous positioning of his knight indicates that Cooper would counterstrike should Earle take his pawn. Did Cooper have a strategy and was the knight part of it? The replacement of Pete as the primary black player prevents us from ever knowing.

The episode ends with a powerful scene: Cooper and Truman rush into Eckhardt's room only to find him shot and Josie brandishing a gun. Josie is unapologetic but begins to crumble at the sight of Harry. She seems to faint but actually dies (from fear, viewers learn later). The Little Man From Another Place and Bob appear and are followed by one of the most memorable images from the second season: the face of a screaming Josie merging into the nightstand's wooden drawer pull. Its meaning has been the subject of some debate, but a literal interpretation seems evident: the scene is a pictorial representation of the term, Ghostwood—that is, Josie is now literally a ghost in wood.

Bob's taunting question about what happened to Josie adds to the growing theme of fear. Josie died from fear (she was "frightened to death" though Cooper does not yet know this) and Bob's question demands attention to this fact. For many episodes (starting with the season premiere), the series has been carefully establishing the danger of fear to Cooper, (and anyone else, for that matter). Hawk tells Cooper that imperfect courage (i.e., fear) can totally annihilate your soul. Here, now, we see an actual example of how fear can kill. Arguably, Josie's fear "annihilated her soul" and her dramatic death should have been an alarm and warning to Cooper: *Fear will be his greatest enemy.* But Cooper seems oblivious to this warning; he soon becomes distracted by Annie Blackburne and pays scant attention to Josie's death. His startling vision of Bob fades from his memory much the way his dream did in episode 2. Only later will Cooper get a better grasp of the power of fear and how it can be harnessed to access the Black Lodge.

After episode 23, ABC television pulled *Twin Peaks* from its schedule and put the show on a six-week hiatus. The series would not return to the airwaves until March 28. Given the dramatic and eerie final sequence, this lengthy pause in the narrative was similar to what happened at the end of the first season—fans were left wondering what was about to happen, especially with the return of Bob to the story. Clearly, Leland's death did not mean the end of Bob, and his reappearance led many to wonder if there was more to the Laura Palmer story. Suspending the series here, as the show promised to return to its strongest storyline, was a tough blow for hardcore followers.

Additional Notes:

Windom Earle appears in this episode disguised as a trucker dining at the Double R. Later, he appears in the same disguise at the Roadhouse as Audrey, Shelly, and Donna meet to compare notes. The series never makes clear why Earle makes the effort to send pieces of the poem to the three girls.

While Annie does not appear in this episode, Norma does talk to her on the phone—Annie will be taking the next bus into Twin Peaks.

This episode marks the first appearance of John Justice Wheeler.

The first draft of episode 23 was completed on December 5, 1990, and was later revised five times. The final draft was completed on January 3, 1991.

Notable Deleted Scenes

Act 1: At the Blue Pine Lodge, Josie returns, sees Andrew and faints. One telling line was omitted from the televised version. Catherine looks down at Josie and says, "Poor thing. Couldn't even pull off a simple murder." This important line was scripted to remind the viewer that Josie had attempted to kill Andrew. It may have been removed because of the confusion it might have caused. The Josie/Andrew subplot was never a major storyline in the series and viewers might not have remembered to which murder Catherine was referring (quite a few murders had happened in recent episodes). This line, however, like later dialogue from Albert, illustrates the dangerous nature of Josie.

Act 2: At the Great Northern, Thomas Eckhardt hands Jones, his assistant, a stack of cash. He tells her it is "the entire amount." Jones looks pleased with the money. Eckhardt then instructs her to "finish the job, regardless of what happens tonight." He pulls the garrote out of Jones' bracelet and wraps it around her hand. He kisses her and then tells her to "Drive north, for a day. I'll wrap up my affairs and be gone by morning. Come back tomorrow night and finish up." This scene is clearly designed to establish suspense. With it, viewers would be wondering what Jones' mission is. The scene clarifies Jones' role (she is apparently a paid assassin), and reveals her weapon (the garrote) in advance, but it adds little to the narrative. In fact, removing the scene made Jones more of a mystery and heightened the tension when she appeared in Truman's bedroom at the end of episode 24.

In Ben Horne's office, John Wheeler, Jerry Home, Bobby Briggs and Audrey listen to Ben explain their new effort to save the Pine Weasel. The script contains some funny lines by Jerry that were cut from the televised version. Ben tells all, "I've been taking a good hard look at my own soul, and I've decided its high time Ben Home give something back to society." Jerry says, "Ben, not the hotel." Ben replies, "No. Not the hotel." Ben explains his desire to save the Pine Weasel. As in the televised version, Jerry explains that "they're incredible, roasted." But the script has him go further, as he explains how you prepare the weasel with a "ginger and garlic marinade" and serve it with a "glass of Sauvignon blanc." These funny, absurd lines were probably cut for time constraints. Still, this is the last episode featuring Jerry Horne and it would have been nice to include the extra lines so he could go out in style.

Act 3: In the final scene, James meets Donna for a picnic to say goodbye. James tells Donna that he loves her, but she says, "I remember when I thought love was simple. But look at us. Nothing we do seems to matter. Maybe love isn't enough." These short lines help better explain why Donna is so willing to let James go. They also foreshadow the same lines spoken by Major Briggs in episode 27 in which he declares his fear of "love being not enough."

Cast and Crew Comments

Chris Mulkey: Hank was totally on his own agenda. Always. He never once looked back. He would do things with people, he'd incorporate them into his plans, but he was ultimately going to screw them, too. So he was just really kinda' close to the devil incarnate. I mean, we talk about Bob. I think he was really close to Bob.

I think I found out [I was leaving the show] a couple of weeks [earlier]. Whenever you got the scripts it was at the last minute—all of a sudden they whipped them out. But that's TV writing under the gun. It was a time when the tone of the show took a network turn. I think it got weirder [but] in a way it lost an edge. And I'm not speaking metaphorically about Hank going away.

I was pissed! I thought, "Hank's goin' back to jail! Oh, no—I don't want to do that!" Because I wanted to do more. I wanted to make more money. But after I went away, the show took on a softer, goofier direction that I didn't like very much. Some of the characters that were introduced were softer. I liked more mystery and more danger.

Kenneth Welsh: Julie, the costume designer, would allow me to do anything every week! When I came in she'd say, "What do you want to do on this episode? What about this character?" And I'd say, "Well, I think I'd like to be a fat biker!" She said, "Hey! Don't we have some padding over there? Bring that padding and put it on him." They dressed me up right on the spot. It was a wonderful improvisational possibility we had there.

Michael J. Anderson: I think that maybe because my character stands between the Black Lodge and the White Lodge—in the waiting room—I really represent a chaos or uncertainty. Have you ever experienced something that was so outside what you normally believe that for the next few minutes you were likely to believe anything? Certain traumatic events can do that to you. That is what my character really is. Everybody is asking, "Is he this? Is he that?" Yeah, he's *all* of those things. He is as much as that moment of uncertainty offers. I think he represents straight trauma. That's what my character is. Josie was killed on the bed and that trauma stayed with the bed.

James Marshall: I heard that the ratings stayed pretty strong; the network just dropped the show. Hollywood is about power. It's a very weird business. They have a problem with something when it becomes so powerful and can exist on its own. It's that classic thing—"Let's get him big and famous, and once he is really high let's shoot him down and make fun of him as he goes down. Then, let's feel sorry for him and help him come back." Then he's the "come-back man," the underdog. It's been going on forever.

Twin Peaks took off like a gigantic rocket. And as it was flying there was suddenly this reaction: "*Whoa! Whoa! Whoa!* What do we do? I can't take credit for it. It's all Lynch! Well, fuck Lynch! And I'm not gonna let Mark Frost have another ground-breaking hit! Are you kidding?!" That's what it looked like to me. I grew up watching somebody like Martin Sheen go through his ups and downs. So I thought, "Oh, here we go." The first year it was so big it was almost as if it could breathe on its own. No other series did that, *ever*. You could see a picture from *Twin Peaks* and it was almost transcendent. They looked at it and said, "How dare you come in here and really do this?" [Hollywood] was like, "What are you doing? You don't just come in here and swing a giant stick!" It's too depressing to think about, but that's how it goes.

Episode 24 (Script number 2017; First televised March 28, 1991)

Special Guest Star: Billy Zane (John Justice Wheeler)

Guest Starring: Heather Graham (Annie Blackburne), David L. Lander (Tim Pinkle)

Co-Starring: Brenda Strong (Jones), Ron Blair (Randy St. Croix), Julie Hayek (Model), Betsy Lynn George (Teen Model)

Written by Barry Pullman; Directed by James Foley; Edited by Jonathan P. Shaw

Wednesday, March 22, 1989:

> Prologue: Cooper dictates to Diane about "recent developments." (This prologue served to recap the show's various plotlines because *Twin Peaks* had not aired for six weeks.)

> Act 1: A despondent Truman drinks and remembers Josie. Annie Blackburne arrives at the Double R. The Log Lady notices Major Briggs's tattoo. Windom Earle is outraged by Cooper's attempt at stalemate. Jack Wheeler asks Audrey out for a picnic. Cooper provides a blunt report on Josie's criminal life. Truman tells him to get out.

> Act 2: Jones gives Catherine a puzzle box from Eckhardt. A disguised Earle gives Donna a gift for her father—a small, wrapped package. Pete reports that there is no stalemate game that doesn't involve the loss of pieces. The Log Lady has a tattoo similar to Briggs's. She remembers a light in woods from when she was a child; she also had the same experience when her husband died in the fire.

> Act 3: Doc Hayward opens the box and finds a black pawn with a note: "knight to king's bishop 3." Ed wants a divorce but Nadine thinks they are simply breaking up. Donna spies Ben paying an affectionate visit with her mom, Eileen. Cooper notices scars on Annie's wrists. Cooper tries to talk Truman down from his rage. Truman breaks down and Cooper embraces him.

> Act 4: Cooper and Hawk put Truman to bed. Ben hosts the "Stop Ghostwood" fundraiser. Pinkle shows off a real pine weasel which bites Dick on the nose. It then escapes into the audience, terrorizing the fundraiser attendees. Audrey is knocked off the stage into Wheeler's arms. Jones knocks out Truman's guard and climbs into bed with Truman.

This episode challenges episode 19 as the worst in the series (and like that earlier episode, has a great number of scenes played for laughs). Poor scenes proliferate: Truman's drunken binge (complete with a faux *film noir* ambiance and an embarrassing performance by Ontkean); Annie's introduction (and later, Cooper's first meeting with her); the Wheeler/Audrey picnic (with Wheeler singing!), Ben's visit to Eileen; Mike and Nadine's visit to the Great Northern; the "Save the Pine Weasel" fashion show (with a pine weasel on the loose), and on and on. It proves that no series is too good to avoid self-destruction if diligence is not maintained. In interviews, director Foley talked about how unhappy he was working on *Twin Peaks,* and given the episode he ended up directing it's easy to understand why. The episode ends with Eckhardt's assistant Jones slipping into bed with Truman—a scene that, as we see in the next episode, makes no sense.

Though Heather Graham performs quite well, the material she has to work with in this episode is not strong. Harley Peyton was aghast at the turn the show had taken and the idea of Annie's backstory: "She came out of a nunnery! It was ridiculous. It was just a mess. It was a mess!"

Fortunately, a couple of scenes are entertaining. Welsh conveys a subtle creepiness in Earle's visit with Donna, and it's even creepier in retrospect when we learn that he's pretending to be Dr. Hayward's deceased college roommate (whose phone number is actually one for a cemetery). Also, during the fashion show (an excruciating scene that never should have made it on the air), there's a brief interlude with Catherine and Ben that is well played by the two actors, despite some mediocre dialogue. Finally, Jones' delivery of the mysterious box to Catherine begins an intriguing plotline that nicely represents the show itself—boxes locked inside other boxes, all containing puzzles and secrets.

Earle delivers his next chess move: N-KB3 (Nf3) in a small gift box, which Dr. Hayward opens. The box contains a black knight, tagged with Earle's move written on a scrap of paper. There was no reason for Earle to melodramatically include an actual chess piece with his move; it merely added confusion to the story. Was Earle moving a black knight? (Impossible, since he was playing white.) Or was Earle *taking* a black knight? (Impossible again: none of the pieces were positioned to allow the capture of a knight.)

This was the first episode to air on ABC after the six-week hiatus and there was much at stake regarding ratings. *Twin Peaks* was losing viewership and the network was uneasy about renewing the show. Had this episode done well there may have been a new hope for the series. As it was, the episode garnered a low 5.1 rating (and 10 share)—not enough to keep the show alive. Could a stronger episode have helped? Not likely. But this weak episode may have sealed the show's fate.

TV critic, David Bianculli noted in an interview with *Wrapped In Plastic*: "I think that unfortunately for *Twin Peaks*, when it needed to have a good episode the most was when it fell down. It seemed when it was coming back from a hiatus, or when it was coming back off of a cliff-hanger, it was always a let-down. But then the episode after *that* was always magnificent. It was maddening. I think particularly the last time they came back from hiatus it would have just renewed interest in the show rather than help dilute it."[1]

Additional Notes:

Tim Pinkle returns for the first time since episode 12 (where he tried to sell Shelly a device to raise and lower then-paralyzed Leo into bed).

This episode marks the first appearance of Annie Blackburne. (The script for episode 24 spells Annie's last name as "Blackburne" but her name also appears as "Blackburn," specifically in the credits to *Fire Walk With Me*.)

The first draft of the screenplay for episode 24 was completed on December 11, 1990. It was revised five times and completed on January 11, 1991.

Notable Deleted Scenes

Act 1: At the sheriff's station, Hawk reports to Cooper about Truman and they discuss Josie's death. The scene is virtually the same as what aired, but with two crucial differences. In the televised version, Cooper is dressed in his civilian garb (a flannel shirt), but the script describes Cooper as outfitted in "full deputy dress." It's hard to imagine Cooper dressed in a deputy's uniform—he would have looked foolish and character would have been further diminished. What's more, it would have made little sense for him to seek out such a uniform and don it so quickly after Truman's departure, especially since he hadn't been wearing a uniform since being deputized. Fortunately, this element of the scene was dropped. A small line of dialogue was also appropriately cut from the televised version: When Cooper asks about Truman, Hawk says, "His vacation days'll be used up soon." This line either implies that Truman has been out of the office for some time (even though it has only been one day since Josie died) or that Truman has *very* few days of vacation.

Act 3: A "regretful" Truman relives Josie's death: "I know she was evil. I looked into her eyes . . . and saw the life drain out of them . . . she was so helpless . . . she needed me and there was nothing I could do." These interesting lines show that Truman has accepted Josie's criminal side, and also reinforce the mysterious nature of her death. Earlier dialogue explains that Josie was "frightened to death" and in this scene Truman describes how the life drained out of her. The death of Josie was a fascinating mystery that was unfortunately never developed. The strange circumstances surrounding her death, and later clues indicating a potential "haunting" of the Great Northern (see episode 27), position the Josie mystery to be as intriguing as the mystery surrounding Laura Palmer. Had *Twin Peaks* survived to a third season this story could have developed into a substantial and satisfying story arc.

Cast and Crew Comments

Heather Graham (*Annie Blackburne*): David Lynch did these commercials for Calvin Klein perfume, Obsession. He did four commercials using some of the *Twin Peaks* people. I was in one. We went one day and they put us on tape. They asked us some questions and I came up with some bizarre answers. Lynch then chose us to be in these commercials. I met him from that. I had also known the casting director, Johanna Ray, who he uses all the time on his movies.

One day they called and said, "We want you to be Dale Cooper's love interest." I went to David's house and talked to him about it. He was really cool, because with a lot of directors, they have to see you reading. But David goes more with a gut feeling after meeting and talking with you.

People were a little bit frustrated [on set]; I think by the fact that David wasn't around as much and they felt the story was being dissipated. I couldn't really understand because I was so excited to be there! But everyone seemed jaded about it. They had been through so much hype and all that.

Some of the people were really friendly. [But] they were already a family. They had been through a lot together and it felt like walking into a place where everyone else is in the group and you feel like an outsider. It didn't feel the same as when you start out on a job and everyone starts off new.

Kimmy Robertson: At that time, the whole second season felt to me like, "Whatever we do, it has to involve prettier and prettier young actresses." It seemed like that was the focus and the story was second. But maybe that was because my character was lost by then. Gone. That was my feeling at the time.

Everett McGill: I didn't notice too much of a difference between seasons. After the first four or five years of doing movies, I realized that acting wouldn't be enough for me, in terms of making a living. I set about finding another way to make money. So I got involved with real estate development. I had a business going at the same time as the series, and I would go back and forth. I would come in for a day or two, depending on how much was involved, to do all my scenes. I wasn't as aware, personally, of the second season malaise. I was hearing it from other actors who were supposedly not as happy with how things were going, or that there was a certain tension on the set.

Harley Peyton: If they had put us on Wednesday night at ten it might have been a completely different experience. I don't know, and I don't want that to sound like sour grapes, but I don't think the network knew what to do with the show. Putting it on Saturday was supposed to be this experiment, which clearly failed. It just hurt the show more and more. On our end, as the seams started to loosen, it didn't help either. It was difficult to preside over that because we all loved the process and we didn't want it to end. It was such a delicate balance that didn't hold. It isn't really about heroes and villains, that's just what happened. Mark and David had this unbelievable relationship, but it wasn't something that was meant to last. I don't think that's a secret.

Episode 25 (Script number 2018; First televised April 4, 1991)

Special Guest Star: Billy Zane (John Justice Wheeler)

Guest Starring: Heather Graham (Annie Blackburne),and David Lynch (Gordon Cole)

Co-Starring: Brenda Strong (Jones), Robert Bauer (Johnny Horne), Ron Blair (Randy St. Croix), and Jack McGee (Bartender)

Written by Harley Peyton and Robert Engels; Directed by Duwayne Dunham; Edited by Paul Trejo

Thursday, March 23, 1989:

> Act 1: Jones tries to strangle Truman, but he knocks her out. Truman and Cooper believe Eckhardt was jealous and wanted Truman dead. Gordon Cole arrives with the Windom Earle dossier. Earle listens to their conversations through a bug he placed in the Truman's office. Cole reports that Earle was on Haloperidol (the same drug used by the One Armed Man) to fake his illness. Earle was working on Project Bluebook, investigating UFOs. Cole reinstates Cooper in the FBI. Earle says he will kill the winner of the Miss Twin Peaks contest.

> Act 2: Donna sees her mother meet Ben. Eileen and Ben discuss their old relationship. Audrey and Donna spy on them. Cooper sketches the tattoo symbols. Annie flirts with Cooper. She notices Cooper's sketch and says it looks like the symbol from Owl Cave.

> Act 3: Donna asks her father about Eileen and Ben. Hayward brushes the whole thing off. Audrey bumps into a disguised Earle at the library. Cooper and Truman examine Pete's latest chess move then leave to explore Owl Cave. Ben offers Audrey a partnership in his business. Wheeler tells Ben he is falling in love with Audrey.

> Act 4: Hawk, Andy, Truman and Cooper explore Owl Cave. They find the symbol sketched on the cave wall. They find a stone handle in the wall. Annie is amazed and stunned at being out of the convent. She tells Cooper that she "failed" before and is afraid it will happen again. Cooper offers to help. Earle enters Owl Cave and turns the handle. The cave wall begins to shake.

Episode 25 has a distinctly different feel to it than the past few installments. It is stronger in content and theme, the characters are better defined, and there is a more relaxed, confident feel to the production. The televised episode follows the structure of the script, but much of the dialogue is slightly different, as if the actors weren't following their lines word-for-word, but, rather, using the script as a basic outline for what to say. What's more, there seem to be a few ad-fibbed lines in the televised version, usually at the end of scenes.

Why is this episode different? It is probably due to David Lynch's presence on the set (he reprises his role as Gordon Cole in this episode), and because of his working relationship with director, Duwayne Dunham. Dunham may have consulted with Lynch on various scenes, and the two men could have bounced ideas off each other regarding dialogue and camera movement. Whatever the reason, episode 25 shows the series moving in the right direction. Here, it shakes off some of its irksome, nonsensical sub-plots, and returns to a unique blend of surreal mystery and dark humor.

The overall pace of the episode is more energetic; in the previous episode the characters just seemed to be killing time. Cole's return is always welcome and he seems to bring out the best in Cooper. (As soon as Lynch returns, Cooper is back to wearing standard FBI business attire of suit and tie.)

As mentioned, Lynch may have had some miscellaneous input during shooting. For instance, in act 3, before Ben tells Audrey that she's "his man," Johnny Horne is visible outside, yelling and pretending to shoot buffalo. That scene is not in the original script, and represents the kind of oddball moment common to the show's first season. There's also an interesting unscripted line by Cooper: After Andy accidentally exposes the petroglyph in Owl Cave, Cooper declares, "Fellas, coincidence and fate figure largely in our lives."

This episode does have a few problems. The scene with Jones at the beginning makes no sense. If her assignment was to kill Truman, why not kill him while he sleeps? Instead, she strips down to lingerie, slips into bed and *then* tries to kill him!

The postcard from James to Donna is also problematic. James drove away from Twin Peaks on Tuesday (episode 23), but by Wednesday he was already in San Francisco (820 miles from Seattle; even more from Twin Peaks). Somehow he got a card to Donna in just one day! While the original episodes aired almost two months apart (February 16 and April 4), only two days have passed on the show.

Donna's suspicion about the relationship between her mother and Ben Horne starts to grow in this episode. By the end of the series the mystery turns out to be rather anti-climactic. Still, the plotline is more engaging than the Audrey/Wheeler and Nadine/Mike romances (and is even more interesting than the Cooper/Annie relationship, which got off to a cloying start).

The ability of Cole to hear Shelly seems like a bit of typical, unexplained and arbitrary *Twin Peaks* weirdness. Maybe that's all it was intended to be (it was added at Lynch's request) but it works as an amusing sidelight to the main events.

Earle disguises himself as Edward Perkins (presumably a poetry professor) as he bumps into Audrey at the library. He identifies the poem she received as that of Percy Bysshe Shelley (1792-1822). The entire poem, titled, "Love's Philosophy," reads:

The fountains mingle with the river
And the rivers with the ocean,
The winds of heaven mix for ever
With a sweet emotion;
Nothing in the world is single,
All things by a law divine
In one another's being mingle—
Why not I with thine?
See the mountains kiss high heaven,
And the waves clasp one another;
No sister-flower would be forgiven
If it disdain'd its brother;
And the sunlight clasps the earth,
And the moonbeams kiss the sea—
What is all this sweet work worth
If thou kiss not me?

Shelley's poem describes the interconnectivity of all things in the world. It could be argued that the "philosophy" of love is that the world (perhaps the universe, itself) holds little meaning without love as a unifying force. This fascinating poem hints at the philosophy of Major Briggs and recalls the description of his dream in episode 8. It also foreshadows his revelation in episode 27 that his greatest fear is "the possibility that love is not enough."

In the following episode, Cooper reveals to Truman that he once sent this poem to Caroline.

Additional Notes:

In act 3, Ben tells Wheeler that Audrey is off to Seattle to talk to "environmentalists." The script, however, has Ben saying that Audrey is off the visit "The Sierra Club." If you look closely at the scene, you can see that the word "environmentalists" is dubbed-in, replacing the phrase, "Sierra Club." (The editors try to cover the dub with a quick edit away from Ben in mid-sentence.) Why did the makers of *Twin Peaks* make such a minor change? It could have been for legal reasons and concern that the Sierra Club would not want to be associated with show and its fictional environmental cause. Whatever the reason, the producers did not want to specifically name The Sierra Club in the story.

Pete delivers another chess move to Cooper: P-QR3 (a6). Cooper realizes that the pawn is in danger from the white bishop, but trusts that "Pete knows what he's doing." (Although this move may not provide Cooper with any advantage over Earle, it is still relatively safe since the pawn is protected by both the rook and bishop.)

This episode reveals that Earle was involved in Project Blue Book, the secret governmental investigation into UFOs. Cole gives Cooper a folder containing that information. Recall that Major Briggs had previously mentioned Project Blue Book to Cooper in episode 20.

Cooper confirms that this episode takes place on Thursday (and, hence, March 23, 1989) when he makes a recording for Diane and notes that it is "Thursday, 9:05 p.m."

The first draft of the screenplay for episode 25 was completed on January 9, 1991 and later revised six times. Its final draft was completed on January 24, 1991.

Cast and Crew Comments

Harley Peyton: David was a more active presence during the second season. At least in reading scripts and asking for changes. And while he may not have directed as many episodes in the season, his character appeared in many and this led to increased involvement as well. Mark was prepping *Storyville* during the latter part of the second season, so David's participation increased to an even greater extent.

Kenneth Welsh: Windom is a master impressionist. I was given the opportunity to exercise this part of my craft which I love—to be able to disappear into these different kinds of characters. Like that Englishman in the library scene. That was my choice. I said, "Well, I think he should be English. He should be a librarian, or somebody very bookish."

We had so many good directors. That was another thing I loved about it. I played all these bad guys before I played Windom, but he was the ultimate. There's something in my eyebrows that makes me do this.

Heather Graham: [Annie's] background regarding the story of the boy she once knew was not made any clearer to me. What David Lynch told me was that [Annie] was like a finely-tuned machine that is very delicate. The slightest thing can set her off. He said that Cooper was going to be helping me and that would be the basis for us starting the relationship.

I don't know if this is true or not, but I had the feeling sometimes that they were making it up as they were going along! [*laughs*] They didn't take me aside and tell me anything so I have to assume that they either didn't want me to know or that maybe [they didn't know.]

Richard Beymer: I think Ben Horne changed more than anyone on the show. He went through more experiences of change. The other characters did not. He was a Southern general—he was all over the place. Most other folks—the sheriff, and others—stayed the same. So it was great fun. I had no idea it was going that way.

Episode 26 (Script number 2019; First televised April 11, 1991)

Special Guest Star: Billy Zane (John Justice Wheeler)

Guest Starring: Heather Graham (Annie Blackburne), Robyn Lively (Lana Budding), David Lynch (Gordon Cole)

Co-Starring: John Boylan (Mayor Dwayne Milford), Ted Raimi (Heavy Metal Youth), and John Charles Sheehan (Bellman)

Written by Mark Frost and Harley Peyton; Directed by Jonathan Sanger; Edited by Toni Morgan

Friday, March 24, 1989:

Act 1: Cooper, Truman, Hawk and Andy see a detailed petroglyph in Owl Cave. Earle recounts details about the White and Black Lodges to Leo and a "heavy metal youth," whom they've promised beer and a party. Catherine asks Pete for help with the box from Jones. Bobby insists Shelly enter the Miss Twin Peaks Pageant. Shelly recites the poem she received form Earle. She shows Cooper the written fragment and he keeps it.

Act 2: Cooper tells Truman that Earle's poem is the same one Cooper once sent to Caroline. Briggs recognizes the petroglyph: The silhouette of a hooded figure passes the drawing, a star field fills the screen, an owl flies toward the camera and the screen fills with flame. Cooper recognizes Leo's handwriting on the poem fragments and knows that Leo is with Earle. Leo refuses to get an arrow for Earle and is given a shock. Earle kills the youth.

Act 3: Ben wants the topic of the Miss Twin Peaks speeches to be about the environment. Catherine shows Truman the puzzle box. Pete drops it and finds another box with strange symbols on it. Cooper asks about Annie's past. Annie believes she can trust Cooper. Earle watches them from shore.

Act 4: Dick hosts a wine tasting fundraiser for the Stop Ghostwood project. Wheeler gets a telegram and announces he must immediately leave. Donna is angry about her mother's secrets and announces she had entered the Miss Twin Peaks pageant. Cooper is called to the park where the police have found a giant crate in the gazebo. The box opens to reveal the heavy metal youth, dead, inside a giant black pawn. A sign attached to the pawn reads, "Next time it will be someone you know."

Heather Graham delivers a fine performance as the haunted Annie Blackburne and makes the character engaging and compelling. Still, the early scenes between Annie and Cooper are not particularly good because something about MacLachlan's portrayal of Cooper is off; there's a fine line between Cooper's joy at simple pleasures (hot coffee, donuts, a hand-carved whistle) and his enraptured gaze at the new waitress. Everything improves in the rowboat scene, however, as the silly grins give way to troubled pasts. The writing is solid, and Graham elevates it with a strong performance—Annie is a character unsure of herself, yet working toward a new beginning and taking tentative steps without allowing fear to bind her. In response, MacLachlan reverts to the reliable Dale Cooper. It's not a flashy scene, but, combined with the perfect Badalamenti soundtrack, it sets the right tone.

The show returns to the theme of fear in Cooper and Annie's conversation—more specifically, the power of fear. As noted before, this theme runs throughout the second season. In the premiere, Cooper, while possibly dying from a gunshot wound, says, "On balance, though, being shot is not as bad as I had always imagined it might be, if you can manage to keep the fear from your mind. Then again, I suppose you could say that about almost anything in life: it's not so bad if you can keep the fear from your mind." In episode 18, Hawk warns Cooper about the Black Lodge: "You may be fearless in this world, but there are other worlds. There you will meet your own shadow self. But it is said if you confront the Black Lodge with imperfect courage, it will utterly annihilate your soul." And, of course, Josie Packard died of fear. The warnings keep piling up, but Cooper does not dwell on the topic. Not yet.

Here, Annie tells Cooper that she had to return to Twin Peaks once she realized that secluding herself in a convent would not help: "I realized that I was just hiding, and that running away from my fear didn't make the fear go away." Cooper responds, "It made it stronger." Annie: "Yes. So I had to face it. I had to face myself. And I have to do it here." Annie's experiences probably parallel Cooper's, who also had a past traumatic experience that emotionally damaged him. The implication here is that Cooper has not resolved his fear regarding Caroline Earle's death. In fact, that fear may be stronger in him because he has run from it. Cooper, too, will have to face this fear. And he will have to do it in Twin Peaks.

All of this was to come to a head in the final episode until Lynch's re-write of the script altered the themes and direction. In the original script for the last episode, Cooper discusses Earle's plan with Truman: "To fear the worst often causes the worst. He's going to terrify her, Harry. He did it to me. It's what he did to Caroline." Earle, like Cooper, has learned that fear is the key to opening the door to the Black Lodge. In episode 28, Cooper tells Truman that Josie was "trembling with fear" when she died—a fear that attracted Bob because it gave him sustenance. Major Briggs specifically tells Cooper that "Fear and love open the doors" to the Black and White Lodges. Earle's plan, then, is to capture the "queen," drag her to

Glastonberry Grove, and induce fear. In fact, the script for episode 29 says that Annie is "terrified," and the doorway to the Lodge opens.

Lynch's re-write of episode 29 altered the story, though even in the original version it's unclear whether fear played a part in Cooper's rescue of Annie in the Black Lodge. In that original, scripted version, Cooper willingly offers his soul to Earle in exchange for Annie's freedom. But Bob intervenes and says that Cooper is being coerced by Earle. Bob will punish Earle but also attack Cooper. At this point, Laura Palmer intervenes and apparently saves Cooper. Still, the final scene shows Cooper possessed by Bob. Are we to infer that Cooper succumbed to fear after all? Perhaps this would have been explored more extensively in the third season if the show had been renewed.

Back to this episode: Ben proposes a new theme to the Miss Twin Peaks committee: saving the forests. Yet the contest is just two days away, certainly too late to change an entire theme! Dr. Hayward responds by saying that the committee will "take it under advisement." How much longer can they delay making a decision? And why would Mayor Milford be allowed to judge a contest in which his fiancée is a participant? None of this plotline makes any sense, and it doesn't get better as the series continues. After all, Annie will get her own sister's vote in the contest!

Another unfortunate sequence is the wine-tasting party hosted by Dick Tremayne. Though not as bad as the fashion show, it still relies too much on goofy, slapstick comedy more akin to sitcoms than *Twin Peaks*. Buchanan's performance is pretty good—too bad it was wasted on such a superfluous scene.

The episode contains a minor error that was corrected in post-production. In act 3, Ben sees Bobby sitting with Mike and Donna. In the script, Ben reminds Bobby of the wine-tasting party to be held later that night at the Great Northern. It was probably shot that way and then, in postproduction, Ben's line was dubbed with another: He reminds Bobby to pick up the dry cleaning. (Bobby's response, "Thank you," seems odd, unless he was responding to something else—the original wine-tasting invitation, most likely.) Ben's line was likely removed because Bobby was not in the later wine-tasting scene.

The episode ends on a high note as Cooper again demonstrates his shooting prowess. Cooper's incredible marksmanship was first revealed in episode 4 during target practice at the sheriff's station shooting range. This reminder that Cooper has almost super-human abilities is a nice throwback to the first season and a sign that the series may have been finding its footing again, at least in regards to the Cooper character.

The end of the episode also reveals Windom Earle's next (and final) chess move: BxP (Bxa6). Cooper believes that Earle is playing "off the board" since Earle didn't tell him his move (although it's rather obvious that the move had to be BxP). This move marks the end of the game. In the next episode, Earle sweeps his chess pieces off the board and turns his attention toward the Owl Cave Petroglyph. He has obviously abandoned the match. Cooper ignores it also—it's his turn to move, but he never replies. Pete, too, seems to forget the game.

The first draft of the screenplay to episode 26 was completed on January 16, 1991 and later revised six times. The final draft was completed on February 7, 1991.

Notable Deleted Scenes

In act 3, Truman asks Catherine about Josie. The script contains some lines of dialogue cut from the televised version: Truman says, "I want to believe she wasn't all bad. There was something good there. Decent." (In the televised version, these lines are changed to Truman's simple comment, "I need to understand.") Catherine attempts to explain: "It was probably something she had no choice about. And I think that eventually became the largest truth in her life. In time she no longer knew who she really was. She, I don't know quite how to say this . . . she lost her . . . center." These lengthy lines were probably cut because they concerned a character that wasn't immediate to the series. And yet the presence of Josie persists in the *Twin Peaks* narrative in almost every episode after her death, as if the writers of the series still had a mystery left to solve. (And perhaps they did—the viewers of *Twin Peaks*, like the characters, never fully understood what happened to Josie when she died.) The next episode hints at the intriguing possibility that Josie's spirit lived on after death. Catherine's description of Josie's loss of identity makes the fate of the character even more mysterious.

Later in act 3, Cooper enjoys a quiet boat ride with Annie. The script contains some lengthy lines, cut in the televised version, in which Annie describes her emotional past and reasons for going to the convent: "I was so frightened for so long. Of everything. Of life. Everybody here thought I was nuts. And when you think about it, it was such a weird nineteenth-century thing to do. To think I could remove myself, as if that could stop all the noise in my head, when the problem was me, it was always in . . . me." These lines better establish the background of the Annie character and help explain why she left Twin Peaks for the convent. Annie's past is never adequately addressed in the televised version and there's an element of absurdity to the fact that she has been to a convent. It's a story point that demands elaboration, for explanation as to why the character would do such an unusual thing. This scene provided it, but, unfortunately, all the pertinent lines were cut.

Cast and Crew Comments

Ted Raimi (*Heavy Metal Youth a.k.a. Rusty Tomaski*): I was at a commercial audition where I was auditioning for this assistant-teacher [role]. I had on a corduroy jacket, my classic brown glasses, jeans, and hush puppies! [*laughs*] And I get a call from my agent, who says. "You gotta run down to the Valley to audition for *Twin Peaks*." I said, "What's the part?" "You're playing a punk rocker." I said, "Are you kidding me? First of all, I'm the farthest thing from it; secondly, you picked the worst day, because I don't have a change of clothes." He said, "You gotta go now." So I went down there, and in the waiting room there are maybe ten guys who are serious punk rockers—real punk rockers. I walk in and go, "Oh brother, let's get this over with, *fast*. Get me out of here."

I walked in and I read. David Lynch was there. And I said, "You know guys, look"—and I know you should never do this in auditions—"frankly, I don't think I'm right for this part, but let me show you what I got." So I read it and I went all out. Just let it go. And they were laughing pretty hard. I got home that afternoon and they called and said, "They want you for the part. Not only that, they want you for other episodes, too."

Robert Engels: I know David saw everything. He may have been gone but we were getting notes from him. I know he was on top of all that. As an executive producer he did not have to be there all the time. The cuts always got to him and the notes were always extensive. He was still very much like most of those guys—he was giving you notes on stuff you already shot. I remember that in the second season: "Yeah, that would have been nice, but it's done!" [*laughs*]

Harley Peyton: David wouldn't really read scripts until the night before they were to be shot. So then he would call in and say, "Really, you ought to do this, this, and this." And the director would say to me, "You can't do this, it's ruining everything I've planned." I would call up Mark and say, "Mark, you've got to talk to David, because I'm not going to do it. I'm going to tell the director to do what he planned." Mark would say, "No problem, I'll talk to David." But then, because Mark was working on his own movie at the time, he never really had a chance to talk to David. Soon, David would blame me for not carrying out the changes. It got pretty ridiculous.

Robert Engels: In any show, once things are not as sensational as [they were] before, then everybody starts to pull different ways. When we didn't get off to a booming start, we suddenly were not the redeemers of television anymore. Where Mark was much more educated in the ways of television—he knew how to go through it—David didn't have patience with that.

Harley Peyton: At one point David wanted us to write a scene so that he could kiss Mädchen Amick. You know, as Gordon Cole. I had a hard time motivating it, and then—and okay, I was being a little thorny—I wrote a line of dialogue for Bobby Briggs when he witnessed the kiss: "Hey, why are you kissing that old guy?" Needless to say, the line was cut from the script.

Heather Graham: I really loved [Kyle MacLachlan's] character from watching the show. As a person he was nice enough but he was kind of distant. But I enjoyed working with him.

I think that in some ways they wrote each character for the [actor], after they got a sense of them. I didn't tell them, "Oh, I want to be like this or that." They wanted Annie to be good. She was with Cooper because he was so good. The producers seemed to like actors and liked to take what people could bring to their roles, their own personality.

Ted Raimi: [Kenneth Welsh] was just great. That guy is just terrific. First of all, I think he's at the top of his craft. But he's a really funny guy. He doesn't look funny when he's acting; he's so serious. But he's hilarious. He's the kind of actor I'd like to be at that age, because he doesn't care what people think about him being weird and bizarre. He doesn't really care. That's a great attribute, because as time goes on you become more reserved and concerned about keeping your image—or you go the other way. Very few actors go the other way, and I'd like to become one of those.

Episode 27 (Script Number 2020; First televised April 19, 1991)

Special Guest Star: Billy Zane (John Justice Wheeler)

Guest Starring: Heather Graham (Annie Blackburne), Robyn Lively (Lana Budding), and Dan O'Herlihy (Andrew Packard)

Co-Starring: Willie Garson (Heavy Metal Roadie), John Boylan (Mayor Dwayne Milford), Carel Struycken (the Giant), Ron Blair (Randy St. Croix), Ron Kirk (Cappy), Ted Raimi (Heavy Metal Youth), Frank Silva (Bob), and Layne Robert Rico (Pilot)

Written by Harley Peyton and Robert Engels; Directed by Stephen Gyllenhaal; Edited by Jonathan P. Shaw

Friday night, March 24, through Saturday, March 25, 1989:

Act 1: Cooper believes that Earle is playing "off the board." Hayward wants Ben to stay away from Eileen. Donna finds her birth certificate. Briggs plays an old video of Earle who says, "These evil sorcerers, Dugpas, they're called, cultivate evil for the sake of evil." The Dugpas have found a secret place of evil called the Black Lodge. Cooper suspects the petroglyph holds the answers. The arm of an elderly patron at the Double R starts to shake. Milford plots with Lana so she can win the pageant. Cooper tells Donna, Audrey and Shelly that they are in danger.

Act 2: Earle threatens to kill Shelly. Audrey learns that Jack has left and hastily leaves. Ben hears a noise and turns around in shock. At the same moment, Pete, staring at a wall in the Great Northern lobby, says, "Josie I see you face." Cooper thinks about Annie as Truman remembers Josie. Cooper's arm begins to shake. Earle and Leo, dressed in a horse costume, accost Briggs. Earle shoots him with a tranquilizer dart.

Act 3: Cooper asks Annie out for dancing. Audrey arrives at the airport and stops Wheeler's plane. Earle injects Briggs with Haloperidol, and then asks him, "What do you fear most in the world?" He answers, "The possibility that love is not enough." Briggs says he first saw the petroglyph in his dream. He then recounts the detail about his disappearance. He speaks what sounds like gibberish (actually "That gum you like is coming back in style" backward—"Taht mug uoy ekil si gnimoc kcab ni elyts.")

Act 4: Andrew smashes the puzzle box open with a rolling pin and finds a small metal box. Cooper and Annie dance. Annie decides to enter the Miss Twin Peaks contest. Cooper calls her the queen. On the stage, the Giant appears, shaking his head and mouthing the word, "No." Earle realizes that the cave painting "is not only an invitation, but also a map! A map to the Black Lodge!" The giant fades away. A montage of images follow: the Roadhouse, the stoplight, the Double R Diner, a corridor at the high school, a hallway at the Great Northern, the interior of the sheriff's station, the petroglyph, tree branches blowing in the wind. At Glastonberry Grove, Bob emerges from a bright light.

This episode has a sharper focus than other recent offerings, as the writers seem to be getting as much extraneous material as possible out of the way so that the primary conflict of Cooper versus Earle can come to the fore. Also, Gyllenhaal's directing is clever and captivating: a sequence of scenes toward the end the episode—slow tracking shots down empty hallways—conveys a sense of unease and unearthliness. It feels like what *Twin Peaks* should be.

The episode contains the memorable scene in which Leo finds the control for his electric collar and tries to attack Earle with it, only to shock himself. Welsh's and Da Re's performances are notable: Da Re portrays Leo's confused surprise at being shocked, and Welsh moves seamlessly from uproarious laughter at Leo to deadly menace as he threatens to teach "the value of hate." In fact, Welsh is terrific throughout the episode. His interrogation of Major Briggs is by turns both whimsical and threatening. He's even entertaining in the episode's most absurd scene in which Earle and Leo are dressed up in a horse costume. (Like Ben Horne's elaborate Civil War outfit, just where did Earle find the horse get-up?) Earle may be a master of disguises, but this one was ridiculous. Luckily, Welsh's skillful performance salvaged this truly asinine idea.

And it's not the only curious scene. Both Annie and Audrey are encouraged to enter the Miss Twin Peaks contest one day before the event (and one day past the ludicrously-late entry deadline). There's also the Audrey/Wheeler fling in his private jet before he returns to Brazil. In less than four days, and on the basis of a single picnic date, Audrey has fallen completely under Wheeler's spell. As a result, Audrey seems diminished by these hasty passions. This rushed romance (paralleled by the Cooper/Annie story) suggests that the writers were ignoring the one episode/one day format. (Of course, by this time in the production they were likely wearying of the demanding *Twin Peaks* story structure.) But more importantly: What exactly was the point of introducing Wheeler to the story, if only to have him dash off so quickly? Was it to move Audrey beyond her infatuation with Cooper? As is, her speedy leap toward Wheeler seems absurd.

This episode contains the notable line from Windom Earle in the Project Blue Book videotape: "These sorcerers, dugpas, they call them, cultivate evil for the sake of evil and nothing else." This line appears, almost word-for-word, from a 1926 novel by Talbot Mundy, titled *The Devil's Guard* (aka *Ramsden*). In it, adventurers Jimgrim and Ramsden face an agent from a place called the Black Lodge. Such agents are called dugpas, which the book describes as "sorcerers who cultivate evil for the sake of evil." (The book goes on to describe a secret war between the Black and White Lodges.) The placement of this line into the narrative is curious; Mark Frost, Harley Peyton, and Robert Engels all deny having read the Mundy book. While it's possible that Lynch supplied the line, it seems more likely that one of the other writers came across the line in *another* work that was citing Mundy. (As for the Lodges, Frost has acknowledged that he got the Black Lodge idea from Dion Fortune's *Psychic Self-Defense*—see episode 18.)

Although the Earle-Cooper chess game lasted through fourteen episodes it vanishes from the storyline as if it had never existed at all. Windom Earle, to whom chess represented all of life, sweeps the game away three episodes from the end of the season. Dale Cooper, who knew only that Earle had taken another pawn and promised to take yet more pieces, never mentions chess again. The game was explicitly abandoned by both players—and, obviously, by the show's producers. Only the idea of "capturing the Queen" remained, where, interestingly, playing cards became the dominant image, not chess pieces.

From the start, chess was set up as the primary metaphor representing the Earle-Cooper relationship. But then the game was gone. This poorly executed endgame (or lack, thereof) to the Earle-Cooper chess match is just one of the creative missteps in the show's final few episodes. It could have continued to be a great story but the game was not allowed to fulfill its original potential.

Speaking of missteps, when Donna examines her birth certificate, she's shocked to see that there is no father listed. She should also have been surprised to see her mother's maiden name listed as *Hayward*, which is extremely unlikely (unless, by wild coincidence, Eileen and Will Hayward shared the same last name before they were married). The certificate also lists Donna's middle name as "Marie."

The Giant makes a brief return, trying to warn Cooper that Annie should not enter the Miss Twin Peaks contest. The Giant appears just as Cooper utters the word, "Queen." Cooper either ignores the warning or, more likely, he doesn't understand what the Giant is trying to convey. Still, this is another frustrating incident of Cooper's blasé response to startling, otherworldly warnings. He saw Bob only a few nights earlier but seemed unfazed by the vision. Now, the Giant sends a not-so-subtle alert. But Cooper appears simply lost.

As Audrey leaves Ben's office to chase after Wheeler, Ben senses something behind him and suddenly turns around. What does he see? Could it be Josie (or the spirit of Josie)? Immediately following Ben's sharp about-face, the scene cuts to Pete, standing in the Great Northern lobby, staring at the fireplace mantle and saying, "Josie, I see your face." These linking scenes strongly imply that Ben may have seen Josie (or some aspect of her).

This episode introduces a recurring motif of shaking right hands accompanied by a weird tingling sound effect—the first occurrence is at the Double R Diner with one of the patrons. A short time later, it happens to Cooper in Truman's office, then to Pete at the airport. Though the scenes are never explained exactly, they presumably have something to do with the return of Bob to Twin Peaks. Note that the final shot of the episode has Bob emerging from Glastonberry Grove, right hand first.

The shaking arms scenes, the shot of Ben Horne's startled reaction to something or someone, and Pete's line about Josie were not part of the final script for the episode. These last-minute additions indicate that the producers may have been laying the groundwork for a third season. The shaking hands element is quite prominent in the episode, especially since Cooper, himself, experiences the phenomenon. What did the shaking hands mean? The series never supplied a definitive answer. (A "numb-arm" plot point will occur in *Fire Walk With Me* and Robert Engels may have brought the idea from the series to the film. The "numb arm" element in *Fire Walk With Me* seems to connect to the Man From Another Place, who calls himself "The Arm.")

Maybe—just maybe—the creative team on *Twin Peaks* knew the end of the series was near and felt liberated to experiment with the show, to create a few "off-the-wall" bits which "felt right" but might not have meant anything. If so, they were following the spirit of the early episodes and David Lynch's experimental philosophy. Whatever the case, these bits remind us again: This episode felt like what *Twin Peaks* should be.

Additional Notes:

The televised version of episode 27 is one of the most altered episodes (from script to screen) of the second season (not counting, of course, the final episode). The order of most of the scripted scenes was dramatically rearranged for the televised version. A few scenes were cut (as usual), and one—Nadine's slideshow—was re-written to be included in episode 28. Finally, much of the scripted dialogue was slightly changed during the shoot, probably because the director, Steve Gyllenhaal, encouraged improvisation.

Episode 27 marked the last regular broadcast of *Twin Peaks* as a weekly television series. ABC cancelled the show and removed the final two episodes from the critical May sweeps period. They announced that these final two episodes would be broadcast back-to-back (as a TV movie) on June 10, 1990.

The first draft of the screenplay to episode 27 was completed on January 30, 1991 and later revised six times. The final draft was completed on March 12, 1991.

Notable Deleted Scenes

Act 2: At the Roadhouse, Bobby helps Shelly rehearse her speech. This scene was substantially re-written after the script was completed. The draft history on the script indicates that this scene was re-written and re-shot on March 12—a full month after the last revision was completed (in fact, it was probably re-written at the time the episode was being shot). The re-write of the scene takes the action from the Roadhouse to the Double R, and changes the tone of the scene. In the original draft, Bobby is more of a schemer, more interested in what it will mean to him if Shelly wins the pageant. The speech he writes for Shelly is inept and irrelevant: "I believe there are so many beautiful things in the world that should be admired and be thankful for. For example, Detroit auto makers reported a record year of sales for sports cars." Shelly is unimpressed and uncertain of the speech, but Bobby is enthused. He dreams of what he sees as an inevitable outcome: "Shel, you're gonna be wonderful. You'll win in a walk. And then we are off. Fade out on Twin Peaks. Fade up on Hollywood. Raider games. Sunset Strip. Easy street, baby. Just like you always wanted." He looks Shelly over. "Maybe a new hairdo. Or some signature makeup. We got to mesmerize."

In this original scene, Bobby behaves in the same selfish manner as he did in earlier episodes. His motivations are the same—to get money, to get out of Twin Peaks, to have an easy life. The new scene—the one that was used in the televised version—has Bobby much more aware of Shelly's needs. Her speech is more appropriate to the pageant theme, and the scene ends with Bobby pledging himself to Shelly. In some ways this new scene (and another one between the two characters in the final episode) provides some closure to the Bobby/Shelly relationship. The two seem happy together, and it may be that the characters were being set up for the return of Leo to the story (had there been a third season). In the current episodes Leo seems concerned for Shelly's safety. It's not hard to imagine a storyline in which Leo returns, healed and rehabilitated and ready to start anew with Shelly (though it is debatable whether such a story would work). Whatever the direction of the story, it's clear from the televised version that Bobby was no longer being portrayed as a tricky hustler.

Act 3: At the Blue Pine Lodge, Catherine and Andrew struggle to open Eckhardt's second box. The script explains that Andrew "pushes the zodiac buttons, tries different combinations." In the televised version, the box does not contain zodiac symbols, although the dialogue (and action) in both versions is identical—Andrew opens the box by pushing buttons which correspond to "his birthday, Eckhardt's birthday and the date the gift arrived." Because the box seen in the televised version is not the same as the one described in the script, Andrew's action (pushing zodiac signs which correspond to birthdays) is meaningless. Eckhardt's box represents a sloppy effort on the part of the *Twin Peaks* production. If the prop department could not create a box with twelve zodiac symbols, then the writers (or director Gyllenhaal) should have altered the dialogue to match the action. Although the error is minor, *Twin Peaks* rarely featured mistakes as obvious as this one.

Act 4: Wheeler arrives at the airport in a taxi owned by Tim and Tom's Taxidermy. Tim Pinkle rides in the passenger seat. His blind brother, Tom, is behind the wheel. Wheeler exits the cab with relief. He stares at Tom, incredulous that the blind man drove him to his destination. Tim explains his brother: "He loves to stuff, and he loves to drive. Otherwise he sleeps." Wheeler makes a hasty goodbye, and Tim reminds him that he and his brother will "stuff anything." The two drive away with Tim giving his brother directions on where to steer the car. If shot, this scene may have been cut for time constraints; it is also possible the scene was cut because the absurd humor of a blind man driving a taxi was too much, even for *Twin Peaks*.

Cast and Crew Comments

Robert Engels: Our offices were right above the soundstage. The directors would come in to prep and many of these guys were feature [film] guys. Television producers don't usually hire guys of that stature. With a lot of them you could say, "Give me your prep. Show me what you're doing." I can remember once with Steve Gyllenhaal, Mark said, "Do you know what he's doing? He's walking around. What is he doing?" [*laughs*] We worried he wasn't doing anything! So I went down to ask Steve what he was doing. I caught up with him and started shooting the shit with him. He was walking around the set and he had a little pocket notebook. He was flipping it open and he was just drawing stick people. The script was in his head and he was doing the shots. He was doing great prep! Once I saw that, I didn't need to ask him anything

Kenneth Welsh: Steve Gyllenhaal was a wonderful director. He was very sympathetic. Steve's creativity was in how he seemingly hadn't thought of anything until he was actually doing it. I believe he did a hell of a lot of homework. But he made it look like he was inventing on the spot. There was this one camera shot he did from above—Windom was in the kitchen or something. Steve said, "Well, just kind of improvise a little. Go on the script then go off the script." He was the kind of director who loved to give you the feeling of improvisation, although I felt that he totally knew what he was doing all the time. He's brilliant.

John Boylan: I didn't like the injection of [the Giant] into the [Roadhouse] scene. To a more learned person than I, it may have vast meanings. But to me, it was an intrusion into a scene. I felt that if it's capably acted and honest work—and the script is good enough—it would go by itself. That's my opinion.

Ted Raimi: What they were going to do was, after [my] character died on the show, Windom Earle was going to reincarnate me and bring me back; I'd be doing his bidding. Like a zombie! It was so crazy. I just respect that so much, that they weren't too worried about the falling ratings. It was a true artist's show.

There was sort of a snicker around the set—they knew it was ending. It was like a big wink to everyone on the set, "Well, we ain't got much time, so let's give it all we got." Like, "If we're going to go down, let's paint the ship orange and blue. Let's throw sparklers off the edges." I think that was the mood; I don't think it was really bleak.

Mark Frost: I don't know that [dugpa line]. Harley might have known about that. Now that I think about it, he did find a reference to the dugpas somewhere else.

Harley Peyton: It doesn't ring a bell at all. When we were working on that show we always had these weird reference books. I had a reference book for demons, and you'd go in there and take stuff out for episodes. Maybe I looked it up. I had this one reference book which was about gods and devils. In theory, I could have looked in there to get it. I must say, though, it doesn't ring a bell at all. So maybe Bob did it. I'll pass the buck to him. Dugpas—I've never heard of them! [*laughs*]

Robert Engels: That's got to be David. I wrote a lot of that Earle stuff. I remember the night we did that because Ken Welsh was wearing a rug. It sounds like it comes from one of those meditation books by Blavatsky. But if it's got a Tibetan connection it strikes me as something from David.

Episode 28 (Script number 2021; First televised June 10, 1991)

Guest Starring: Heather Graham (Annie Blackburne), David L. Lander (Tim Pinkle), Robyn Lively (Lana Budding), and Dan O'Herlihy (Andrew Packard)

Co-Starring: John Boylan (Mayor Dwayne Milford) and Jill Engels (Trudy)

Written by Barry Pullman; Directed by Tim Hunter; Edited by Paul Trejo

Sunday, March 26, 1989:

Act 1: Leo frees Briggs from his shackles and says, "Save Shelly." Earle returns to find Briggs gone. He smiles and his teeth and mouth are black, a demonic visage. Ben wants Audrey to enter the pageant for the good of the "Stop Ghostwood" campaign. Cooper believes that fear killed Josie. He thinks Bob was attracted to Josie's fear. Cooper wants to find his way into the Lodge before Earle does. Earle leaves Leo shackled and clutching a piece of twine in his mouth which is connected to a cage of spiders suspended over his head.

Act 2: Lana lures Dick into a storage room and seduces him. Annie and Cooper discuss the forest and, metaphorically, Annie's past. Nadine shows slides of her wrestling to Jacoby, Mike, Ed, Norma. Ed tells Nadine that he and Norma are getting married. Nadine says she and Mike are getting married, too. Hawk finds Briggs by the side of a road.

Act 3: Cooper and Truman tend to Briggs. Andrew shoots the box open to reveal a key. Cooper believes the petroglyph tells when and where a door will open. Briggs mutters, "Protect the queen" and "Fear and love open the doors." Cooper realizes that the queen must mean Miss Twin Peaks. Cooper and Truman hastily leave for the pageant.

Act 4: The pageant contestants dance. Bobby approaches Earle, who is dressed as the Log Lady. Earle smashes Bobby in the head with his log. Donna confronts Ben. Annie gives her speech and impresses the judges. Andy promises Lucy he will be a great father. Hayward announces the new Miss Twin Peaks—Annie Blackburne. Suddenly the lights go out. Smoke fills the hall. Nadine is hit on the head by a sandbag. Earle abducts Annie. Andy tells Cooper that the petroglyph is a map.

Unlike episode 27, the televised version of episode 28 follows closely to what was scripted. Directed by Tim Hunter, arguably the best director of *Twin Peaks* after David Lynch, episode 28 surprisingly lacks the visual flair of Hunter's previous *Twin Peaks* episodes. In an interview with *Film Quarterly* in 1993, Hunter explained his straightforward approach to this episode: "The show had fallen prey to a certain kind of directorial overachieving, so I decided to do the next-to-last-episode without any camera movement. . . . I tried to give David [Lynch] the cleanest possible episode to set up whatever extravagant finale he had in mind."[2]

Although Hunter refrained from camera movement, his artistic talents are evident in other ways, especially in how he chooses to frame certain scenes. Look, for example, at an early scene between Ben and Audrey. The camera is placed outside the room looking through a doorway at the characters; in effect, creating a double frame that distances the viewer from the action. This is a good example of what Hunter describes as a "clean" approach to the episode.

The episode begins in Windom Earle's cabin where Leo frees Major Briggs. Later, Earle returns to find Briggs gone. He tells Leo he has a surprise and holds up a bag with something moving inside. Earle then appears from behind the bag exhibiting a white face and blackened mouth—a visage not unlike brief glimpses of Leland and Laura in *Fire Walk With Me*. Did Hunter introduce this unusual element? Maybe. But David Lynch could certainly have had input to this episode. Hunter was friendly with Lynch, and since Lynch was preparing to direct the next episode the two may have briefly discussed some elements of this one.

For several episodes the writers appear to have forgotten that the series followed sequential days in the life of the town. Because of this oversight, storylines such as the Cooper/Annie romance, the Wheeler/Audrey romance, and the preparations for the Miss Twin Peaks pageant, were compressed into three- or four-day arcs. A better plan would have been to put several-day gaps between some of the episodes (as was done between episodes 16 and 17).

Also, because the story is supposed to take place in 1989, a problem occurs with the date of March 26, which was Easter Sunday. There are no references (even visual clues in the background) to connote the day, and it is highly unlikely that the pageant would ever be scheduled on Easter. At this point in the series, however, the calendar was probably the last thing on the minds of the producers, who were busy just trying to keep the show afloat. With Mark Frost gone for a good part of the second season (and Lynch offering brief comments over the phone), the rest of the production staff was tasked with running a complex mechanism on a strict deadline. Harley Peyton has compared running a TV series to "taking nine months to shoot a movie where you re-write the script every week."[3]

The scripts to *Twin Peaks were* being re-written and these revisions frequently resulted in inferior material. The Miss Twin Peaks "umbrella dance," for example, represents another of the series' lowest moments. And it seems to last forever. Almost as bad is the "talent" portion of the pageant, an embarrassing segment that further harmed the episode. The pageant ends with a couple of awkward speeches by Audrey and Annie. After Annie is crowned, however, the final few minutes improve dramatically. A strobe-light (foreshadowing the Red Room in the next episode) and sudden eruption of smoke create the chaos and diversion Earle needs in order to kidnap Annie. It's beautifully shot and directed.

Additional Notes:

Two themes involving fatherhood come to a head in this episode's fourth act. Donna concludes that Ben is her real father (she's curiously shocked and horrified, even though she's suspected it for a while), and Lucy "chooses" Andy as the father of her baby.

Earle sneaks into the Miss Twin Peaks pageant disguised as the Log Lady. His strategy is clear—once Miss Twin Peaks is crowned, he will knock Nadine unconscious during the pandemonium (he cannot risk getting into a tussle with her, considering how strong she is) and temporarily immobilize Cooper, thus clearing the way for his escape.

Because of the show's declining ratings, this episode and the finale were aired together as an ABC "Movie of the Week" on June 10, almost two months after episode 27. Today, the five-to-six million viewers the series had at its lowest point would qualify as a sizable audience, but in the early Nineties these were disastrous ratings for a series that had garnered as much publicity as *Twin Peaks*. Even worse, the ratings had significantly declined since the first seven episodes of the season (which had been averaging around nine million viewers). The final two episodes (with 6.7 million viewers) fared well compared to other late-season episodes, and ABC probably could have counted on a reliable base viewership of five million; but, again, at the time, this was hardly enough to secure the show's renewal.

The first draft of the screenplay to episode 28 was completed on February 5, 1991 and later revised five times. The final draft was completed on February 22, 1991.

Notable Deleted Scenes

Act 2: At the Roadhouse, Tim Pinkle coaches the pageant contestants in a dance rehearsal. The scene contains a number of minor lines cut from the televised version. Donna and Shelly make fun of Pinkle; Nadine expresses excitement at being on stage; Annie proclaims the rehearsal, "the weirdest thing I've ever seen;" and Lana says the pageant is the greatest thing that has ever happened to her. One other change was made: Much of the dialogue for Nadine and Lucy in the televised version was *originally* scripted for Audrey. (One cut line has Pinkle taking a particular liking to Audrey: "I think I can make dancers out of you. Especially you, Miss Horne.") Audrey's absence in the televised version could be due to scheduling conflicts, scene reshoots, etc. But it is also possible that Sherilyn Fenn did not want to participate in such an absurd, frivolous scene. (See Heather

Graham's comments below.) Fenn may have balked at the scene and refused to play it. (This may have been the case with Lara Flynn Boyle and Mädchen Amick, whose lines were also cut from the scene.)

Act 4: Cooper spies Windom Earle on a catwalk above the stage. He leaps onto the stage and climbs to the catwalk where he confronts his old partner. Cooper levels a gun at him, but Earle is unfazed. Smiling, he tells Cooper, "Our little game of four-dimensional chess has concluded. And once again, dear, dim, Dale—you have left your queen unprotected." He giggles and then continues, "Forgive me. I amuse myself. You see, twenty years ago I made a promise. And tonight I keep it . . . in the Black Lodge." Smoke bombs suddenly erupt and a strobe light begins flashing (a sequence used in the televised version). Earle grabs the confused Annie as Cooper leaps into the *melee*. The smoke clears, the lights come up, and Annie is gone.

The scripted version of the episode's finale is more rewarding than the televised version because it provides a confrontation between Cooper and Windom Earle. The scene on the catwalk, though brief, contains some strong Earle dialogue, and would likely have been quite intense, especially with Cooper training his gun on his arch-enemy. Unfortunately, this scene was not to be. For that matter, it may never have been shot. The staging of the televised version's final act suggests that Hunter may not have bothered choreographing the complex catwalk scene. Quite possibly, he assumed the inevitable confrontation between Cooper and Earle would come in the next episode. David Lynch, of course, radically re-wrote the script for that episode, removing a scripted showdown between the two foes. Because of that decision, Cooper and Earle never confront one another.

Unknowingly, Tim Hunter had the opportunity to film what would have been the only major face-to-face conflict between Dale Cooper and Windom Earle. Had he known what Lynch intended for the next episode, Hunter may have shot the final act of episode 28 differently.

Cast and Crew Comments

Kenneth Welsh: Tim [Hunter] showed you that he knows more about the technique of film-making than anybody else who worked on that show. He would talk about the kind of lens he wanted, the kind of shot he wanted. He talked the technical language of film-making with the Director of Photography, with the guys in the crew, and everybody else around him. He knows every single aspect of film-making. I think he knows everything about every film that anybody ever made! You could probably ask him about the lens that John Huston used in such-and-such a film and he would tell you! I remember somebody did that to him once. You could put Tim on the spot about anything that had to do with the craft of film-making, and he's your man. He knows it all.

He's a very precise director. He'll tell you exactly the shot you're in, exactly what kind of frame you're in, what kind of possibilities you had in terms of movement. He would give you the parameters, totally and exactly. It was really delightful to work with him.

Kimmy Robertson: Mark came up to me and said, "We want you to choreograph a dance for the next episode." I said, "*What??*" He said, "We know you dance so we want you to choreograph a dance." I choreographed that dance to "Mack the Knife" and it was supposed to be cheesy. But I don't think anybody got that. I mean, with the big jump with the split at the end? You can't get cheesier than that! Plus, I'm supposed to be pregnant? [*laughs*] I was approaching my character like Nadine. It was like my character had gone insane.

Heather Graham: I think that a couple of the actresses really were unhappy with [The Miss Twin Peaks Pageant] and didn't want to be in it. It seemed kind of silly, and I just thought of it as a funny thing. I didn't take it too seriously, I guess.

Charlotte Stewart: What I think happened was that David kind of dropped out of the show. David went off to do a bunch of other stuff. He had other people writing and other people directing and then, all of a sudden, all these other characters came in. We were asking, "Who is this? I don't even know who these people are." So a lot of characters went by the wayside for a while.

Harley Peyton: [The network] had no concept of what the show was about. But, frankly, they scheduled it so miserably that they can share as much blame as anybody for what happened to it. The fact of the matter is they had a show that probably had more favorable publicity than any television show in the ten years [previous]. Maybe twenty years? It had become a national thing. It was on the cover of *Time* magazine and all this stuff was occurring. Their first decision was to put it on Thursday at nine, which was almost the worst timeslot in television. The next thing was this cockamamie idea of putting it on Saturday night!

Chris Mulkey: All those guys at ABC got pissed at Lynch and started [messing] with his show and saying, "Hey, you have to do this and you have to do that." And that, ultimately, was the demise of it. They were threatened by the show and by David. And then what happened is, they started moving the show around—a show that was incredibly popular, incredibly great in every sense: look-wise, content-wise, acting-wise, the music, the writing, the whole deal. And they start moving this thing around and nobody could find it. A show that was on the cover of *Time* Magazine! [*laughs*] So now, no one can find it. All these people are [wondering], "Is it on Saturday, Thursday, Sunday? They moved it again. They pre-empted it!" Unbelievable.

211

Everett McGill: With so many characters, I'm sure that the story sessions with David and Mark had to be give-and-take. And I think ABC could have been searching for a way to get better ratings. Maybe they were asking for things. I know sometimes the sexual references were oblique and well-disguised. I remember that the staff at ABC in charge of censorship would send stuff back that was red-lined and it was so far off the mark! They were so suspicious that even the most innocent line would be red-lined! Simple things! Crazy things! They were all twisted! [*laughs*]

Harley Peyton: There are all sorts of reasons why I think [*Twin Peaks*] failed. Which is not to say that it was anything less than interesting. That whole second year was very difficult for a lot of reasons. One of them was that the relationship between Mark and David was becoming less and less fruitful. It wasn't that they were battling, it was [that they were going separate ways] and I was in the middle. During that time David and I had had a rather large falling out. It was kind of a big falling out.

It wasn't about anybody being a villain. There was a real interesting symbiosis going on in those first seven episodes [and] that sort of fell apart. Simply because Mark wanted to do what he was gonna do, and David was doing what he was doing. So it was a pretty delicate balance and the balance didn't hold. That's probably the most valid description of the process, as opposed to the little details along the way.

David Lynch: A lot of *Twin Peaks* got goofy in the second year. Everything is a mixture, and the balance is critical. And I thought *Twin Peaks* got pretty goofball, and that's not good.

THE LAST EPISODE

The first draft of the last episode of *Twin Peaks* (episode 29) was completed on February 14, 1991, almost the same date ABC Television pulled the show from the regular schedule and put it on a six-week hiatus. The series was barely hovering above cancellation and the mood around the set was tense. Despite the gloomy prospects for the series, Mark Frost designed the final episode to be filled with cliff-hangers (as he did in the first season finale). Two further drafts of the script were completed on February 25 and 28.

Four days later, on Monday, March 4, 1991, David Lynch began shooting the final episode of *Twin Peaks*. We don't know when Lynch first saw the script but it is safe to assume he saw it before March 4 and had time to plan his own vision of the work. With ABC seemingly abandoning the series, Lynch may have felt free to reimagine the episode according to instinct. He began improvising and altering the story while he shot. As a result, no script of the final, filmed version likely exists.

Episode 29 (Script number 2022; First televised June 10, 1991)

Starring: Sheryl Lee (Laura Palmer)

Guest Starring: Heather Graham (Annie Blackburne), James V. Scott (singer), and Dan O'Herlihy (Andrew Packard)

Co-Starring: Carel Struycken (the Giant), Hank Worden (Waiter), Ed Wright (Dell Mibbler), Michael J. Anderson (Man From Another Place), Frank Silva (Bob), Phoebe Augustine (Ronette Pulaski), Jan D'Arcy (Sylvia Horne), Andrea Hays (Heidi), Arvo O. Katajisto (Security Guard), and Brenda E. Mathers (Caroline)

Written by Mark Frost, Harley Peyton, Robert Engels, and David Lynch (uncredited); Directed by David Lynch; Edited by Toni Morgan

Sunday night, March 26, through Monday, March 27, 1989:

> Act 1: Cooper studies the petroglyph and says, "Fire walk with me." Truman remembers there is a circle of twelve sycamores called Glastonberry Grove. Hawk confirms he found the bloody rags and diary pages there after Laura was murdered. The Log Lady arrives with oil. She says her husband brought the oil back just before he died. At that time, her husband said, "This oil is an opening to a gateway." Cooper has Ronette Pulaski smell the oil and she gets scared. She remembers it from the night Laura Palmer was killed. Earle arrives at Glastonberry Grove with Annie. She acts as if hypnotized. Earle says, "I tell you they have not died. Their hands clasp—yours and mine." Earle and Annie part red curtains and disappear. Hayward treats Nadine and Mike while Ed and Norma flirt. Nadine regains her memory. Norma is stunned.

> Act 2: Ben and Eileen try to keep Donna from leaving home. Hayward strikes Ben, who hits his head against the fireplace. Cooper finds the grove and then passes through the red curtains and disappears. Truman sees him go. Cooper enters the Red Room and sees the Little Man from Another Place dancing as a man sings a song ("Sycamore Trees").

> Act 3: Ten hours after Cooper has disappeared, Truman and Andy sit and wait. Audrey arrives at the Twin Peaks Savings and Loan and chains herself to the vault to protest the bank's involvement with the Ghostwood Development Project. Pete and Andrew arrive and enter the vault. They pass Audrey. Andrew opens the deposit box. A bomb explodes and blows out the windows of the building. At the Double R. Bobby tells Shelly they should get married. Dr. Jacoby arrives with Sarah Palmer. Jacoby says Sarah has a message for Major Briggs. "Channeling" an unidentified persona, Sarah says, "I'm in the Black Lodge with Dale Cooper. I'm waiting for you."

Act 4: Cooper is seated across from the Little Man From Another Place who says, "When you see me again it won't be me." He tells Cooper he is in the "waiting room" and that some of Cooper's "friends are here." Laura Palmer walks in, snaps her fingers and tells Cooper she will see him again in 25 years. She says, "Meanwhile," and places her hands together strangely (one hand vertical and palm forward, the other hand horizontal and palm up). The old room service waiter from the Great Northern Hotel appears and makes a "whooping noise" and then says, "Hallelujah." The waiter offers Cooper coffee. He is replaced by the Giant who sits next to the Little Man and says, "One and the same." The Giant disappears and the Little Man rubs his hands together. Cooper tries his coffee but is puzzled as the liquid changes viscosity. The Little Man says, "Wow, Bob, wow," and "Fire walk with me." Cooper crosses the room and exits. Cooper finds himself in a hallway. He enters a second room but it is empty of occupants. Cooper turns back the way he came and enters another room. The doppelgänger of the Little Man says, "Wrong way." Cooper turns back. In the next room, the Little Man's doppelgänger introduces the Madeleine Ferguson doppelgänger as "another friend." She says, "Watch out for my cousin." Cooper turns back the way he came. The next room is empty. The Little Man appears and confirms his identity as a doppelgänger. Cooper sees the Laura Palmer doppelgänger. Her hands are in the same position as when he last saw Laura. She repeats the word, "Meanwhile." She screams and approaches Cooper. The image of Windom Earle's face flickers across hers. Cooper runs down the hall and into another room. He staggers, clutches his stomach, and sees blood. Cooper notices a bloody trail of his own footsteps behind him. He turns and follows them back. Cooper enters another room and is startled to see a vision of him lying beside Caroline Earle. He calls her name but the vision changes to one of Cooper lying beside Annie (who is wearing the same dress as Caroline). Annie sits up. Cooper yells, "Annie!" A dissolve edit transitions to a point-of-view shot of the connecting hallway. Cooper calls, "Annie!" again. Cooper enters another room and sees Annie who is replaced by Caroline Earle. Annie and Caroline exchange personalities as they speak with Cooper. Laura's doppelgänger appears and screams at Cooper. Earle appears and tells Cooper he will let Annie live in exchange for Cooper's soul. Cooper agrees. Earle stabs him. There is a shot of explosive fire and the sequence reverses: Earle "unstabs" Cooper. Bob appears beside an agonized Earle. He tells Earle to be quiet and then tells Cooper to go. He says that Earle is wrong: "He can't ask for your soul." Bob says he will take Earle's soul. Earle screams as a column of fire appears behind him. Bob pulls his arm away and Earle is silenced. Bob laughs. "Cooper" turns and walks away. After he leaves, another "Cooper" emerges from the red curtains. He crouches next to Bob and laughs, and then follows the first Cooper. The first Cooper encounters the Leland doppelgänger who says, "I did not kill anybody." The second Cooper enters the hall. The first Cooper exits as the second shares a laugh with Leland. The second Cooper gives an evil smile to the camera. The first Cooper runs and the second follows. The second Cooper overtakes the first and leaves the Red Room. Bob laughs at the camera. The second Cooper appears in Glastonberry Grove with Annie lying unconscious beside him. Truman notices their reappearance and rushes to their aid. At the Great Northern, the second Cooper awakens and says he needs to brush his teeth. He enters the bathroom, squeezes toothpaste into the sink and smashes his head into the mirror. Truman and Hayward are startled. Now bloody, the second Cooper sees the image of Bob staring back at him from the broken mirror. The second Cooper smiles, laughs, and says—again and again—"How's Annie?!"

David Lynch returns to direct *Twin Peaks* for the first time since episode 14 and creates a powerful installment, drawing superior performances from the entire cast (most noticeably MacLachlan, who at times during the second season lost sight of how to portray Cooper). Lynch creates riveting moments from the same story material that previous directors struggled to elevate. The quality of the finale is due to his ability to develop a uniquely *Twin Peaks* atmosphere for every scene. Perhaps no scene better epitomizes this than the return of Nadine's memory in act 1. The script is slightly humorous but also contains some harsh dialogue from Nadine when she regains her memory. Lynch removed this dialogue, transforming Nadine from aggressor to victim. As a result, Lynch's version takes on a tragic air as Norma and Ed come to realize their hopes of a life together have been dashed. Sadness pervades the scene, despite its inherent absurdity. Here, Lynch introduces tonal extremes much like he did in early episodes of the series. This kind of approach had been missing from *Twin Peaks* for many, many months.

Frost and Peyton were understandably dismayed at some of Lynch's script changes, not because the alterations weren't well-directed or that they didn't capture the proper *Peaks* ambiance, but because, according to Peyton, Lynch "wasn't following the linear narrative that we were trying to lay down."[1] Frost admitted that had the show been renewed for a third season, "We would have had a little bit of trouble getting back to where we needed to go."[2] Still, Lynch's efforts here result in an unforgettable episode.

The series finale is such a complex and unique episode that it demands a detailed, act-by-act analysis.

Act 1: After a brief scene with Lucy and Andy, Lynch sets the tone for the rest of the episode with a compelling scene at the sheriff's station. The Cooper-of-old seems to have returned, as MacLachlan's portrayal is precise and restrained. There's an inexplicable and quirky logic at play, too, as

Truman connects the twelve rainbow trout in the back of Pete's truck with the twelve trees at Glastonberry Grove. (One should have nothing to do with the other, but in the world of *Twin Peaks*, these connections have meaning.)

Lynch adds appearances by the Log Lady and Ronette Pulaski to restore a connection with earlier stories. Cooper's unusual deductive abilities are also back on display as he is able to predict The Log Lady's appearance one minute before she arrives. As with the best *Twin Peaks* episodes everything is heightened and slightly skewed: A subtle and mysterious atmosphere pervades every scene.

Kenneth Welsh once again excels at portraying the mad former agent, Windom Earle, perfectly treading the line between insanity and menace. Even with subpar scripts over the past several episodes, Welsh delivered a commanding performance. Here, he's even better. Lynch eliminates huge chunks of dialogue, preferring to find the one precise line to convey the threat of Windom Earle. This keeps the episode from relying on exposition and gives each line proportionally more weight and importance.

The first act ends with Nadine's recovery. This scene contains the first of many "head injuries" that become a recurring motif—both Nadine and Mike have their heads bandaged due to earlier wounds. (In a continuity error, however, Mike mentions being hit by a log during the scramble at the end of the Miss Twin Peaks contest, even though Bobby was attacked and hit by Earle. Lynch, who added the line, was likely more concerned about depicting matching head injuries than with continuity.)

Act 2: The melancholy atmosphere that ended act 1 continues at the beginning of act 2, which has Donna leaving home, suitcase in hand. Frustrated with the apparent lies that her family has been perpetuating, Donna refuses to listen either to her mother or to Ben. Dr. Hayward arrives and Ben asks him for forgiveness for telling the truth to Donna. Hayward insists that Ben leave, and Donna hugs Hayward, calling him "daddy" over and over. Sylvia Horne arrives and upbraids Ben. Just when it appears that there will be a happy ending, Hayward lunges toward Ben and slugs him. Ben hits the fireplace mantel and falls to the ground, leaving a bloody mark on his forehead—the second head injury of the episode. Hayward kneels in emotional agony, and the scene ends with everyone in turmoil. This scene is a perfect example of how Lynch draws extreme amounts of emotional energy from his performers.

Cooper finds his way into the Red Room in a manner that Lynch may not have preferred but could not avoid due to the dictates of the script. For Lynch, the Red Room was entered through dreams (such as in episode 2) and is a place that may not have a physical existence. But a major storyline in the second season—almost certainly Frost's creation—was establishing the Black Lodge as a physical place of evil. Because the second half of the second season was leading toward a showdown between Cooper and Earle in the Black Lodge, there was no practical way to avoid this new interpretation of the Lodge.

Act 3: Ten hours later, it's Monday morning in Twin Peaks, and Truman and Andy are still waiting for Cooper. Audrey chains herself to the Twin Peaks Savings and Loan, and Andrew and Pete arrive to see what's in Eckhardt's safety-deposit box. The box is rigged with a bomb and explodes. The episode never resolves who, if anyone, survives.

In a Double R scene created by Lynch, Bobby asks Shelly to marry him and then starts barking like a dog—a reminder of the way Bobby barked at James in the pilot. In another reference to the pilot, Heidi-the-waitress arrives late to work. As with the scorched engine oil and Ronette's appearance in act 1, Lynch is closing the circle, connecting the final episode with elements from the beginning of the series. In a particularly strange scene, Sarah Palmer—making her first appearance on the series in many episodes—arrives to deliver a message to Major Briggs: "I'm in the Black Lodge with Dale Cooper. I'm waiting for you." Whom she is channeling is unclear, though the scene harkens back to Sarah's "gifted" nature, alluded to in the first season. The scene suggests that, had the series returned for a third season, Briggs would have been instrumental in rescuing Cooper. (And Sarah Palmer may have had a role, too.)

With the status of all of the major characters updated, Lynch devotes the entire fourth act to his own version of Cooper's Black Lodge ordeal.

Act 4: Following this chapter, the essay, "Half the Man He Used to Be: Dale Cooper and the Final Episode of *Twin Peaks*," presents a detailed analysis of what happened in the final act of the final episode. The essay argues that Cooper enters the Red Room a whole person but, in the course of events, splits into two beings—a "good" Cooper and a "bad" Cooper. (This argument challenges the idea that Cooper was possessed by Bob at the end of the series.)

Additional Notes:

The episode ends with the third head injury, when Cooper smashes his head against the hotel's bathroom mirror.

Laura Palmer makes a final appearance during the end credits as a reflection in the coffee cup.

Ronette's name is spelled "Ronnette" in the end credits. It is always spelled with one "n" except in the pilot and in *The Secret Diary of Laura Palmer*.

There is some confusion on how to spell the word, Glastonberry. The script to episode 29 spells it as "Glastonbury" throughout. But some sources have it spelled as "Glastonberry." (These include *The Twin Peaks Access Guide to the Town* and the script to *Fire Walk With Me*.) "Glastonbury" is the original spelling in texts referencing King Arthur. "Glastonberry" may be considered a regional spelling of the locale.

This episode marks the first appearance of the Red Room singer and Dell Mibbler.

From Script to Screen: Changes to Episode 29

The final episode of *Twin Peaks* is unique because what appears on-screen is not what was originally scripted. David Lynch was unhappy with the tone and direction of the series during the second season and, when directing the final hour, chose to discard much of what had been scripted by Mark Frost, Harley Peyton, and Robert Engels. Instead, Lynch improvised a very different approach to the existing storylines. Stresses on-set were high and, shortly after the series ended, Mark Frost noted, "When he [Lynch] got on the set he . . . threw out the script, which didn't please me all that much. He would go off and do his own thing."[3]

It is impossible to simply list the scripted scenes that were deleted. Unlike the typical cuts a director or editor might make when assembling a final version, David Lynch essentially rewrote the episode, reimagining entire sequences (including practically all of act 4), severely cutting some scenes and actually *lengthening* others. Almost every line of dialogue was changed in some way. Sometimes the changes were minuscule: Nadine claims to be 37 in the script, but only 35 on the show. (This change was maybe not so miniscule: if Nadine and Ed had been married for 20 years, Nadine was fifteen years old at the time of the wedding!) In other cases, the changes were dramatic: the script portrays Earle as a comical jester with an evil underside, but in Lynch's version there's nothing funny about the character—he is evil, perverse, and very cruel.

What follows, then, is an analysis of the script with occasional comparison to the final version to see where and why Lynch made changes so as to realign *Twin Peaks* to his specific vision. The result, of course, was a transformation of the final episode of *Twin Peaks* into a brilliant and indelible work of art.

The scripted version follows a standard television format: four acts of roughly the same length, each ending at a critical moment in the plot or at a "cliff-hanging" moment of intensity

Act 1

The scripted version of act 1 is far more fast-paced than Lynch's. The original version sets up a very real "race against time" as Cooper and Truman attempt to catch Earle before he can enter Glastonberry Grove. Scenes alternate between Earle racing through the woods and Cooper hot on his trail. Cooper almost catches Earle, grabbing his leg as he enters a "hole is space" (the doorway to the Lodge). Truman watches as Cooper "disappears into the hole." The script makes it clear that Cooper's entry into the Black Lodge is inadvertently caused by Cooper's attempt to catch Earle. (Lynch's version treats Cooper's entry as voluntary and deliberate, almost as if Cooper deciphered a hidden code that allowed him access to the Lodge—a code that neither Truman nor Andy was able to fathom.)

Earlier, the urgency of the original act 1 is evident when Cooper and Truman attempt to decipher the Owl Cave Petroglyph at the police station. Cooper is described as "edgy," and the characters "hurry to the door" after recognizing Glastonberry Grove on the petroglyph. (Lynch's version is considerably slower; Cooper is calm, cool, and in command.)

Meanwhile, in the script, Earle takes Annie into the woods. His behavior is that of a demented jester. He leers at Annie and says, "Has anyone ever told you, you look a lot better than Leo Johnson? Smell better too." Later, as Earle and Annie are about to enter the Lodge, Earle imitates a railway conductor: "Toot, toot, 'board. . . . Get ready for first class despondency and madness." When Annie insists that Cooper will rescue her, Earle responds that Cooper is dead: "Good riddance to bad rubbish."

The first act of the script hints that the Black Lodge traps its victims by showing them what they want to see. Annie resists entry until she sees the image of a "kindly, smiling Mother Superior Nun" welcoming her. The nun turns into Earle, and then Annie is captured.

Meanwhile, Nadine regains her memory. The scripted dialogue is mostly humorous, with Nadine acting as the stereotypical nagging and bullying wife. She is shocked when she sees Mike and tells him to, "Take a hike, bozo." She then commands Ed to, "Put those muscles that aren't between your ears to work and give this punk the heave-ho."

Act 2

In the scripted version, act 2 begins just after Cooper has disappeared into the "hole in space." Sheriff Truman and Deputy Andy are left in the woods wondering what happened to Cooper. They find Earle's horse costume (used in an earlier episode to capture Major Briggs), and a note reading, "Don't look a gift horse in the mouth." The next scene shows Leo struggling with the spiders, attempting to call for help.

Ben Horne and Will Hayward have a confrontation at the Hayward house. Little was changed from the original version, although in the script Ben is pushed toward the front door by Dr. Hayward and then falls, hitting his head on a coffee table. Dr. Hayward kneels in grief, praying, "I'm sorry, Ben. My God, I'm sorry." The script leaves the possibility that Ben's fall was an accident.

In the script, act 2 ends as Cooper enters the Black Lodge, a place described as a dark, limitless space. Before he can even move he encounters The Guardian (presumably the hooded figure seen in past episodes).

Cooper asks, "Where am I?" and there is a flash of light. He finds himself standing in a "shabby motel" lobby. A motel clerk wearing "a bizarre orthopedic brace and a tracheotomy plug in his throat" appears and says, "Home." Cooper is suddenly depicted as a ten-year-old boy, then back to his adult self. The clerk is replaced by an old man, whom Cooper recognizes as his father (reinforcing the idea that the Black Lodge shows its victims who or what they want to see). The old man gives Cooper a key. Cooper takes it, there is another flash of white light, and act 2 ends.

Lynch totally abandoned the scripted version of the Black Lodge and any reference to Cooper's father. Lynch's version is mysterious and obscure, but familiar to both Cooper and the viewer. The scripted version, on the other hand, seemed to be directly connected with the recently published *Autobiography of Dale Cooper*. Later acts of the scripted version also make connections with this work.

Act 3

The scripted version of act 3 begins with Major Briggs and Hawk on their way to Earle's cabin. Briggs is able to remember the way back because the drug Earle gave him has "heightened his sense data." Briggs claims that his brain "is better able to interpret and define reality." The two men find Earle's cabin and burst in. Leo, desperately biting the string that holds the spiders above him, smiles and says, "Hi." The scene ends with an exterior shot of Earle's cabin and the sound of screaming and gunshots.

At the Twin Peaks Savings and Loan, Audrey arrives and chains herself to the vault in protest of the Ghostwood Development Project. In the script, she asks for a glass of water but never gets it. (Lynch's version, however, features the bank manager's long walk to the water cooler and back. Once again, Lynch seems to delight in extending scenes, sometimes to an excruciating degree.)

Pete and Andrew arrive after Audrey and make their way into the vault. In both versions the bomb in Thomas Eckhardt's safety deposit box explodes, leaving the fates of all the characters uncertain. There is little difference between the original and broadcast versions of these scenes.

The scripted version of act 3 returns to Andy and Truman who have a conversation about breakfast. Andy leaves to get the food, and Truman sees something happen in Glastonberry Grove: "The air seems to shift shape, move and alter." Truman moves closer and is startled to see a white shield and silver sword appear. Then, a woman wearing chainmail appears. She holds the sword out to Truman, but disappears before he can move.

The appearance of the woman in chainmail extends the King Arthur motif started earlier in the episode, when Cooper, Pete, and Truman discuss Glastonbury Grove (the burial place of King Arthur). Who this mysterious woman was and how her appearance would have affected future plotlines may never be known. It's possible that this woman represented what Truman most wanted to see, that she was the Black Lodge's attempt to lure him in. Such an interpretation is not necessarily far-fetched; Truman could envision himself as a defender of Twin Peaks, both as town sheriff and as leader of the Bookhouse Boys (a modern day Knights of the Roundtable?). Lynch opted to remove the entire scene, however, leaving students of the show to only speculate about where this unusual subplot may have eventually led.

The original script ends act 3 in the Black Lodge. Cooper finds himself in a "dark, ominous version of the Great Northern . . . where everything is in black and white." Cooper sees his doppelgänger approaching from down a long corridor. To his left he sees Earle in another corridor, beckoning to him. In a room to his right he sees Annie. Before he can get to her, however, a door slams in his face, and act 3 ends.

Clearly Lynch's version of the Black Lodge, and the events that transpire there, are dramatically different from the original script. Yet, despite these differences, it is interesting to note that Cooper's doppelgänger was a fundamental part of the original version and not something that Lynch invented solely on his own.

Act 4

Except for the final scene (and one brief interlude featuring Annie, Caroline, and Cooper) the Lynch version and scripted version of act 4 are completely different. The scripted version continues the conflict between Earle and Cooper. To escape his doppelgänger from act 3, Cooper chooses to confront Earle. The dialogue between the characters again makes references to material in the *Cooper Autobiography*. Earle asserts, "I know all about those three 'missing years,' Tibet, and your pathetic eager-beaver globetrotting quest for enlightenment."

Another white flash and Cooper comes upon Annie "at a sink in a small kitchen area." In this scene, Annie switches personalities between herself and Caroline (much the way Lynch actually filmed it). Earle forces Cooper to confront hard memories, as a flashback shows Earle being interrogated by police officers, then confessing to the murder of Caroline.

Cooper pleads for Annie's life, and Earle cuts a deal. The characters are suddenly in a doctor's office. A dentist's chair sits on an elevated rostrum; Annie is trapped in a medical supply cabinet. Earle explains that in order to become king, someone must voluntarily offer their soul to the Lodge. Cooper agrees to do it in exchange for Annie's life.

Earle sits in the dentist's chair as a man in a dentist's smock appears and approaches Cooper. Suddenly, Earle is trapped in the chair, and the "dentist" is revealed to be Bob. Bob claims that Earle broke the rules because "offered" souls don't count when someone is "coerced." But Bob wants Cooper's soul, anyway. Holding a "nasty, huge syringe" he approaches Cooper and tells him the syringe is for "extracting." Before he can use the syringe, however, a hand reaches out to stop him. It's Laura Palmer. A white light fills the room, and Cooper and Annie are back in Glastonberry Grove.

The final scene is almost exactly the same as Lynch's version: Cooper lies in bed at the Great Northern, gets up to brush his teeth, and as he looks in the mirror Bob is "staring back at him."

Act 4 of the scripted version focuses more on the conflict between Cooper and Earle as well as Cooper's past. Despite providing added background to these characters, however, the original version seems uninspired and sometimes ridiculous. Earle is portrayed, once again, as a jester, going as far as to dress in top hat and tails to sing snippets of "Anything Goes." Later, he sings "Back in the Saddle Again" while sitting in the dentist's chair.

The dentist scenario is also rather silly. Throughout the series Bob was portrayed as an evil force that had inhabited the woods surrounding Twin Peaks. His every appearance was shocking and frightening partly because of his mundane look: jacket, jeans, and work boots. Bob was powerful, yet simple; he could have been anyone (and, indeed, this is a fundamental facet of Bob's character). The scripted version of the final episode has Bob dressed as a dentist—an act which shatters the paradox of the character. A dentist is too easily perceived as a person of power and someone who can potentially inflict pain. Inexperienced horror writers and filmmakers often resort to making their "psychopaths" doctors and dentists because the audience already knows what it is like to feel vulnerable to these people. Making Bob a dentist was an easy way for Frost, Peyton, and Engels to portray him as more frightening but ultimately such a depiction would have betrayed the character.

The original version does make it clear that it is Cooper (possessed-by-Bob) who leaves the Black Lodge, and not the doppelgänger. In this version, Bob suffers defeat at the hands of Laura—he is unable to trap Cooper's soul in the Black Lodge. The episode implies that Bob settles for the next best thing: possession of Cooper in the real world.

***

One wonders what Lynch was thinking when he so dramatically altered the final episode of *Twin Peaks*. The fact that he changed the Hayward/Horne confrontation, diminished the role of Windom Earle, established a connection between the engine oil and the Black Lodge gateway, abandoned the Leo subplot, and threw out any information regarding Cooper's past, suggests that he no longer cared for the serial nature of the show and simply made the episode the way he wanted. On the other hand, because he introduced the Major Briggs/Sarah Palmer subplot, brought back Sylvia Horne, increased the role of Laura Palmer, and kept the Cooper-as-Bob cliffhanger, it's unlikely that he had abandoned *Twin Peaks* entirely. (Of course, the fact that he made *Fire Walk With Me* is confirmation of his continued interest.)

While David Lynch was an active presence during much of the second season, he was uncomfortable with certain plot developments and directions the show was taking. As a result, he changed the final script to his own liking, leaving the viewer with more questions than answers.

To be sure, Lynch's version of the episode is far more striking and powerful than the scripted version, but it suffers from a lack of connection to recent episodes of the series. Frost's version continued the established narrative, but it lacked the eerie, unsettling and subtle aspects of the earlier episodes, resulting in an almost farcical interpretation of the show.

Perhaps if Lynch and Frost—the two people who originally created *Twin Peaks*—had worked closely together on the final episode, the series would have ended in a more satisfying way. (Perhaps this is yet to come. Future collaboration between these two artists could return *Twin Peaks* to its former glory. Time will tell.)

Cast and Crew Comments

Mark Frost: I liked [the second season]. You know, we had such bad luck. ABC moved the show to Saturday nights at ten, which was a completely inexplicable decision. It was actually willfully destructive, I thought. And then we ran into a bunch of pre-emptions, which again was a network decision. It made the show very difficult to follow because it wasn't the kind of thing you could miss for a few weeks and pick up right where you left off.

I feel very good about it. I always intended the show to be very subversive to the medium. David didn't really have any experience with TV and didn't really have a philosophy about television. My sense, having worked in it as much as I have, was that it's generally a pretty destructive force in people's lives at a very subconscious level. It works as a sort of hypnotic tool for advertisers. It's like a perfect tool for mind control, if you think about it. So I wanted to create a show that undermined that and actually was a show that you had to pay attention to; that you couldn't watch passively, or else you wouldn't get it. And that was always my intention. And so I'm really glad, in a way, that the show didn't run on into a fifth and sixth season and become a stupid self-parody, which I think most shows tend to do after being on that long.

Harley Peyton: The episodes that David directed are all my favorites, so it's not personal. But, the last one—all the things he put in there were really things he culled from episodes he directed. Whether one feels he was successful or not, he still wasn't following the narrative. There's nothing wrong with that. He and Mark were this unbelievable team and I think they would both say it got real hard to hold that together.

Robert Engels: I knew working on the last episode that [what I wrote] was never how it was going to be. I had a blast writing the stuff because I thought, "This isn't going to happen." I think other members of the production were thinking, "Oh, he's just fucking with it!" [David] was the director and he was going to do it his way. He was having a ball.

There's a great part of *Twin Peaks* that's built on sort of an altered reality. That there is another reality just behind the reality that is happening. The exact same thing is happening two nanoseconds behind the thing that you're seeing. Or there is another one just in front of it that's exactly the same. For me, that means the Red Room is much more metaphysical. That would explain the two Coopers very easily—there is another Cooper just behind the other Cooper. It wasn't that we consciously put those things in the series, but David I talked about that. It was a cool thing to think about as you wrote. For me, to have those things in mind when you're dealing with the Red Room, it's harder to think it is a place of "consummate evil." Though, of course, it *is*. It is easier for me to think, "This is a place where spirits are fractured." Evil is there and good is there. If you could go into some metaphysical state that would explain reality, it would look like the Red Room. You could make that argument.

In many ways [The Red Room] is the perfect setting for what David loved about the series. There would be this place with beautiful music and love; it seems like a dream but there's some pretty fucked-up stuff going on there! Which is kind of like life.

David Lynch: You've got your own feel, and those feelings are based on ideas, and you just be true to those things and go along, and go in as deep as you can. The thing is that it's the experience of getting it to feel correct. That's the number one thing. It's a process, and there are good days and bad days, and there's next-door-to-hell-type days. But then there's these sublime, heavenly days. And it's this process.

Michael J. Anderson: [Cooper] was following Bob's footsteps in a tight circle. It was the fact that Agent Cooper was so close to Bob that it affected the whole quality of the waiting room. It made the waiting room into the Black Lodge.

The second time Cooper came into the Black Lodge he had already fallen in love with Laura Palmer. Now, he was on the track of who had killed her. But Agent Cooper is analogous to the detective within us all, which is the seeker. The seeker of the truth. By the time he came to the Black Lodge the second time he was seeking her killer. Not necessarily the person, but rather the state. If Laura Palmer was so beautiful, what could have killed her? That was what he was looking for.

Everett McGill: [In the scene with Nadine and Norma] there are a number of layers that are going on at the same time. That's another thing that David handles so well. I mean, there's a sense of loss. And these characters are so noble. They all have a cross to bear and they do it. They don't shirk their responsibilities. My responsibility to Nadine is a noble one. It's very complex because I owe her so much. She's so dedicated to me. But the sense of loss of a true love with Peggy—that's a powerful thing that I think David felt was important to have. Nadine, in her insanity—which was somewhat self-induced—would not be able to cope with the possibility of losing me. There's pain that we all have to live with and make adjustments for and find ways to wade through. David handles that so well.

Jack Nance: Lynch has this fixation with human infirmities or shortcomings. We all have them. If you are doing a scene with a close-up, and there's a make-up girl covering up a zit on your nose, David is going to get a tighter lens to make it look that big on the screen! [*laughs*]. It's not like a human freak show, but he will exaggerate human frailties and shortcomings.

David Lynch: Characters are in that world and they need to be a certain way. The world has got to be a certain way. It's a film world but it has its own reality and things have got to be a certain way. And that "certain way" comes from the ideas. You just stay true to the ideas as you translate them to some medium. If you stay true to them, you'll be OK.

Heather Graham: I remember certain segments where David would make it up. A couple of times when I was there he was listening to music on headphones and he'd be directing along to the music. I think there was one scene where a curtain opens, and he was directing the opening and closing of the curtain along to the music he was listening to on his headphones. [*laughs*] It was kind of fun, feeling that you weren't going along to some script, that whatever you were doing could be altered at any moment by the person who was the creator of the whole thing. It was exciting because you were there at the moment the idea was coming—[you] were part of whatever chemistry was there that day.

The thing that I really like about David Lynch's work—and being there as an actor—was that it didn't follow a linear story, but yet seemed to have an overall strong emotional impact. It seemed really raw and not follow any conventional pattern of storytelling.

Being there that day, what I sensed that they were going to do was add into the series that Cooper [had become] his evil side. That was going to be the continuing story. He had basically gone there to try to save me, and was now coming back into the world as this evil person. The rest of the story would now be: How could he stop himself? Which is really interesting. I think Kyle MacLachlan was very excited to be evil!

Michael J. Anderson: I think that my character actually declares that it was the waiting room. But the Black Lodge itself [could have been] covered in red curtains. I don't think there is a dramatic difference between the Black Lodge and the waiting room. As a matter of fact, I think one of the scary things about the Black Lodge and the waiting room is how slippery the edges are, so that you're not sure which direction you're going, or facing, or how far you've gone, or where you really are.

Kenneth Welsh: After all the build-up, I thought, "Oh my God. How is Windom finally going to confront his old enemy and partner?" But the way David handled it, we were fascinated by walking and talking backwards— the theatrics of it! Down there in that realm, no one has any control except the Lord of the Underworld himself—David! [*laughs*] So I just went along with it. I really had no image of how this would happen because we had no idea what the next script would be like. So I couldn't imagine how we would have this face-off. I knew it wouldn't be anything conventional. And then when Bob pulls that flame out of my head—well, you can't really beat that! [*laughs*] Because if you gotta go, that was one of the best ways.

Kimmy Robertson: We were on the set—David was really upset. But he had a hernia, so he was in pain. And I was crying because I was sad. I said, "I know we're never going to come back here. I just feel sad that this isn't going to happen anymore." He said, "Oh we'll be back, we'll be back."

Jack Nance: Pete wasn't as easy to kill as people thought. At the Saturday serials they'd show you an episode every week and there'd be a cliffhanger at the end. You were sure the hero was dead. There was no way he could escape from that. Then you'd go back to the next episode and see that at the last minute the hero dives out of the car or something like that. We wanted to try and do something like that.

Kenneth Welsh: I remember in that last episode, David loved to improvise—we did all that talking backwards and walking backward. He's so spontaneous, the man. He's beautiful to behold! I had this one scene where I stole the truck and captured the Queen—Annie—and I take her down to the red curtain. I had this big, long speech: "I'm Windom Earle, blah, blah, blah." David said, "No, Ken, I don't think we'll do that. Instead, tell you what: Get into the truck. You grab her by the hair, you smash her face against the back window, and you say, 'Oh look at that: Twelve

Rainbow trout!' All right, let's go! Good deal!" He's a funny guy. He'd go meditate in the trailer and drink six cups of coffee. He's a total yin-and-yang.

Heather Graham: I think when he slammed my head into the windshield I actually did hit it in one take—and I think they used that one! [*laughs*] I did hit it, but it didn't seriously injure me or anything, I just had contact with the window. We did that scene at night and it was in this dark, foresty area. Some of the other actors were there. I think one of the other actors was in his trailer and was yelling these lines from *Blue Velvet*! [*laughs*] It had this sense of being not totally normal. It was late at night, and it was getting later, and you entered into that sleep-but-still-awake feeling.

Don Davis: I'd been told [I'd play a part in Cooper's rescue]. That's all I know; that if it went on, my character would have become much more evident. I was so disappointed when it didn't go on. But whether or not that really would have happened is anybody's guess.

Richard Beymer: No one called my agent to say that was the last show. I don't know whether [Lynch] was improvising. There was a sense that this was it. There were always stories from the network, and we were always sort of borderline, and we knew the network was trying to get us off from the beginning. They didn't understand it, they didn't want it, and it was always the audience who kept bringing it back. But there was a sense that this wouldn't happen again—that we wouldn't be resurrected again.

Charlotte Stewart: It was winding down. I think that we were all aware that it was over. It had run its course. I was sad because I thought it could have been handled better. I thought that some of the really interesting characters in the piece—Grace [Zabriskie] and Catherine [Coulson]—could have been used more. They had such a good nucleus. Then, all of a sudden, all these new people came in. I didn't care to watch it anymore.

Richard Beymer: With David and that group, it was fun. The people were fun. We had a neat family for a while. We were having a good time together and no one was pulling rank. After a while it started happening, but there was a point there where we were all cooking together. How can you keep a family that big, and with that many actors, and with that many egos, together? The only one who could was David. And even he couldn't convince Kyle to do certain things.

Robert Engels: There was an article in the LA *Times* saying "*Twin Peaks* would have been better [if it had] stopped at seven episodes." The article said the consensus is we should have stopped. But that isn't the consensus. That's the consensus of people who don't want you to do a series like that anymore. It's not the consensus of people who worked on it. It's the consensus of people who didn't like it going on and on. It's like watching the *Twin Peaks* movie leak into a profit. What I'm getting at is, when people look at *Twin Peaks* they need to put it in a category so that they're comfortable with the fact that it is still unlike anything else. *Northern Exposure* copied/borrowed [from us] and still never got to where we were. They never got there. They pretended to be surreal but it wasn't surreal. And it wasn't elevated.

Harley Peyton: [*Twin Peaks*] was almost like seven years of television crammed into one year. With the big success, then this, then that, then [people] got tired of it. It was a real roller-coaster ride. It happened very quickly. But, again, it was based on this rare thing where these two guys came together and put something magical together. Maybe it's best that it didn't last. But I do think it could have gone on, just because those characters were so much fun. Why watch *Northern Exposure* when you can watch this? "I like these characters better—they're more fun." I think there were a lot of ways we could have gone that people would have followed. Mark and I both shared a weird sense of humor, so you put some of that stuff in. It wasn't like it was this dark, moody show all the time. There was a lot of weird stuff in there that I think was fun for television.

Catherine Coulson: There's always something new to discover in the stories. It makes you think about your own town where you live in a way that's unique. Other people have tried to do more unusual kinds of programming as a result of the phenomenon of *Twin Peaks*. Certainly there have been other shows that have taken chances with people's imaginations, like *The X-Files*. But I think television isn't going to change that much because it satisfies a certain kind of basic need for people's entertainment, where they don't have to be too challenged. I think *Twin Peaks* does stand alone in a sense, but I also think it impacted the way people allowed themselves to take chances in television.

James Marshall: Look at what came off of *Twin Peaks*—shows like *The X-Files*. Nobody could even admit [the influence] for five or ten years. They're just admitting it now. I knew it at the time. With Sherilyn Fenn, *Twin Peaks* came on and effortlessly destroyed every other show's sexuality. Then there was this sense of mystery that made everything else look like *The A-Team*.

Robert Engels: You are so aware, in television, of when your "pick-up" [network renewal] comes. If you haven't heard by a certain time then it's a bad sign. I don't think we ever got serious about that third year. I like the idea—which I think was Harley's—to jump ahead [ten years]. It was perfect for the problem that a number of the actors were not going to pass for high school students, and it was a very funny idea. I don't think we got any farther than saying the characters would be different. Like, Cooper would be running a pharmacy. Cooper stayed while other people left.

This whole idea of "ten years later" would have shown us whose life turned to shit. That's a cool way to do it. But the fact of the matter is, when you try to do that to a series the network just goes lunatic. The reality is ABC would not have allowed us to do that.

Harley Peyton: We were so desperately trying to hold it together that there was no thought of going on. It would have been fun, it would have been great. *Northern Exposure* proved you can stay on the air and do a show like that; [although] that show was a little gentler. But, no, I don't think there were ever any plans for a third season. Obviously there were a lot of places to go, given the way the show ends.

Robert Engels: I think David was uncomfortable with the ending. I also don't think David wanted to just wrap it up *to wrap it up*—to fade to black with all the loose ends tied-up was not a satisfactory ending.

Mark Frost: I had a vague blueprint [for a third season]. I had already seen the writing on the wall from ABC. And the way they treated us was so awful, that I wasn't going to put any more effort into the show, given the lack of encouragement we got from them.

We all felt like we should have done one more year. That would have been great, I think, because we would have had a chance to right the ship and bring a lot of things into focus and give people a good send-off. Beyond that, I don't know if I would have been interested in doing it. But that's the one regret I have, that we didn't have a chance to come back and maybe redeem the wayward nature of the last half of the second season.

I wasn't happy that *Fire Walk With Me* was the last view that people had of the show. I just didn't think it was a satisfying experience in terms of finishing the story and moving you ahead. "Never say never," I guess.

Harley Peyton: David was and is brilliant. and while I remain a diehard Frost partisan, it is also accurate to suggest that it was David's world, and we were just living in it. And I remain grateful for the opportunity.

Catherine Coulson: I don't think [David] was ever deciding purposefully to put final touches on anything. I don't think it's definitely a done deal. Who knows what the future will bring? I don't think that he thinks that way. He just stays open. Part of its long life may be that we didn't get too much of it. I think *Twin Peaks* stayed with us this long and stayed this popular with so many people and became such a frame of reference because we didn't get enough of it. We'll never get enough, but we'll always look back and get more out of it.

Mark Frost: Television doesn't do very well in remembering its own history. It's so much a creature of the moment. A lot of shows, as soon as they are a few years old, look like stale toast! I think the *Twin Peaks* episodes have held up pretty well.

David Lynch: It's a mystery, and I think people always love a mystery. But there are plenty of mysteries, and they don't travel like *Twin Peaks* travels, you know, to different cultures and different countries like that. And that is something that you just can't figure. I think it's a combo of things that just clicked, and it's like if you could say what those things were, and control things, you'd just do it time and time again. I love the doing, and what happens after that is anybody's guess.

Everything's relative! [*laughs*] There are some people that love it, and there are others that go about their lives not knowing the first thing about *Twin Peaks*.

HALF THE MAN HE USED TO BE:
DALE COOPER AND THE RED ROOM

"And now an ending. Where there was once one, there are now two."

—*The Log Lady, introduction to the last episode of* Twin Peaks

Introduction

Of all the episodes of *Twin Peaks* none is more baffling and beguiling than the series finale. Directed by David Lynch, the last episode of *Twin Peaks* features an extended foray into the Red Room (a.k.a. the Black Lodge) by Agent Dale Cooper. Cooper enters the Red Room to rescue the woman he loves, Annie Blackburne, from Cooper's nemesis, Windom Earle. Once inside, Cooper is subject to the unpredictable laws of the Red Room. Wandering back and forth between nearly identical "red rooms," Cooper encounters various denizens of this other-worldly place, including the Little Man From Another Place, the Great Northern room service waiter, the Giant, Laura Palmer (and doppelgänger), the doppelgängers of Madeleine Ferguson, Leland Palmer and Caroline Earle, as well as the malevolent Bob and, finally, Cooper's own evil twin.

Cooper finds Annie but whether he "rescues" her or not is uncertain; Windom Earle is suddenly and effortlessly dispatched by Bob and Cooper finds himself fleeing the Red Room with his evil side in close pursuit. In the end it seems that Cooper has escaped (along with an unconscious Annie), but the final scene reveals a dreadful image: Cooper, after deliberately smashing his head into a bathroom mirror, sees the reflection of Bob looking back at him.

What happened in this episode? The extended final act is so perplexing and complex that meaningful answers are hard to develop. The task of deciphering the episode is made more complicated by the fact that David Lynch practically re-wrote the entire final act while on set.

Lynch's version is a radical alteration of the original script and seemingly complicates some of the established tenets of the series. Up until now, the demonic presence of Bob took possession of a whole person, forcing that person to commit vile acts. But here, in this final episode, an evil Cooper *coexists* with Bob in the Red Room. The good Cooper apparently flees from his evil half and *someone* emerges back into the real world. But who? Cooper-possessed-by Bob? Cooper's doppelgänger (who may *be* Bob)? Or someone (or something) else?

For a while no one could be sure of an answer. A year after the final episode aired, the feature film, *Fire Walk With Me*, provided the most telling clue. In it, Annie Blackburne appears to Laura Palmer and says, "The good Dale is in the Lodge and he can't leave." Then, in 1997, David Lynch offered an uncharacteristically explicit comment about the series finale: "Coop wasn't occupied by Bob. Part of him was. There are two Coops in there, and the one that came out was, you know, with Bob." [1]

So the obvious question was answered: The evil Cooper, occupied by (or in league with) Bob, came out of the Red Room while the good Cooper was trapped.

Despite knowing this answer, however, we are still left with the puzzles of the final episode and the apparently contradictory denouement they provide the series. We may know how the episode ends but it is hard to know what transpired in the Red Room to lead to that ending. The episode's final sequence is comprised of variably startling and confusing scenes. But do they make sense as a whole? Do they add up to anything? And if they do, does the *Twin Peaks* finale fit—structurally and thematically—with the rest of the series?

David Lynch is a deliberate filmmaker who, although sometimes prone to improvisation, is specific about the way he shoots and edits scenes. No matter how convoluted or contradictory Lynch's films appear, they are carefully crafted to convey particular information. So it is with the final fifteen minutes of *Twin Peaks*. As this essay shows, the complex, dream-like presentation of the final act of the last episode of *Twin Peaks* has specific and decipherable meaning.

Dale Cooper's Fading Light

The last episode of *Twin Peaks* was originally meant to be a climactic chapter in the ongoing Windom Earle/Dale Cooper conflict. The story in previous episodes revealed how Windom Earle—Dale Cooper's former partner and mentor—had gone insane as was ostensibly seeking revenge on Cooper because of an affair Cooper had had with Earle's wife, Caroline. But Earle was after more. He knew about a place called the Black Lodge ("a secret place of great power, where the cultivation of evil proceeds in exponential fashion") and had discovered that the entrance to the Black Lodge was in Twin Peaks. Earle sought to tap the power of the Black Lodge and use it to exact revenge on Cooper.

The script for the final episode describes what happens when Earle and Cooper enter the Black Lodge: Earle takes Annie Blackburne captive and forces her through the doorway to the Lodge—a "hole in space." Cooper jumps into the hole behind them. Inside, Cooper searches for Earle and encounters various apparitions, including a "Guardian," Cooper's own father, and a "black-eyed double" of himself. Finally, Cooper finds Earle in a black-and-white version of the Great Northern. Earle floats above Cooper and taunts him. He shocks him with a remote control and tells Cooper he is "useful for FUN." Pressing the button again, Earle and Cooper appear in the Red Room. Cooper asks where he is. A sign falls into view reading, "PITTSBURGH, STUPID." Cooper sees Caroline in a kitchen. She turns into Annie, then back into Caroline. Frustrated by these games, Cooper demands to know what Earle wants. Earle appears in "top hat and tails" singing "*Anything Goes*" to big band music. He then appears behind Annie brandishing a "thin, gleaming medical instrument." A flashback shows Earle admitting to police that he stabbed Caroline and Cooper. Cooper sees a vision of his black-eyed double lying next to Annie. The double opens its lifeless eyes. Cooper again cries to Earle, "Tell me what you want!" Earle tells Cooper he needs him to volunteer for something. They enter a "throne room"—a doctor's office with a dentist chair. Annie is trapped behind the glass door of a medical supply cabinet. Earle tells Cooper he will release Annie in exchange for Cooper's soul. Cooper agrees. Earle happily sits in the dentist chair and sings, "*Back in the Saddle Again*." Bob appears in a dentist uniform and traps Earle in the chair. He promises to punish Earle, and then attempts to extract Cooper's soul with a giant syringe. Laura Palmer suddenly appears and stops Bob. There is a great noise and a blinding light and Cooper and Annie return to Glastonberry Grove. Later, Cooper wakes in his hotel room, enters his bathroom and sees the face of Bob staring back.

David Lynch had little to do with the Black Lodge storyline and was dismayed by the events he found depicted in the final script. The story violated his perception of what *Twin Peaks* was about. Specifically, Lynch was unhappy with the way events in the Red Room/Black Lodge were portrayed and, perhaps more importantly, the way the once resonant character of Dale Cooper had been reduced to a mere object of the plot.

From the start of the series, Dale Cooper shined brightly as a singular creation. He was a radiant, utterly unique individual who subverted the norms of the traditional fictional detective. More than a mere FBI agent, Cooper was that rare type of character whose complex, sometimes contradictory characteristics elevated him beyond the trappings of the narrative. Cooper *by himself* was fascinating. Had he been separated from the "plot" he would still have been interesting to watch. Cooper was essentially an autonomous being, a rounded character who could not be summed up with convenient labels such as "detective" or "crime-fighter."

During the first half of *Twin Peaks* David Lynch ensured that Cooper remained distinct. (Lynch directed seven of the first 17 hours of the series.) He intimately understood the character whom he considered "fully formed." Lynch also felt that actor Kyle MacLachlan was "born for the role." Portraying Cooper was a delicate thing, however, and Lynch knew that MacLachlan required a particular kind of direction to fully embody the character: "I'm not saying that he wasn't Cooper when other people directed him—but sometimes I would have to kick him up to another gear. It's right inside him but he might get laid back . . . . and not have the energy, alertness and spark that Cooper has."[2]

Lacking a dominant, driving storyline, *Twin Peaks* lost some if its edgy atmosphere during the second half of the second season. At times the series even descended into absurd camp and banal melodrama. Along the way, the character of Dale Cooper lost some resonance. Cooper became encumbered by the weight of the story, his behavior dictated by exigencies of plot. Although Cooper remained vibrant and engaging, the qualities that earlier made him so unique and unusual became diluted.

Despite a presence on the set, Lynch could not alter the way Cooper was portrayed: "In the second season, Cooper ceased to be 100 percent Cooperesque for me . . . . He's got to be specific. Cooper is a certain way. It's necessary."[3] Lynch's view of Cooper—the *necessity* for the character to propel the narrative—was missing in the script for the final episode. Where Cooper was once a "fully formed" character existing independent of plot, his identity in the second season was subject to his various roles in the story. Cooper was "defined" through his interactions with others—through Annie he became the love-struck paramour willing to sacrifice himself; through Truman he became the "good buddy" ready to serve as a sheriff's deputy; and through Windom Earle he became a defender of the community, responding to Earle's evil schemes.

Cooper could only *react* in these stories; his quest for enlightenment and his search for inner truth were no longer facets of his character. A once luminous presence in the narrative, Cooper, by the season finale, had been reduced to mere reflection.

Lynch's Revision

For David Lynch the important conflicts in *Twin Peaks* were never about heroes versus villains, the kind of plots found in traditional narratives. Rather, Lynch was interested in the internal conflict—how a protagonist had to struggle with him- or herself. Lynch was (and is) intrigued with how "good" and "bad" can coexist within anyone. That's what the story of Laura Palmer was all about—her dual nature, her contradictory behavior, her struggle to find a balance between ruinous self-indulgence (drugs and illicit sex) and over-charitable benevolence (participating in Meals on Wheels, tutoring the handicapped, etc.).[4]

When Lynch was presented with a final episode of *Twin Peaks* that described Dale Cooper being manipulated by an external force (i.e., Windom Earle), he refused to accept it. This conflict was, according to Lynch, "completely and totally wrong." For Lynch, the only satisfying and interesting conflict was the one between Cooper and himself. Therefore, Lynch re-wrote and reoriented the final act of *Twin Peaks* so that Cooper would confront the darker aspects of his own psyche. Along the way, Lynch discarded almost every scene that showed Windom Earle toying with or manipulating Cooper. Because the Red Room had always been a place of psychological reflection, Cooper would face manifestations of his fears and doubts. In effect, Lynch set about constructing a finale that would, as Lynch described it, set Cooper "up against himself."[5]

Lynch also recognized the importance of the cliffhanger convention of serial television. In the script, the entire Cooper/Black Lodge plotline leads toward that final moment of shock: The face of Bob staring at Cooper from the mirror. Lynch understood that the show needed to end with that indelible image. He therefore constructed the finale in such a way as to deliver that ending while still being true to what he believed was the essence of *Twin Peaks* (the internal struggle, the nature of duality, the quest for psychological balance).

Up until now access to the Red Room had been solely through dreams, underscoring the Red Room's nature as a reflection of the subconscious. But in the final episode Cooper was *physically* entering the Red Room, a circumstance Lynch probably regarded as ill-conceived. For Lynch, the Red Room had been a place of free association and infinite possibility—a place unbounded by the laws of physical reality. If the real-world entity known as Dale Cooper was entering a realm of the mind, Lynch knew that such physical entry must result in physical consequence. The original script posits a supernatural (and possibly psychological) consequence—Bob's "possession" of Cooper. Lynch radically changed the outcome so that Dale Cooper *divides* into two physical beings: a "good" Cooper and a "bad" Cooper. Once divided, only one flesh-and-blood entity could return to the real world.

In order to fulfill the episode's cliffhanger ending Lynch had the bad Cooper escape, leaving the good Cooper trapped. What's more, the bad Cooper was not possessed by Bob but in alliance with him. He and Bob have the same agenda. This cliffhanger is essentially the same as what Frost, Peyton and Engels intended in the script—release of the chaotic and dangerous potential of "Bob" into Twin Peaks.

Through David Lynch's careful and meticulous craftsmanship the *Twin Peaks* finale evolved into one of the most hypnotic and unforgettable episodes of the entire series. To Lynch's credit he never compromised on his vision, producing an hour of television that both bewildered and bewitched. Even today it remains unlike anything else ever broadcast on television.

But the brilliant finale of *Twin Peaks* is often overlooked. The series is remembered for its earlier episodes—those shows which captured the public's imagination and which were embraced by critics and fans alike. To be sure, the first half of *Twin Peaks* represented a captivating new direction for television, but the series finale served as both a reminder of *Twin Peaks'* former brilliance and as an example of the show's endless ability to surprise. The Lynch-directed finale is a masterpiece and deserves wider attention.

Split Personality

In order to understand what Lynch was doing with the Red Room sequence in the *Twin Peaks* finale we need to analyze the sequence scene-by-scene. This analysis will show how the sequence was designed to pit Cooper against himself, how Cooper's fears and self-doubts were manifested in the Red Room, and how these fears and doubts upset the psychological balance between the "good" and "bad" aspects of Cooper's personality, resulting in a physical division of Cooper into two separate entities.

Although this analysis attempts to reconcile many of the confusing images and incidents in the Red Room sequence it does not explain everything that Lynch creates. There are elements of the sequence that continue to mystify. Rather than force an interpretation onto every confusing element it is better to acknowledge those pieces of the sequence that remain ambiguous or contradictory.

Prologue

When Cooper first enters the Red Room he sees the Little Man from Another Place while a singer (blues vocalist, Jimmy Scott) performs the song, "Sycamore Trees." Not surprisingly, there's "always music in the air" as the Little Man described during Cooper's first dream of the Red Room (episode 2).

The Sycamore Trees scene occurs early in the episode and serves primarily as a prologue and introduction to the final sequence. This scene is not part of the final segment; it is separated from it by other scenes and commercial breaks. Although the scene may be important it was not essential to the last act, which Lynch designed to be one continuous sequence, uninterrupted by commercial breaks. In fact, Lynch structured the entire final episode to allow for a lengthy final act. Where most commercial breaks occur roughly every 12 minutes in hour-long dramas, Lynch "front-loaded" this episode with commercial breaks, which occurred less than every ten minutes. With all the commercials "out of the way" Lynch had more time (over 18 minutes) to devote to the final segment and had the freedom to design it as a miniature film, complete with beginning, middle, and end.

The Waiting Room

The final act begins with Cooper seated across from the Little Man From Another Place. The Little Man says, "When you see me again it won't be me." He then explains that Cooper is in the "waiting room" and that some of Cooper's "friends are here." Laura Palmer appears and tells Cooper she will see him again in 25 years. Then, cryptically, she says, "Meanwhile," and places her hands together strangely (one hand vertical and palm forward, the other hand horizontal and palm up). It is impossible to know what Laura's hand signal means. Knowing the eventual outcome of the sequence, however, leads one to believe she is signaling imbalance and division.

The Little Man and Laura could be telling Cooper similar things: that Cooper won't be seeing either of them again—at least not for a while—despite the fact that he will shortly encounter aspects of both. They seem to be preparing him for the concept of the "double self." (In fact, the Little Man's double will explicitly state, "doppelgänger" in a later encounter.)

After Laura delivers her message she disappears. The old room service waiter from the Great Northern Hotel appears and says, "Hallelujah." Although no evidence suggests the waiter has died, his presence in the Red Room suggests he probably has. (With the exception of Earle and Annie, the only other people Cooper encounters are deceased.) The waiter rises from his seat next to the Little Man and offers Cooper coffee. He is replaced by the Giant who returns to sit next to the Little Man and says, "One and the same." Whether the Giant is referring to himself and the waiter or himself and the Little Man is unclear. Because the Giant *takes the place* of the old waiter and returns to the seat he just vacated (and because the Giant appeared in conjunction with the old waiter in the real world) we assume he is referring to himself and the old waiter. Still, the Giant is sitting next to the Little Man as he speaks. The possibility exists that he and the Little Man are "one and the same." If so, we don't know the significance of this revelation.

The Giant disappears and the Little Man rubs his hands together. Cooper tries his coffee but is puzzled as the liquid constantly changes viscosity. The Little Man offer a few more cryptic comments: "Wow, Bob, wow," and "Fire walk with me." These lines are followed by an image of explosive fire, the sound of a scream and a strobe-light effect. The Little Man disappears and Cooper crosses the room and exits.

As the Little Man explains, the first room is a "waiting room." It is a place where Cooper prepares for his impending journey. None of the other rooms he visits (including what appears to be a return to the first room) has the same function. The waiting room is a place of relative safety for

Cooper. The entities who appear to him are autonomous beings (as opposed to reflections of his psyche) and are either benevolent (the Giant, the old waiter, possibly Laura Palmer) or at least neutral (The Little Man and, again, Laura Palmer). None is a white-eyed doppelgänger. These entities appear to offer clues and direction to Cooper for his upcoming journey. As we said, the Little Man and Laura hint at the idea of doppelgängers and opposite selves. Similarly, the Giant's comments about being "one and the same" indicate that two entities can be one, that they can occupy the same space. In fact, they are describing Cooper's current condition—he is a whole Cooper, comprised of both a good self and a bad self. Although separate selves can exist, this is not yet the case for Cooper; he is still complete. But the cryptic comments from the Little Man, Laura and the Giant all serve to warn Cooper that division can occur—that, in fact, the balance Cooper maintains between his good and bad sides will be threatened.[6]

Whether Cooper understands this or not is uncertain, so the Little Man offers more warning and advice. "Wow, Bob, wow" is almost certainly a warning: Bob exists and his presence is alarming. In the *Twin Peaks* narrative Bob functions both as a tangible antagonist and as a metaphor for an individual's evil side, his dark impulses. The Little Man is telling Cooper that he will confront Bob—both figuratively and literally. Finally, the Little Man exclaims, "Fire walk with me." In the context of Cooper's current situation the phrase implies balance. The dark side (represented by fire) must be kept in check; it cannot be allowed to dominate, to race forward and overwhelm the psyche. The dark side must be accepted and controlled, to be made to "walk" beside the good self in order to maintain balance. When the Little Man says, "Fire walk with me," there is an accompanying shot of explosive flame, an image of the uncontrollable fury of fire and a visual metaphor for the chaotic nature of the bad side. After the fire image appears, a strobe light flashes—another visual signal of the balance between good and bad.

Once Cooper has been given his clues and warnings he chooses to walk across the room and begin his exploration (and search for Annie). He is about to embark upon a journey that will lead him back and forth between similar red rooms—rooms that will symbolize the dual halves of his mind. His movement back and forth will signify the oscillating condition of his psyche as his good and bad sides start to seesaw out of control.

A Cycle of Six Rooms

After Cooper exits the waiting room he enters a realm dictated (in part) by his own subconscious. The Red Room(s) may be another plane of existence—a palpable, otherworldly dimension—but it is also a province of the mind. As such, it takes on distinct characteristics for each visitor. According to Lynch, "It changes depending on whoever walks into it."[7]

These "changes" result from the unique mind of each visitor as their fears, doubts and beliefs find manifestation in distinct ways.

Cooper's visit to the Red Room challenges the balance between his opposite selves. As soon as Cooper leaves the waiting room imbalance begins, but it begins slowly. Upon exiting the room, Cooper finds himself in a hallway. An armless statue stands at the end of the passage and it will remain there during Cooper's first few traversals between rooms. The statue could be viewed as a symbol of solidity, an indication that Cooper's psyche remains anchored to a single physical body.

The second room Cooper enters looks the same as the first (the waiting room) but is empty of occupants. Cooper returns back the way he came and into what appears to be the first room, but is not. Here, the doppelgänger of the Little Man (though not identified as such) tells him, "Wrong way." Cooper turns back. But does Cooper turn the "right" way? Or is the Little Man's statement actually a signal from Cooper's subconscious that his mere presence in the Red Room is wrong—that no matter which direction he takes it will lead to disaster?

Cooper has little choice but to turn back again and repeat the pattern. Each "back and forth" cycle he undertakes, however, will become "psychologically" more intense.

In the next room the Little Man's doppelgänger introduces the Madeleine Ferguson doppelgänger as "another friend."[8] She warns Cooper to "watch out" for her cousin.

Maddy's is the first doppelgänger of a "real" person that Cooper meets. She and the subsequent doppelgängers are all aspects of people whose deaths are connected to Cooper in some way. Cooper investigated the murders of both Laura and Maddy and he was present as Leland died, offering absolution and guidance to his departing soul. He was also with Caroline Earle when she was killed and, due to his lack of vigilance, is partially responsible for her death. These half-souls haunt Cooper on his passage deeper into the Red Room, reminding him of his failure to prevent their deaths and, of course, alerting him to the real possibility of psychological division. Interestingly, all the doppelgängers Cooper encounters are impotent apparitions incapable of inflicting any physical harm. Their psychological and emotional threat, however, is considerable.

Cooper turns, yet again, back the way he came. The next room is empty and Cooper walks in. The Little Man appears and confirms his identity as a doppelgänger. Cooper suddenly sees Laura Palmer. Her hands are in the same position as he last saw her and she repeats the word, "Meanwhile." But this is not the same Laura he previously encountered; she, too, is a doppelgänger. She screams in a horrific way—a mix of terror and anger. As she approaches Cooper the image of Windom Earle's face flickers across her own. Cooper reacts with fear and turns to run.

Lynch's choice to superimpose Windom Earle's face over Laura's reinforces the idea that Earle is merely an observer in Cooper's psychological drama, and not an active participant. Earle is not manipulating these events (unlike in the original script) but he is still a gleeful spectator, reveling in Cooper's trauma.

Cooper's fear and his retreat from Laura mark a severe break in his psyche. He is still whole—but barely. Shaken by the ominous and startling specters of the Red Room Cooper is now vulnerable to division. Only a few critical incidents are necessary to sever his fluctuating good and bad sides.

Cooper flees down the hall and into another room. He begins to stagger and, clutching his stomach, sees blood oozing between his fingers. He is wounded—the memory of the stabbing he suffered at Windom Earle's hands. The flickering image of Earle coupled with Cooper's own fear may have triggered that memory. Cooper notices a bloody trail of his own footsteps behind him. He turns and follows them back. When he exits into the hallway the armless statue is gone (and it will not be seen again in any subsequent traversals of the hall). The missing statue signals Cooper's fading solidity and that his physical body is irreparably damaged. Although still "whole" at this point, Cooper's body has been violated—the first physical damage he's suffered in this realm of the mind. His division is now inevitable.

Weakened in both mind and body Cooper enters another room and is startled to see a vision of himself lying beside Caroline Earle. He calls her name but the vision changes to one of Cooper lying beside Annie (who is wearing the same dress as Caroline). Annie sits up with a vacant, searching look on her face. Cooper cries, "Annie!" But his fear for Annie's safety and his doubt that he can save her from the same fate that befell Caroline overwhelm his psyche. And here, now, he literally comes apart.

It is Cooper's own fear and uncertainty that lead to his downfall. No outside force can be blamed. In the unstable realm of the Red Room where "anything can happen"[9] Cooper fails to master his own weaknesses. This failure makes Cooper susceptible to the dangerous and darker aspects of subconscious. He pays a profound price—the imbalance in his psyche results in his division into two physical beings.

Lynch's cinematic construction of the scene employs visual and auditory techniques to convey a sense transformation without explicitly showing Cooper's division. What's more, Cooper's fearful reaction to seeing Annie on the floor occurs at the midpoint of the episode's final act, effectively splitting the sequence into two halves (the first part featuring a whole Cooper, the second featuring a divided Cooper). When Cooper reacts to seeing Annie he is illuminated by a strobe light, signifying his duality. When the camera cuts back to the floor, the prone Cooper and Annie are gone. The shot is accompanied by a sound effect, a low humming noise—the

241

sound of something heavy passing. For the first time, Lynch uses a dissolve edit to transition scenes: the empty, flashing floor fades into a point-of-view shot of the connecting hallway. The dissolve edit visually conveys the dissolution of Cooper's mind. A new, "half-consciousness" comes into being as the point-of-view moves down the hall. The frantic voice of Cooper calling, "Annie!" accompanies the shot, implying this is Cooper's point-of-view. But Cooper's voice calms as the "camera" approaches the next room; his frantic cries of "Annie!" change to placid inquiry ("Annie?") then to calm repetition of her name ("Annie"). As Cooper divides, the emotional tone of his voice changes. The next shot we see is "Cooper" entering another room. But this is not the Cooper we last saw. This is half-of-Cooper—the good self, separated from the bad.

The Final Room

The good Cooper enters the last room of the journey. Now unencumbered by the weaker and dangerous aspects of his personality, the good Cooper moves immediately to his goal—the rescue of Annie from Windom Earle. Cooper sees Annie as soon as he enters but, unbeknownst to him, she is under a hypnotic spell.

Annie is a passive presence in the Red Room; she behaves as if her mind has been turned off. There are two possible explanations for this. One may be that because Annie was forced to enter the Red Room (as a captive of Windom Earle) she becomes psychologically mute and therefore immune to the effects of the place. Or, second, the prayers she chants before being pulled into Glastonberry Grove are answered and she is granted protection by a higher power (just as Ronette Pulaski was saved by prayer in *Fire Walk With Me*). Either way, Lynch deliberately positions Annie as a passive occupant. He knew she had to be "cancelled out" of the equation in order for him to focus on Cooper's ordeal. If Annie were an active and willful presence in the Red Room then she, too, would have had to face aspects of her inner self. Rather than over-complicate the sequence, Lynch deliberately neutralizes Annie.

That doesn't explain Windom Earle, however, an active and willful entrant into the Red Room. Before this episode, the storyline had employed Earle as an elementary plot device—a basic antagonist in conflict with Dale Cooper. The story had failed to elevate Earle beyond cliché—he was a power-hungry madman hatching an evil scheme. To Lynch, then, Earle was already imbalanced—so severely that he was powerless against the psychologically-reflective forces of the Red Room. Lynch's view of Earle as unsubtle and uninteresting may have led him to eliminate the character from the story after only the briefest of confrontations with Cooper.

The good Cooper sees Annie as soon as he enters the room. But Annie's identity becomes conflated with Caroline Earle's. She and Caroline exchange personalities as they speak with Cooper:

ANNIE:	Dale. I saw the face of the man who killed me.
COOPER:	Annie. The face of the man who killed you?
ANNIE:	It was my husband.
COOPER:	Annie.
ANNIE:	Who's Annie? It's me.
CAROLINE:	It's me. It's me.
COOPER:	Caroline.
ANNIE:	You must be mistaken. I'm alive.

At the end of this conversation Laura's doppelgänger again violently screams at "Cooper." Unlike his last encounter with her, however, "Cooper" is not scared, merely startled. The same holds true for his reactions during his conversation with Annie/Caroline; the good Cooper is not frightened by Annie's declaration that she has been killed (unlike the "whole" Cooper, who reacted with fear upon seeing the stabbed Annie). The good Cooper cannot feel fear, nor is he subject to the self-doubt that disabled the whole Cooper. There is a marked difference between how "Cooper" behaves now and how he behaved previously.

Annie, meanwhile, is being manipulated by an outside force; but it is difficult to determine who or what is manipulating her. It appears to be Windom Earle who, as Lynch established in an earlier act, seemed to hypnotize Annie upon bringing her into the Red Room. Using Annie as a tool (and perhaps accessing his own memories of Caroline) Earle taunts "Cooper" with the two women. But Earle's efforts are wasted. As he will soon discover, he has no power over "Cooper."

Earle tells "Cooper" that he will let Annie live in exchange for Cooper's soul. Without hesitation, the good Cooper agrees. Earle stabs him. There is a shot of explosive fire and then the sequence reverses: Earle "unstabs" the good Cooper, who remains unharmed.

Bob suddenly appears. He crouches next to an agonized Earle who is now clearly under Bob's control. Bob seems irritated, even angry at Earle for having invaded the Red Room. He treats Earle as nothing more than a nuisance, a mere mortal who has ventured into a realm beyond his control. Bob tells the good Cooper to go. He then explains that Earle is wrong, that "he can't ask for your soul." Bob's statement can be interpreted two ways: first, that Earle does not have the power to ask for Cooper's soul or, second, that Earle cannot take what is actually only half-a-soul (which is all the good Cooper can offer). Earle's stabbing/unstabbing motion supports the latter interpretation: Earle seems capable of taking a soul and makes an attempt, but his action is immediately negated since "Cooper" no longer has a complete soul to give.

A vastly different Bob/Earle/Cooper confrontation is contained in the original script. There, Earle offers Annie's freedom in exchange for Cooper's soul and Cooper agrees. But Bob interferes, explaining, "The fool broke the rules. It doesn't count if you're coerced." The script offers a more definite reason for Earle's failure—he "broke the rules" by negotiating for a "coerced" soul. But in the script Earle never makes an attempt on Cooper's soul. Lynch, on the other hand, explicitly shows Earle stab Cooper in a futile effort to take his soul.

The good Cooper remains undisturbed as he faces Bob, even when Bob violently removes the soul from Earle's body. Bob has already told Cooper to go. So Cooper does. He calmly turns and walks away. The good Cooper does not confront Bob. He has no reason to. "Cooper" has no fear of Bob now. As for Bob, he knows that Cooper has divided into good and bad. He knows that Cooper is already defeated.

The good Cooper also seems unconcerned for Annie's safety. He does not act as if Bob is any threat to her and his behavior suggests he believes she is now safe. The good Cooper intuitively understands that Earle's plan has failed and that Annie is free.

Divided, He Falls

After the good Cooper leaves, the bad Cooper emerges from the red curtains. He crouches next to Bob, laughs and then follows the good Cooper. Meanwhile, the good Cooper is unhurriedly winding is way out of the Red Room maze. He does not feel threatened and has no reason to rush. The bad Cooper is in pursuit, not to catch (i.e., defeat) the good Cooper, but to outrun him. Although it appears the bad Cooper is *chasing* the good Cooper, he is in fact *racing* the good Cooper to the exit.

The good Cooper, unaware of his double self, encounters the Leland doppelgänger who says, "I did not kill anybody." This curious statement is open to many interpretations. If, however, the apparitions "Cooper" sees in the Red Room are, in fact, partial reflections of his subconscious this encounter may be a way for Cooper's psyche to acknowledge a truth he has so far kept suppressed—that the "whole" Leland (not just the "evil" side) was responsible for killing Laura and Maddy and Teresa Banks. Cooper realizes that it is insufficient to blame one part of a personality for the actions of the whole. Worse, it is immoral to place blame entirely on the concept of demonic possession. Whether Bob truly exists or not, Leland is ultimately responsible for allowing Bob to gain control.

Just as Cooper was "wholly" responsible for failing to protect Caroline Earle, Leland was wholly responsible for his murderous acts. Neither Leland nor Cooper was capable of controlling their weaker sides. Granted, the darker side of Leland was strong, but his good side allowed that side to take over. Cooper had rejected this notion in an earlier episode. When Leland dies, Cooper offers Leland absolution for his sins. Blame for his actions is placed on Bob, an outside force one character labels, "the evil that men do." But Cooper knows this blame is misplaced. Only now, divided, can he realize this truth. Through Cooper's encounter with Leland, Lynch suggests that people are wholly accountable for their actions; placing blame on demons or personal weaknesses is an effort to excuse behavior and avoid responsibility.

Leland's doppelgänger delays the good Cooper long enough for the bad Cooper to catch up. Looking down the hall, the good Cooper sees the opposite self for the first time. He now realizes what's at stake: Only one physical Cooper can leave the Red Room. The good Cooper begins to run, not out of fear for himself, but out of duty to those who are in the real world.

In the end the good Cooper fails. The bad Cooper overtakes him and leaves the Red Room. The good Cooper remains inside and, as Annie explains in *Fire Walk With Me*, can't leave.

When the bad Cooper appears in Glastonberry Grove, Annie is lying unconscious beside him. She has blood on her face, possibly from wounds she received from Windom Earle when he hit her face against a truck window before entering the Red Room. Truman notices their reappearance and rushes to their aid.

Later, at the Great Northern, the bad Cooper awakens in his room. He asks about Annie, either to fool Truman and Doc Hayward into thinking he cares about her, or because he needs to know whether she's alive (since she can provide damaging testimony as to what transpired in the Red Room). "Cooper" enters the bathroom and smashes his head into the mirror. Now in possession of a physical body the bad Cooper rejoices in pain and self-abuse. (This behavior is not unlike Laura Palmer indulging in drugs and promiscuous sex.) To the bad Cooper, the body is just another thing to treat with reckless disregard. What's more, the bad Cooper laughs mockingly at his earlier inquiry ("How's Annie?"). He doesn't care about Annie and finds it funny that anyone would think he does.

Of course, when "Cooper" looks into the mirror he sees Bob staring back. This is the ending Lynch made sure to keep. But Bob, staring from the mirror, is not in possession of Cooper, he is allied with him. Lynch avoids using the word "possessed" when describing the bad Cooper's relationship with Bob. He says, "Bob was, you know, with him"—a deliberately vague statement. Lynch is uncomfortable with anything more specific. Bob is *with* the bad Cooper. They are essentially in league. No more details are necessary.

Conclusion: In the End there is no End

Is this how *Twin Peaks* was *supposed* to end? Did David Lynch intend to forever doom Dale Cooper to division? The answer is no. Even though he altered and diverted the original Cooper/Earle/Bob plot Lynch was

245

conscious of the story's possible continuation and explicit about the design of the finale, declaring the episode, "*not* the ending. That's the ending people were stuck with. That's just the end of the second season."[10]

A better question, however, might be: Is this ending *enough*? Does the story of Dale Cooper come to any kind of conclusion? The answer, quite possibly, is yes.

By staying true to *Twin Peaks'* signature themes of duality and balance, David Lynch performs a nearly impossible trick—he creates a concluding episode that provides both finality and possibility. In it, Cooper is defeated and saved while the storyline ends and advances.

The last image of *Twin Peaks*—Bob victorious, an evil Cooper released—is devastating. Dale Cooper, a mythic and enigmatic character, has been reduced to mere rudiments. Cooper, who was once complex and rich, has been distilled into components of "good" and "bad." Whole, Cooper was more than the sum of his parts. Divided, he becomes a lost soul. It is a bitter ending.

Granted, this ending is made bitterer by the good Cooper's entrapment. Would the ending be more palatable with the good Cooper free and the bad Cooper trapped? Of course—Bob would be defeated and the evil would be purged from Cooper. But even this ending would leave "Cooper" diminished. He would still only be half-a-person. He would, in all likelihood, be incapable of comprehending the human condition, of understanding the impulses and emotions and weaknesses that contribute to the full essence of human behavior. What's more, his abilities as a detective would be immediately handicapped; it would be impossible for the good Cooper to comprehend the motives and attitudes of criminals and suspects.

Ultimately, Cooper's division (no matter which side escapes) is a tragedy for the character. Sadly, the series ends with the worst of two possibilities—the bad Cooper triumphant.

But this ending, bad as it may be, is more hopeful than the one the script would have left. Had the series ended with Cooper wholly possessed by Bob the tragedy would be complete. With no additional episodes to continue the story Cooper would become hopelessly doomed to defeat.

While Lynch's episode is also left open and incomplete, it provides the possibility for closure. Laura tells Cooper she will see him in again—evidence that Cooper's two selves will someday (25 years from now) reunite and make him whole again ("meanwhile" he is trapped in a double existence). What's more, the presence of Cooper's good self, trapped as it may be, mitigates the certainty of defeat. Cooper's good self remains a potential positive force. This force manifests itself in *Fire Walk With Me* when the good Cooper guides Laura Palmer to salvation and happiness.

Perhaps this aspect of Cooper *needed* to be in the Red Room for Laura's sake.

Lynch probably did not realize this specific potential for the good Cooper until he scripted *Fire Walk With Me*. At the time of shooting the final episode he was performing his own balancing act, one that required him to provide a cliffhanger ending without violating the "logic" of the Red Room. Amazingly, Lynch succeeded.

Lynch demonstrates a remarkable awareness of the conventions of television—specifically of serial television—in his version of the finale. His two years working in the medium probably taught him some lessons about the mechanics of serial story-telling. Despite his drastic alterations to the final act Lynch understood that the story would continue should the series enter a third season and so structured the episode to allow for that possibility.[11] Lynch stayed true to the script's first three acts in which a number of cliffhangers were introduced. He also *added* a scene in which Sarah Palmer—"channeling" an unidentified persona—contacts Major Briggs to declare, "I'm in the Black Lodge with Dale Cooper. I'm waiting for you." This fascinating scene is full of potential. In it, Lynch unmistakably opens the door for continuation of the Red Room storyline. Briggs is informed of Cooper's status and essentially summoned to come look for him. (The persona speaking through Sarah Palmer is never identified; it could be anyone. One possibility is Laura, since her mother serves as the conduit of communication. Another possibility could be Annie, since she delivers a similar message in *Fire Walk With Me*.)

In previous episodes Lynch showed a fondness for the Briggs character. The Lynch-directed season-opener featured an eloquent speech by Briggs in which he recounted a dream about meeting his son in heavenly place of peace: "He was happy and carefree, clearly living a life of deep harmony and joy. We embraced, a warm, loving embrace, nothing withheld." This speech marked a reconfiguration of the Briggs character who had been, in the first season, a rigid disciplinarian. In the finale Lynch returns to the Briggs character and positions him as a crucial player in any future Red Room storyline. (Sadly, the death of Don Davis, who played Briggs, effectively eliminates the character from playing a prominent role in the Showtime *Twin Peaks* series.)

Finally, Lynch improves the episode by providing a reason for the cliffhanger ending. The script inexplicably ends with Cooper possessed by Bob, as if the need for such a moment of shock superseded the logic of the story. But the script's ending makes no sense. How could Cooper fall prey to Bob? What weakness in character did he exhibit to allow the possession to take place? The script's ending posits a far darker universe than the one Lynch imagines—for if Cooper can become a victim of Bob, what protection do any of us have from evil?

Lynch provides Cooper with partial salvation while reaffirming a universe where a person can still affect his destiny. Lynch also rescues Cooper from the trap of plot contrivance. By reorienting the finale so that Cooper confronts his inner fears, Lynch shows how Cooper ultimately defeats *himself*. This approach to the material enriches both the character and the narrative: Cooper, despite his failure, remains enigmatic and alluring. The drama of the final episode of *Twin Peaks* is no longer driven by arbitrary plot twists and clichés; instead, it is fueled by the complexity inherent in Dale Cooper's character.

What Lynch proves with his version of the *Twin Peaks* finale is that he was not treating the episode—or the series—with reckless disregard (as some critics have suggested). Lynch respected every aspect of *Twin Peaks*—its themes, its characters, and its narrative structure. He also respected the work of his co-producers. He may have felt their concept of the Red Room was wrong but he did not discard their version wholesale, he merely adapted it according to his interpretation of what *Twin Peaks* was about.

Twin Peaks was important to Lynch: "I love the mood and the characters. I love the possibilities for stories. There's a magical thing that can take place in my mind in that world."[12] Magical things were in Lynch's mind while he was shooting the finale. Others may have dismissed *Twin Peaks* as a failed series but Lynch was still fully engaged by the show. He proved this by directing a final episode that would forever embody the mystery and the wonder and the *magic* that was *Twin Peaks*.

FIRE WALK WITH ME:
REMEMBRANCES FROM CAST AND CREW

Early Stages

The script for Fire Walk With Me *went through a number of revisions. A pre-release draft dated July 3, 1991 features Agent Dale Cooper as the lead investigator in the Teresa Banks murder. When Kyle MacLachlan limited his participation in the filming to only one week, many of the lines for Dale Cooper were assigned to a new character: Chet Desmond, (to be played by actor and musician, Chris Isaak). The shooting draft for* Fire Walk With Me, *featuring the Desmond character, was completed on August 8, 1991.*

Robert Engels: (*co-writer,* Fire Walk With Me): Somewhere in [the second season] David and I started to work more together and Mark and Harley worked more together. Then David and I started another project, and another project, which grew into us being writing partners for about three-and-a-half years.

We started writing a script called "In Heaven" together. We had actually worked out a whole story and a very rough first draft. It was a story about a guy forced to marry an ugly woman and then she becomes more beautiful. Then David got the idea to do a prequel to *Twin Peaks*.

I can remember arriving at David's and he said, "What do you think about doing *Twin Peaks*—a prequel?" I said, "That would be fun." David said, "Well, you know, we have to spec it out." David specs everything out. I said, "I think we can find somebody who wants to do that." And away we went. Then David went to the French and they added it to his deal.

We talked endlessly about how far back we should go and where Mike and Bob came from—all that stuff—a lot of which David had thought about, and a lot that we thought up together. We were going to start jumping ahead but then Kyle didn't want to do the movie for a while. So that changed the script. But a lot of the process was just talking through it and doing a real rough outline.

Mark Frost: I was not involved at all. David and I had a disagreement about what direction a movie should go. I felt very strongly that our audience wanted to see the story go forward. So I declined to be involved in the movie.

Harley Peyton: I think David wanted to make a movie that represented his vision of the television series. So that's what it was. Because I was involved in the other vision, that was kind of maddening. As always with David there was incredible stuff in the film—stuff that no one else does.

I think [Kyle Maclachlan] was just tired of being Agent Cooper. He didn't want to do that anymore. I suspect they had those problems with a lot of people. The cast was determining [which characters] were going to continue.

Robert Engels: Chet Desmond was born from Kyle's reticence to be in the movie. Then we re-thought who this person was and it became a full-blown person who we thought was pretty cool. *Chet*, from Chet Baker; and *Desmond* from Norma Desmond—it's a *noir* name. Both David and I love Chet Baker. But all these things work as a plus. Now we had two agents and to use a musician [Chris Isaak] was pretty cool .

David Lynch (*co-writer and director*, Fire Walk With Me): I'm a huge fan of Chris Isaak's. I hooked up with him on *Blue Velvet* and I wanted to use two songs but I didn't want to use the vocals. Chris said, "Fine," and we went into a studio—the studio he used in San Francisco—and he and his band recorded these new tracks for us. It was fantastic. That started the thing rolling.

Richard Beymer: I didn't like the script. I wanted to see—and I think the public wanted to see—the cast of *Twin Peaks*. Not new people coming in, although I can understand a couple of new people. But not this whole other direction. And in the script there was just a token part [for me] that you knew was never going to end up in the movie, anyway. Ben was just a coke dealer. I didn't want to do that. I could see doing that if there was some sort of buildup to it, and there was a character involved. But I saw no reason to push that at all. And it had nothing to do with the plot. It was just a device.

Miguel Ferrer: There were some weird things that went on with *Fire Walk With Me*. There were a couple of actors, who shall remain nameless, who were saying things like, "I don't know if I want to do this. The script isn't good enough."

I was really upset by that. I was really upset that those individuals were acting like a bunch of spoiled children. And I picked up the phone and I said as much. It really made me sick. It really bothered me, how they turned their backs on [David].

Actress Moira Kelly played the part of Donna Hayward for Fire Walk With Me *(replacing Lara Flynn Boyle, who had played Donna in the series). Sheryl Lee had worked with Moira Kelly in the TV film,* Love, Lies, and Murder.

Sheryl Lee: David called to ask me if I knew about this young actress, and I said, "Oh my God, yes! I worked with her!" It was wonderful synchronicity. I just adore her. I think she's wonderful. It was really great for me when she came in to do *Fire Walk With Me* because we already had a friendship and a trust that was very, very strong. So it was just effortless for that relationship to develop. It was right there from the beginning.

Gary Bullock (*Sheriff Cable*): Johanna Ray was casting. I think she had called me once before for something and all of a sudden this just popped up. It was the most unique audition I've ever had. It was just with David and we just sat and talked about this, that, and the other—nothing to do with the script. I had read it so I knew what the character was about. I was pretty comfortable with that; it was a pretty real character to me. I am from a small town in Tennessee and it wasn't hard to figure this guy out. And that was that.

Pamela Gidley (*Teresa Banks*): I met [David Lynch] initially for the series and [then] something happened—I was doing some other film and couldn't do it. I think, if I remember correctly, [I auditioned for] the Mädchen Amick role. I'm pretty sure. But he doesn't audition—he just sits down and talks to you. And he said that was the character I was supposed to look at.

And then I got called back for the movie, which was great. For some reason David just really insisted that I play that role. I was doing another movie at the time and he really went above-and-beyond to get me to do that role. He worked out the schedule so that I would fly in for a day, fly out, work on this other movie for a few days, fly in. He took full responsibility for whatever happened in case I couldn't make it on the other movie, to cover the insurance costs. I mean, it was crazy. But that was great. It worked.

David Lynch: I guess I go by a feel, or you could say intuition. In talking to somebody—and it's not just me, I think anybody could—you hear that person, you see their eyes and you run them through the script as they're talking. And some will hit a bump and they won't work for that particular part but they're still very interesting people. So you can learn things by talking to someone that could be used later in another thing, or they might be good for another character. You just talk to them and a feeling comes over.

Dana Ashbrook: It was on and then it was off. I heard it was supposed to happen, then it wasn't going to happen. Then, all of a sudden, they called and said it was on. I was shooting a short film in the panhandle of Texas—a thing called *The Coriolis Effect*—and I had to fly out of there to go shoot in Seattle. So I remember leaving that set and going straight to the set of *Fire Walk With Me* and doing the scene where we're on the couch in the basement and talking about the drugs.

Lenny Von Dohlen: I was doing another movie called *Leaving Normal* in Canada at the time. I was to go right into *Fire Walk With Me*. I think I knew that it was a prequel. I think there had been some talk about it and what characters would show up and who wouldn't. I didn't know I would be in it until they asked me.

Heather Graham: It seems like David Lynch likes to work with [certain] people. So I think he basically stuck me in there, which was fun for me. I [thought] it would be something that didn't necessarily make sense. At first they had different ideas about what to do and then I knew it was going to be a prequel. There was one scene that was shot that was actually a flash-forward, kind of like a sequel.

Walter Olkewicz: I met David for the first time at the [first season] wrap party. He came over to me and said, "I just saw your stuff and it's great, incredible. We're going to have you back next year." I said, "David, I died in the last episode." It was great, he said, "Bullshit; we got flashbacks, dream sequences. We'll find a way, trust me. You'll be back." Sure enough, when he wrote the movie I got an intricate part, because it was before Laura was killed.

Shooting

Principal photography for Twin Peaks: Fire Walk With Me *began on Wednesday, September 4, 1991. Cast and crew were on location for four weeks in North Bend, WA and surrounding areas. In early October, the production moved to Los Angeles to shoot on-set.*

Gary Bullock: I think I understood what [David Lynch] was saying. I don't know why, it was just an instinctual sort of thing. He said, "Slow down, slow down; so slow that it feels uncomfortable to you. Then it will be just about right." One remark he did make—and this is the key—he said, "What you don't realize is I'm hearing the music in my head." And I thought, "Oh, yeah. There's that slow, heart-beat pace of the opening music to *Twin Peaks*." And then I remembered the way that all the scenes [from the series] took their time. I remembered Kyle MacLachlan and how some of his scenes just slowed way down. They were not in a rush to get anywhere. They just took their time. I thought, "Ok, I got it." And we just did it.

Robert Engels: Carl Rodd—that's the character Harry Dean [Stanton] plays. Harry Dean loves doing that stuff and we thought, "Why shouldn't Carl Rodd be part of this whole mythology?" Part of it is because he's Harry Dean and he's so great. I was there the day they shot [his scenes] and it was just a real cool thing that happened. He's a "salt-of-the-earth" guy and something really fucking weird happened to him. Maybe stuff has happened to him before. We sort-of scripted that but it's not in any draft. We always did some writing on the set and I'm sure it sprung from Harry's and David's friendship.

Frank Silva: I came back up [on location] the last week that they were here and I was on-call for the entire week. Every day they'd put me on-call; I'd be at the hotel and David would say, "Frank, what are you doing here?" And I said, "Well, I think I'm here to work." We had planned on doing the killing scene in the original train car. That was why I was here that last week—we were going to actually do the murder scene on location. But they ran out of time and they said, "We're going to do the killing scene in LA. We're going to build a set."

Lenny Von Dohlen: [My scene] was done in Encino. They had this studio. They had taken over this warehouse and they had their own little world out there. It was wonderful, except for the freeway. For some reason they had torn the original set down, so, for the film, they approximated it. I remember because there was a thing I had about the couch in the series. I kept picking things off it. Harold was one of those people. Then there was a different couch and there was nothing to pick!

Michael J. Anderson: I really like the whole David Bowie character. He's like what could [someday] happen to Agent Cooper. The FBI really represents higher intelligence, in general—higher intelligence in an effort to combat some abstract concept of evil. The idea of the investigative agency was to find out things about the other side. I think David Bowie represented an agent who had learned so much that they no longer had a good hold on him. It wasn't clear to him, or anybody else, who he belonged to or where he was. Even as he was walking down the hall they weren't quite sure. It was almost as if [Cooper] was seeing himself a little further down the road. David Bowie's character knew too much.

Miguel Ferrer: The thing that I remember most about *Fire Walk With Me* is a brief story that sums up the nature of David Lynch. I remember we were shooting this scene in the FBI office with David and Kyle and David

Bowie—who was great, by the way. He was so cool. We were just about to roll camera and Lynch comes up to me and—he always called me Albert—he said, "Albert, that's David Bowie!" I said, "Yeah, I know." He said, "Pretty cool, huh?" [*laughs*] Then he just walked back, sat down and said, "Roll camera!" There's something so child-like about him, which I just love. With all he's accomplished, and the impact he's had, and the contribution he's made, he's still not jaded. He's still star-struck. And I love that about him.

Phoebe Augustine: [David] struck me as a very innocent soul. Very innocent. I remember he would do this thing where, to give you an incentive to get the scene done and get it right, he would put a stick of chewing gum up on the camera. When you finished the scene you could have the piece of gum. [*laughs*] I thought that was nice.

Gary Bullock: They were shooting the scene with David Bowie in the office. That's where I met Kyle. We rode up in a van to the site and while they were doing their thing I went with the photographer [Laurie Sebastian] to a little park [to shoot the "Cable Bends steel" photo]. She took the shot. But the actual piece of steel was the funny part. They didn't have their prop rebar—the stuff you can easily bend—handy at the time. So they had a piece of *real* steel rebar. And they couldn't get it bent! They were trying to figure out how to bend the damn stuff. Nobody there could possibly move it. So they took the lift on a grip truck, raised the lift, put the rebar under it, and lowered the lift on it. That's what they actually used to get it bent! It was heavy son-of-a-bitch! [*laughs*]

Dana Ashbrook: The very first day was hard. David was really patient and helpful. He talked to me a lot about each line and what was going to happen. He brought me back there—David took us back to the time. He said, "This was what was going on with the drugs and everything."

It all made more sense [especially] by the time we did the scene in the woods. That is one of my favorite scenes in all of it. It's a long scene and complicated and it was cold and we were fighting it. It came out really cool. It was one of those "go-with-what-David-says" things. He explained what he wanted and I tried to get at what he wanted but I didn't really know what it was. That was hard for me.

The end of that scene was the hardest part. I was so confused, and Bobby is supposed to be confused about Laura and the part about Mike. In my mind, as an actor being Bobby, I chalked it up to her just freaking out. Bobby didn't really get in to the whole supernatural thing. That's not Bobby's thing. He was probably the most in-tune guy in Twin Peaks. He just didn't get into any of that. If you think about it, there was always a real fear that

Bobby felt. It was never a supernatural fear. It was always that somebody was trying to shoot him or kill him.

In an early scene, Bobby confronts Laura outside the high school and she charms him into backing down. As he leaves, he starts walking backward into the school.

Dana Ashbrook: We were trying to re-create the same thing from the pilot—where I'm walking backward into the principal's office. He wanted me to do that again. He had everybody dancing at some point. He had music cranking on huge speakers. After a few takes he had everybody dancing. I don't know how much he ended up using.

James Marshall: There was something about the way we did [my] last scene in the movie—maybe it was the writing. It seemed like Mark Frost was great at setting up characters and plot lines—at orchestrating the show—but David was able to make the dialogue incredible. Each person has his strength and I think when David was on, he did this incredible dialogue. Every time he wrote the dialogue I was better able to click-in to the character. That last scene was really cool.

In the writing [of the series] the dynamics went flat; it became one-note. I never found my character at all [during the series.] It was always mushy or "almost there." How much mystery do you keep? There's not much character in brooding. It became mystery, then brood, then mope. I had all this past and I was trying to play too much at once so it would jam up. I didn't find the character until we shot the last scene in *Fire Walk With Me*. The last scene that I ever did in the last movie! I said, "This is it! Here is where he needs to be!" There was something in that scene—it had all these different possibilities for emotion.

Walter Olkewicz: [David] just really took care of you. I mean, that scene in *Fire Walk With Me* where I'm on the ground, knocked out, and people keep coming in and out of the cabin—every time the camera stopped he had three assistants running over, putting blankets under my head and keeping me warm. He was just making sure that if I was sacrificing to make the scene work, he would make sure that I was as comfortable as possible. When the cameras weren't rolling he just made sure the actors were totally taken care of. He was really wonderful to me. I loved him.

Lenny Von Dohlen: [David Lynch and I] had talked during the series a bit. I felt like he and I were on the same page. He seemed to encourage me to do what I was doing. Also, by that time I knew and trusted Sheryl. We became great friends. That kind of jumping off of a very high board together was like going through Outward Bound together. You're tied together! Of course, you may never want to see that person again, but that was not the case with Sheryl.

Sheryl Lee: I trust [David Lynch] so much. You have to relate it to life. We don't know what's going to happen to us next. We have no idea. In fact, some directors go so far that they don't let the actors see the whole script. And they shoot it in sequence, because people don't know what is going to happen to them. You have to be completely in the moment. It's very easy for me, in that sense, to trust David because he knows more than I do. He knows where he's going to go with something.

Lenny Von Dohlen: I remember David screaming at his assistant: "Deepak! Never schedule the most important scene in the movie for four a.m.!" Now, that's either amazing, if that's true, or, more likely, it's a very clever director trying to get two tired actors to step up to the plate at four a.m. Of course, at the time I thought he was serious and I dug in!

Laura and Harold had a lot going on, separately, but when it came together it was supercharged. Nobody probably knows how many levels that scene plays on. By the end of it we were both shaking. Sheryl was really shivering. She had put herself through it. I was worn out, too. When it was over I saw some movement out of the corner of my eye. David was dancing a jig! I thought, "Wow! That's what it should be about." He was celebrating the exploration. He acknowledged the moment. And that is very, very, very, very rare. It was just the most thrilling way to work. I don't know how he did it, really. It was never like some directors where they say, "Make that face like you did in that other movie." He is an intellectual but he is also an alchemist.

Sheryl Lee: By far, the most difficult nude scenes I have ever done in my career are in the nightclub. When you are doing a love scene you're nude but so is the other person. You're looking into their eyes and you trust each other; there is somebody with you. But in *Fire Walk With Me* there was nobody in there with me. It was me, by myself, in a bar full of people. David is so highly respectful—and we had a First Assistant Director named Deepak [Nayar], who was also highly respectful. They would clear the set as much as they could but we still needed all those extras. Most of the extras were professional strippers so they couldn't have cared less! [*laughs*] That was actually good for me because I got to see how relaxed and comfortable they were, and that helped me a little bit.

James Marshall: David was standing in the middle of an empty parking lot at night [for] the scene with the gun on the sign of the "Bang-Bang Saloon." It was raining and he was just staring down—the bill of his hat was straight down. I was way across the lot with the trailers and everything. I came walking across to make sure he was OK because he was in the same position for a very long time. [*laughs*] He said, "It's just beautiful!" I looked down and the "bang-bang" was reflected in the puddle, and one "bang" was on a cigarette butt and the other "bang" was on a different cigarette butt. Then there was this stick that was the gun. He said, "Should I shoot it?" I am standing here—a kid who grew up with *Eraserhead*—and David Lynch is asking my advice! That was so cool!

Walter Olkewicz: He was so funny, David, because he was just so great at telling stories. He was telling us how they were building this new addition to his house. Frank Lloyd Wright, Jr. had designed his house! We were preparing for the scene and all of a sudden he'd go off on this tangent telling us about his house and how they're building it. Then the cinematographer came in and said, "David, we're ready." He said, "We're working on the scene, just a few more minutes." We weren't preparing for the scene at all. That's his way of preparing, because he's bonding with the actors and making them comfortable and making them feel the mood he wants them to be in.

Phoebe Augustine: I was sitting in the set of the cabin with the door closed and four of us in there, and David telling us stories—weird stories about his Russian neighbors and how he saw this little kid running along who then disappeared and reappeared ten feet farther along, and other dimensions and things like that. It was just a long time for being on a set, where time is money, and just talking, relaxing, and telling stories. And then Deepak [Nayar], first A.D., would come running in: "David, we have to hurry, we have to hurry up." "Oh, Deepak, not yet! Longer!" That's my favorite time—talking to David.

Jack Nance: There's nothing on the set that's not exactly right before he cranks the camera. Not one little thing out of place before he cranks the camera. Which makes it nice. It's kind of a long set-up to get everything just like that. But once you start to shoot it's done in a quick minute. It's a real neat way to do it.

James Marshall: It's hard to explain [Lynch's directing style]. It's sort of like, "less is more." When he does something it definitely means something. He does very little. Not out of insecurity—he just doesn't want to disturb the water. Lynch has a really good balance, plus he has a comedic sense. It's not "comedy"—it's a flair. Lynch allows the organic. He allows things to grow. That's really what it is. He'll take something that is comedy and say, "Now, wait a minute; that is funny but I don't need to play it as a comic scene. That is just a part of life." He can add a giddiness to the whole thing. His comedy becomes a drama—just like life. It has a certain amount of angst and giddiness to it. And it can depressurize the whole thing.

David Lynch: The world changes. People change. Always. Every day, every second. It's one of those things you can't figure on. And that's what I'm saying: A person better enjoy their work. They say, "Don't do the work for the fruit of the action, do it for the doing. Do it for the happiness you get doing that." Then you're a winner. Because you can't tell what's going to happen afterwards. So you'd better enjoy the work.

Catherine Coulson: He's just gotten better and better. But he's always been a real genius. He really has. I remember saying on *Eraserhead* that I felt like I was the handmaiden to genius. He's a real regular guy, you know, he's just a really regular, sweet, very nice person who knows exactly what he wants and knows when it's not right. And I think he's just honed his talents as he's gotten older. But he has this incredibly youthful enthusiasm. He never slacks off. When he works, he gives his entire self to the work.

Post Production and Deleted Scenes

Mary Sweeney (*editor*, Fire Walk With Me): I don't like to be on the set too much because I like to be very virginal in terms of what I'm going to see and make sure that it matches what the spectators are going to see, and there are a million ways in which you're influenced by what you witnessed if you watched the filming.

David's pretty good about indicating his preferences to the script supervisor, so I have a lot of information to go ahead and assemble a scene without seeing the dailies with David, and without him sitting there telling me what to do. I know him very, very well, and I know the way he works, and I know how much I can rely on his notes, and I know if there's something in particular he will have communicated that to me. So, inevitably, when we sit down and see the first assembly, which is generally within a week or so after he finishes shooting, there are things I've totally missed, and "not the way I wanted that cut," or whatever. But at least we're ahead of the game, and I have it assembled, and so we generally see that first assembly, which is always very long,.

In the first assembly [of *Fire Walk With Me*], I put everything and the kitchen sink in there that David shot. I try to put in as much as I can so that he's satisfied and that I'm not arriving at a polished cut without him having enough input. So it was big and fat and ugly in the first cut. And so definitely it got trimmed and we move things around.

Michael J. Anderson: Every day they'd present you with a re-write. [*laughs*] But I do know this: we shot a lot of things for *Fire Walk With Me* that didn't appear in the film.

Robert Engels: The series was unusual in that a lot of people who were in the show had stayed friends. They were close. So when we started to write the script we wanted to service everybody. A lot of that script was really a wish list. We were hoping to make it a long movie. As it became [shorter], it had to be focused on Laura. When we realized we had to bring it down to a certain running time we knew we couldn't have stuff like Ben Horne's son's birthday party in there. And once we said it was going to be about Laura then all these scenes had to go. You couldn't have just one of these nice little scenes. There were cuts of wonderful stuff. Some of it was cut because it couldn't be as long as we wanted [but] also because it was free-form. David would start to look at something and say, "I think it is more interesting to go this way." It was hard because we shot all that.

Mary Sweeney: The fact of it being a prequel was not a challenge for me as the editor. I think it was a challenge for the writers and for David as the director. The main challenge of that job was how much material there was and how long it was. It was like a five-and-a-half-hour first cut. There were a lot of scenes in there that spoke to particular characters and their side stories that really didn't drive the central story of Laura Palmer's demise. We just had to sacrifice them because they were appendages and we just couldn't have them in the film. So that was the toughest thing, because they were all really great scenes and really great characters from the TV series. That was the hardest part, to pick and choose what to loose.

Michael J. Anderson: Lynch throws the scenes together and looks at them later and figures out what they mean. He discovers it as he goes along.

Mary Sweeney: David does improvise on all of his shoots, but he also, very much more than people expect, adheres to his script. He definitely shoots almost everything that's in there, and if he gets some ideas on the day, he'll shoot some things that aren't there. But it's really tangential. It's what adds flavor and tone and mood to his movies, but the narrative he's pretty much got clear in his mind. He's a very responsible filmmaker. He makes sure he gets what he needs. He just thinks in the language of cinema.

Robert Engels: Working with David, nothing becomes solid until they're shot. The shooting script of *Fire Walk With Me* describes the bar scene as "everybody getting roasted and toasted." That's all it says. It's what David decides to do, then. He'll decide what it is.

David Lynch: Here's the deal—something isn't finished until it's finished. When you start focusing on something, [it] gets a kind of an energy going and things begin to flow. But ideas don't come when you just snap your fingers. They come along out of who-knows-what. But there is this focus that pulls them, I think. I always say, "You should always be aware." You might think your script is complete but it may not be. There may be opportunities and ideas coming that are so valuable. You have to stay feeling [it], and focused all the time. Lots of things will start talking to you. It's just the way. It's got to all feel correct to be finished. You've just got to be with it.

Robert Engels: You have to go back to the fact that he's a trained painter. So much of it is, "Does that image belong in this frame?" I don't think he just throws things in there. He will know, viscerally, something should be there. But it may not happen until that day and in that way. He would have faith that he's picking the right thing.

Gary Bullock: We spent a good bit of time on [the fight between Cable and Chet Desmond]. It was all afternoon. We were losing the light by the time we got to the end of it. In fact, most of the time I spent up there was rehearsing for that scene. I rehearsed with Jeff Smolek, the stunt coordinator, and Chris [Isaak], to work out all the moves.

Then it was all gone. So there is this blank spot where he says, "You're not taking that body anywhere," and then they're taking it. What was supposed to happen was, he challenged me and I said, "Why don't we step out back." We go out back and have the fight.

And you know how they do blood splatter scenes—like when the mynah bird was killed? There was a blood splatter shot in the fight scene, too. When he is beating the hell out of me, the secretary and the deputy are watching and all of a sudden you see the splatter go all over them! That's gone, too.

Pamela Gidley: We shot the scene where [Teresa calls Jacques]. I don't know why it was cut out. Maybe it had some story flaw in it that didn't work in the long run. Lucky for me, that was the only thing that was cut out.

Charlotte Stewart: There is a scene where Laura comes to see Bobby and as she walks through the house. There is a shot of Garland reading the Bible to Betty. There is opera playing in the background and you get this picture of what their home must be like. It is so dry. It was just odd and it didn't fit.

Don Davis: I had a ten-week contract on a film called *A League of Their Own*. It shot pretty well concurrently with *Fire Walk With Me*. It was shooting over in the Midwest and I couldn't be released in order to go over and work on the other. Originally, I think there were going to be a couple of scenes with me. All we wound up shooting was one scene with me sitting and reading from Revelations. Then I don't think it appeared.

Dana Ashbrook: The script had me in a telephone booth. I don't know if there was a whole bunch of dialogue. Then I think [David] might have just wanted to put something in. I remember it was definitely improv—he told me what to say and I just said it. I loved it, though. That was unusual for me. I'd never done one like that.

Grace Zabriskie: Whenever I read about people talking about things that didn't make the final cut I think about one scene that upsets me most. It was the scene where Leland comes home and tries to teach us Norwegian. That was not a light scene. What happened was, we worked toward hysteria. Yes, we all laughed, but it turns into full-fledged hysteria—laughing and crying at the same time.

There may have been a bit of a psychological game going on in terms of his power trip, and mine and Laura's attempt to resist that. But we get sucked into it and found where the laughter came. I believe David made it clear that it was to go on and on, and turn into this other thing. We did it a number of times.

Everett McGill: It's kind of funny; throughout the series David had always said to me, "Well, we're gonna try to get you and Peggy in a pickup truck sometime in the near future." [*laughs*] We never did. And that's what he wanted, to have it happen in the movie!

Norma and Ed had had a couple of drinks and were happy and delighted to be with one another. We were absolutely free of life's burdens. For us it said everything about why we loved one another. So it was completely different for me—because both Peggy and I carried a certain burden throughout the series. In this scene we had none of that. I was surprised he had to cut it. That was a pretty substantial scene. It went on for quite some time. There was no way to shorten the scene and maybe that was the reason he had to lose it.

I remember a phone call David left on my machine. He left a long message where he said he had to lose those scenes. I can't remember why, but he was real disappointed that he had to.

Kimmy Robertson: We shot a big scene where we talked about raccoons. I think that was a ten-hour movie when he finished it! [*laughs*]

Heather Graham: We did film a scene where I am asleep in a hospital bed. I have a ring on my finger and a nurse steals the ring off of my finger. I think at some point there may have been some person appearing by the side of the bed. I'm not sure.

I wonder what would have happened. [*laughs*]

Reaction

Fire Walk With Me *had its world premiere at the Cannes Film Festival on Saturday May 16, 1992. It opened in the United States on August 28. Reactions at Cannes were quite negative; reviews in the US were also harsh. The movie was probably David Lynch's worst-received film.*

Jennifer Lynch (*author,* The Secret Diary of Laura Palmer): I think *Fire Walk With Me* is one of the finest pieces of work on film, period. I also think it is one of the greatest films ever about child abuse. That is so rarely brought up about the film. Too often, in order to avoid that subject, the content of the film is described as, "Very Lynch." Sure it is. But it is also an incredible observation on the torment and on the "dis-ease" of abuse—that terrible unrest in families and in people that is, I'm sure, much more prevalent than any of us want to accept. I thought everybody in it was at their finest.

Gary Bullock: The funny part is, that whole first part of the flick was like a different movie. It was completely different up until the part where Chris Isaak disappears. Then, all of a sudden—bang!—we are back into Twin Peaks again. Here's Agent Cooper and all that stuff. It is like two separate things. I remember talking to Harry Dean Stanton and he said, "Well, I understood what I was doing and I understood what you were doing. But that's about it."

Robert Engels: I think David knows [how the story works] in that dream-like way. I think he does know but I don't think it is a literal answer. I don't think it's anything you can jot down. It's as if the dreams he has are tactile to him. He sees it; he understands it. Certainly, more than anybody else that I know, he does have it figured out—the whole picture of life, in that sense. And that allows him to move with such confidence. To the viewer, it's like, "Wow! We are in good hands here."

David Lynch: Talking about a film is sort of absurd. Because there's the film and it is a complete thing. That should be the thing that goes out. Anything you add to it is not necessary and anything you subtract from it would be bad and hopefully unnecessary. It's a tricky thing. These days everybody's talking about things. It just becomes something that people do and I think it diminishes the films.

Robert Engels: He's reticent to talk about all of this. It's not out of any arrogance or disdain. He would like you to figure it out. In a fun way. So much of what he does [gets the reaction:] "Isn't that cool!" [David would say,] "What do you think is cool about that? I'm happy you found something cool." It's so much like a painting. You look at it and you experience it. Those [ideas] are real fun when they happen.

David Lynch: Like I always say, "During the day you can laugh, you can cry, you can get angry, you can get happy—there is always a mixture of things." In a film, there is a certain feel. It's like a glue. You've got to go down a narrow path with these ideas and a wrong turn can break it all.

Lenny Von Dohlen: To be honest, I am thankful I am in it only as little as I am. It was such an assault on my psyche while watching it. I'm not saying that [such a thing] can't be a criterion for great art but I don't know that I want my daughter to see it. At the same time I recognize that it is tremendously exciting to see someone with a vision, someone who has such a strong view on the world. Everybody is cookie-cutter now. [It is exciting] for David to be so brazen and bold and horrifying.

Walter Olkewicz: I went to Cannes with David. It was a pretty incredible couple of days in Cannes; the main theater is like a 2,000-seat theater—it is immense. The first time it screened the audience just booed, they hated it. I was just heartbroken.

That movie is hard to like the first couple of times. It's hard to ask your friends to go see it four times. But you'll really start liking it. I've seen it now about eight times and I like it more every time.

David Lynch: Every viewer, no matter what film they are looking at, has a different reaction than another viewer. It's just the way it is. Everybody is at a certain place and they have so many internal things going on. The frames of the film are exactly the same [but] every screening is different, every individual reaction is different. It's just the way it is.

Sheryl Lee: I felt really great about [making *Fire Walk With Me*] because I never felt complete with Laura. I never got to be Laura alive, except in flashbacks. It allowed me to come full-circle with the character. She always had a tremendous amount of life. For two seasons everybody talked about her, yet I didn't get to do those things and be her. So it was good in that way.

The film had so many mixed responses that I don't know whether people think it was better left unsaid. But that really doesn't matter to the artist. For us, it was a great experience.

Jennifer Lynch: It was very unpopular to talk about the grace and power of *Fire Walk With Me* because it was about such a touchy subject. It has staying power. I would love for a critic to have said, "You know, I saw it last week and I'm still not ready to talk about it." What a great compliment that would be: To say, "It is lingering inside me and I have not digested it." How many great dates do we go on where we don't know how we feel about the person but they've stayed with us? How many great conversations? To have this ability to present something that people really take home with them is a gift. For people to have criticized it in such a base way was really disappointing to me. I don't know if he would ever openly admit it but I know it really struck my father in a sad way. Because he could tell people weren't seeing the movie at all.

Robert Engels: I was recently talking with someone and he said, "I saw your movie the other night. That's pretty good!" They're really saying, "I'm sorry. I didn't mean to pound you like that." Because it *is* pretty good. There has been re-evaluation. When it shows on Bravo, invariably someone calls up and says, "Oh, that was a good movie."

David Lynch: I always say there was a black cloud over me, at least during those years. It's like sometimes, the expression is, you just can't get arrested. [*laughs*] That was happening. And like Peggy Lipton said—she felt that it was not the spirit of *Twin Peaks*, that it was too dark. The Laura Palmer story had some goofball stuff, but it also had some torment, and I think this business of incest upsets people. It's not a feel-good picture, but it's got some beautiful abstractions that I just love. I always say that with *Dune* I know I sold out, so it's a double failure because it didn't do so well at the box office or reviews, and I felt bad. But on *Twin Peaks: Fire Walk With Me* I felt real good, even though the reviews were terrible. It just didn't matter to me.

CRITICAL REACTION TO *FIRE WALK WITH ME*

When *Twin Peaks: Fire Walk With Me* premiered in the United States it was ignored by many major film critics. Their opinions of the movie—a major film from a renowned and acclaimed director—were never made public. This silence spoke volumes. The snubbing of *Fire Walk With Me* was a clear rebuke of the film and its director, David Lynch. There's little doubt that most of these quiet critics did not like the film and felt that the kindest way to treat it was to remain silent.

Others, however, were not so restrained. A great many critics excoriated the film, hating it in vicious, sometimes gleeful prose. It was a feeding-frenzy of insults and denunciation that, in retrospect, revealed an inadequacy and immaturity in popular film criticism of the time. A negative review can be welcome and valuable, of course, as long as it's a substantive critique; but almost all the critical reaction to *Fire Walk With Me* was empty and mean-spirited.

Fire Walk With Me is a difficult film on many levels. First, it requires knowledge of the television series that preceded it, and second, it demands viewers face some challenging and uncomfortable subject matter. It is not an easy film to digest quickly. For many, it has taken years and multiple viewings to parse the cryptic nature of the film. In short, *Fire Walk With Me* is (and was) too difficult to interpret on a deadline. The path of least resistance for many critics at the time of release was either silence or rejection.

Fire Walk With Me has become better appreciated in the decades since it came out. Many critics have spent time with the film, re-evaluated it, and come to realize that the movie has much to offer. But in those first few days of the film's release, a collective blindness to its potential merits descended upon the critical establishment.

What follows is a sample of some of those 1992 reviews from around the country. Some are startling to read at this remove; they display a nastiness and simplicity that serves little purpose other than to insult. Few reviews bothered to tackle *Fire Walk With Me* on its own terms—as a complicated (and, yes, possibly flawed) piece of art.

***

The most notable critic to ignore *Fire Walk With Me* was David Ansen from *Newsweek*, a critic who had always been kind to Lynch films. Ansen liked *Dune* when it was being universally assailed, calling it "richer and stronger than just about anything commercial cinema has to offer." He strongly praised *Blue Velvet* ("It's one of those uniquely unnerving visions...which will be argued about and cherished for years to come"). Ansen, however, had nothing to say about *Fire Walk With Me*.

Richard Corliss of *Time* also ignored the film, despite having devoted ample space to reviewing Lynch's work in the past. (*Time*'s lack of mention of *Fire Walk With Me* is exceptionally surprising considering that Lynch was featured on the cover of the magazine only two years earlier.) *Playboy*'s Bruce Williamson did not like *Blue Velvet* ("It lapses into gratuitous violence and vulgarity. Lynch went overboard while testing how far a maverick movie-maker can go") or *Wild At Heart* ("An enticing but disturbing follow-up to *Blue Velvet*"), but had nothing to say, good or bad, about *Fire Walk With Me*. This is somewhat surprising, given that *Playboy* had featured major articles on both Lynch and Sherilyn Fenn in the recent past. Plus, they had run pictorial references to *Wild At Heart* and *Twin Peaks* in their 1990 cinema summary. Clearly, *Playboy* saw a market for Lynch and *Twin Peaks* at one point, but felt that that market was no longer there for *Fire Walk With Me*.

Finally, and most notably, was the silence from one of the nation's premiere critics at the time: Gene Siskel. Two years earlier, Siskel had warm things to say about *Wild At Heart*, calling it "a great, rowdy, passionate love story." But he was mute when it came to *Fire Walk With Me*.

Siskel's long-time associate, Roger Ebert, remained only partially quiet. Ebert had never cared for Lynch's work up to that point; he claimed to be "underwhelmed" by the *Twin Peaks* pilot and had instigated the booing that greeted Lynch when he accepted the *Palme d'Or* at Cannes in 1990 for *Wild At Heart*. At the time of the film's domestic release, Ebert chose to stay silent about *Fire Walk With Me* in his column and on the TV show he co-hosted, *At the Movies*. Although he wrote no official review, Ebert posted electronic dispatches to the online service, CompuServe, from the Cannes Film Festival in 1992. There, he wrote a mini-review of the film after seeing the world premiere.

Ebert quickly condemned *Fire Walk With Me* as, "shockingly bad . . . simple-minded and scornful of its audience." (He was the first reviewer to claim the movie didn't know its audience, a sentiment echoed by other critics in later reviews.) Ebert went on to claim the Deer Meadow sequence (the half-hour prologue to the movie) was a "meaningless 30-minute introductory sequence" and that the audience "essentially has to start all over at the half-hour mark."

But then Ebert really piled-on, as if airing a personal grudge against the kind of films David Lynch makes: "The rest of the film is a mixture of the usual Lynch hallmarks: screams, rapes, satanic dwarfs, sadists climbing up ladders into bedrooms, wood paneling, many trees, ghost horses, angels, bureaucratic jargon, cocaine abuse, wounds under microscopes, clues that lead nowhere, and tableaux of sick middle-class family life. Of more than a dozen U.S. and Canadian critics I talked to, one liked the film and the others resorted to sign language, such as rolling their eyes and sticking their fingers down their throats."

Ebert's cruel dismissal of *Fire Walk With Me* does not warrant a lengthy response. But one of his comments requires a short rebuttal: the casual labelling of the prologue as "meaningless." It's clear now, many years later, that the Deer Meadow prologue is deftly connected to the rest of the film. Sure, it takes some work to make the various connections but the prologue gives the movie an elegant balance. Ebert wasn't interested in investing any deeper analysis to *Fire Walk With Me*; calling the prologue "meaningless" showed his lack of understanding about both the film and the television series.

Ebert was the first of many, many critics to publically condemn the film. Michael Snyder (*San Francisco Chronicle*) called it "haphazard" with a "muddled script." *Interview Magazine* said it was, "an ill-structured, lurid, shock-crazy prequel to a once-popular saga. . . . This is torture." Russel Smith (*The Dallas Morning News*): "A collection of creepy atmospherics, gratuitous freakiness, corny gags, and David Lynch visual clichés." Susan Wloszczyna (*USA Today*): "A morbidly joyless affair." Owen Gleiberman (*Entertainment Weekly*): "The movie is a true folly—almost nothing in it adds up." Vincent Canby (*The New York Times*): "It's not the worst movie ever made; it just seems to be." It went on and on—a devastating avalanche of negativity.

Most of these negative reviews aren't worth discussion or rebuttal; a few, however, require some comment. David Kehr of the *Chicago Tribune* observed, "The details of this *Twin Peaks* are slight and repetitious, and their meanings are numbingly obvious." He later took aim at one of the central themes of *Twin Peaks* (and Lynch films in general): "This simplistic, puritanical division of the world into 'good' and 'bad' is what stands behind the 'Twin Peaks' of the title, and never, in Mr. Lynch's proudly naïve universe, do the twain meet." The most astonishing thing about this statement is how Kehr completely misinterprets Lynch's work. *Fire Walk With Me* is partly about how the "twain meet" in the person of Laura Palmer. The categorical realities of good and evil are objective, of course, but Lynch's characters are continually struggling with which side they will let take control. Kehr, here, is blind to the obvious.

Like Roger Ebert, Jay Boyar of the *Orlando Sentinel* had an odd perspective on the Deer Meadow prologue, calling it a "deliberately flat half hour." The use of the word "deliberate" is strange—it's hard to imagine David Lynch *purposefully* making the prologue uninteresting. In fact, the events in Deer Meadow were engrossing, perplexing, and haunting. Boyar goes on to decry the lack of humor in the film, stating that the "funny frills" of the series were gone; that Cooper's character was used only "seriously," and that even the Log Lady made a "non-comedic" appearance. This was a common complaint about the film and it shows how many people (including long-time *Twin Peaks* fans) may not have been ready for the dark tone of the film. Lynch's vision of Laura as a tormented victim of incest (and the supernatural) would have suffered from the addition of humor; his decision to exclude potential comic relief was deliberate and wise in light of the harrowing narrative.

Jay Carr of the *Boston Globe* also noted that the film contained "no comedy," but went on to say it had "nothing surreal, just wave after wave of titillation." Again, here's a critic who seems to be seeing only part of the film. How can anyone claim there is nothing surreal in *Fire Walk With Me*? Perhaps Carr missed Phillip Jeffries' recount of his visit to the convenience store meeting, or Laura's mesmerizing dream, or Ronette's desperate prayers being answered. These are scenes that offer far more than simple titillation.

But Carr was just getting started. He next claimed that the film "proceeds from no artistic conviction;" that it "shows how quickly a creative impulse can be exhausted—from quirky originality . . . to dispirited quasi-porn." Here, Carr reveals a laziness in his analysis, an inability (or refusal) to look past the surface images of the film. To call *Fire Walk With Me* quasi-porn is completely unfair. The sex and "titillation" in the film served a specific purpose, showing Laura's tightrope walk between good and bad. And Mr. Carr's claim that Lynch made the movie only for money ("a cynical desire to squeeze a few more bucks from the already over-worked corpse of Laura Palmer") is totally unfounded and shows a complete lack of familiarity with David Lynch. Surely, Lynch could have delivered what an audience wanted: a continuation of the story from the TV series, complete with all the humor and quirkiness he could fit into it (obviously, the kind of film Mr. Carr wanted to see). But Lynch chose not to simply remake *Twin Peaks* for film; he went into other directions with a story that was ripe with potential. The world of *Twin Peaks* fired David Lynch's imagination and he was brave enough to eschew economic temptations to make a bold and challenging work.

Despite Lynch's reputation as an artist, however, there was probably little he could have done to evoke any praise from New Orleans critic David Baron of the *Time's Picayune.* Baron got personal with his attack, calling Lynch a "repellent director" and *Fire Walk With Me* "a lurid monstrosity." Baron conceded that the movie could have had a "workable premise" if "[Laura] Palmer seemed intriguing enough for the audience to care about her fate." Here, again, is another ill-informed opinion of *Twin Peaks.* On the series, Laura appeared only as a corpse, in flashbacks, and in a dream, yet she was perhaps the most intriguing character of all. The intrigue of her "many secrets" arising from her dual nature and identity provided depth and mystery. Even after the murder was solved there remained unanswered questions about her. *Fire Walk With Me* answered many of those questions and further defined her character, showing aspects of her personality only alluded to on the show. The film was, in part, a character study of Laura Palmer. (Viewed from the perspective of the series, the Laura of *Fire Walk With Me* becomes both victim and victor—finding peace in the end by transcending the dual nature with which she struggled.) But Mr. Baron revealed his distaste for Lynch up front, and this distaste colored his judgment of the film's main character. There is no question that Laura was intriguing—even those who never watched the television show could see this. Too bad Mr. Baron missed the boat.

People Weekly went nationwide with criticism that insulted film, director, and audience. Tom Gliatto proclaimed *Fire Walk With Me* a "nauseating bucket of slop" appealing only to those fans "willfully perverse enough" to watch all thirty episodes of the series. Never mind that this throw-away aside provides no insight into the movie. It does, however, provide insights into Gliatto as a critic. Even if he hated *Fire Walk With Me* (which he obviously did) readers deserved more than simplistic bumper-sticker quotes (even if they *were* reading *People Weekly*).

Many critics, while taking pains to explain how an audience would respond to the film, didn't realize who the film's core audience actually was. While *Fire Walk With Me* had the potential to please those who had never seen the show, it was actually a film designed for a specific audience: those viewers who were ensnared by Lynch's powerful story on television and who followed it through to the end. Michael Wilmington of The Los Angeles *Times* was one of the few critics who recognized this fact. In one of the better-written reviews of the film (which was mixed), Wilmington stated "*Fire Walk With Me* is the real last act of the *Twin Peaks* saga . . . it caps off a pop cultural landmark." And *TV Guide* acknowledged this, too, when it praised Lynch "for taking one last trip to *Twin Peaks* for true believers."

All-in-all, most of the reviews were heavy-handed and unfair, and it seems that almost every critic had prepared to eviscerate the film going in. Movie-making is a challenging and powerful forum, and movie critics share in that power, for they can either evaluate a film to give the public a better understanding of it, or they can merely pass judgment on whether it is good or bad. The reviews of *Fire Walk With Me* show that many of the major film critics in the U.S. did not have the skills to do the former and were surprisingly ill-equipped to do even the latter.

Few of the national film critics made any effort to review the film in a systematic or substantive way. This is a shame, and a bit surprising, for while many fans never expected reviewers to embrace *Fire Walk With Me*, they did expect an informed evaluation. Only in a few rare instances did critics attempt to examine the film's merits and faults in a meaningful manner. *Twin Peaks: Fire Walk With Me* was not for everyone, but it was a powerful movie nonetheless. It required more critical acumen than most critics were able to give it.

THE REALIZATION OF LAURA PALMER

David Lynch is not known for making "easy" movies. A Lynch film almost always demands its audience to pay attention, to reject commonplace assumptions about narrative, to question the meaning of the images and the context in which they are presented. Even Lynch's most basic films (*The Straight Story, The Elephant Man*) contain confusing and potentially contradictory elements. It is not surprising, then, that Lynch's "difficult" films receive the most debate and analysis.

If we measure Lynch's films by comprehensibility or by how many baffling and contradictory elements they contain, then Lynch's most difficult film is certainly *Twin Peaks: Fire Walk With Me* (that is, arguably, until *Inland Empire*). Ironically, this film has received less academic examination than other Lynch movies perhaps because *Fire Walk With Me* seems so perplexing. "An impossible film," according to Lynch essayist Michel Chion, the 1992 prequel to the television series, *Twin Peaks*, is also arguably Lynch's least accessible: "[It] operates on an impenetrable, unreadable surface . . . . It is seamless; there is no way in."[1]

To even begin appreciating the film's themes and storylines one must have some familiarity with the original *Twin Peaks* television show (co-created by Lynch and writer/producer, Mark Frost) that aired on ABC TV during 1990 and 1991. Although *Fire Walk With Me* was designed (and can function) as a stand-alone film, knowledge of the series certainly makes the film a richer and more rewarding experience.

This lack of knowledge about *Twin Peaks* likely contributed to the harsh critical reception *Fire Walk With Me* met when it was released. In fact, *Fire Walk With Me* received the most scathing reviews of any Lynch film: Roger Ebert called it, "meaningless [and] simpleminded;" Owen Gleiberman of *Entertainment Weekly* said, "The movie is a true folly—almost nothing in it adds up;" and Jeff Shannon of *The Seattle Times* said, "The film is an incoherent travesty of loose and dead ends."

These extreme reviews are knee-jerk reactions to the difficulties inherent in *Fire Walk With Me*. But rather than give David Lynch some artistic

271

benefit-of-the-doubt, too many critics angrily dismissed the "incoherent" *Fire Walk With Me* as either "scornful" (Ebert), "sophomoric" (David Baron, *The Times-Picayune*: New Orleans) or, worse, "lacking any artistic conviction" (Jay Carr, *The Boston Globe*).

There is no question that some movies are bad (for any number of reasons) but some movies are labeled as bad simply because people don't "get them." Often these are challenging, experimental works that require more from an audience (and from critics) than most films. To declare that *Fire Walk With Me* has no artistic conviction or that portions of the film are meaningless proves that many viewers of *Fire Walk With Me* do not appreciate David Lynch's unique approach to filmmaking; nor do they understand—in this specific case—how David Lynch was trying to further expand and explore the intriguing world he helped establish on the television series.

This essay will show that despite its seemingly irreconcilable narrative, *Fire Walk With Me* remains a meaningful and cohesive film, one that tells a satisfying and complete story about its doomed protagonist, Laura Palmer. This essay will provide the most comprehensive examination of the Laura Palmer character to date, analyzing how she changes and grows through the course of her story. Further, the essay will show how David Lynch, in seeking to make Laura a complex, fully-realized character, found it necessary to make unforeseen edits to the film (particularly the scene depicting Laura's murder) and alterations to the already-established Laura Palmer backstory. These changes, necessary as they were, transformed Lynch's original vision of *Fire Walk With Me*. Once enacted, Lynch's modifications heightened the film's ambiguity and made deciphering *Fire Walk With Me* a more difficult and problematic affair.

Part 1: The Journey of Laura Palmer

David Lynch said he made *Fire Walk With Me* because he was fascinated with the Laura Palmer character. She was "radiant on the surface but dying inside. I wanted to see her live, move and talk." Lynch also explains, "I was in love with that world and I wasn't finished with it."[2] *Fire Walk With Me* was Lynch's effort to return to *Twin Peaks*, to uncover more of its secrets and—most importantly—to bring Laura Palmer to life.

Fire Walk With Me tells more than one story but most of the film is devoted to the events of the week leading up to Laura Palmer's murder. The subtitle of the film, found on the shooting script and on the film's overseas theatrical ads, reads, "The Last Seven Days of Laura Palmer." Why are these seven days important? What happens in them? In short, what story is there to tell about Laura Palmer?

From the series we know that Laura was extremely troubled. "She was two people," according to her psychiatrist, Dr. Jacoby: She exhibited destructive behavior (prostitution, taking drugs) while simultaneously showing an altruistic side (volunteering for the Meals On Wheels program, tutoring the mentally handicapped, Johnny Horne). Laura was frightened of a menacing figure named "Bob" and, just before she was killed, she became despondent about "Bob" and his true identity. According to Dr. Jacoby, Laura "may have allowed herself to die" (episode 8) and according to Laura herself (through her diary), she "had to die because it is the only way to keep Bob away from me" (episode 16).

As the series progressed, Agent Cooper learns that Laura's father, Leland Palmer, was Laura's killer and he was probably "possessed" by the demonic figure Laura called "Bob." When Leland died (in episode 16) he explained, "Bob made me do things . . . he wanted others, others they could use, the way they used me. . . . They wanted Laura . . . they wanted her but she was strong. They made me kill that girl, Teresa. They said if I didn't give them Laura, they'd make me kill her, too."

Fire Walk With Me explores the relationship between Laura and Bob and it reveals more about the death of Teresa Banks at the hands of Leland Palmer. During the last seven days of Laura's life, she confirms the identity of Bob and comes to realize that her father killed Teresa, and—as Bob—has been sexually abusing her for years. The story of *Fire Walk With Me*, then, is the story of that realization and the consequential despair Laura suffers. Laura's "double life" is depicted as an internal struggle as she attempts—and fails—to resist a life of depravity and self-abuse. The "good" side of Laura erodes as she is consumed by self-loathing and a feeling of inescapable doom. But this good side is never extinguished; Laura manages to keep the evil forces (led, apparently, by Bob) at bay. She does this by never physically hurting another person. She refuses to allow "them" to use her as a means of inflicting pain on another. This is crucial. *Laura's descent into evil is never complete because she is strong enough to resist hurting others.* When the bad side of Laura is manifest, she only hurts herself. The undying element of good in Laura ultimately leads to her salvation. At the very end of her life she knows she will die a good person.

Fire Walk With Me charts the struggle between the two people that are trying to be Laura Palmer. This struggle (or imbalance) in an individual is a theme Lynch has explored in other works. Before scripting and shooting *Fire Walk With Me*, Lynch directed the final episode of *Twin Peaks* in which Dale Cooper physically enters the subjective realm of the Red Room/Black Lodge. Lynch re-worked the original script of this episode, transforming it into a conflict between the good and bad sides of Dale Cooper. (The original script had Cooper pitted against Bob and Cooper's arch-nemesis, Windom Earle. In it, Cooper was battling an external force, something Lynch likely found of little dramatic interest.) Ultimately, the bad side prevails as Cooper physically divides into separate entities. ("There are two

Coops in there," according to Lynch.[3]) The bad Cooper escapes while the good Cooper remains in the Lodge.

When Lynch turned his attention to *Fire Walk With Me* he continued to explore dual personalities and the struggle to keep a dual nature in balance. In *Fire Walk With Me*, Laura does not face the threat of physical division but confronts her binary nature through a more complex, internal conflict between "good Laura" and "bad Laura," both of whom vie for dominance.

A Building Crisis (One Laura)

When Laura's story begins she acknowledges that she has already changed in some way. She tells her boyfriend, James Hurley, "I'm gone . . . long gone." Significantly, Laura refers to herself in the first person; she is still a unified whole. Her bad side may lead her to indulge in drugs (she snorts cocaine in the girl's bathroom at school) but her good side loves James and recognizes the goodness in him. Laura's good side is strong and functions as an effective counter-balance to her darker nature.

Later, Laura's best friend, Donna Hayward, reminds Laura of James's quality, referring to him as "the one" and someone who loves with "true love." Laura is uncomfortable with Donna's comments and dismisses them. Soon after, Donna poses a philosophical question to Laura: "Do you think that if you were falling in space you would slow down after a while or go faster and faster?" Laura responds, "Faster and faster. And for a long time you wouldn't feel anything. Then you would burst into fire . . . forever. And the angels wouldn't help you. Because they've all gone away."

Laura's despair is evident. Her comments about angels not helping reveals a hopeless state of mind. She believes that angels exist—but not for her. She has been abandoned; there is nothing good in her life (not even James). Laura is alone.

Despite this despair, Laura does not feel threatened, nor does she sense any urgent danger. Her hopelessness and despair comprise a pervasive sense of *ennui* in Laura. She is adrift (falling in space) and will be "for a long time." Though Laura acknowledges a sense of loss, she chooses to ignore its causes. A passive figure, Laura accepts the pain in her life, but so far shows no fear.

This all changes when Laura arrives home to discover pages have been torn out of her diary. This crisis will propel the rest of the narrative: Laura recognizes, for perhaps the first time, the depths of violations she has suffered. The absence of the pages triggers a realization within Laura, made evident when, in panic, she rushes to tell her friend, Harold Smith, that Bob took the pages. (As established on the series, Smith was an agoraphobic shut-in whom Laura befriended during her Meals On Wheels work.) Interestingly, Harold insists that Bob is not real. He has known Laura for some time, and although she has evidently spoken of Bob in the past she must have portrayed him as a figment of her imagination. But now Laura asserts that Bob *is* real, and this realization overwhelms her. She emphasizes again, "He's real;" then she elaborates: "He wants to be me . . . or he will kill me." Here, Laura finally admits to herself the severity of the danger she is in. And for a moment, Laura loses control—the delicate balance she's been maintaining between her two selves dissolves. The evil in Laura surges through the crumbling façade of her denials and she screams the words, "Fire walk with me" while her appearance transforms into the demonic.

This manifestation is short-lived, and "Laura"—that balanced composite of good and bad—reasserts herself. But she is scared. She now acknowledges that Bob is real, but she does not seem to know who he is. She either realizes that Bob masks himself in the identity of someone else, or she retreats into another safe-haven of denial, postponing the devastating acknowledgement that Bob is, in fact, her father.

But whether Laura knows Bob's identity or not, she cannot avoid the truth much longer. Laura's dual nature is now critically destabilized. At home and in a daze, Laura hears the taunting voice of Bob demanding to "taste through [her] mouth." The film dissolves to an image of the Red Room curtains signifying that Laura's crisis is building. Her world is bleeding into another realm.

Agent Cooper senses this. The image of the red curtains dissolves back to Cooper in Philadelphia, where he describes Laura to Albert. He feels she will be the victim of the same murderer who killed Teresa Banks. He also tells Albert that Laura is "crying out for help." Cooper is right to a certain extent. Laura is crying out—but only he can hear her. So far she has made ambiguous comments to Donna and James about her loss of identity and helplessness. She has explicitly sought help from Harold Smith, but only in the task of hiding her diary. Laura's cries for help are muted in the physical world, but they ring loudly in the world of dreams and the subconscious— the realm of the Red Room. This is a world to which Cooper is tuned, and it is from there that he perceives her plight.

At the moment Cooper discusses Laura with Albert, the realm of the Red Room intersects with Laura's waking life. Outside the Double R Diner, Laura receives a visit from Mrs. Tremond and her grandson. These two characters appeared briefly in the series, where they were established as otherworldly beings. (They also made an appearance earlier in the film during the Deer Meadow "prologue," where they were again established as denizens of the Red Room.) The Tremonds give Laura a framed picture depicting a room with flowered wallpaper and a dark open doorway in its corner. The grandson delivers a warning to Laura: "The man behind the mask is looking for the book with the pages torn out. He is going towards the hiding place. He is under the fan now." The line, "The man behind the mask" is important because it confirms to Laura that Bob hides his identity inside another.

Frightened by the message, Laura rushes home, where she finds Bob searching for her diary behind her dresser. She flees the house in terror and hides behind a bush. Looking back, she sees her father, Leland Palmer, leave the house. In a moment of horrible clarity, Laura realizes that Bob may be her father. It is a sickening realization, a trauma that causes near physical pain. Laura is overcome by grief and collapses into sobs. (The script interestingly describes this scene as "Laura is coming apart.")

Laura, now at her most vulnerable and susceptible to the darker side of her psyche (like she was at Harold's), denies what she's seen. Somehow the good side of Laura rallies and keeps her focused long enough so she can seek solace in her best friend, Donna Hayward.

Donna is crucial to Laura. She is a figure of goodness and purity, and she serves as a stabilizing influence in Laura's life. That is why Laura goes to her at this moment. Laura does not go to James or Harold (or even to her psychiatrist, Dr. Jacoby). She goes to Donna, because Donna loves her unconditionally. She needs to hear Donna say that she is Laura's best friend. (A deleted line from the script has Donna also say, "I'm your friend no matter what way you are." Even though this line is not spoken in the film, its meaning is still conveyed when Donna embraces Laura and says, "I'm your friend always.")

Laura returns home, but her trauma is renewed when an oppressive Leland confronts her at dinner. Intimidating her about her relationships, and then insisting that she "wash her hands," Leland effectively reduces Laura to a child, someone who has no autonomy and no power. Laura, here, is nothing but a victim.

Although *Fire Walk With Me* is about Laura, an important subplot in the film is the story of Leland Palmer. ("It [deals] with the torment in the father—the war in him."[4]) The series reveals Leland to be a serial killer: He murdered Laura, Madeleine Ferguson (Laura's cousin), and Teresa Banks (a young girl who was killed a year earlier and whose murder investigation is detailed during the film's first half hour). The series explains that Leland was possessed by the demonic Bob, but it never makes clear just how responsible Leland was for his crimes. In fact, the series tries to have it both ways—to depict Leland as a victim (Cooper tells Sarah Palmer in episode 17: "Leland did not do these things") and as a culprit (Cooper also believes Laura "forgave him," suggesting that Leland held some responsibility for his actions). The film muddies the issue further: Leland is given a motive for murdering Teresa (she tried to blackmail him) but he also behaves like a puppet under Bob's control. This latter characteristic is most evident after the dinner table scene: Leland sits on his bed in what appears to be a seething rage. Then the fury drains out of him, as if Bob has released the strings with which he manipulates Leland. Leland goes to Laura's room to tell her, "I love you. I love you so much."

Poor Laura is further traumatized. (According to the script, she "can hardly speak.") She knows that Leland's love is real, but she cannot deny the likely truth that Leland is Bob. In a moment of utter helplessness, Laura looks at a painting of an angel on her wall and asks, "Is it true?" Laura's appeal to a divine power marks the fall of the mental barriers she's been using as a refuge. She can find no way to reconcile two truths—that her father loves her and that her father is Bob. Laura looks to a source outside herself for answers but finds none. The truth is inside Laura, and it is horrible. Finding it impossible to view her father as a victimizer (and her herself as his victim), Laura places blame on herself. She has no other recourse at this point: In her mind her "bad" behavior is the cause of her suffering.

Laura's "bad" side is now poised to take control. She has endured too many emotional and psychological blows (seeing Bob at the dresser, connecting his presence to Leland, being humiliated by her aggressive father, then feeling genuine love from a man who could quite literally be a monster) for her fragile psyche to remain intact and balanced. What's more, Laura views herself as so worthless, that she is beyond salvation. Her angels have abandoned her. As a result, Laura retreats into passivity and self-doubt. Like other Lynch protagonists (Diane in *Mulholland Drive* and Henry in *Eraserhead*), Laura works against herself—her confusion and doubt entrap her.

Laura, like Agent Cooper in the final episode of *Twin Peaks*, is caught by her own flaws and uncertainty. She sees no way to break free and (like Cooper) her identity becomes fractured. In *Twin Peaks*, Cooper fails to keep his two selves in balance, and his good side literally flees from its intolerable opposite. In *Fire Walk With Me*, Laura's good side cannot *physically* escape, but it can retreat into the deeper reaches of her mind much the way Henry in *Eraserhead* retreats into the mental fantasy world of the Lady in the Radiator. In effect, Laura's situation resembles a complex fusion of what happened to the Henry and Cooper characters: Laura's good side sinks into her psyche (à la Henry's escape), leaving her bad side on the surface (like Cooper).

This division is not sudden; the process has only just begun. Laura's burgeoning bad side will find release while she sleeps, during a powerful, unsettling dream. After the dream, Laura's darker side will be dominant and her good side suppressed.

Laura's Dream

Laura dreams of the picture given to her by the Tremonds (the room with the door). Her point-of-view is inside the picture, moving through the open door. She sees Mrs. Tremond beckon her further in; she sees the grandson who snaps his fingers, effectively placing Laura in the Red Room. There, she sees the Owl Cave ring on a table. Agent Cooper enters the room. The Little Man From Another Place asks Cooper, "Do you know who I am?" Then he identifies himself as "the arm" and makes a "whooping" noise. The Little Man picks up the ring and holds it toward Laura (her point-of-view). Cooper turns toward "Laura" and says, "Don't take the ring . . . Laura, don't take the ring." At this point, Laura seems to wake up. She is in her bed. She turns to look at her bedroom door and discovers she cannot move her left arm. Laura sees a bloody Annie Blackburne in her bed. Annie identifies herself and says, "I've been with Laura and Dale. The good Dale is in the Lodge and he can't leave. Write it in your diary." Laura looks at her door again and when she turns back, Annie is gone. Laura realizes she is clutching something in her numb hand. She opens it and sees the Owl Cave ring. She is horrified. She becomes distracted by a noise outside her room (the distorted sound of her name being called). She opens her door to look out on a dark, empty hall. She looks back at the Tremonds' picture and sees herself in the picture standing in the doorway. A close-up of this second Laura reveals a look of loss and sadness on her face, as if she no longer knows who she is. At this point the dream truly ends and Laura wakes up.

Laura's dream is possibly the most important sequence in the film. Dreams have always been a significant element of Lynch's work. Through dreams Lynch has the freedom to explore the inner workings of his characters' minds. Dreams are of particular importance in the *Twin Peaks* universe because they provide access to the mysterious world of the Red Room. This "free zone" (as Lynch describes it[5]) is a place that reflects the consciousness of the person who enters ("It changes depending on whoever walks into it"[6]). It is a place of transformation, as is obvious from the *Twin Peaks* finale. It is also a place where the buried or concealed aspects of a person's subconscious are made manifest; those who are vulnerable or unprepared for what they encounter in the Red Room can be psychologically wounded as a result of their "visit."

Laura journeys into her dream in a state of doubt and hopelessness. The Little Man (or "arm") holds the ring before her as she hears Cooper's warning. Laura "wakes" from this part of the dream to discover her left arm is now paralyzed and, like the "arm" in the dream, it holds the ring. Laura is not shown physically taking the ring, but in her weakened, passive state she is vulnerable to it. She either acquiesces to the ring, or, more likely, it is *imposed* upon her. Either way, she makes no deliberate effort to take it— when the Little Man picks it up, Laura receives it.

The film so far has established the ring as a dangerous thing. But its exact nature is ambiguous. Earlier in the film, the Little Man talks about the ring with Bob, where the ring is linked with Teresa Banks's murder. Bob is said to have "fell a victim," and the Little Man says, "With this ring, I thee wed." Ownership of the ring ostensibly marks a person as Bob's victim, but only if the Little Man "weds" Bob to his prey. Teresa Banks had the ring for some time, and her arm was reportedly numb, implying that she, too, somehow accepted the ring from the Little Man.

The ring seems to be an object of power that can do great harm if wielded by a malevolent entity. The Little Man forces the ring on those too vulnerable to resist. Using the ring, he binds his victims. He entraps them. Cooper senses this and wisely warns Laura not to take the ring. What Cooper really wants is for Laura to resist the ring, to turn away from it. And, arguably, Laura does not "take" the ring. It is thrust upon her. Given her mental state, she has little strength to refuse it.

Accepting the ring in the dream results in a different kind of danger for Laura than receiving it in the waking world. Once Laura is given the ring, her psyche shifts balance, and her good side is trapped. Annie Blackburne hints at Laura's situation when she explains that there is a "good" Dale who has also become trapped. Like Cooper, Laura's good side is caught. Shortly after Laura receives the ring, she sees herself in the Tremond's picture—a signal that the good side of Laura is now locked deep in her subconscious. She has effectively become divided, her good self imprisoned within the painting

Laura's journey in and out of her dream (and the Red Room) is a damaging experience. Other critics, however, regard Laura's dream as one of positive transformation. Martha Nochimson, who has written one of the most insightful analyses of *Fire Walk With Me*, argues that two Laura's emerge from the dream—a wounded Laura (the one at her bedroom door) and a "visionary" Laura (the one in the painting). After her dream, "wounded" Laura has the ability to free herself and become visionary. In this way she is able to perceive deeper truths: She will know when Donna is in danger, recognize the true identity of Bob, and understand the liberating power of the Owl Cave ring.

It can be argued, however, that Laura has always been visionary, hence her ability to see Bob and the Tremonds in the first place. What's more, the "visionary" Laura whom Nochimson identifies in the painting is a forlorn figure, one who appears bewildered and despairing rather than someone who has "acquired the hopeful power of the subconscious."[7]

It is true that the Laura who wakes from her dream is a different person than the one who fell asleep. But it is a darker Laura who emerges, not a "visionary" one. Unencumbered by her good side, the bad Laura boldly asserts herself. The first time we see Laura after the dream she is dressed provocatively and preparing to go out and prostitute herself. This post-dream Laura is clearly not a positive figure. She is dangerous and frightening.[8]

Two Lauras and a Pink Room

The following night, Donna arrives and is startled by Laura's appearance. Laura brushes her off, showing a marked difference in her behavior toward Donna than she did a day earlier. Donna reminds Laura that she is her best friend—the same declaration that Laura so desperately needed to hear the day before. Today, the words have no meaning. Laura discards Donna without a second glance and leaves the house.

Laura arrives at the Roadhouse. Before she enters, however, she is startled by the appearance of the Log Lady (who somehow knows to be there). The Log Lady delivers an important message: "When this kind of fire starts, it is very hard to put out. The tender bows of innocence burn first and the wind rises—then all goodness is in jeopardy."

The Log Lady plays a crucial role at this juncture. Her presence counters the appearance of the Little Man and the effects of the Owl Cave ring. Her admonition that it is hard to put out "this kind" of fire alerts Laura to the consuming presence of her darker side. The Log Lady essentially tells Laura that her good side is in danger. More than simply provide a warning, the Log Lady attempts to steer Laura back in the "right" direction and, in effect, free the good Laura from the trap within Laura's mind. This development is emphasized when Laura turns to see her reflection in the Roadhouse door. Once again, two Laura's appear on-screen, recalling the dream sequence in which Laura sees herself in the painting. This time, however, Laura's reflection signals liberation rather than entrapment.

The darker Laura is weakened, her determination partially diffused by the re-awakened good side. Laura is obviously affected by the new shift in her psychological balance and is now in a position where she can choose to either indulge her bad side or empower her good. She has become the "two people" that Dr. Jacoby perceived.

These two Lauras imply a third "Laura"—a conflicted presence that flickers back and forth between good and bad. Before her dream these two "Lauras" were integrated into a blended whole. Now, the whole has become divided and "Laura" cannot find balance between her two selves. "Laura's" psyche is confronted with dissolution as she struggles to keep the her dark side from entirely consuming her good. (She is trying to control the fire that has started—the one that "jeopardizes" her "goodness.")

This struggle is evident when "Laura" sits at a table in the Roadhouse. Emotions wash over her, and she breaks down, crying. She must decide which side will have control. But "Laura" has convinced herself that she has been abandoned and that her situation is hopeless. Her feelings of indecision and loss are underscored by the words Julee Cruise sings on the Roadhouse stage: "Why did you go? Why did you turn away from me? Was it me? Was it you? Questions in a world of blue."

"Laura" chooses. She takes the path of least resistance. She gives a nod to Jacques Renault at the bar, signaling that she is ready to sell herself to men. Her darker nature has prevailed.

Two truckers arrive at her table and give her money. "Laura" is angry, however. She knows her bad side is strong and winning and she lashes out at the men, physically accosting them. Like a caged animal, "Laura" is frightened and hostile. As long as "Laura" allows her dark side to hold sway, however, she is helpless to break free and save herself.

Laura resigns herself to the situation when Donna arrives at the table. Disgusted by the effortless goodness in Donna, Laura's bad side secures control. She allows her anger to spill over against Donna, targeting her friend and calling Donna's bluff to come with Laura and her two "johns." Laura knows what dark passages they are about to tread, but she allows her innocent friend to come along anyway.

For the first time, Laura is poised to hurt another. This is a critical juncture. So far, Laura has only hurt herself when she has been "bad." If she were to purposefully and seriously hurt someone else, however, her good side would be irretrievably lost. This is what Bob wants. This is what Bob (and his ally, the Little Man) have been driving Laura toward.

In the cosmology of David Lynch films, violence against another irrevocably leads to doom. In *Eraserhead*, Henry stabs the baby and suffers a mental collapse, retreating into his mind to escape the horror he caused. In *Lost Highway*, Fred Madison kills his wife and seems damned to retreat forever on an endless nighttime road—a "lost highway." In *Mulholland Drive*, an envious Diane hires a hitman to kill her perceived rival (and ex-lover), Camilla. As soon as she commits to the killing, she literally sells her soul to the malevolent derelict behind the restaurant. (Diane faces a "go/no-go" choice when the hitman informs her, "Once you hand this [money] over, it's a done deal." When he asks, "You sure you want this?" she replies, "More than anything.") In *Blue Velvet*, Jeffrey suffers lesser, but still dire, consequences when he submits to Dorothy's pleas to "hurt" her. Shortly after slapping Dorothy, Jeffrey meets the evil Frank Booth. What follows is Jeffrey's short-lived journey down a hellish "lost highway" of his own. He suffers humiliation and torture at the hand of Frank, who reminds Jeffrey, "You're just like me." (This is a critical line because, as David Foster Wallace explains, Frank is one of Lynch's "bad guys"—characters who are "exultant, orgasmic, most fully present at their evilest moments: . . . they have yielded themselves up to a darkness way bigger than any one person."[9] By hurting Dorothy, Jeffrey, too, yields himself to a darkness bigger than himself and, in a sense, he becomes "just like Frank.")

Time and again Lynch posits that negative or hurtful actions against another lead to damnation. The demonic Bob wants to be Laura, but he cannot fully possess her until she hurts someone else. Bob and his associates have slowly weakened Laura's psychological defenses, setting her off-balance and positioning her to take the rage and hate she feels against herself and unleash them upon another.

Laura is about to do just that. She has brought Donna into her frightening world as the two girls and the truckers travel to "Partyland," a seedy bar described in the script as a "border truck stop" between Canada and the United States. Identified as the "Pink Room" on the *Fire Walk With Me* soundtrack, Partyland arguably represents a real-world (or waking-world) version of the Red Room—a place that literally straddles borders. As such, Partyland threatens to be another of Lynch's "free zones." It is a dangerous place, especially for the unprepared Donna. Laura watches as Buck, one of the truckers, drugs Donna's beer. Aware of its danger, Laura still encourages Donna to drink. Laura has now participated in hurting another.

Once Donna is drugged, she withdraws from the scene. At the same time, Ronette Pulaski replaces Donna at Laura's side. Ronette is an associate of Laura's, a dark-haired girl who, like Laura, has participated in prostitution. As such, she functions as a counterpart to Donna: a corrupted version of Laura's friend. It is significant that her first appearance is here in the Pink Room. In this real-world version of the Red Room, Ronette is not unlike Donna's doppelgänger—her shadow-self (to use a term from the series). Laura ostensibly exchanges Donna for Ronette and, in a drug-addled haze, blissfully forgets the harm she has caused her "best friend."

Ronette's connection to Donna is further reinforced when she later spies Donna in a dangerous situation and alerts Laura. Ronette essentially "reconnects" Laura with Donna. Once she serves this function, she is no longer necessary to the scene; Donna's presence reasserts itself in Laura's life. and Ronette seemingly fades away.

Laura sees an oblivious Donna who has become vulnerable to the predatory sexual advances of Tommy (the other trucker), and all Laura's instincts of goodness and friendship resurface. A bright white light shines down on her, signaling the resurgence of Laura's good side. Laura panics at the imminent threat to Donna and takes action to save her.

Nochimson argues that the bright light that bathes Laura's face "makes her aware" of the threat to Donna: "Shocked into action, visionary Laura finds the power to protect Donna."[10] Nochimson's analysis implies that a force outside Laura brings Donna's plight to her attention. This is possible, though the identity of this force is never defined. Still, this is a curious scene. Until this point of (literal) illumination Laura is unaware or doesn't care about Donna. When she actually sees Donna on the threshold of rape—a true, lasting injury, the kind which may damage Donna beyond repair—Laura acts to save her friend. This action and awareness comes from Laura, not some outside force.

The Log Lady's earlier warning implies that Laura has the power of choice. She says, "When this kind of fire starts *it is very hard to put out*." The message? "You have the ability to extinguish this fire. It won't be easy. But you can *choose* to put it out."

Why else would the Log Lady deliver this message if not to inform Laura she still had the power to change her fate? This message has been ringing in Laura's subconscious the entire night. She has been sorting the Log Lady's words, making sense of them. In a desperate moment of clarity (arguably the white light) Laura understands the Log Lady's warning.

The Log Lady's words are doubly significant when Laura sees that Donna's "tender bows of innocence" are burning, that Donna's "goodness is in jeopardy." She recognizes that Donna is succumbing to the same dark impulses that are consuming Laura. But her "good" side will not allow it; "Laura" chooses to do the right thing and rescues Donna.

Confidence and Over-confidence

Her raucous night over, a quiet morning and gentle conversation with Donna helps restore some balance to Laura. She is fragile, however. Her talk with Donna is strained, and although her good side has been freed, Laura is still damaged from her dream two nights earlier.

Laura is under assault by forces beyond her understanding. These forces have so far manifested themselves as Bob, the Little Man, and possibly the Tremonds. They sense weakness in Laura and capitalize on it as they attempt to de-stabilize her fragile psyche. But Laura has just survived a grueling test of her conscience and has emerged a stronger character.

After Leland picks up Laura at Donna's, he and Laura are accosted by yet another mysterious being, Mike, the One Armed Man—who drives up beside them and, in a cacophony of revving engines, horns and screams, attempts to warn Laura: "It's your father!" and cryptically threaten Leland: "The thread will be torn, Mr. Palmer!"

This unsettling encounter scares Laura and Leland both, releasing disturbing and uncomfortable memories in each. Anger, fear and confusion course through Laura and, for the first time, she cautiously questions Leland about his secret, wondering if he had been home "during the day" last week. This question shows Laura at last willing to explore a potentially harsh truth. Early in the film Laura was a passive figure, resigned to a life of loss and despair. Now, bolstered by the increasing strength of her good side (and her choice to do good in the Pink Room), she challenges Leland, someone who wielded such oppressive authority over her just a few days earlier.

Later, at home, a bolder, more aggressive Laura is further evident as she pieces together the Owl Cave ring puzzle, recalling the instances in which she has seen the ring (on the One Armed Man, held by the Little Man and, most importantly, on Teresa Banks). Laura has been actively sorting through her memories and experiences—much different behavior than that of the passive, oblivious Laura a few days earlier.[11] When a bright light interrupts her thoughts, Laura looks up, angry. Addressing an unseen Bob, Laura demands to know, "Who are you? Who are you, really?" Significantly, Laura does not cower; she does not retreat the way she did when she saw Bob at her dresser. This Laura is forceful. She is on the threshold of taking control of her life.

But confidence leads to over-confidence and maybe even foolishness. Laura returns to an over-indulgent use of drugs, a dependence and habit she is not yet strong enough to break. Because Laura's life frequently dissolves into repetitive behaviors, it easy for Bob to wait until Laura's new-found confidence is weakened by her addictions. Her habits are all part of Bob's plan to constantly chip away at her resolve.

Buoyed by a new drug-induced high, Laura and Bobby rendezvous late at night with a drug dealer (Deputy Cliff, from the film's prologue). The deal goes bad, and Bobby shoots and kills the dealer. But Laura is only briefly startled. She laughs at the outcome. Then, in a drug-induced misinterpretation of identity, Laura confuses the dealer for Bobby's friend, Mike. "You killed Mike," she insists, causing Bobby also to wonder at the identity of the victim. Although Laura's mind is muddled, she shows little, if any, fear in face of such a horrific act. Laura is detached from the event. She takes on a mock-superior tone with Bobby, chastising him for what he's done. Laura then giggles dismissively at the whole thing as if she is psychologically and emotionally immune to the sudden death of another human being.

Devastation

Laura's returns to drug use shows that she is weak despite her surface confidence. She still seeks escape from the psychic wounds inflicted upon her during the dream and the hard realities she has faced in the waking world. (James realizes Laura is "on something again" when he visits her outside her house the next morning.)

Still, Laura has exhibited more strength than usual and this has likely alarmed Bob and his associates, who have so far not succeeded at weakening Laura. (As the dying Leland confirmed in episode 16 of the series, "Laura was strong. She fought them. She wouldn't let them win.") None of their tactics has worked: The appearance of Bob at the dresser, the appearance of the ring and her dual self in the dream, the harm inflicted on Donna in the Pink Room. Laura has overcome each one of these psychic blows. Now, as Laura becomes increasingly determined to resist Bob's various violations, she must face the most horrific shock of all. And for this she is woefully unprepared.

Late at night, Bob enters Laura's room and begins to rape her.

Laura is again in a drug-induced haze. Part of her responds to Bob's sexual advances. Another part resists, seeking again and again to know: "Who are you?" Laura struggles for a truth that seems too elusive to grasp. Bob's "identity" continually slips away from her vision. She literally grabs Bob's face in an attempt to hold it still long enough to truly see it. Finally, she does. The script describes the revelation as: "Slowly, what she always knew deep inside of her becomes clear. BOB BECOMES LELAND." When he does—when Laura finally recognizes that her father has been abusing her for so many years—she screams in terror and the screen goes black, implying (and the scripts confirms) that she has passed out.

Why does Laura learn the truth about Leland/Bob at this moment? One common supposition about this scene is that there is no particular reason for Laura to make the discovery now—she just does. Many serious reviewers of the film assume that Laura happens to learn Bob's identity as if by accident. These reviewers are handicapped by the knowledge of the series—they already know Laura will learn Bob's identity and are not surprised when she does. There is no revelation for them. (As a result, these viewers make fewer demands of *Fire Walk With Me* than they might another film. They are satisfied as long as *Fire Walk With Me* shows them story events they already know.)

This kind of viewer fails to anchor Laura's discovery to the structure of her story, fails to credit Lynch and Engels for constructing a narrative that logically leads to this specific revelatory moment.

In point of fact, Laura learns Bob's identity *because Bob wants her to*. He needs to wound her like never before. He needs to ruin her, to sap her of her will, to leave her senseless and vulnerable. That is why he comes to her now. He must hurt her before she can grow stronger.

Not everyone sees the scene this way. Martha Nochimson argues that Laura's dream gave her visionary power "to discover Bob's true identity when he next invades her room."[12] This is a robust theory because it identifies Laura as an active character, one who is driving her own story. But it still fails to explain why Bob's identity is revealed at this moment in the story. Why did Laura's visionary power not work earlier? After all, she was in the car with Leland and suspected the truth. Yet she still didn't see Leland as Bob. (Nochimson might argue that Laura needs to be in the physical presence of Bob-as-Leland, not simply Leland himself. Once Bob (as Leland) comes to Laura's room, she sees his true identity.)

Nochimson's argument provides a valuable way to view the post-dream Laura, but the "visionary" theory still remains suspect. Since her dream, Laura has faced the other-worldly bright light and failed to determine his (or its) identity. What's more, a visionary Laura is hard to reconcile with a Laura who so easily mistook the identity of Bobby's gun-shot victim. Why did she so readily perceive the drug-dealing deputy as Bobby's friend, Mike?

Why do her supposed powers of perception fail her? These questions pose serious challenges to the idea of a visionary Laura.

Lynch critic, John Alexander, offers one explanation for Laura's misperceptions about Bob/Leland: Although Bob and Leland are "obviously one and the same person . . . Laura denies the truth, choosing to live in self-manifested illusion."[13] In other words, Laura is preventing herself from learning the truth because "what she always knew deep inside her" is too horrible to accept. This is evident from Laura's reaction to the truth. The fact that Bob is Leland devastates her. She passes out and then spends the next day in numb shock: "Laura's perception of reality dissolves into vagaries—school is a daze of Dutch angles and blurred images. The monster of her dreams has erupted forth into her waking life, to drag her down into the underworld."[14]

If Laura's powers of sight allow her to at last pierce the mask of her oppressor—to see his true face—why does she collapse into ruin once she does? Has the truth helped her? Has it freed her? No. The truth about Bob debilitates Laura; it does not empower her. She finds herself adrift in a distorted world of pain and despair. Laura has not escaped Bob; rather, she has become further victimized by him.

This was Bob's intent. He chose to reveal himself to Laura—she did not discover the truth on her own. The script explains, "Bob *becomes* Leland" the truth "*becomes* clear." This use of passive voice mitigates any action by Laura (she does not "discover" or "unmask" Bob, or participate in any other active way at learning the truth). Lynch shoots the scene with deliberate obfuscation: In dream-like agony, Laura struggles to make herself aware—to stay in the moment and to "see" who Bob is. But she loses her focus, acquiescing to the drugs and sensations of her body. The figure above her seems to oscillate between Bob and Leland. At the last moment, Laura sees Leland on top of her, and she screams.

Lynch renders the scene this way because he wants to convey the idea that while Laura seeks the truth, she is also afraid of it. As Alexander notes, Laura has always known the truth but has always denied it. Bob capitalizes on this uncertainty. He allows Laura to see his other face because he knows it will destroy her growing confidence and control. It will leave her helpless to his psychic advances and his goal to be her—to taste through her mouth.

Bob is the active agent in this scene. He imposes the truth upon Laura so that it will irrevocably destabilize her. In this way Bob resembles Bobby Peru from Lynch's previous film, *Wild At Heart*. Just as Bob preys upon Laura, Bobby Peru targets Lula, another young woman in denial. Peru visits Lula in her motel room where he cruelly victimizes her. Like Bob, he forces himself upon Lula, and while he does not go so far as to physically rape her, he effectively does so verbally. Peru seeks to ruin Lula, to leave her powerless. His verbal and physical assault succeeds: "Lula is so defeated by being victimized this way that, when she realizes that Sailor [her boyfriend] is also in danger of becoming Peru's victim, she cannot summon the energy to aid him."[15]

Lula, like Laura, is resistant to Peru at first—she pushes him away and tries to stop his advances. But when Lula gives in to the sensations Peru evokes from her body, her resistance breaks down and she acquiesces to his demands. Once she does, Lula is forced to realize a truth about herself that she has long denied—that she enjoys a reckless, promiscuous life. This truth cripples Lula—Peru's intent all along. According to Lynch, what Peru did "pointed out that Lula plays tricks on herself, like we all do. She blocks out many parts of reality so she can still continue to be Lula."[16]

Laura, too, has blocked out parts of reality. She has always known the truth about Bob, but she has successfully suppressed it so she can go about her everyday life. Knowing that Laura "blocks out reality," Bob forces her to see behind her self-imposed barriers. *He makes her see Leland as Bob.* The effect is overwhelming, and Laura crumbles.

The next morning Laura can hardly lift her head at the breakfast table. She tries to crawl inside herself to escape the harshness of a now undeniable reality. Leland innocently questions her, and Laura leaves the table. He pursues her, and Laura turns on him, hissing the words, "Stay away from me." She still has her anger and some sense of self-preservation, but she is a defeated character.

The Last Day

This defeat is evident throughout Laura's last day. The walk to school is painful. The real world seems foreign as it spins and tilts away. Laura has become disconnected from reality—time seems to race forward and backward. As she sits in school, her world shifts and blurs, and Laura is powerless. Beaten, she dissolves into sobs.

To facilitate some kind of escape from this hellish waking-world, Laura seeks drugs from Bobby. She returns home and prepares to go out and meet Leo Johnson and Jacques Renault—hard men, the kind to whom Laura submits in times of greatest depression. She dresses promiscuously and snorts her cocaine.

All traces of self-esteem are gone. This loss is reinforced when Laura looks at her angel painting and, to her horror, sees the angel fade from the picture and completely disappear. Laura's abandonment is confirmed. Her angels have gone, and her prediction that they will not help her has come true.

It is a dark Laura who later meets with James. When he tries to kiss her, she pushes him away and then turns on him. She hits James and says she pities him. James does not back down. Instinctively, he knows she needs help and he tries to reach her. Quite possibly, James succeeds. He arguably awakens the implied "third" Laura—the unbalanced persona who struggles to find equilibrium between her good and bad selves. Detached and resigned, however, this Laura merely despairs at the growing strength of her darker side.

In fact, she reluctantly acknowledges the victory of her dark self when she says to James, "You don't know me . . . Your Laura disappeared. It's just me now." This dialogue significantly contrasts with Laura's earlier exchange with James at the school. There, despite her sense of loss, she referred to herself solely in the first person. Now, she uses both first and third. She is not a "whole" Laura—she is a divided Laura who insists that one of her two selves has gone. ("It's just me now.")

Once again, Laura plummets into a world of indulgence and abuse. She makes her rendezvous with Jacques, Leo and Ronette at Jacques' cabin deep in the woods. There, she engages in an orgy of intoxicants and brutal sex. Leland/Bob follows to observe. When he stares through the cabin window, Laura is once again bathed in white light. But this light does not bring the power of vision or escape, rather it brings a reminder to Laura of Bob's inescapable power.

Death and Salvation in the Train Car

Time passes. Laura and Ronette are bound and left in the cabin. Leland enters and gathers up the girls. He marches them into the woods toward an abandoned train car deep in the forest.

Does Bob plan on killing the girls at this point? If so, why take them to the train car? Why not just do the deed in the cabin? And finally, why does he need to take *both* girls?

Once again, Bob is the active agent here. He is following through on the plan he set into motion when he revealed himself to Laura the night before. Possessing Laura is his goal and now, in this all-or-nothing moment, he brings Laura to a specific place where he can perform the ritual required for him to gain control. The ritual requires him to bind Laura's hands behind her back and place her above a mirror. Here, so close to Glastonberry Grove—the gateway to the Red Room/Black Lodge—Bob intends on finally "taking" Laura. He is not expecting to kill her. Not now. Not unless he has too.

His reasons for bringing Ronette along are less clear. The series provides few details about what happened to Ronette the night Laura was murdered. We know she was with Laura in the train car and that she saw Bob. According to Agent Cooper in episode 8 (directed and co-written by Lynch), "Using a blunt object [Bob] hit Ronette and knocked her unconscious. He must have been so intent on killing Laura he didn't realize Ronette regained consciousness and escaped." But this still doesn't explain why Leland/Bob would bring Ronette along. She was not Bob's target and as a witness to his crimes she would have to be killed (something Bob may have attempted in episode 10). So why didn't Bob simply kill Ronette in the cabin?

At the time the series was written, Ronette was an incidental character, and her presence with Laura the night of the murder was explained as happenstance. Naturally, Ronette's presence could not be overlooked in the film. Surprisingly, Ronette's role in *Fire Walk With Me* is given more meaning than the series ever hinted.

Earlier, a tenuous connection was made between Ronette and Donna Hayward. Ronette and Donna are parallel figures in Laura's life, and are counterparts. Donna functions as the friend of "good" Laura, Ronette as the friend of "bad" Laura. Significantly, Ronette was introduced in the Pink Room, emerging from the shadows just as Donna withdrew into the darkness. In this way Ronette represents the perverted Donna—the kind of character Donna might have become if she had continued to wear "Laura's stuff."

A darker Laura came close to harming Donna, but the good Laura asserted herself and rescued her friend. Now, inside the train car, the presence of Ronette provides another potential victim—not for Bob but for Laura. If Laura is made to kill Ronette she will have forever abandoned her good side and, like Leland, have irrevocably given control to Bob.

And Laura's transformation into Bob begins. Horrified, she looks into the mirror and she sees Bob's reflection staring back. The process is underway. Bob's plan is succeeding and Laura, so lost and broken, is losing control. She is opening herself to the ultimate violation.

Suddenly, there is a moment of hope. It comes from Ronette, of all people. Ronette, the perverted Donna—a girl no better than Laura at her worst—Ronette Pulaski begins to pray and her prayers are answered.

An angel appears above Ronette, its presence made known by a bright white light and a sudden silence. The angel brings with her a sense of calm and protection. The horror of the events in the train car—the screaming and the torture—are cancelled out, an effect Lynch accomplishes by dropping the pulsing music and sound effects from the soundtrack. Ronette looks up at the angel and realizes her prayers have been heard. She has asked for forgiveness ("I'm sorry. I'm sorry."), and after she does her bound hands are freed.

Laura sees all this and suddenly realizes that salvation is possible. She now knows a truth even deeper than the reality of Bob's identity—she knows she was wrong about the angels. Having blamed herself for her horrific misfortunes, Laura felt she didn't deserve angels. She turned away from them, convincing herself that is was *they* who had abandoned *her*. She then chose to let her good side disappear, to let the fire consume her. Bob made every effort to push her toward this choice—he abused her, victimized her, stripped her of her self-esteem so that Laura would feel unworthy of angels. But Ronette's angel proves to Laura that she, too, is a good person, and the angels have never left. In this moment, her strength returns, and her ability to resist Bob is assured.

It is also at this moment that the Owl Cave ring finds its way to Laura. The One Armed Man arrives outside the train car and, with the help of Ronette, manages to slide open the door. Leland/Bob reacts, throwing Ronette out and closing the door. But not before the ring leaves the One Armed Man and rolls across the floor. Laura sees it, and with her new-found strength, puts it on. The result is a Lynchian moment of power unleashed, a moment akin to when Henry stabs the baby in *Eraserhead*, "setting in motion a flow of forces."[17] Leland screams, the Little Man shudders, static electricity floods the frame. Leland, forced by Bob into action, screams, "Don't make me do this!"—and plunges a knife into Laura again and again until she is dead.

What happened here in this sudden few seconds? Why does Laura dare to put the ring on when she has been so explicitly warned against it?

Laura Palmer has chosen good over evil. Once she does, the Owl Cave ring poses no threat to her. It cannot ensnare her, nor can it enslave her. Significantly, the ring has not been imposed upon her by another being. The Little Man has not "wed" Laura with it, and although the One Armed Man may have thrown the ring into the train, he does not force Laura to take it.[18] The ring is not placed on Laura's finger; it comes to her at a moment when she can choose to put it on.

Laura did not have this freedom of choice in her dream. There, the Little Man held the ring out to Laura—who later found it clutched in her hand. Weakened by the machinations of Bob, she was too vulnerable to resist. Cooper, who had sensed Laura's weakened state and her "cries for help," was wise to warn her against the ring. He recognized the threat of the Little Man and he hoped Laura would be strong enough to turn away.

The ring is clearly an object of power. If wielded by malevolent entities it can do great harm. But if held by a person of goodness (as is Laura when she takes it) it can lead to salvation. Robert Engels (co-writer of *Fire Walk With Me*) explains that the ring can be both good and bad depending on who has it: "For [some] people it empowers them."[19] Laura knows she cannot escape death, but she also knows she has the power to resist Bob. She boldly takes the ring—this object of power—and fearlessly puts it on. Perhaps she knows this action will force Bob to kill her. If so, she faces death with bravery and a certainty in her own goodness.

Laura must know that the ring and angels are connected, that the angels have delivered the ring to her. Realizing all this with sudden clarity, Laura embraces the potential of the ring. It cannot harm her; it can only "empower" her. This is why the Little Man is suddenly so afraid; Laura has turned the tables—she has wrested power away from him and Bob. Laura's choice does more than save her, it gives her victory over Bob and his associates. Laura has stolen their greatest weapon.

But an empowered Laura represents a threat. Bob knows Laura cannot be allowed to possess the ring. She has to be killed.

Once Bob kills her, however, Laura has escaped and the ring is lost.

***

Laura's escape brings her to her own Red Room where she sits confused and dazed. Her ordeal still resonates, and the consciousness of her afterlife (her soul, if you will) is befuddled. Laura has escaped—but not through easy means. She has endured a brutal death, and upon "awakening" in this new place she is both sad and uncertain.

She is startled by Dale Cooper who gently places a hand on her shoulder. Cooper smiles and his presence is reassuring. In an instant Laura's confusion and despair evaporate. Cooper's presence makes perfect sense to her as she realizes her destiny has always been connected with his in complex and subtle ways.[20]

An angel appears. Laura is filled with joy because she knows this is *her* angel. When she sees it she recognizes the truth of her escape. Her "goodness" has won. She has defeated her dark impulses and, by extension, the external evil forces that oppressed her. She has triumphed. She has escaped. She is free.

Part 2: Remaking *Fire Walk With Me*

Laura's journey in *Fire Walk With Me* was not a gentle one. She suffered and despaired and in the end, before receiving the helpful guidance of Dale Cooper, she remained confused. Those who watch *Fire Walk With Me* might also suffer and despair. Certainly most emerge from the experience confused.

Fire Walk With Me is not an easy film. It is difficult to watch, and it is difficult to comprehend. Familiarity with the series provides some guidance but also, surprisingly, some impairment. In an effort to explain David Lynch's intent with *Fire Walk With Me*, essayist David Foster Wallace has this to say:

> [*Fire Walk With Me*] sought to transform Laura Palmer from dramatic object to dramatic subject. As a dead person, Laura's existence on the television show had been entirely verbal and it was fairly easy to conceive her as a schizoid black/white construct . . . . But the movie . . . attempts to present this multivalent system of objectified personas—plaid-skirted coed/bare-breasted roadhouse slut/ tormented exorcism-candidate/molested daughter as an integrated and living whole: these different identities

> were all, the movie tried to claim, the same person. In *Fire
> Walk With Me*, Laura was no longer "an enigma" or "the
> password to an inner sanctum of horror." She now
> embodied, in full view, all the Dark Secrets that on the
> series had been the stuff of significant glances and
> delicious whispers.[21]

In effect, Wallace claims, Laura (of the series) was not a character; she was simply a plot-point. She embodied the mystery that motivated *other* characters to action. In *Fire Walk With Me*, however, Laura was no longer incidental to the story, she *was* the story, and as the dramatic subject of the film she had to drive the story through her choices and responses.

So does she become an "integrated and living whole?" Wallace maintains that Lynch didn't "entirely succeed at the project he set for himself in *Fire Walk With Me*,"[22] that the transformation of Laura from object to subject was "maybe an impossible thing." Wallace's careful choice of words like "maybe" and "not entirely" shows how difficult it is to pin down what happens in *Fire Walk With Me* (and that even an accomplished thinker like Wallace will not commit to claiming *Fire Walk With Me* either a success or a failure). Wallace refuses to say whether Laura was satisfactorily re-imagined as a dramatic subject because he knows that the film is ambiguous and open to contradictory interpretations.[23]

But Laura's success as a dramatic subject is crucial for the success of *Fire Walk With Me* as a whole. The film works only if the audience can see Laura as someone actively charting the arc of her own story. Such a character is defined by their ability to change and to experience revelation. What's more, such a character must be different by story's end than she was at the beginning. In *Fire Walk With Me*, Laura needed to be capable of action. But Laura was not "active" in the TV series—she didn't "do," she was "done to."

In creating a film about Laura Palmer, Lynch ran up against the barriers of the already-existing story. *Fire Walk With Me* was a prequel depicting certain events that could not be changed: Laura had to be killed by her father (who was arguably possessed by the demonic Bob), the murder had to take place in a train car in the woods. These things, among many others, could not be changed, even if they seemed counter-intuitive or didn't feel right to Lynch. Still, David Lynch needed to make Laura Palmer a well-rounded character who was more than a victim—more than a dead body on a lakeshore.

Lynch had never faced a situation like this before when making a film. He always had the freedom to tell a story exactly as he saw fit, even when adapting the work of another (e.g., *Dune* and *Wild at Heart*). To Lynch, filmmaking is a process of exploration and possibility. There are no boundaries. "As soon as you start something, all these things start kicking in, you are in a process, a beautiful, beautiful process with ideas and getting them onto some medium."[24] Even finished scripts remain malleable, serving as guideposts that Lynch uses to navigate the making of movies: "A script is only a way to get a kind of structure . . . . You might think a script is complete but it might not be . . . there might be opportunities and ideas coming that are so valuable."[25] For Lynch, the ideal approach to filmmaking is to be open to change and to rely on intuition.

In *Fire Walk With Me*, Lynch committed to bringing Laura to life, but had to follow her story to its pre-defined end—the one in which Laura is killed. How could he make her an active character in this scenario? How could she grow and change and take action? She couldn't simply choose to die (as the series suggested), she had to take some active role in her death.

David Lynch knew all this, but the circumstances of Laura's pre-existing story gave him little room to maneuver.

Opportunities and Ideas—Changing the Script

Lynch and Engels originally conceived the story of *Fire Walk With Me* to be one in which Laura Palmer sought escape from the oppressive presence of Bob. There were few choices for Laura to make and no real change for her to undergo. Bob was the antagonist, and Laura had to find a way to elude his growing power. This story was more in keeping with the facts and backstory established in the series.

At some point between completing the script and shooting the film, Lynch realized that he and Engels had failed to make Laura Palmer a fully-realized character. The script still depicted Laura as a helpless victim whose despairing behavior and tragic death resulted from outside forces. Clearly, the film needed a dramatic ingredient that would strengthen her character.

Lynch found that in the angels—a story element that does not appear anywhere in the shooting script. (Laura does not mention angels to Donna; she does not see one disappear from her bedroom painting; Ronette does not see one in the train car; and Laura does not see one in the Red Room at the end of the film.) But in Lynch's version, Laura speaks of angels, telling Donna that they will not help her, that they've "all gone away." This crucial line (the most important one in the film) establishes Laura's state of mind, and shows that she has imposed boundaries on herself

The added angel line shows that Laura has resigned herself to (and, in fact, *expects*) a tragic fate. She has given up on herself, asserting that the angels have gone because she cannot, and will not, believe she has any value. She is unworthy of salvation.

But Laura is wrong, and Lynch cleverly constructs the Laura-Donna scene to signal her mistake. Lynch shot the scene using a dramatic camera angle to show that angels do, indeed, watch over Laura. The girls are viewed from high above as they talk, a shot that reflects "an angelic presence," according to *Fire Walk With Me* cinematographer, Ron Garcia.[26] Cinematically, Lynch informs us that the angels have not left. Although Laura believes the angels are gone, it is *she* who is "gone . . . long gone" (as she explained to James in an earlier scene). Like most Lynch protagonists, Laura has "trapped" herself.

This, of course, makes Laura a far more interesting person. The introduction of the angels in *Fire Walk With Me*—and Laura's belief they have abandoned her—repositions the character of Laura Palmer in the narrative. She becomes someone who must recognize her own mistakes before she can grow and change and escape the trap in which she has placed herself.

In the train car, when Laura sees that the angels have not abandoned Ronette, she realizes she was wrong about herself. At that moment, Laura undergoes believable and meaningful change.

Once Laura undergoes change, however, she must take some sort of definitive action. But there was none to take, at least according to the way Lynch and Engels originally wrote it. When Laura is brought to the train car she realizes that Bob is about to possess her, and she knows her only escape from such possession is death. (Again, this harks back to the series where Laura explicitly states she "had to die because it was the only way to keep Bob away from me.") Lynch and Engels give Laura as much autonomy as they can: In the script she says to Leland, "You have to kill me." She looks at Bob in the mirror and says, "No! You can't have me." Then, again, to Leland she commands, "Kill me." And Leland does.

Lynch probably shot the scene the way it was scripted, assuming that Laura's explicit decision to end her life was a sufficient conclusion to her story (and, of course, one that perfectly fit with the facts as described on the series). Once it was shot, however, Lynch saw that such an ending was still weak and unsatisfactory.

As scripted, Laura Palmer, despite her strength of character and her conviction to die, is still incapable of effecting her own fate. Arms bound, she can only order Leland to kill her. The decision is hers, but the crucial act is Leland's; she is dependent on what he does. Leland takes center stage in this important final sequence as he, now freed from Bob, performs the ugly but necessary act of murder. As a result, Leland frees Laura from possession. Further, he "re-sacrifices" himself to Bob as a consequence of Laura's escape. Scripted, the scene is essentially about Leland, not Laura.

Lynch must have seen the flaws in this scenario. The story could only succeed with Laura taking action. Lynch was faced with a hard reality—he had to find some way to restore Laura as a narrative centerpiece.

This is where David Lynch redefined and expanded the meaning of the Owl Cave ring. He saw that it did not have to be an object of entrapment, that it could be a path to empowerment. If the ring could make its way to Laura, she could put it on. She could take action and chart her own path.

So far, Lynch and Engels had carefully established the ring as a dangerous object: The ring was connected to Teresa Banks, whose arm went numb and who then suffered a gruesome death. Dale Cooper, a clever, intuitive, and above all, *reliable* character, explicitly warns Laura not to take the ring when the Little Man offers it. Finally, a scripted scene (that Lynch shot) shows a nurse steal the ring from an injured Annie Blackburne, and "selfishly" put it on. The accumulation of all these incidents clearly pointed to a dangerous and evil Owl Cave ring.

Remarkably, Lynch saw beyond the existing narrative constraints of the ring, and envisioned a scene of liberation rather than doom. He saw the ring not as an object of evil but as an object of power. Laura could be perceived to be *stealing* the ring from the malevolent beings who wielded it, and then turning it against them. A few careful edits were all Lynch needed to accomplish this revision. First, he needed to remove the scene with Annie and the nurse; it contributed little to the narrative and would, in fact, weaken Lynch's new vision of the ring. Second, Lynch needed some new, minor footage to insert into the train car murder scene. Three shots were required: 1) a shot of the ring rolling across a straw-strewn floor; 2) a shot of a woman's hand placing the ring on her other hand; 3) a shot of the hand with the ring held up before a bright white light. These three simple inserts were likely produced after the initial filming of the train car scene.[27] Lynch did not have the luxury or opportunity to reassemble his cast and shoot new material with the actors. Like the edits he made to the film's prologue (see next chapter), Lynch dramatically altered the murder scene in the editing room.

David Lynch opened himself to those "valuable opportunities and ideas" that come to him during filming. The "idea" of angels and the "opportunity" of the ring presented themselves, and Lynch intuitively knew they were right for *Fire Walk With Me*, and that they made the film "as free and experimental as it could be within the dictates it had to follow."[28]

Yes, it's true that Lynch's new edits introduce ambiguity to the film, and yes, it appears as if *Fire Walk With Me* abandoned narrative continuity, and *yes*, multiple valid readings of the film were suddenly made possible. But the new version of the murder scene—the one after Lynch's edits—becomes more complex, more daring, and more rewarding. The Laura Palmer of the film suddenly becomes different that the Laura Palmer of the series. On the show, Laura reportedly "allowed herself to die." In the film, however, Laura escapes from Bob *before* she dies. Her realization of her own goodness—her acceptance of the angels—makes her untouchable.

In *Fire Walk With Me* Laura does not escape through death, she escapes because she has the power in herself to do so. In this way, Laura is decisively and explicitly transformed from dramatic object to dramatic subject. She at last succeeds at becoming a "living and integrated whole."

Even though the new elements of guardian angel and redefined ring complicate the narrative as presented on the television series, they succeed in the way they lift Laura Palmer out of the narrative dead end of the film's script.

When Lynch places the ring and the angel in the train car, he allows Laura to become a fully realized character. He found a way for her to choose good over evil. Once she does, she leaves this world to begin a journey into a larger, more profound universe.

Conclusion

No other David Lynch film requires as much attention and contemplation as *Fire Walk With Me* does. It is exactly because the film offers such challenges that it warrants comprehensive and exhaustive analysis. *Fire Walk With Me* deserves reconsideration so that it can take its rightful place among Lynch's other great works.

Part of the reason *Fire Walk With Me* is rarely analyzed by academics, or infrequently considered by writers who wish to discuss Lynch's *oeuvre*, is because the film offers no easy point of entry. How does one approach *Fire Walk With Me* in order to study its themes, analyze its character dynamics, or deconstruct its narrative? Is the movie a stand-alone film, or should it be considered as another episode of *Twin Peaks*? A more common (and frequently asked) question is: "Should a new viewer to *Twin Peaks* watch the film *before* or *after* watching the series?"

Many feel strongly that *Fire Walk With Me* should be saved until after the series. The film reveals too many of the show's secrets and it obviates the "Who killed Laura Palmer?" mystery. But the series imposes a certain narrow view on both the Laura Palmer character and her backstory, and it arguably handicaps attempts at open, freer interpretations of the film.

Those familiar with the series watch *Fire Walk With Me* and find themselves reassessing Laura and reconstructing a narrative they thought they knew. Those who have never seen the series watch *Fire Walk With Me* and find themselves suddenly immersed in a confounding, Byzantine milieu from which they must assemble a comprehensible story. No wonder Michael Chion believes, "There is no way in."

But there is.

As this essay has shown, the key to appreciating the film is Laura Palmer. Those who have never experienced *Twin Peaks*—who do not know the difference between the Black Lodge and the Roadhouse, or the identity of Annie Blackburne and the Log Lady—need only focus on Laura. The film provides a complete, satisfying story arc for her character.

Laura Palmer also provides a point of entry for long-time fans of the series who, when confronted with the film, sometimes fail to see that Lynch was asking more from them than the he was on the series. "Indeed, *Twin Peaks: Fire Walk With Me* demand[s] a degree of belief in the fate of Laura Palmer that surpassed the comfort level of many of the series' original viewers."[29]

Lynch designed *Fire Walk With Me* to actualize Laura—to "realize" her. Once long-time viewers start seeing Laura as more than a plot component, she becomes, as Wallace observes, "complex, contradictory, real"[30] and the film achieves new power.

***

After making *Fire Walk With Me*, Lynch returned to the world of *Twin Peaks* again, writing and directing the "Log Lady introductions" to accompany episodes of the series as they were re-broadcast on the Bravo cable network. In the introduction to the pilot of *Twin Peaks*, Lynch emphasizes the importance of Laura Palmer in the *Twin Peaks* narrative, explaining that *Twin Peaks* is a story of "many but it begins with one. . . .The one leading to the many is Laura Palmer. Laura is the one." Here, in yet another emphatic comment about the character, Lynch is asking viewers to assess (or reassess) the series with a different Laura Palmer in mind—the Laura Palmer who was so vividly brought to life in *Fire Walk With Me*.

It probably doesn't matter to Lynch if viewers watch *Fire Walk With Me* before or after the series. What is likely, however, is that Lynch hopes viewers will seek out—or return to—the series after seeing the film.

Because *Fire Walk With Me* is more than a simple "prequel" or "sequel" to *Twin Peaks*. It functions as an informative new pathway back to the television show. The film reorients both audience and narrative so that each might envision a new Laura Palmer; it revives Laura, reifies her, and gives her a fresh presence in the televised story.

Fire Walk With Me is David Lynch's reinvestment in *Twin Peaks*. For all its power and complexity, its intensity and emotion, *Fire Walk With Me* succeeds because of one simple thing: It forever reminds us that Laura Palmer invigorates *Twin Peaks*.

DREAMS OF DEER MEADOW

"I think fragments of things are pretty interesting. You can dream the rest. Then you're a participant."[1] – David Lynch

David Lynch's most bewildering and complicated work may be his sixth feature film, *Twin Peaks: Fire Walk With Me*. The motion picture prequel to the TV series is filled with cryptic dialogue, seemingly abandoned plotlines, and baffling characters. The film is distinctly divided into two parts, a thirty-minute prologue that features the investigation into the murder of a young woman named Teresa Banks, and a two-hour primary story about the last week of Laura Palmer's life and the events that led to her murder.

Audiences (whether they are familiar with the series or not) often feel that there is a lot more going on in the film than is immediately apparent. The movie offers what seems to be a restricted glimpse into a larger universe; it hints that there is a great deal more happening behind the picture, outside the frame and between the scenes. It tantalizes by what it does not reveal.

Deciphering *Fire Walk With Me* is a game that has been played by fans and scholars for years. Numerous theories about the meaning of the film (how its narrative works and why the characters behave the way they do) have been proposed. Still, the film has always managed to mystify.

David Lynch's work since the release of *Fire Walk With Me* in 1992 provides some guidance about his approach to storytelling and his problem-solving techniques while making films. If we look at these works—particularly at *Mulholland Drive*—can we learn anything about his directorial approach that provides perspectives on *Fire Walk With Me*? In short, can we deduce more satisfying answers about the film?

The answer is: Yes.

The history of *Mulholland Drive* is particularly instructive. As many know, Lynch filmed and edited an open-ended pilot for a network TV series to be called *Mulholland Drive*. When the network did not pick up the series, Lynch was left with an incomplete work. Later, he had the opportunity to film new material to complete the project. Rather than finish the story by tying up the loose ends, Lynch re-interpreted the pilot so as to make it a *dream* of a (new) main character. In effect, the pilot became a reflection of a much different story.

Years earlier, Lynch co-wrote and directed the film, *Lost Highway*. Like *Mulholland Drive*, *Lost Highway* has a bifurcated narrative—a story about one character that shifts into a seemingly different story about another. Both films suggest that one of their two stories is real and the other is a dream (or mental fantasy) of one of the characters. *Fire Walk With Me* contains a similar, though less obvious, narrative framework.

Due to circumstances beyond his control, Lynch was forced to make *Fire Walk With Me* in ways he did not originally intend. This led to some storytelling experimentation as he struggled to maintain his vision. As a result, Lynch found new ways to structure narratives and tell stories. In later films, he would continue those experiments. In fact, a study of *Fire Walk With Me* shows that Lynch's approach to his later works took root in this film. It is a point of origin—in essence, an early version of a structure that would be developed more fully in *Lost Highway* and *Mulholland Drive*, where dreams and multiple personalities would become overt parts of the narrative.

As I will show, the first thirty minutes of *Fire Walk With Me* can be interpreted as the dream of FBI Special Agent, Dale Cooper, a character who was supposed to have a prominent role in the original version of the film, and who was, arguably, the most important character in the TV series. Through storytelling experimentation Lynch managed to maintain this prominence. The prologue-as-dream scenario restores Cooper to an active presence in the story, and it resolves many of the film's confusing and obscure elements. In fact, the dream interpretation solidifies the film, making it a more cohesive work.[2]

Visions and Revisions

When David Lynch and Robert Engels began to write *Fire Walk With Me*, they envisioned an ambitious film that would tell a number of complex stories. First, they saw the film as the story of Laura Palmer and her last few days alive. Second, they saw it as the story of Dale Cooper and his investigation into the death of Teresa Banks—an investigation that would introduce Cooper to the arcane world of the Red Room and its denizens. Third, they saw a story about the inhabitants of the Red Room—Bob and Mike—and their efforts to return to their "home." Fourth, they saw a film that would feature familiar characters from the TV series (such as Sheriff Truman, Deputy Andy, Pete Martell, Big Ed Hurley, etc.) in numerous vignettes.

The magnitude of such a task was daunting, but the film presented other challenges as well. *Fire Walk With Me* was designed as a prequel, depicting events that took place before the television show—events that would not be fully resolved until the story "continued" in the series. However, the film was also intended to be a self-contained, stand-alone work—one that provided a definite beginning, middle, and end. Within this difficult framework, Lynch and Engels attempted to craft a film that would tell a familiar story but provide fans with something new. Clearly, this framework meant that Lynch and Engels were limited with what they could do with one of the series' most important "established facts"—the Teresa Banks story. It had to be integrated with the Laura Palmer story, but it could not venture too far into new story territory.

Viewers of *Twin Peaks* already knew Teresa Banks had been killed by Leland Palmer (possessed by Bob) and that Leland/Bob inserted a small scrap of paper imprinted with the letter "T" under her fingernail (as he inserted an "R" under Laura's). The audience also knew that the murder of Teresa Banks would remain unsolved until well into the series: any investigation into Teresa Banks's death in the film would lead to a dead end. Although the Teresa Banks story would allow viewers to learn more about the character and the crime, the fact remained that no meaningful resolution or revelation could be supplied by the film.

So why bother covering Teresa's murder at all? One obvious reason is that the investigation allowed Dale Cooper to be in the film. After all, a *Twin Peaks* film without the show's dominant character would have been untenable. But Lynch and Engels also saw another narrative purpose for the Teresa story: to integrate the character of Dale Cooper into the world of Laura Palmer—to make him a crucial figure in her life (and afterlife).[3]

The TV series hinted that somehow Cooper was a presence in Laura's world before she died. (Episode 16 reveals that Laura and Cooper shared the same dream.) The film, then, would show how Cooper became "connected" to Laura's psyche. Events in the Teresa Banks prologue would trigger Cooper's intuition and alert him to a potential danger surrounding a future, unidentified victim (Laura). This intuitive "alarm" would resonate with Laura; she dreams of Cooper and receives his warnings. When she dies, she is comforted by his presence in the vague world of the Red Room and, arguably, shepherded by him to a place of happiness.

The lives, minds, and spirits of Dale Cooper and Laura Palmer were explicitly intertwined, even though they never physically met. In the world of *Twin Peaks* they are the two most vibrant, important characters, and *Fire Walk With Me* was originally designed to show how the connection between them came to be.

This original vision of the film, which included Cooper's investigation into Teresa's murder (and the other three storylines described earlier), is not what ended up in the final cut. In some respects, this comes as no surprise—such a version would have had a running time of well over three hours. More importantly, actor Kyle MacLachlan refused to commit the amount of time needed to shoot his part, and this led to significant revisions.

Lynch and Engels altered their vision of the film so that Laura's story became prominent. They reduced the Mike/Bob conflict to an echo of its former self; removed the *Twin Peaks* vignettes entirely; and—in the most dramatic alteration—truncated and transformed the story of Dale Cooper into the story of Chester Desmond (played by actor and musician, Chris Isaak). As such, a different FBI agent would investigate the murder of Teresa Banks.

When this shift occurred, a new set of problems arose. First, story continuity was seemingly disrupted. Though not explicitly stated in the TV pilot, it is implied that Cooper had investigated the Banks murder himself. When *The Autobiography of F.B.I. Special Agent Dale Cooper* was published in April, 1991, Cooper is, indeed, the investigating agent.[4] One can argue the canonicity of tie-in books (a strict reading would reject them), but the fact is, the book simply presented what fans had assumed all along. Now, suddenly, the movie would reveal that Cooper did not investigate the Banks murder after all.

A more significant problem was this: having Desmond investigate the Banks murder did not resolve the primary issue of making Cooper an important player in the film. If that was one of the main reasons for including the Teresa Banks investigation in the first place—if not the *main* reason—then why bother with it at all, especially if Cooper was to be relegated to a few minor scenes?

Such questions were certainly in the minds of viewers of the final film. The Teresa Banks investigation, sometimes referred to as the "Deer Meadow prologue," takes about thirty minutes to complete, at which point the film shifts to the story of Laura Palmer. Her story then dominates the rest of the film—almost two hours. Outside of some subtle and minor connections between the prologue and the rest of the film, the two seem like different stories. So the question remained: why keep the Deer Meadow section if there would be no significant presence by Dale Cooper?

The Dreams of Dale Cooper

This essay contends that Cooper's relative insignificance in the prologue is an illusion, and that he is a more dominant presence than first appears. True, Chet Desmond does seem to lead the investigation. But as with many Lynch films, there may be more going on here than first appears.

The original scripts provide some clues. When the investigating agent changed from Cooper (in a "pre-release" draft dated July 3, 1991) to Desmond (in a "shooting" draft dated August 8, 1991), the names changed but the dialogue remained the same. Desmond took on the role originally scripted for Cooper. Almost all of Cooper's original lines were left as they were—including his dialogue with Sam Stanley, who assisted him in the investigation. Despite the fact that MacLachlan pulled out of the project, David Lynch was essentially shooting from his original script of *Fire Walk With Me*.

Some changes, of course, had to be made. Agent Desmond meets a mysterious fate when he inexplicably disappears. Dale Cooper is then introduced to the story and, rather than investigate Teresa Banks's death, he is sent out to investigate Chet Desmond's disappearance. Cooper's role is now minor and passive. He is a seemingly insignificant character in this revised version of *Fire Walk With Me*, absent from many critical scenes and appearing only after the action had transpired. What's more, his investigation in to Desmond's disappearance is brief and essentially fruitless. He leaves the scene as baffled as he arrived. Although his presence in the film provides a critical link to the series, his function in the *Fire Walk With Me* narrative is muted and negligible.

This was clearly not Lynch and Engels original intent. Cooper was supposed to be a more vibrant figure, especially if he was going to play a critical part in Laura's story. Lynch must have understood this, must have recognized that the film was weakened without Cooper playing a more significant role.

Faced with this predicament, I believe Lynch took a bold and risky approach to re-imagining the narrative of *Fire Walk With Me* (the same approach he would take years later when he reworked the *Mulholland Drive* pilot into a feature film). By adding a few critical lines of dialogue and by carefully editing and restructuring certain scenes, Lynch positioned the entire Deer Meadow prologue (from the opening shot of the TV being smashed to Cooper's monologue beside Wind River) as a dream of Dale Cooper. By doing so, Lynch restored Cooper to a more resonant, meaningful presence in the story. The Cooper-as-dreamer scenario allowed Lynch to return to his original concept of *Fire Walk With Me*. It is Cooper—not Chet Desmond—who confronts the mystery of Teresa Banks.

Lynch ensures that Cooper's dream has narrative purpose. He understood that the dream had to be more than mere authorial conceit—the act of "dreaming" had to be necessary for the story, had to contribute something that a reality-based narrative could not, otherwise such dreaming would be arbitrary.

Cooper's dream had to have intrinsic value. And it does. Lynch deliberately composed the dream so that it leads Cooper to a better understanding of the Owl Cave ring (Teresa Banks's ring). Almost every change he made to the prologue—almost every "dream" element Lynch added—was designed to guide Cooper's mind to the secrets of the ring. As we will see, Cooper's subconscious mind is seeking answers through the dream, while, at the same time, otherworldly beings access Cooper's dream and try to help him.

The prologue, then, is not so much about the Teresa Banks investigation as it is about Dale Cooper, and his journey as an FBI agent who will one day use information gleaned here to help him solve the Laura Palmer case.

Remember, the idea that Cooper could be dreaming the events of the prologue is perfectly in keeping with the character (who, in the series, experiences powerful and significant dreams) and with themes Lynch has explored in earlier works. Dream imagery and character preoccupation with dreams in prevalent in almost all of Lynch's previous films, from *Eraserhead* to *Blue Velvet*. (And, of course, these concepts figure prominently in *Mulholland Drive*.)

The Cooper-as-dreamer scenario provides a satisfying explanation for the confusing, sometimes arbitrary nature of the prologue. Its various cryptic lines, narrative dead-ends, and extraneous story content can be viewed as part of Cooper's powerful dreaming subconscious—a mind working to sort facts, process information, and to assign meaning to certain experiences. What's more, dream "logic" explains the shifting reality of the prologue as it moves from Deer Meadow, to Philadelphia, and back to Deer Meadow.

Cooper's dream can also be viewed as a pathway to another world. The dream opens the door to the Red Room "reality," a place which is home to a group of autonomous inhabitants and which is governed by its own baffling rules. As we mentioned, some of these beings will try to help Cooper (just as they did in the series).

Finally, the dream scenario allows the film to become a more organic whole. Cooper's psyche dominates the first part of the film and echoes into the second. Cooper's presence in Laura's story now seems more appropriate. It feels "right" for Cooper to guide Laura through dreams and through death when his mind has already guided viewers through the crucial events that precede her tragic story.

In constructing *Fire Walk With Me* so that it positions Cooper as an active (though dreaming) participant, Lynch transforms the film from a patchwork tapestry of loosely connected scenes into a unified and balanced work.

Inside a Dream

Lynch conveys a sense of dreaming by using numerous instances of "doubling" in the prologue. As we will see, dialogue, characters and events regularly occur twice. This pronounced use of doubling does not happen in the second part of the film (Laura's story); it only happens in the prologue. There are also many lines of dialogue in which characters talk about sleep and dreams. Again, this kind of dialogue is primarily confined to the prologue.

If we look beyond the film and analyze the changes made between the pre-release and shooting drafts of the script, and between the shooting draft and the theatrical cut of the film, we find compelling—almost conclusive—evidence that the first 30 minutes of *Fire Walk With Me* is Dale Cooper's dream. When Lynch changed Cooper into Desmond he made other changes. Some of these occur in the second part of the film but most occur in the prologue, making it more abstract and inscrutable than originally scripted. They are evidence that Lynch was conceptually changing the prologue, altering its narrative status from reality to dream.

Cooper's Dream Part 1: Chet Desmond

The prologue opens with a shot of a static-filled TV screen being smashed with a lead pipe. The next shot shows a body floating in Wind River and is subtitled, "Teresa Banks." These are the first images of Cooper's dream, but they are not figments of his imagination. Teresa Banks really was killed (as later dialogue in the film—and facts established in the series—confirm). As Cooper dreams, he envisions what must have happened to her the moments during and after her death.

Gordon Cole is shown in his Oregon office, ordering one of his two secretaries to, "Get me Agent Chester Desmond on the phone!" As originally scripted, Cole is shown talking into a speaker-phone. By adding the two secretaries, Lynch changed this very simple scene into a slightly more complicated one. The appearance of the two secretaries, each of whom appears separately but performing the exact same action (walking forward from the right side of Cole's desk, toward the side of the frame and then off screen) marks the first significant instance of doubling in the film. Their presence seems redundant—and noticeable. (Why does Cole need both of them?) The two secretaries are blonde and brunette, a scenario that often signifies duality in Lynch's work. *Lost Highway* features the characters Alice and Renee; *Mulholland Drive* has Betty and Rita; *Twin Peaks* has Laura and Maddy. These blonde and brunette character-pairs arguably represent aspects of a single personality. Likewise, the appearance of the two secretaries, in the dreaming mind of Dale Cooper, signifies that one being (Cooper) could manifest as another (Chet Desmond).

Almost all of the Chet Desmond part of the dream is based on Cooper's own memory. In other words, those events that Chet Desmond "experiences" are actually events that already happened to Cooper. His dreaming subconscious has transformed himself into a new, slightly different, personality. It was really Cooper—not Desmond—who traveled to Deer Meadow with Sam Stanley. It was Cooper who confronted Sheriff Cable, viewed Teresa Banks's body, spoke with Irene at Haps, questioned Carl Rodd, and who, finally, was left stymied by the case. This was the story as it was originally scripted by Lynch and Engels. A dream interpretation of the prologue allows these scripted events to still be considered "reality" even though they are not explicitly depicted on screen. Instead, we see them represented through Cooper's dreaming mind.

Lynch's reconfiguration of the prologue employed a clever story-telling tactic. He managed to convey his original scripted concept (Cooper in Deer Meadow) but used a different actor (and different character) to do so. In short, he had it both ways.

The question arises as to why Cooper would dream himself as someone else. Why does he imagine himself as Chet Desmond? The film provides no explicit answer. Perhaps Cooper mentally re-created himself as Desmond because he knows that, in reality, he failed to solve the Banks murder and believes a different detective will have better luck. The dream is, in part, wish fulfillment: Cooper wants to solve the case. But, deep down, he knows that reality cannot be changed, that the insoluble nature of the case cannot be avoided. Just as Cooper failed in reality, so too will Desmond fail in the dream. Once Desmond fails, he is no longer necessary; Cooper's restless, churning mind "erases" him.[5]

But before that will happen, Cooper will "re-live" the events of his trip to Deer Meadow through this different persona.

Desmond arrives in Deer Meadow and meets Sam Stanley and Gordon Cole. Cole introduces Lil, who performs her "coded" dance. A blue rose is pinned to Lil's dress. Desmond explains that he can't tell Stanley what the blue rose means. Later, Stanley enquires about the blue rose when Desmond decides to return to the trailer park. Cooper also mentions the blue rose in his message to Diane, where he describes the Teresa Banks investigation as one of "Cole's 'blue rose' cases." Neither Cooper or Desmond offer any more information about the meaning of the blue rose and it is not mentioned again in the film. It appears to be an aspect of the prologue, only.

So what is the blue rose and why is such an obvious mystery introduced but never resolved? Many believe its meaning is self-evident—a blue rose is an impossibility, something that cannot exist in nature. A "blue rose case" alerts the FBI agent that he's dealing with a potential supernatural phenomenon. This may be true, but notice Desmond uses an interesting choice of words when talking to Stanley: He says he "can't" tell Stanley what the blue rose means, not that he "won't." Desmond can't tell what the rose means because *he doesn't know*. The blue rose is merely a figment of Cooper's mind—a dream-invention that represents the impossibility of the case.

Cooper recognizes that the case potentially involves some sort of otherworldly phenomena and so he introduces a symbol of these phenomena into the dream. To Cooper, the blue rose could function as a subconscious alarm, something that will echo into the waking world and alert him to look beyond the rational. When Cooper travels to Twin Peaks he is prepared to use unorthodox methods of investigation. His mind is open to all sorts of possibilities. Did his dream about a "blue rose" prepare him for this subsequent investigation? Maybe.

The blue rose did not appear in the script until the prologue was changed to feature Chet Desmond. The pre-release draft of the script (which featured Cooper, rather than Desmond) makes no mention of it. Lil does not wear one and Cooper does not speak about it with Stanley or mention it to Diane in his recorded report. Its introduction to the "Chet Desmond Draft" can be considered a major clue to unlocking the mystery of the prologue. The unexplained and unresolved presence of the blue rose is one way Lynch signifies a dream world—the blue rose is but an artifact of a dreaming mind.

Desmond and Stanley arrive in Deer Meadow and confront Sheriff Cable. They gain access to Teresa Banks's body and examine it. Desmond notices that Teresa's ring is not included with her personal effects. This is the first time the ring is mentioned in the story. The missing ring is critical and will dominate the rest of the prologue. Ostensibly, Cooper dreams of the missing ring because he could not locate it in "reality." But more is going on here. Cooper intuits the importance of the ring. He may not have understood its importance during his visit to Deer Meadow, but in his dream he begins to deduce a deeper meaning. The ring becomes the focus of his dream as he "realizes" he needs to know more about it. Of course, he cannot escape "reality"—when he dreams of reaching for the ring (as Desmond does), he cannot grasp it. But finding and holding the ring is not as important as understanding it. And, as we will see, Cooper will come to learn crucial information about the ring before his dream is over.

Desmond and Stanley visit Hap's Diner and speak with Irene. Another instance of doubling occurs when the old patron twice asks, "Are you talking about that little girl that was murdered?" Although the line is repeated in the film, it is spoken only once in both the pre-release and shooting drafts of the script. Lynch uses the line twice in the final edit to effectively reinforce the idea that "Cooper" is investigating the murder of "that little girl" for the second time.

Desmond and Stanley visit the Fat Trout Trailer Park and meet Carl Rodd, the property manager, who takes them to Teresa's trailer. It is here that one of the most fascinating exchanges in the film occurs—an event that strongly suggests the characters are aspects of a dream. After Rodd gives each agent a cup of coffee, Stanley says, "We sure do need a good 'wake-me-up' don't we Agent Desmond?" Desmond mutely looks at Stanley and offers no reply. Stanley repeats the line: "We sure do need a good 'wake-me-up' don't we Agent Desmond?" This seems to shake

Desmond out of his trance and he replies, "Yeah! We do, Sam." At this moment a number of unusual events take place. The film cuts to a point-of-view shot of an unidentified old woman entering Teresa's trailer. Desmond asks if she knew Teresa Banks. The old woman shivers and backs away. There is a shot of a nearby telephone pole accompanied by the Indian "whooping" noise. Rodd seems to go in to a trance and speaks some cryptic lines, "You see, I've already gone places. I just want to stay where I am." Desmond appears puzzled, as if trying to understand what is happening, why Rodd is suddenly behaving so strangely. But before any further inquiry is made, the scene ends. It is an abrupt transition. The scene doesn't properly conclude; rather, it seems to cut off in the middle.

What happened here? Why do all these strange events happen at one specific moment? And why are they not further developed in the film? Stanley's "wake-me-up" line seems to act as a trigger, as if Cooper's dreaming mind is trying to wake itself up. (The "wake-me-up" line is *not* part of the pre-release draft of the script; there, Stanley asks, "You really do like that coffee, don't you Agent Cooper?" Rather than change the single word "Cooper" to "Desmond," Lynch changed the entire line. This important change was deliberate—the new line suggests the idea of a dreaming mind trying to wake itself.) Before Cooper can awaken, however, a different "consciousness" manifests itself within the dream. For the first time, a separate entity, distinct from Cooper's mind, enters the dream and attempts to communicate.

In the TV series, Cooper exhibits a psychic ability to contact other beings (and other worlds) through dreams. He encounters Mike (the One Armed Man), Bob, the Little Man From Another Place, Laura Palmer (and possibly the Giant) all through his dreaming subconscious. In *Fire Walk With Me*, he again receives messages from another, this time unidentified, being. The message, however, is unclear. Rodd appears to be channeling another consciousness. He is afraid and just wants to stay where he is. But why would he (or whoever is speaking) be afraid of leaving? One possibility is that Rodd only exists within Cooper's dream. If Cooper awakens (as he almost did when Stanley spoke his lines) Rodd would cease to exist. Another possibility is that this consciousness wants Cooper to stay asleep, perhaps because Cooper has yet to learn important information.

Admittedly, that there is not enough evidence to support any definite solution to this puzzling scene. Nor is it even certain Lynch knew what it meant. Co-writer Robert Engels recalls that the scene was "a real cool thing that happened." It was "sort of scripted" but "not in any draft . . . . it sprung from Harry [Dean Stanton's] and David's friendship."[6] The scene is a perfect example of Lynch re-working and developing the material as he shot the film. Although the specific meaning of this scene may never be known, I believe the scene, when put in context with the other changes made between drafts of the script, strongly hints that a dream is taking place, that the dreamer (who may be Cooper) is on the verge of waking, and that someone or something is attempting to deliver a message before that waking can occur.

The dream continues as Desmond and Stanley confront Sheriff Cable about taking Teresa's body back to Portland. After they secure the body, Stanley asks Desmond if he is going back to the trailer park for the blue rose. Desmond does not reply. Here, again there is mention of the blue rose. The rose and the ring are two recurring objects fraught with deeper meaning, yet never satisfactorily defined in the film. Could the two items be related? Stanley's suggestion that Desmond is "going back" for the rose, coupled with Desmond's eventual sighting of the ring, implies a connection. The film, however supplies no further information about this potential relationship.

Cooper's dreaming mind could be equating the two items. In "reality" Cooper never found the ring, but in his dream it becomes an important and mysterious object. Like the blue rose, however, Cooper "can't" say what the ring means. But he wants to find out—he wants to "go back for the blue rose."

Desmond returns to the trailer park and after a brief exchange with Rodd, he begins to look around. He seems drawn to a particular trailer. When he looks under it, he sees Teresa's ring sitting on a small mound of dirt. He reaches for it and the screen goes black.

This is a critical transition point in the dream. Although the shooting draft of the script describes Desmond as "disappearing" the image on screen freezes and then fades to black. Desmond does *not* physically disappear. In the dreaming mind of Dale Cooper, however, Desmond ceases to exist.

As we've mentioned before it is difficult to discern why Cooper is experiencing this particular dream. It is obviously based on his own memories of investigating the Banks murder. But is Cooper dreaming to relive the case and this time solve it through a new persona? Or is he trying to escape from the memory of the failed investigation by retreating into an alternate identity? In the end it doesn't really matter because the Desmond character will not (and cannot) solve the murder. Cooper's restless, active mind either submits to the inevitable and erases Desmond; or his retreating, passive mind finally acknowledges his failure and no longer needs Desmond. But the Desmond persona has performed a critical function. Through Desmond, Cooper has had a glimpse of the ring. This sighting opens a doorway into Cooper's mind, allowing him to at last grasp a deeper meaning to the ring. Its appearance triggers the ending of the first part of the dream and the beginning of the second. As we will see, Cooper's dreaming mind will now be more receptive to critical information from otherworldly beings.

Desmond is gone but the dream continues. After the screen fades to black, the film cuts to an establishing shot of Philadelphia, then quickly to the first appearance of Dale Cooper. Cooper enters the story almost as soon as Desmond disappears, reinforcing the idea they are the same character—Cooper has simply replaced Desmond.

Lynch now provides the first of his two most explicit clues that the prologue is a dream. Cooper says to Cole, "I'm worried about today because of that dream I told you about." Cole looks a bit confused and "not sure what to say." Cooper offers no further information. But this line, so early into Cooper's appearance, is a clear signal that dreams play an important role in the story. Cooper's line is a crucial clue regarding the Chet Desmond/Deer Meadow sequence that just ended. It was all part of a dream—Cooper's dream.

Cooper leaves Cole's desk and stands in the hall before the closed-circuit security camera. He then walks into an adjacent room where he checks the image on the corresponding security monitor. Cooper repeats this behavior until, inexplicably, he sees *himself* on the security monitor. At this moment he is in two places at once. Cooper's appearance in the security monitor is open to many interpretations, but, if this sequence is still part of a dream, it hints at the idea that Cooper is a "doubled presence" in the dream, that he has already appeared in the dream under the guise of Desmond.

When Cooper spoke with Cole, he never described his dream. The audience, like Cole, is waiting for him to say more. Cooper says he's worried and indicates his dream was important, but says nothing else. Of course, his subsequent behavior in front of the security camera implies he is either re-enacting, or acting upon, his dream. But nothing is certain in this part of the film.

Neither Cooper's announcement about his dream nor his doubled appearance were part of the pre-release draft of the script. These elements were added later, when the script was changed to accommodate Cooper's new role. As Lynch reworked the prologue, he added Cooper's new dialogue to suggest that part of the film was actually a dream, then included a scene (the two Coopers) to evoke dream logic.

Cooper's Dream, Part 2: Phillip Jeffries

The doubled presence of Cooper coincides with the appearance of Phillip Jeffries, the FBI agent who has been missing for two years. Jeffries, who is confused and erratic, cryptically relates some of his experiences to Cooper and the other agents, then disappears.

The entire Jeffries scene was radically altered from the way it was originally scripted. Even the shooting draft of the film contains a significantly different description of this scene than the pre-release draft. A close examination of the scene, along with a comparison of the filmed version to the scripted one, suggests that Lynch purposely altered it so that it would appear dreamlike. In fact, the final version of this scene (as it appears in *Fire Walk With Me*) is so bizarre that it seems impossible to reconcile it with any waking "reality."

In the *script*, Jeffries walks past Cooper's double and into Cole's office and Cooper follows. Albert and Cole recognize Jeffries, who seems distracted and confused. He points to Cooper and says "Who do you think that is there?" He stumbles to a chair and says, "It was a dream. We live inside a dream." He then tells the tale of his journey to "one of their meetings . . . above a convenience store." The script flashes back to the meeting. We see the Man From Another Place, Bob, the Tremonds and the Woodsmen. The meeting adjourns and the script returns to Jeffries, who is quietly crying, "the ring . . . the ring." At this point Cole asks Albert to leave the room. Cole tries to use his intercom to call for a stenographer. The intercom does not work but Cole continues to try as "static begins to build and the florescent lights start to hum." Cooper goes to the door and looks to see if anyone is coming to help. Cole, meanwhile is focused on the intercom. He turns back to Jeffries. But there is no one there. Cooper and Albert return to the room to find Jeffries has vanished.

Much of the Jeffries scene was changed for the film. The scripted scene has a logical linearity and deliberate pace to it. The on-screen version, however, is chaotic and obscure: Jeffries enters the room and points to Cooper, "Who do you think this is there?" Blue static superimposes the scene. Jeffries tells his tale, but the audience hears only snippets. His story is intercut with scenes from the convenience store meeting; Jeffries' voice fades in and out. The audience hears him say, "It was a dream. We live inside a dream," and, "the ring . . . the ring." Albert and Cooper never leave the room during the story. Jeffries screams and then Cole declares, "He's gone!" There is a shot of an empty chair and Albert announces, "I've got the front desk right now. He was never here."

(The scripted version of the scene also told more about where Jeffries came and went. He is shown in Buenos Aires both before and after his appearance in Cole's office. Lynch cut these scenes. As part of a dream they would be extraneous information. Dream logic requires no explanation about Jeffries' origin. He need only enter Cooper's mind at the right time, tell his story, then disappear.)

The Phillip Jeffries scene is a kaleidoscopic montage of images and sounds that is difficult to decipher. It does seem, however, that Jeffries suddenly disappears right in front of Cole, Albert and Cooper. For three people to witness such an overt supernatural phenomenon—especially when that group includes the no-nonsense, forensic minded Albert—

clashes with the subjective nature of the *Twin Peaks* universe. The "supernatural" in *Twin Peaks* was often tied to the psychology of the individual. Dreams and intuition allowed "the gifted and the damned" to tap into other worlds—to see what others could not—in ways that was unique to the individual. Lynch has said that the Red Room is a place "that changes depending on whoever walks into it."[7] Supernatural phenomena exist in the *Twin Peaks* world, but in ways that uniquely reflect the observer.

In the Phillip Jeffries scene, three people witness the exact same phenomenon. Surely, the witnessing of such of an event would challenge the way Albert, of all people, perceives the universe. Could an Albert who watched another person *literally vanish* be the same Albert who would later travel to Twin Peaks and sarcastically ask Cooper if he's seen "Bob on Earth in the last few weeks" (as he does in episode 9)? Is this the same Albert who will insist on "confining [his] conclusions to the planet earth" (episode 10)? Having Albert witness the Jeffries disappearance contradicts his established character. There is no way to reconcile the behavior of Albert in the series with the Albert from the film.

Unless we accept that the Phillip Jeffries scene is part of a dream.

Conveniently, Jeffries supplies the most explicit, telling clue about the nature of what is happening: "It was a dream. We live inside a dream." Phillip Jeffries, Gordon Cole and Albert Rosenfield—and even Dale Cooper—live inside a dream. What came before—the Deer Meadow prologue—was part of a dream. It is as simple as that. There is no deeper meaning to what Jeffries says, no greater mystery to solve. The characters live inside a dream. This is the proper way to "read" the prologue of *Fire Walk With Me*. Many clues have so far hinted at this interpretation, but here, in *a line that was not part of the original draft* of the film, Lynch exhibits a rare moment of explicitness. He provides a glimpse into the mechanics of the narrative, an invaluable "key" that cracks the code of the prologue.

In a dream, "Albert" is free to witness a disappearing Jeffries. In a dream, Cooper can appear in two places at the same time. What's more, with a dream interpretation we can now venture a guess as to what Jeffries means when he asks, "Who do you think this is there?" about Cooper. Cooper, quite simply, is the *dreamer*. If Jeffries knows that he is inside a dream, he may very well know whose dream. (Another equally valid answer might be that Jeffries recognizes Cooper as Desmond. Again, if Jeffries knows he is in a dream, he may know that Cooper has changed identity.)

Jeffries does not seem to be a creation of Cooper's dreaming mind, but rather an autonomous entity that has found a way to contact Cooper through his subconscious. Jeffries' presence is important—he has vital information to impart, and in a crash of images and sound, he does. Lynch's complex, multi-layered editing of the scene has a dreamlike quality. Cooper's mind is overloaded with the information that Jeffries pours into the dream. Lynch isn't editing this scene merely to show viewers what happened at the convenience store meeting (as the original flashback meant to do), he edits the scene as if the dreaming mind of Dale Cooper is receiving this information and his mind is struggling to process it.

Jeffries succeeds in supplying some crucial information to Cooper: The boy magician looks at Bob and says, "Fell a victim." The Little Man is shown holding Teresa Banks's ring and speaking to Bob. He says, "With this ring, I thee wed." (In yet another line that was not scripted.) This is enough information for Cooper to deduce that possession of the ring probably marks a victim for Bob. It is crucial that Cooper understand that the ring is a potentially dangerous object (at least when taken from the Little Man). Cooper will later appear in Laura's dream and warn her not to take the ring. Cooper can only know the ring is bad if, at some time, he becomes privy to its secret. This is that time. Jeffries supplies the critical information that Cooper will need in order to warn Laura. (It is important to note here that Cooper recognizes the ring as a dangerous object and something that might be a trap. He is right to warn Laura. What Cooper does not know—and what Laura will later come to realize—is that the ring is an object of power, and something that poses no threat to a "good" person.)

Cooper's dreaming mind has been working toward discovery of this information. The entire Desmond/Deer Meadow section is driven by the mystery of the ring. Cooper is either actively seeking it or being guided to it (or both). Either way, once "Desmond" reaches for it, the dream shifts to another level of consciousness. Cooper—as himself—enters the dream and is now positioned to receive Jeffries' crucial information.

But the dream is not yet over. Once Jeffries disappears, word arrives that "Chester Desmond" has also disappeared. This sets up the next scene in which Cooper travels to Deer Meadow to investigate the new mystery. This section is still part of the dream.

Cooper's Dream, Part 3: Dale Cooper

At the Fat Trout Trailer Park, Rodd tells Cooper all he knows about Desmond's last visit. Cooper thanks Rodd and says, "Sorry to wake you." Rodd replies, "That's OK, I was having a bad dream anyway." Here, again, the dialogue returns to the subject of dreams.

After Rodd tells Cooper what he knows, Cooper intentionally walks toward the site where Desmond found the ring. Cooper is known to act on intuition and so there is nothing unusual about him following his instincts and repeating Desmond's steps. But it could be that Cooper "remembers" what Desmond did, because it happened to him in an earlier part of the dream.

Cooper explores the now empty space where the trailer once stood, but there is no mound of dirt or ring to be found. He asks Rodd about who stayed in the trailer. Rodd says it was an old woman and her grandson. They were named Chalfont. Then Rodd says that the previous tenants were also named Chalfont. Here again, there is an instance of doubling. What's more, the fact that there were "two Chalfonts" is emphasized. (Of course, this curious incident recalls the appearance of the Tremonds from the series. Donna Hayward meets Mrs. Tremond and her grandson living in a house next to Harold Smith. When Cooper visits the same home he finds another, different, woman living there who is also named Tremond.) The presence of the double Chalfonts augments the dreamlike nature of the section. Two Chalfonts suggest that Cooper may have been here before—either as himself in "reality," or under another guise (Desmond) in an earlier part of the dream.

Cooper notices Agent Desmond's car and walks toward it. He sees the words, "Let's Rock" written on the windshield, in what looks like bold, red paint. A significant connection has now been made between the film and the series. In *Twin Peaks*, Cooper experiences a powerful dream in which he visits the Red Room and sees Laura and the Little Man From Another Place. The Little Man's first words to Cooper are, "Let's Rock!" Here, in *Fire Walk With Me*, Cooper receives a hint of what's to come—a kind of precognitive echo of his future dream. The "Let's Rock" message is another reminder of the power and pervasiveness of dreams in the *Twin Peaks* narrative. It also marks the third time Cooper has received a message from the "another place" (arguably the Red Room). The first was Rodd's cryptic "gone places" comment, and the second was Phillip Jeffries' appearance. In each of his dream's three segments, Cooper has had contact with another world.

The last moments of the dream come when Cooper dictates his report to Diane. He tells her "Agent Desmond" has disappeared and that the clues Desmond and Stanley found have led to dead ends. He makes special note that the Teresa Banks case is a "blue rose case." Finally, he says he has the feeling the killer will strike again. These notes to Diane are nothing more than notes Cooper is leaving for himself. As his dream ends, he summarizes all that he knows. His mind attempts to impose "order" on the facts. But Cooper knows that there is more to the case than is apparent. His dream has opened his mind to other possibilities and prepared him for the important role he will play later in the film, and especially later in the series. After Cooper finishes his report, the film transitions to the waking world of *Twin Peaks* and Laura Palmer.

If Cooper "wakes up" at this point, the audience doesn't see it. Lynch did not have the same freedom shooting *Fire Walk With Me* that he had shooting *Mulholland Drive*. In the latter case, Lynch carefully redefined his existing material (the pilot) into a dream story, then meticulously crafted a new story from which this "dream" would reflect. He reassembled his cast, shot the new material (including a scene of his protagonist awakening), and finished the film. *Fire Walk With Me* was a different affair. Lynch's solution to re-work the prologue material into a dream was an ongoing process during the shooting and editing of the film. In fact, Lynch may not have fully committed to the dream scenario until he found a satisfying way to make all the pieces of the puzzle fit. By then it was probably too late to shoot anything new. The distinct transition from Deer Meadow to Twin Peaks would have to suffice as the border between dream and reality.

Futures Past

In both the pre-release and shooting drafts of the *Fire Walk With Me* script, the Phillip Jeffries scene happens after Cooper has completed his assignment in Deer Meadow. (Shortly after Laura Palmer is introduced, the script cuts back to Philadelphia and Jeffries makes his appearance.) During the editing of *Fire Walk With Me*, however, Lynch chose to move the scene and fold it into the Deer Meadow prologue.

In order to do so, Lynch had to make significant edits to the scene. As scripted *and shot*, Albert does not announce, "News from Deer Meadow— Chet Desmond has disappeared." Nor does Cole ask (while he is looking at the videotape of Jeffries' arrival), "Where is Chester Desmond?" These critical lines were added *after* the scene was shot. The dialogue was recorded later and inserted into the scene.

It is easy to see where and how Lynch inserted this new dialog: Watch closely as Albert delivers his lines. He says, "I've got the front desk right now. He was never here." The scene cuts to Cole as Albert says this last part. Albert is not shown saying this critical line ("He was never here"). Lynch cleverly employs two shots of Cole during Albert's line—a medium shot, then a close-up. This editing effectively masks the inserted dialogue. The audience focuses on Cole's reaction to, rather than Albert's delivery of, the news. Also watch Cole when, in the security room, he subsequently asks about where Desmond went. Lynch cuts to a shot of the back of Cole's head when he speaks his line—the audience never sees him mouth the words.

Lynch moved the Jeffries scene back to an earlier part of the narrative because he realized it was a necessary part of the dream story. It is here that Cooper learns about the ring, the Little Man and, to some extent, Bob.

Cooper's dream ends with his report to Diane. He says, "The letter below the fingernail gives me the feeling the killer will strike again. But like the song says, '...who knows where or when.'" The dramatic irony is implicit in his remarks. The viewers know the answer and Lynch verifies their knowledge by cutting to the Twin Peaks sign and using the familiar *Twin Peaks* theme. These two scenes had to be placed together; they represent the boundary between dream and reality. (See Appendix 1 for more on the song Cooper references, and how its lyrics provide further evidence that the prologue is a dream.)

If the Jeffries scene was to be part of the dream, it could not take place after the transition. It had to be placed before Cooper's visit to Deer Meadow. But the Jeffries scene is awkward. As written, it is designed to parallel action taking place in Twin Peaks—it does not build toward, nor transition to, another part of the story. Moving it earlier in the narrative meant the scene would require some transitional function. It had to *lead* somewhere.

Lynch deftly places it between Chet Desmond's disappearance and Cooper's subsequent investigation. He radically edits it to be dreamlike and removes Jeffries' extraneous "before" and "after" scenes. Finally, he inserts new dialogue to link the scene to the next part of the film. As a result, Lynch creates a stronger narrative arc to the dream. Desmond begins the story in Deer Meadow; Jeffries acknowledges the dream in Philadelphia; Cooper ends the story in Deer Meadow: A beginning, a middle, and an end.

Dream Logic

The Deer Meadow prologue introduces a number of significant new elements into the *Twin Peaks* universe. But these elements are never mentioned in the series. The obvious reason, of course, is that *Fire Walk With Me* was written after the series; it would have been impossible for the show's writers to acknowledge characters and events that not yet been developed. It is striking, however, that a character like Chet Desmond, or an important case classification such as "blue rose," would be absent from the later part of the story when they have such prominence and importance in the film. Their introduction (and subsequent absence) threatens to disrupt narrative continuity. A dream interpretation, however, diffuses these contradictions. All the prologue's newly-introduced elements become repositioned as artifacts of a dreaming mind. In "reality" there is, arguably, no Chet Desmond, no blue rose cases.[8]

Dale Cooper, however, is real, and his presence in the waking world is an essential component of the story. If the entire prologue is Cooper's dream, the audience only perceives his character through the arbitrary, impulsive nature of his dreaming psyche. In short, they don't get to see or hear the "real" Cooper in the film. In order for *Fire Walk With Me* to function as a stand-alone work, Cooper needs to be grounded in Laura Palmer's world. He has to be part of a shared reality, an individual who is subject to the same physical laws as the other characters. Otherwise, he exists only as an abstraction—a reflection of reality (just as Betty is a reflection of Diane in *Mulholland Drive*).

Lynch solves this problem—but just barely. Cooper appears in one brief scene that is explicitly connected to the waking world of Laura Palmer. In Philadelphia, Cooper speaks with Albert about the Teresa Banks case. His first words are, "Lately, I have been filled with a knowledge that the killer will strike again." This line is almost an exact replication of his earlier message to Diane (in the dream). Here, the line indicates that Cooper has had some vision—some premonition—of the future. He says he has "been filled with a knowledge." But how? When and where did this knowledge come to him? As has already been established in the series, Cooper can gain valuable knowledge from dreams (in episode 2, directed by Lynch, Cooper explains that he "subconsciously gained knowledge" in this manner). The "knowledge" Cooper describes to Albert was also gained from a dream—in this case, the prologue.

Cooper tells Albert they will work together on the next case. Albert then asks Cooper to describe the next victim. Cooper describes, in general terms, Laura Palmer. Then he cements the connection by exactly describing what she is doing at that moment: "She is preparing a great abundance of food." The film cuts to Laura Palmer at the Double R Diner as she prepares the food for her Meal-on-Wheels route.

Cooper is now established as part of Laura's world; his conversation with Albert is not part of a dream. It is Cooper's only real-world appearance in the film. He will show up two more times—once during Laura's dream, once after her death. Both times will be in the Red Room; but he won't really be Cooper. He will be the "Good Dale" (explicitly labeled as such by Annie Blackburne in the film)—the sundered half-of-Cooper that was trapped in the Red Room during the series finale. (Lynch offers nothing more to identify this aspect of Cooper. Annie's brief comment is cryptic, and unless viewers of the film have already seen the series finale they may not fully understand the implication of her statement.)

The Good Cooper serves an important function. He guides Laura and offers advice. He tells her not to take the ring when the Little Man offers it. He knows now, after all his varied experiences, that taking the ring from the Little Man is a bad thing. Later, Laura does take the ring—but only after she recognizes the unassailable goodness in herself and the knowledge that she can defy and defeat the forces that control the ring. Her fate is still initially one of confusion and despair. But Cooper is there for her, a comforting presence who guides her towards angels and an afterlife of happiness. Would Laura find this happiness without Cooper? There is no way to know. But Cooper's experiences in *Fire Walk With Me* (implicit in the dream prologue) prepare him for the vital role he will play in Laura's destiny. *Fire Walk With Me* may be Laura's story, but it is also Cooper's. It is Cooper—not Chet Desmond or Phillip Jeffries—whose life intersects with Laura's. He is the critical player in the narrative and his presence in the story is far more profound if we recognize him as the consciousness that governs the film's prologue.

Laura's Dream

Is it fair to expect a viewer of *Fire Walk With Me* to perceive that Cooper is the dreamer, to arrive at this conclusion without a working knowledge of the series, the various drafts of the film script, or Lynch's previous and subsequent work?

David Lynch is an intuitive director who creates movies that "feel right" to him. Filmmaking is "a subconscious intuition kind of thing ... you can have [a scene] in the script but when it's in front of you, it's fluid. If a line doesn't work you adjust it—you see it has to be this way."[9] Lynch doesn't connect the dots for the viewer, but he does ensure that all the "dots" are in place. When asked about *Lost Highway*, the film he made after *Fire Walk With Me*, Lynch stated, "The clues are all there for a correct interpretation."[10] For Lynch, then, there *is* a correct interpretation, a single, specific way of "reading" *Lost Highway*. He deliberately placed all the necessary clues required to decipher the film. Almost certainly, he did the same for *Fire Walk With Me*.

Dream imagery such as Lil's dance, Chet Desmond's disappearance, Cooper's doubled appearance, and Phillip Jeffries' bewildering visit pervade the prologue. What's more, recurring hints about dreams and sleep come from Sam Stanley, Cooper, Jeffries, and Carl Rodd. Taken together, these clues are almost enough for viewers to unlock the narrative's peculiar structure. But they are not the only clues available to the audience. Dreams are explicitly positioned as important aspects of the narrative when, later in the film, Laura Palmer experiences her own dream, charged with meaning and portent.

Laura's dream is a valuable clue because it echoes the prologue in both narrative structure and story content. Laura dreams of entering the Tremonds' painting. She moves through rooms until she arrives at the Red Room where she sees the Little Man, the ring, and Dale Cooper. Laura does not physically appear in the Red Room, her presence is implied through her point-of-view. Cooper turns to the camera (i.e., Laura) and tells Laura not to take the ring.

Like Laura, Cooper does not "appear" in the first part of his dream. He experiences the dream either as a disembodied observer or by playing the part of Desmond. Either way, his presence is only implied.

Laura seems to "awaken" from the Red Room dream—she is shown lying in bed with her eyes open. But Laura is still dreaming. Annie Blackburne appears and tells Laura about the Good Dale being trapped in the lodge. She instructs Laura to write this message in her diary.

Again, Laura's dream parallels Cooper's. After Chet Desmond disappears (upon seeing the same ring the Little Man shows to Laura), Cooper physically appears. Though still dreaming, Cooper seems to have awakened from "that dream" he told Gordon Cole about. Like Annie

Blackburne, Phillip Jeffries appears[11] with an important message. He wants to tell Cooper, Cole and Albert about his trip to "one of their meetings." Jeffries says the meeting was above a convenience store but he also talking about the Red Room (or lodge, since it houses "woodsmen"). Jeffries, like Annie, imparts his message and vanishes.

Laura gets out of bed and opens the door to her bedroom. She turns back and looks at the Tremonds' picture where she sees herself in the painting, standing in a doorway. Cooper, like Laura, also sees a double of himself. In another notable parallel, Cooper's double appears in a video monitor; Laura's appears in a painting.

As we can see, Laura's dream points back to the prologue in a couple of ways: First, it reintroduces some of the same story elements seen earlier (the ring, the Little Man, the doubled presence of the dreamer). Second, it loosely parallels the structure of the prologue (the dream-within-a-dream, the message from an outsider about the Red Room).

Laura's dream is also worth noting because it presents the same kind of "reality" that manifests in the prologue. Laura may be dreaming but she is also entering another world, one with its own autonomous inhabitants (the Little Man, Annie) and rules. This is the same dream-world Cooper accesses in the series—a place that reflects the mind of the dreamer; a reality that adapts to each individual who visits it.

By placing an explicit dream in the film that resembles and reflects the earlier part of the story, David Lynch provides the final, perhaps most substantive clue that as to the nature of the Deer Meadow prologue. This, coupled with the other clues present in the film, gives the viewer of *Fire Walk With Me* enough information to deduce the "correct interpretation" of the prologue.

Conclusion

For years, David Lynch considered *Fire Walk With Me* to be his "most experimental film."[12] What made it, in Lynch's mind, so "experimental?" Was it because the film was an extension of a previous work, the *Twin Peaks* television series? (Probably not; Lynch was used to telling an on-going story with the series, and *Fire Walk With Me* was just another chapter.) Was it because *Fire Walk With Me* employed a sort of circular narrative which deftly connected the story's final episode with its first? (Possibly, but Lynch had already ventured into this territory during the series finale, an episode that both echoed and repeated the series pilot.) Or was it because *Fire Walk With Me* represented Lynch's first major effort to rework objective story material into a subjective dream narrative—an experiment he would try again, and perfect, in *Mulholland Drive*? This is the likely answer. For the first time, Lynch positioned story material to function as the reflection of a specific consciousness. In this case, Dale Cooper's.

When asked about Kyle MacLachlan's reluctance to commit to *Fire Walk With Me*, David Lynch said, "I love restrictions and I believe in fate. So what he did worked out just fine . . . there's no such thing as a problem, there are only solutions, and you just go forward."[13] Lynch's comments are telling. MacLachlan's limited availability was not a restriction—rather, it led to a solution. This solution may have been to replace one actor for another, but this tactic merely sidesteps the narrative problem Lynch faced when his second-most-important character was no longer viable. I believe Lynch's solution was far more complex and subtle. He took a chance—he "experimented" with the film and found a way to keep Cooper a prominent character in *Fire Walk With Me*.

Although the cryptic dialogue and abstract imagery of Lynch's films are not always immediately comprehensible, Lynch maintains that, "they are, in some way, understandable."[14] He prefers to keep things puzzling and complex because "most films are designed to be understood by many, many, many, many people," and therefore, "there's not a lot of room to dream and wonder."[15] *Fire Walk With Me* has room to spare when it comes to dreams and wonder. But the film is not without purpose, not without design. There is a strategy at work in *Fire Walk With Me*.

When David Lynch added Chet Desmond to the *Fire Walk With Me* story he made other significant changes in order to transform the original, straight-forward prologue (featuring Cooper) into an esoteric, abstract narrative that is strongly reminiscent of a dream. When we identify Cooper as the dreamer, this prologue becomes, for the first time, an integral part of the overall film. It balances the narrative and brings homogeneity to the work.

When Dale Cooper dreams of Deer Meadow, *Fire Walk With Me* achieves a new form of aesthetic unity; it emerges as a cohesive, meaningful film, at last.

APPENDIX 1:
TWO MORE OBSERVATIONS
ABOUT *FIRE WALK WITH ME*

I. Judy, Judy, Judy

In *Fire Walk With Me*, long lost FBI agent, Phillip Jeffries says, "Well now, I'm not gonna talk about Judy. In fact, we're not gonna talk about Judy at all. We're gonna keep her out of it." Among the many fans and students of *Twin Peaks*, however, Jeffries admonition not to talk about Judy is the equivalent of someone telling us not to think of an elephant—once you hear it, it is impossible to do anything *but* think about it.

So we're going to talk about Judy. Who is this mysterious person that Jeffries mentions? What is her purpose in the *Twin Peaks* story? Is she important, or is she some piece of nonsensical fluff thrown into the film by David Lynch and co-writer Robert Engels? Finally, can Judy be identified from clues in the film, script, or series?

The answer to the last question is: yes. But here's the catch—Judy has a different identity depending on which version of *Fire Walk With Me* you examine. Judy is not a single definitive persona; rather she is a character (or idea) that changed as *Fire Walk With Me* evolved through scripting, shooting and editing.

The Judy of Twin Peaks

The most popular theory about Judy is that she represents another missing or murdered girl along the lines of Teresa Banks and Laura Palmer. As such, she fits into a cyclical pattern suggested by the film and series: a girl (Laura, Teresa, Judy) is killed, and an FBI agent (Cooper, Chet Desmond, Phillip Jeffries) is assigned the case. The case (likely one of Gordon Cole's Blue Rose cases) is never completely solved because the agent assigned ends up missing (or in Cooper's case, severely compromised). The film tells us that Phillip Jeffries is "long lost," suggesting that—until the moment of his sudden reappearance—Jeffries has not been in contact with Cole or the FBI. It is not a stretch, then, to theorize that Jeffries disappeared while on some assignment. This theory is strongly supported by the disappearance of FBI agent Chet Desmond who has just been investigating the murder of Teresa Banks (a case explicitly referred to as a Blue Rose case). Finally, we know from the series that at least part of Cooper will disappear after he solves the Laura Palmer case. (Cooper's "good self" will be trapped in the Black Lodge.)

So the pattern is compelling: three agents disappear while on assignment; two obviously investigating the death of a young woman. Connect the dots and surely one can assume that the third missing agent (Jeffries) was also investigating the death of a young woman. Who was she? The film never provides an explicit answer, but Jeffries does mention someone named Judy. Therefore Judy must be another dead girl. So say many fans, including essayist, Tim Kreider, who suggests, "Maybe the mysterious name 'Judy' points to another, unknown girl in the 'Blue Rose' series of cases, victims of the demon Bob—one before Teresa, or one after Laura. There's always another one."[1]

It's a great theory. It fits nicely with the facts established in the series and (apparently) in the film. It's a clean and precise way of tidying up an annoying loose end. And it provides more meaning to the existence of Phillip Jeffries in the story. What it does not do, however, is explain why— at two hours, eight minutes and 21 seconds into the film—an image of a monkey appears on screen and clearly says the word, "Judy." This very deliberate scene suggests something else entirely about Judy. But what?

The Judy of the Scripts

The monkey does not appear in either the pre-release or final draft of the *Fire Walk With Me* script. However, the name Judy does. In fact, the scripts provide some tantalizing clues about Judy's original identity.

In an early draft (dated July 3rd, 1991), Phillip Jeffries first appears in a Buenos Aires hotel where the head clerk hands him a note from a "young lady." Soon after, Jeffries appears in Cole's office in Philadelphia where he tells the assembled agents he's "not gonna talk about Judy." Jeffries says, "I want to tell you everything, but I don't have a lot to go on. But I'll tell you one thing: Judy is positive about this." Then Jeffries drops a fascinating detail: "Her sister's there, too. At least part of her." Jeffries then realizes that it is May 1989 and disappears.

This early draft of the script provides strong evidence that Judy was a living person whose note to Jeffries compelled him to go to Philadelphia to tell Cole, "everything." (After all, "Judy is positive about this.") Jeffries comment about Judy's sister is tantalizing—he says her sister is "there" but never says where "there" is. Then he adds that at least *part* of Judy's sister is there. This comment opens all sorts of possible interpretive paths, especially given the nature of the *Twin Peaks* universe where divided personalities are quite possible.

So now we have a second mysterious person to identify—Judy's sister. Some believe the sister may be Josie Packard who "died" in the TV series but whose spirit seemed to live on in the walls (and drawers) of the Great Northern hotel. Robert Engels attempted to clarify some of these early draft mysteries in an interview that appeared in *Wrapped In Plastic* 58: "The thing behind Judy has to do with where David Bowie [Phillip Jeffries] came from .... He was down there [Buenos Aires], and that's where Judy is. I think Joan Chen [Josie] is there, and I think Windom Earle is there. It's this idea that there are these portals around the world, and Phillip Jeffries had one hell of a trip to Buenos Aires and back! He really doesn't want to talk about Judy because that reminds him of whatever happened to him." When asked if Josie, therefore, could be Judy's sister, Engels replied, "Yes. Yes, I think that is true."

Lynch and Engels originally envisioned "a whole other set of mythology" that was eventually abandoned. Judy's existence in the final film is clearly a product of that mythology. By the time Lynch and Engels revised the script, Judy's presence in Jeffries' story was altered. In the shooting draft (dated August 8th 1991) Jeffries still receives a note from the head clerk (who says a young lady left it), and Jeffries also tells Cole that "Judy is positive about this." But he makes no reference to Judy's sister. Instead, he says he "found something in Seattle at Judy's." This intriguing line gives us a bit more information about Judy: We know she lives (or lived) in Seattle. This line naturally links Judy to Teresa Banks and Laura Palmer—all three women lived in Washington State. This geographic proximity once again suggests that the women may have known one another, or at least been in contact. It also suggests that Judy could have had some interaction with the Lodge residents (particularly Bob) who obviously exist in the Pacific Northwest (where they physically manifest themselves).

The Judy of the Film, Fire Walk With Me

Now we know that Judy could be related to Josie. We know that she could be alive and in Buenos Aires. Or she could be dead and from Seattle. But, in fact, we really don't know anything since all this evidence about Buenos Aires and Seattle and Josie was deleted from the final version of *Fire Walk With Me*. All we know for certain is that Phillip Jeffries mentions Judy, and 100 minutes later so does the monkey.

So we are back to the question: Who is Judy and why does the monkey say her name?

It seems evident that Judy's true identity simply changed as Lynch and Engels developed the material. Engels explained, "There was a thing that was going to happen with Josie and Windom and Judy. In our original planning of the prequel there is a whole other section about all this." But little of this complex back story went beyond the planning stages. After some revision, the shooting script simply put Judy in Seattle.

Lynch likely shot the Phillip Jeffries scene according to these later revisions. (In fact, the full scene does appear in this format on "The Missing Pieces" supplement to the *Twin Peaks: The Entire Mystery* Blu-ray collection.) When editing the film, however, Lynch realized the Judy remained a frustrating loose end—an idea that his already complex film could not satisfactorily sustain or explain. So he cut as much of the Judy material as he could (Jeffries' line about Seattle and his line about Judy "being positive" were deleted). But Lynch could not successfully delete *all* the references to Judy.

Jeffries makes a dramatic entrance into Cole's office, and his very first line—the dialogue that introduces Jeffries to the audience—is the one about Judy ("I'm not gonna talk about Judy"). It's a great line, wonderfully delivered by David Bowie. What's more, it establishes a detached and incoherent feel to Jeffries, and it reinforces his other-worldly nature. The line is also a part of one long continuous take in which Jeffries enters the office and confronts the agents. As such, there was no way for Lynch to remove the line without disrupting Jeffries' introduction to the scene. In other words, *there was no way to edit the line out of the shot*. It would have been impossible for Lynch to bring Jeffries into the office, establish his physical position in relation to the other characters, and also delete the line. If the line had been removed it could have created a noticeable, amateurish, jump-cut in the scene, something that Lynch would never allow. (Lynch could have looped new dialogue into the scene—essentially erasing the Judy line—but that might have been equally awkward.)

So Lynch was stuck with a line he simply could not remove. But if the original identity of Judy was to be deleted, Lynch had to provide a new identity for the mysterious Judy, especially since Lynch was trying to make *Fire Walk With Me* a stand-alone, possibly insular film.

And that's just what Lynch did. He found another persona to attach to the name. This persona was Laura Palmer.

Lynch reintroduces the name Judy to the film after Laura Palmer has been killed. He deliberately places a close-up shot of a monkey uttering the word, "Judy," just before he cuts to a close-up of the dead Laura Palmer. This simple edit between these two shots obviously establishes a connection between the name and the character: "Judy" is said/Laura is shown.

(This begs the question: Who—or what—is the monkey? One good guess is that the monkey is Phillip Jeffries. Remember, Jeffries said he had "been to one of their meetings" above the convenience store. Sure enough, a monkey does peek from behind a mask during the convenience store scene. Coincidence? Probably not.)

So, OK, if Judy is Laura, what's it all mean? Admittedly, there is no easy—or exclusive—answer to this question. Any interpretation is subjective. The short and simple answer is that Laura Palmer was a convenient candidate for the identity of Judy. Lynch needed to provide someone, and who better than Laura?

Of course, we expect that, in Lynch's mind, there is some deeper meaning—some substantive connection—between Laura and Judy. Perhaps in a self-contained, "stand-alone" *Fire Walk With Me*, the mysterious Judy simply becomes a "code word" for Laura, a symbolic representation of the *idea* of Laura Palmer.

Names and identities have always been fluid concepts in Lynch's work. Any casual study of *Lost Highway* or *Mulholland Drive* proves that theory. *Fire Walk With Me* merely provides another example. Perhaps Judy functions as a "secret name" for Laura, one that empowers her in some way. David Lynch's lyrics to the song, "Floating," from Julee Cruise's 1990 album, *Floating Into the Night*, contains the intriguing lines: "When you told your secret name/ I burst in flame and burn." Remember also Laura's comments to Donna about falling in space: "For a long time you wouldn't feel anything. Then you would burst into fire … forever." Are secret names words of power? Do they tap into an energy unfathomable in "reality?" Lynch's investigation into the slippery nature of names and identity hints at these provocative themes.

Assigning meaning to Lynch films is always a tricky proposition, and nowhere is that more true than with *Fire Walk With Me*. The film was continually evolving through scripting, shooting and editing. The purpose of characters, scenes and dialogue changed as Lynch sought to create a consistent, cohesive work that transcended the trappings of the televised series. Lynch resisted committing to any specific backstory, and was open to changing and redirecting the story material as the process continued. Robert Engels explained that the story behind *Fire Walk With Me* was never concrete: "It was free-form—David would start to look at something and say, 'I think it is more interesting to go this way.'"

So with that in mind, Judy could be anything or anybody: A living being, an unknown victim—or Laura Palmer. Or maybe she is nothing more than the original inspiration when Robert Engels wrote the script: "Judy—the name is from my sister-in-law. I think that's where it came from."

II. Songs of Deer Meadow

This section is an extension of Chapter 12 (Dreams of Deer Meadow), which posits that the first 30 minutes of *Fire Walk With Me* (the Deer Meadow prologue) is actually a dream of Dale Cooper's. There is compelling evidence in the film to support this claim. Since writing the original piece I discovered additional, persuasive evidence to support the theory. This evidence comes from lyrics to the two songs alluded to in the Deer Meadow section of *Fire Walk With Me*: "Good Night Irene," and "Where or When."

Before considering the evidence, let's distill the dream theory to its critical points:

- Before events in the film, Dale Cooper (with Sam Stanley) investigated the Teresa Banks murder but failed to discover the culprit. (This fits with facts established in the series, *The Autobiography of F.B.I. Special Agent, Dale Cooper: My Life, My Tapes*, and the original draft of the *Fire Walk With Me* screenplay.)

- As *Fire Walk With Me* begins, Dale Cooper dreams about his original investigation of the murder. In the dream, Cooper takes on the persona of "Chet Desmond." The dream allows Cooper to tap into the "Red Room realm" and gather clues he could never find in the real world.

- In "Philadelphia," Cooper expresses concern about his "dream" just as Phillip Jeffries—a long-lost agent—appears to tell Cooper they "live inside a dream." He also mentions the Owl Cave ring.

- Cooper returns to Deer Meadow ostensibly to find a missing Chet Desmond but examines the location where he "saw" the ring. Cooper receives another message from the Red Room realm—the words, "Let's Rock" painted on the windshield of a car.

In summary, the dream theory repositions Cooper in the film as a more active participant in the story. Cooper learns about the ring so he will be able to warn Laura Palmer about it in her own dream. *Fire Walk With Me* becomes a more balanced and unified work under this interpretation.

Two real-world songs are alluded to in *Fire Walk With Me*. The first is "Good Night Irene" (words and music by Huddie Ledbetter). A sleep-deprived Chet Desmond and Sam Stanley visit Hap's Diner to learn about Teresa Banks' past. This scene opens *in media res* in the back room of the diner where Jack, the diner's manager, is addressing Desmond and Stanley. Jack says, "Ask Irene about that. Now, Irene is her name and it is night. Don't go any further with it. There's nothing good about it." Here, Jack is making a coded reference to the song, "Good Night Irene." (It is *night*. Her name is *Irene*. There's nothing *good*.)

Jack's line may be nothing more than clever, comical nod to a piece of real-world pop-culture. But look past the song's title to the lyrics, and you find a potential clue to the nature of the film. The refrain to "Good Night Irene" reads:

Irene goodnight,
Irene goodnight.
Goodnight, Irene, goodnight, Irene,
I'll see you in my dreams.

The song contains an obvious reference to dreams—an assertion, in fact, that Irene will be seen in dreams.

What is the purpose of the Jack scene? On the surface it seems to simply introduce Irene and then direct Desmond and Stanley into the dining section of the diner. But the scene stands out as an odd detour in the narrative, especially because it is so brief. The viewer barely has time to process the scene, to make any sense of it. Without transition, Chet Desmond and Sam Stanley go from the morgue to the back room of the diner for their curious exchange with Jack (they are not shown entering the building or the room). They leave the room almost immediately, emerging into the diner proper.

The whole sequence seems abrupt and jarring. It makes sense, however, if one thinks of the agents' movements from one location to another as part of an unfolding dream in which a sleeping consciousness (Cooper's) is "jumping" from place-to-place.

The actual scripted scene with Jack is much longer than what appears on screen. Desmond and Stanley meet with Jack in his office, and Jack explains that the FBI had been there before, "Back in the fifties when Hap was running the place." Jack explains that Hap is "good and dead." When Desmond asks about Teresa, Jack says "Sheriff Cable already asked me about Teresa Banks." He then explains that he never saw Teresa with any friends, nor did she mention any. Jack then tells Desmond and Stanley to talk to Irene (using the "Good Night Irene" lines that exist in the final film).

Lynch ultimately deleted most of the scene, probably because it provided little new information to the viewer. But why did he keep the last few lines of dialogue? Why didn't he delete the *whole* scene? Lynch could have simply opened with Desmond and Stanley speaking with Irene in the diner. It seems a more sensible place to start. At 138 minutes, *Fire Walk With Me* was already a long film and Lynch admits, "I had a limit on the running time of the picture. We shot many scenes that—for a regular feature—were too tangential to keep the main story progressing properly."[2] Yet, despite the film's time-limit, Lynch makes certain that the "Good Night Irene" dialogue is included. Why? Could it be because the dialogue is yet another clue (among many) that points to a dream interpretation for the Deer Meadow sequence?

Like Lil's coded dance earlier in the film, Jack's dialogue cleverly incorporates the necessary clues to decipher the title, "Good Night Irene." But the title of the song is not a clue in-and-of-itself. Astute viewers of *Fire Walk With Me* recognize that the song's *lyrics* are where the clue truly resides.

Such is the case with the next song mentioned in the film. Cooper makes a reference to the song, "Where or When" (music by Richard Rodgers and lyrics by Lorenz Hart) in his recorded report to Diane at the conclusion of the Deer Meadow prologue. He says he has "the feeling the killer will strike again. But like the song says, '. . . who knows where or when.'"

Remember, I contend that the Deer Meadow sequence is not only a dream, but also a *re-enactment* of Cooper's real-world investigation into Teresa Banks's death. The lyrics to "Where or When" are highly supportive of this claim. They read, in part:

Sometimes you think you've lived before
All that you live today
Things you do come back to you
As though they knew the way
Oh, the tricks your mind can play!

Later lines reinforce the cyclical nature of the Deer Meadow sequence (and of *Twin Peaks* as a whole):

Some things that happened for the first time
They seem to be happening again
...
But who knows where or when?

Doubling and circular imagery are prevalent in the *Twin Peaks* narrative. (In the series, The Giant famously warns Cooper that "It is happening again," when Killer Bob is about to kill Madeleine Ferguson.) The song, "Where or When" certainly alludes to these themes. If a deliberate reference on David Lynch's part, this may be *all* the song was intended to do. But how appropriate—and haunting—that the very last lines of the Deer Meadow sequence reference the idea of a world re-experienced in the realm of the mind, a world so often visited in the works of David Lynch: The world of dreams.

APPENDIX 2:
THE FRANK SILVA INTERVIEW

Frank Silva (1950-1995) is known throughout the world for his powerful portrayal of "Killer Bob" in both the *Twin Peaks* TV series and the film, *Fire Walk With Me*. Frank's distinct features and growling laugh easily made Bob one of the most memorable characters from the show. In fact, Bob has come to represent *Twin Peaks* almost as much as Dale Cooper or Laura Palmer.

Frank Silva worked with David Lynch for years as a prop-master and on-set dresser. Silva's anonymity, however, vanished once *Twin Peaks* became a hit. He came to the part of Bob by accident, in an incident that has now become legendary among *Twin Peaks* fans. Silva was the on-set dresser for the show's pilot. While Lynch was shooting a scene in Laura Palmer's bedroom, he told Silva to move so as not to get caught on camera—but then changed his mind. As Silva told it at the 1993 *Twin Peaks* Fan Festival, "A blood vessel kind of like burst in [David's] head, and he said, 'Frank! Get down at the end of the bed, just crouch down there, and act scared!' And I went, 'What?!' 'Just act scared!' And that was how Bob began." Silva went on to play the menacing Bob in a number of *Twin Peaks* episodes and the feature film, *Fire Walk With Me*.

Wrapped In Plastic editors Craig Miller and John Thorne had the pleasure of interviewing Frank Silva in 1993 at the Twin Peaks Festival in Issaquah, Washington. We enjoyed Frank's lively stories and outgoing personality. He, in turn, enjoyed speaking with fans and was pleased to be back in the Pacific Northwest. Clearly, Frank was nothing like his on-screen persona. During our interview, Frank explained how difficult it was to portray Bob: "I don't recognize him. During the series I had a rough time watching it. It really disturbed me. And it still disturbs me when I see it, but I also know that that's not me."

After the interview we drove Frank Silva into Snoqualmie. During the ride, Frank spoke of his admiration for David and Jennifer Lynch. He recounted a number of fascinating anecdotes about his friendship with the two filmmakers. Frank told of the time he and Jennifer rented a videotape of *Eraserhead*, and how David stopped by to provide a live running commentary as they watched. Frank explained how he would troubleshoot for David while working on *Wild At Heart*. Lynch required a shot of a decapitated head hitting the ground. Frank laughed as he explained that he filled the prop with cow brains (which he bought at a local butcher) to give the scene the proper effect! As we drove through Snoqualmie, Frank pointed out various landmarks and told stories of shooting the pilot in the area.

Years later, we had the pleasure of speaking with Jennifer Lynch about Frank Silva:

Jennifer Lynch: When Frank and I met I was instantly in love with this man. There are just some people you know that you can't have a life without having a friendship with them. He and I met when my father was working at DEG [De Laurentiis Entertainment Group] where I was my father's personal assistant. Frank was in the office working on another production. I was looking for an apartment and Frank said, "There is one open in my building." And so Frank and I not only worked in an office together, we became neighbors. We were right down the hall from each other. I, still, to this day, consider myself a luckier person for having known Frank.

It was funny [that Frank got the role of Bob]. I remember giggling and saying, "God! That's perfect!" He called me and said, "Hey, your dad wants me to memorize these lines. I'm going to be in a scene after lunch." He had ended up in the mirror and nothing had been creepier than that. I said, "That's the universe talking, Frank; you've got to go with it." It was so great because I knew him as such a gentle, laughter-filled person, and yet what sort of giggly, creative person doesn't want to play bad sometimes? So he became my wicked pervert. He had no idea how he was going to handle the manifestation of Bob. But it handled itself.

***

Frank Silva did not have the chance to give many interviews. At *Wrapped In Plastic*, we felt honored and lucky that we could speak with him at length about his career and work. The complete interview with Frank Silva was originally published in *Wrapped In Plastic* #8 (December, 1993), an issue that is long out-of-print and difficult to obtain. Because Frank Silva shared so many insights and memories about his time working on *Twin Peaks* and with David Lynch, the full interview is reprinted here and has been edited for clarity. (Note: a few parts of this interview do appear elsewhere in this book, specifically in places where Frank Silva's comments highlight scenes or provide insights about *Twin Peaks*.)

WIP: We wanted to start by asking about your actual work—Are you a "set designer" or "set decorator?" What's your actual title when you're working?

Frank Silva: It's a mixture of a lot of different things. I try not to put "boxes" around my job description. I art direct. I set decorate. I do light design because that was what I went to school for. I do a mixture of things.

I started out as Patty Norris's assistant on *Tap*. That was my first movie. Patricia Norris was David [Lynch's] production designer and costume designer. This was at the time I was with DEG [De Laurentiis Entertainment Group]. David walked out because he was tired of Dino's crap: "Yeah, you'll have the money next week, David!" Next week would come: "Uh . . . next week, David, you'll have the money!" So David came into the office—*One Saliva Bubble* was ready to go—and said, "Let's get out of here." So he left. Well, when they left, I remained friends with Jennifer [Lynch], and David, and Johanna Ray. In fact, Eric DaRe was Johanna's assistant. He was his mom's assistant in casting back in "Dino Days" for *One Saliva Bubble*. We had a nickname; we called him "Deranged." Eric Deranged was his name. It was like this little happy family at Dino De Laurentiis!

So Patty was leaving and she said, "I think you're wasting your talents here. If you ever want to leave, give me a call." I knew Dino was folding at the time because he was going bankrupt. It was around Christmas and I was getting ready to go on my vacation. I had this feeling that when I came back my office wouldn't exist any longer. It was one of those things, you know? They're moving furniture out slowly, and I thought, "They haven't told me anything yet, but I do get the feeling!" So I called Patty before I left on my vacation and said, "I think I better get out of here." And she said, "Great! Take your vacation. I'm starting a new movie in January and I'd like you to help me." And that was *Tap*. I was her right arm for two or three weeks during pre-production.

A week into filming she realized she needed an on-set dresser because she had no one to fill that job. Apparently things were just going crazy on the set. So she put me on the set and said, "Just do it." I had no idea what I was doing, but I kind of just winged it.

What was your actual job on the Twin Peaks *pilot?*

I was called the "On Set Dresser." That was my credit. Leslie Morales was the Art Director, and Patty Norris was the Production Designer. In fact, Leslie also linked up with Patricia Norris on *Tap*. That was Leslie's first movie working with Patricia Norris.

331

Had you worked with David on anything before Twin Peaks, *either* Dune *or* Blue Velvet?

No. *Dune* was a bit earlier. *Blue Velvet* was shot in North Carolina and then he came to L.A. and that's when I met him. I linked up with Patty and worked with her for a few movies.

David had been hired by French TV to do a five-minute film. It was a five-to-ten minute thing. Four directors were going to make a short film to fill an hour or half-hour slot for TV. David wrote this thing called *The Cowboy and the Frenchmen*. It was not for the States, but for French TV. Patty called me and asked if I was available and I said, "Sure." So basically Patty and I were the entire art department for this short film. We were doing everything. We were doing costumes. We were doing art. We were doing the locations. Harry Dean Stanton was in it. He plays the cowboy. There were lines in the script calling for things like, "Flapjacks as big as a saddle blanket!" So we were in this makeshift kitchen, cooking these flapjacks in this pan, trying to flip them over! I would say, "Patty what are we going to do?" And she would say, "Let's just try it!" We were running out to the set and saying, "David, is this OK?" "Yeah! Yeah, perfect!" It was wild! Then, to top it all off, I think it was a two-day shoot for what was supposed to be five-minute film, but David, of course, couldn't get it down to five minutes. It ended up being, like, twenty minutes! So I did that project with David, and then I went off and did some other films.

Do you get specific directions when you work with Lynch? Does he know exactly what he wants, or does he just give you a general idea and it's up to you to put that into concrete form?

He knows what he wants. I've learned from working with David that less is more. I notice when I've worked with him, the less you have in a room, the less you have on a table, the less you have on the walls, is the best way to go. Make sure that the pieces you have in the room are wonderful, interesting pieces. When we did the high school scenes [for the *Twin Peaks* pilot] up here, we basically went into those high school rooms and utilized them as they were. In that one classroom, where all the shots were done, there was orange and yellow paper all over the walls. But it was also filled with stuff—filled with paperwork and filled with artwork. Immediately, David said, "Frank, take *everything* off the walls. Everything. And I want the American Flag over here. And get me a picture of George Washington!"

You know that deer head during the safe deposit box scene? That was an add-on scene. That was not originally scripted. That was shot at the high school also, in this little cubicle. The thing about the deer was [*laughs*] . . . we wanted that deer on the wall but it wouldn't stay up. And we wanted to mount this deer head on this kind of plaque. Well, that plaque is a real trophy! On the back it's got all these brass plates on it! We turned it over and we were trying figure out how to mount this deer and David said, "It's taking too long! Just throw it on the table and we'll make like it fell off the wall!" We were trying to distress the wall, and I'm saying, "David this is the school building!" "Oh, we'll pay for it!" That's how we operate. That's the beauty of David, to be able to do that kind of stuff.

At the sawmill, the desk in Jack Nance's cubicle was filled with stuff. David immediately said, "Take everything off! Leave the telephone, and put a pencil on it." Now, when working with David I'll go into a room and just start cleaning. That's how he likes his sets, very minimal.

There's a scene in the Twin Peaks *pilot when they go into the morgue to identify Laura's body, and the lights are flickering. I've heard rumor that was not intentional, that the lights really were not working.*

No, that was intentional. What happened was, somebody was playing with the lights and David liked that. He wanted to keep that effect. Somebody was actually on the switch, just playing with them. Then it kind of stuck throughout the entire story because that also happens with the Log Lady in the town hall scene. She's flicking the lights off and on.

There's a whole theme of electricity that runs through Fire Walk With Me. *Does David have a fascination with the idea of electricity and electrical currents?*

You see it in the Lynch-Frost logo. I think that basically started with the pilot. I always think he's been fascinated by that. And also the sound you get next to those big huge power things, that humming, crackling energy? He's real fascinated with sound, that's a real important thing to him. When he directs, the earphones are always on. He's so into it. Sometimes he'll have his soundman play music through the headphones so that he can hear music while the scene's going on.

He actually watches a monitor, yes? He doesn't watch the actors?

That's a new thing because he never used to do that. I don't know if he did that on *Blue Velvet* or not, but I know on the original pilot we never had a monitor. We shot it straight out. On *Wild At Heart* he started using a monitor.

You were working with him on Wild At Heart, *also?*

Right, I was the prop master on *Wild At Heart.*

How was working on Wild At Heart *different than the* Twin Peaks *pilot?*

The only difference I could see was the time allotment. Working on a feature film gives you a chance to be a little more relaxed and things aren't as hurried. When we worked on the *Twin Peaks* pilot we were on a TV schedule, which is real different. They want you to shoot it between 18 and 22 days and we went well over that. I think we went to 31 or 32 days. But with features it's a lot more kick-back. There's a lot more waiting.

What are the actual responsibilities of a prop master?

Basically a prop master's responsibilities is [to oversee] everything an actor touches or handles. Also rings, sunglasses, wristwatches. Anything that an actor would touch is your responsibility. And you're responsible for all the stuff nobody else wants to do! Like special effects, if they're too cheap! "Props! We need smoke here. We need rain here." Sometimes if there's no gun-wrangler you'll have to do guns, which I'm not fond of. There were lots of guns in *Wild At Heart*. It spooks me, especially with all the stuff that's gone on in these last few months with the guns. See, that's where I just get to a point. I'm a creative person and to me being a prop master was creative up to a point, then it just really shuts down and there's not much creativity going on. Granted, you can look for a wristwatch that typifies the character and that sort of thing. Beyond that, there's not much to it. To me it's boring. I really don't want to spend my life being a prop master.

Well, you're certainly getting recognition for something else!

But I haven't quit my day job! I mean, the acting thing doesn't have everything.

Were you responsible for any of the technical aspects in Fire Walk With Me *or were you just an actor in that?*

I was just an actor. I wasn't part of the crew at all. I thought it would be better not to be part of the crew. Since I was an actor in the film, I thought it was time to make that separation. I thought it wouldn't look right, being part of the crew and also acting in it. I thought, just give that part up for now and go in and do the acting gig.

We'd like to talk a little bit about Bob, and how Bob came about. It was a happy accident that occurred during the filming of the pilot, correct?

Yeah, it was an accident. But I really had no idea that it would go anywhere. I thought, "Well, you know how David is, this could be a spur-of-the-moment kind of thing." I never, ever thought that it would lead to what it actually lead to. I thought, "Oh, it's not going to make it into the [pilot]. I'm not going to be in the series or anything; it's just going to be a perchance kind of thing."

When we actually did that [European] ending with Bob being shot by the One Armed Man—when we did an entire huge scene with Bob—I thought, "This isn't really going to go anywhere. It could possibly be the ending to this movie, or it could possible *not* be the ending to this movie." Apparently it was the ending to the European version. But at that point I never thought they'd be calling me for the series.

I thought it was all a joke and then they'd call and say, "David wants you here at the set." "What for?" "We don't know. He just wants you here. And don't forget, bring your clothes!" [*laughs*] Because the Bob wardrobe was what I was wearing to work that day! And he hasn't changed since!

So, the denim jacket is yours?

Yeah! That's where it all came from. They would say, "Don't forget, bring your clothes." So I would go in and there would never be anything scripted for Bob. I'd go in and sit there, and I'd wait, and I'd wait, and I'd wait. They'd start getting lighting ready for the scene. But no one ever told me what I was going to do. And David never told me what I was going to do. Then, at the last minute, David would say, "I want you to do this, this, and this."

Sometimes David wouldn't say that much. It would be generalizing. Like the scene with Maddy, Donna, and James. David would say, "Well . . . I think I want Frank to walk into the room, and maybe *leap* over the sofa!" That was it. And he'd tell the cameraman and they'd light it. Then they'd call the first team—that's first team on the set. I was standing there and David walked up to me in the dining room of the Hayward house and he said, "Frank, just walk in, blah, blah, blah . . . you know what to do!" [*laughs*] I would turn around and say, "I know what to do?!" "Yeah, you know what to do." Then he said, "Action!"

Instead of leaping—I didn't feel comfortable leaping—I just crawled over it. As I started crawling over it, and got over the sofa, David said, "Keep crawling." So I kept crawling and he didn't say anything. He didn't say, "Stop." He didn't say, "Cut." I kept crawling, and I kept crawling, but I was always taught that you're not supposed to look at the camera or look at the lens of the camera. So I crawled to the side of the camera, just alongside of the camera. And David said, "Cut! That was great, Frank! Do it again, and crawl right into the camera!" And so we did it in two takes. I crawled right into the camera.

So, you're responsible for a lot of that Bob imagery?

I guess! The intensity, I guess. That's the thing; a lot of us didn't know what Bob really was. I don't think David did. I certainly, at first, thought he was real. And who knows, he still could be—he still could be reality. I just thought he was this really whacked-out, crazy guy. An intense, crazy guy. David and I never really sat down and discussed this character or discussed the characterization. He would just say, "You know what to do." When we were doing the murder scene in the train car for that dream sequence he would say, basically, "Get down at that mound of dirt. Play with that mound of dirt. Now, walk towards the camera. Now, scream." This character just kind of grew.

I think you said in another interview, that David didn't really have a killer in mind at first, and it just gradually evolved into Bob. At what point do you think they said, "Let's make him the killer"?

I keep going back to when we did that dream sequence in the train car. That was a pretty powerful scene when we filmed it. When we did that, Bob, to me, was still a reality. Before I did that scene, I turned to Sheryl Lee and I told her, "Look, we're going into the playpen. Let's just pretend that this is playtime now and this is not reality."

When I was playing that scene I thought Bob was a reality. Being a whacko, crazy guy who has killed someone—to him, it was almost as if it was a sexual act. The killing was having sex. As I was doing that scene the screams happened after the killing, not so much during the killing. And I was feeling that they were screams of terror and also of sorrow. Almost like a release. A lot of those screams ended in screams of crying, to me.

It was almost screaming as a release—to let the tears of remorse flow after what had just happened. I don't know if David picked up on that. I have a feeling he did and he saw something there—that maybe Bob was someone else (or someone else was Bob) and this was the remorsefulness coming out. Maybe David clicked that together. Rather than Bob just being one person, maybe he was two, maybe he was three—or he was this entity that possessed people and there was this sense of remorse after it all happened. Because that's what I got from doing that scene.

I remember watching that scene for the first time as you were letting out those screams, I was thinking, "Is he screaming with—"

Glee?

Glee. Or screaming with sadness?

It's a strange scream that's going on there. That's what I felt. You weren't quite sure where it was coming from. And I'm wondering if David maybe picked up on it because that scene wasn't done until the second season. At that time we still wanted to keep the killer a secret. Everybody was saying, "Is Frank really the killer? Is Bob really the killer?" Because why would David be so explicit as to show this scene with Bob as the killer? Everybody was freaking out and saying, "Who is the killer? Is it Bob?" David wasn't letting on to anything. I think he had somewhat of an idea but I think it may have turned into something [else] there.

I think it was Bob Iger who said there would be resolution to the mystery and the killer would be revealed in the first episode of the second season. That was promised.

I don't think they knew at that point. I do think that the turning point was when David did that scene in the second-season premiere. I think that could have been the turning point.

Someone pointed out to Mark Frost, during an interview at the time, that Robert Iger had said, "Bob is the killer," and Frost said, "Well, that's his opinion."

And there were so many theories because of that show! The freeze-frame, at the end, of me screaming where I'm digging into her with a knife—a lot of people were reading into that, saying, "He wasn't killing her, he was trying to save her! He was giving her CPR!" Uh huh. *Sure.*

One of the other scenes that had that interesting duality was the killing of Maddy, which for many is the most powerful scene in the entire series. It was so intense.

It was so intense to do.

As I was watching I couldn't tell whether he was attacking her or hugging her, is he kissing her, or is he killing her? There was a sense of duality. You kind of interpreted that as Leland's hugging her, Bob is killing her. But even when it's just Bob there was still that struggle.

There was a lot of sexual stuff going on between Bob and her. Part of that killing scene is dancing with her. The slow dancing with her in the super slow motion. When we were doing that David's only direction was: "Dreamy. I want it dreamy. Make it dreamy." And that was what he wanted in that scene. He wanted it dreamy and sexual and really slow, and almost, as I take it, animalistic. That's how I sense Bob anyway. He's more animal than anything. So I played him more like an animal. I wanted that feeling for him. But that was like the big thing for the dance, he kept saying,

"Dreamy." For all of us, for when Leland did it, for when I did it, for when Ben Horne did it.

That scene was so horrific to do. I remember when we did the master of me doing it; I was so exhausted towards the end because we had shot the master all in one sequence. At the end, where I shove her head into the painting of Missoula, Montana—I fucked up the line, too; I kept saying Missouri—we were both so exhausted. She falls to the floor and I was so exhausted I fell to the floor with her, over her body. It ended with me animalistic, over the body, kind of licking the body and hovering over the body. It was such an intense thing to do. Of course, Sheryl Lee—

She had to do it two more times!

And close ups! We had to do coverage on it! And she had to do *everything!* We had breaks, taking turns, but she was like minced meat.

Was this scene with all three of the different actors and Sheryl shot on the same day?

Oh, yeah.

How long was that whole filming sequence?

An entire day. Probably a fifteen- or sixteen-hour day.

That's got to be the most intense scene in Twin Peaks, *and probably the most violent thing I've ever seen on network TV. Did they edit things out that were even more extreme?*

No. Everything was there.

It's amazing that all that got on the air.

I was shocked myself. I was real shocked. But *everything* was there.

As we have said, it's certainly the most effective scene and one of the most memorable scenes on the series.

Well, another thing that I always found really interesting—and this was one of my big fears as I was doing the series—is that every time I did get the call to go in I always worked with David. I had never worked with any other director for the series, except the second season! All the times I had gone in, David was the director. And I had known David for a long time; our relationship and friendship is there and I feel real comfortable with him. Of course I'd get nervous, but I understand him. So, when they called me to go in they said "We need you here for one of the episodes." And I said, "Oh, OK, what I'm I doing?" "Well, umm, we don't know exactly yet, but just come in." And I went in and it was Tim Hunter directing. I said, "Oh, no! This is really scary! A real job with a real director!" [*laughs*]

Had you seen his film, River's Edge?

Yeah. I had been an admirer of Tim Hunter but I had never worked under another director before; I was used to David. This was like really weird— going in and working for a real director! I mean, David is a real director but it wasn't the same thing!

It worked out extremely well, though. We think that Tim was probably the second best director on Twin Peaks.

Absolutely! It was real interesting working with Tim. With David, I would go in and usually we got it in one take—whatever I had to do was usually done in one take, maybe two, but usually it was there in that first one. It was right on, it was perfect. Lighting was fine, I hit the marks, and it seemed to be the right intensity.

Now, with Tim I went in and I was used to already playing Bob. I had an idea of what I thought Bob was. He would say, "Let's try it," and I'd do *my* Bob thing. Then he'd say, "Frank, let's try it again, but let's do something with the hands, let's do something stranger and weird with the hands." So I would do what he wanted, something weird with the hands. And then he'd say, "Frank, you're right. Don't do the hands." [*laughs*] So it was real interesting in that respect, working with another director, because I had never done that. And I worked with another director, very briefly.

The Josie sequence. Where Josie dies.

Yeah, Lesli Glatter. Lesli was great because she said, "Frank, you know what to do." It was great. But there was another director I worked with, too—

When Bob came out of Glastonberry Grove?

When I was in the rear-view mirror in Leland's car. That's all I had to do, just adjust the mirror. It was the first time, too, that Bob had been in daylight. That freaked me out. It was really weird; I was sitting in the car and I said, "I don't know about this. This is the first time Bob's been out during the day. I don't know if he goes out during the day."

You had mentioned that most of your scenes were done with David. Did he shoot lots of material or did he realize what the television restrictions were?

He did shoot lots of stuff for the episodes he actually directed. But once David knows what he wants, and the actors and everything else are there, he knows when he's got it. I mean, he's definitely one of those directors who knows when he's got it. He knows he shouldn't take it any further; he knows that he doesn't need another cut or anything like that.

If he knows he *doesn't* have it, that's when he'll go after it and keep going. Like the day we shot the hospital scene where I'm running down the hallway. My call wasn't until three or four in the afternoon. I got there and they hadn't gotten their first shot of the day yet—and they had started at seven or eight that morning. What happened was, they got there and David hated the scene. So he rewrote it and everyone just sat around waiting for him. They finally got the first shot at three or four in the afternoon. But that's another big thing David does, he'll look a scene over and sometimes rewrite the entire scene, then and there.

Let's talk a little bit about Fire Walk With Me. *I guess we could extend the same question we just had. There was a lot of film footage for* Fire Walk With Me *that never made it into the final cut, at least the theatrical cut we've seen. Was there a lot of Bob that was filmed that never made it to the final version?*

Well, a lot of Bob was in the scene at the convenience store, which was a much larger scene. It's something that I'm in a lot more than what was actually seen. The Red Room scene where I take the pain from Leland's body and throw it on the floor, that scene was much larger. The intercourse scene is all there. The scene with the dresser is all there, although it may have been a little bit longer.

Another thing I noticed from this last time that I saw it, is that Bob talks to Laura a lot. You hear Bob's voice talking to Laura: "I want to be you, I want to taste through your mouth" that kind of stuff. The first time I saw it I just heard it that one time when she's in the hallway, below the ceiling fan. I noticed that there was more stuff [where] Bob was speaking to Laura. I never picked up on that the first time I saw it.

The killing scene basically had a lot more. We did the entire killing scene like the Maddy scene, where Ray had to do it and then I did it. I think [David] wanted to make it more explicit that Bob was possessing Leland; he wanted to see more of Leland doing it rather than Bob doing it. So in that stuff I'm just there every now and then.

It's kind of fitting—in the series we've got Bob's aspect doing that killing, and then in the movie we've got Leland's.

Absolutely. Yeah, because the story basically dealt with Leland and Laura. It was the relationship between those two characters and the fact that it was a real screwed-up family, really fucked-up.

Did you and Ray Wise get together and ever say, "OK, we're kind of playing the same character, let's trade notes?"

Uh uh. Never.

Because he did a wonderful job, too.

Oh, absolutely!

There are certain sequences where you see his face just change, you almost feel as if Bob is there.

Ray and I got to know each other a lot on the series. Basically, I didn't spend much time with Ray during the movie because I wasn't really there all the time. I came up for three days the first time, here in Seattle, and they were running so far behind that they never used me. So they sent me back home, and then I came back up the last week that they were here. I was on call for the entire week. And every day they'd put me on call, I'd be at the hotel, and David would say, "Frank, what are you doing here?" And I said, "Well, I think I'm here to work." He'd say, "Well, I don't know about that. I don't think we're gonna ever get to it." Every day I'd get that from David! "Frank, what are you doing here?" "David, I'm here to do that scene!" "Well, I don't know. I don't think we're gonna get to it."

We had planned on doing the killing scene in the original train car. That was why I was here for that last week; we were going to actually do the murder scene here. But they ran out of time. In fact, I was here for an entire week and the only thing that I shot was when Leland's dumping the body in the river and he turned and walked away. That's it! That's what I came here for. For, like, nine days, that was it. And they said, "We're going to do the killing scene in LA. We're going to build a set."

I think that everyone who is interested in Twin Peaks *has this question, and we have to ask you. Do you think there will be more?*

That's really hard to say. I would hope that there would be some sort of closure.

You'd be interested in doing it?

Oh, of course. I think there should be some sort of closure. I guess it does kind of close, in a way, when you look at *Twin Peaks: Fire Walk With Me*. But I also think that there are a lot of unanswered questions. And maybe we could finally put it all to rest—have that third part of the trilogy.

If David Lynch said, "We want to end this with Bob possessing Cooper," that would have been some kind of closure. But then the movie states that it was actually the bad Cooper who got out, and maybe the good Dale is still trapped. The whole thing is open—

To all kinds of things. And maybe he did that for that reason. Maybe he is planning on doing something as a closure. Maybe that was an open ending to be able to close it. I don't know. I think it could have that third part of a trilogy. I think it could have a closure movie; you know, with the pilot, and then *Twin Peaks: Fire Walk With Me,* and then a final episode to end it all. Maybe he is planning on it. No one knows with David. He could lose interest in it. And then again it could be one of those things that's burning in him. It's that thorn. He wants to close it off.

But if it were just up to him, he would love to keep going?

Oh, of course he would! It all boils down to that money game. That's what Hollywood is all about. And that box office thing about making money. [Some other interviewers] were asking the question, "Well, *Twin Peaks: Fire Walk With Me* wasn't a success. How do you feel about that?" To me, it *was* a success. As far as dollars-and-cents at the box office—it wasn't a success. But I don't go to movies for those reasons. I go to movies that I want to go to. I don't care whether they got critical acclaim or not. I still want to go to a movie and find out for myself whether it's going to be a good movie or not. But that old Hollywood crap is the bucks. That's all they care about. If the movie makes money they don't care about anything else. They would make their money back by foreign distribution, video, and all that stuff. I mean, twelve million dollars, thirteen million dollars—what it took to do *Fire Walk With Me*—is not a lot of money. That's still considered low budget. I'm sure that they could make that kind of money back.

Is it awkward or uncomfortable to go to a movie like Fire Walk With Me *and see yourself on the screen as this really bizarre kind of character?*

Yeah.

Have you seen the movie very many times?

No. This was my second time seeing it [at the Festival]. The first time I saw it was at a cast and crew screening at the Director's Guild. It was packed and I sat towards the back.

What was it like?

It's real strange. It's very strange. First of all, now—and even back then—I don't recognize that person up there. Because, to me, it's not me. I don't recognize him. Now, I can sit and watch it. During the series I had a rough time watching it. It really disturbed me. And it still disturbs me when I see it, but I also know that that's not me. It's weird, it's different, and it's kind of spooky. But I think for any actor, no matter who they are, the roughest thing possible is to sit and watch yourself on the big screen. I think that's pretty scary. I don't know how they do it.

Piper Laurie said that she would never watch her work, but she would watch Twin Peaks *because of all the other actors in it.*

I don't understand how the actors go and see their dailies every day. That, I think, would be totally excruciating, especially if you're still struggling with the character and have that facing you every day. I would never want to go see dailies. I think you would be better off divorcing yourself from that and to just do it. Just do the character, go into it, do it.

Another thing that I never did when I was on the set, as Bob, was look in a mirror. When I went into the make-up trailer, whenever I would get near a mirror, I wouldn't look at myself. I couldn't, even in those mirror scenes. Those were the most horrific scenes for me to do, to play those scenes looking at myself. It was really bizarre. That scene in *Fire Walk With Me* in the train car, when I turn into Laura when she's looking in the mirror—when I did that scene I went off into another plane. Something happened. Something happened when I looked into the mirror and did that scene. David yelled, "Cut!" and I walked away, and David said, "Frank! Frank, come here. You've got to see this." And I said, "What?" And he said, "Come here, you've just got to see this." David had frozen that scene on the monitor. I said, "David, I don't want to look at that. I was in some strange place." And he said, "I picked up on that, too." There was something happening that he saw and I said, "I don't want to see it because I was somewhere I don't want to be again." It was real weird.

You say that when you see Bob on TV or film it's actually spooky to you. Obviously it's spooky to a lot of people—Bob is a scary character. How is it for you when you go out into the "real world?" Do people shy away from you?

Absolutely. That's usually the first instinct. They'll recognize you and feel strange about it. You can always tell when somebody is recognizing you. I get a real kick out of it because you can see what the changes are with them. They kind of get freaked-out and weirded-out by it, and it takes them a while before they'll actually come out and acknowledge me and say, "Are you that guy from *Twin Peaks*?" Or they'll usually say, "Are you Bob?" That's usually what it is: "Are you Bob?"

I got this one letter from a fan—he was so cute—his name was Chad. He kept writing to me; and Gaye [Pope] said, "You better answer this yourself." He was totally flipping out about Bob. He's been a horror-film freak for years. He was like fifteen-years old. Apparently, Bob was disturbing to him and also mesmerizing. He had every picture he possibly could of Bob around in his room. He would watch the series and then run upstairs and lock himself in his room. And he couldn't look in mirrors because he might see Bob. He was really out there. He wrote me this letter and he wrote his phone number. So I thought, "Instead of writing him it would be really great to talk to him in person." I called and his little sister answered the phone and she said, "No, Chad's not here, he's out bobsledding." So I called, like, three or four days later. When I called, immediately the phone went up and it was Chad; I had this vision of him sitting by the phone because I didn't call him back right away. And I felt so bad because I had this vision of him [picking up the receiver] every time the phone rang. [*laughs*] He picks up the phone and I said, "Chad?" And he said, "Yeah?" I said, "I hear you were out *Bob*sledding!" And he totally freaked out! [*laughs*] And so we chatted; and every, like, two minutes he would ask, "Is this really you? I can't believe it: This is not Bob. Bob can't be calling." I said, "It is." Then he said, and this was really great, he said, "I gotta ask you one question. How long did it take to get into your make-up?" And I went, "Chad. I'm not wearing any make-up." And he said, "Oh! *Really*?" And I said, "Yeah. Thanks a lot, Chad." [*laughs*]

APPENDIX 3:
GEORGIA COFFEE COMMERCIALS

In an unusual return to the world of *Twin Peaks*, David Lynch directed a four-part series of commercials for a Japanese coffee drink—Georgia Coffee. All the commercials were set in the world of *Twin Peaks* and featured a number of actors from the series. The four-part story was about Agent Cooper's search for a missing Japanese woman. In each commercial, Cooper gains clues toward discovering her whereabouts.

The commercials were shot over a one-week period in 1992. Each commercial aired for two months in Japan, starting in January, 1993. The "story" concluded in July of that year.

Starring Kyle MacLachlan (Cooper), Catherine Coulson (Log Lady), Michael Horse (Hawk), Harry Goaz (Andy), Kimmy Robertson (Lucy), Mädchen Amick (Shelly); **Directed by David Lynch**; *English with Japanese subtitles, (30 seconds each; color).*

Commercial #1:

The story opens in the conference room of the Twin Peaks Sheriff's station. Ken, a Japanese man, has come to Twin Peaks to enlist the help of Agent Cooper in finding his girlfriend, Asami. She sent Ken a postcard from the Great Northern Hotel and then disappeared. When they searched her room, they found a picture of Asami and a mounted deer head. Cooper says, "Let's think about this over a coffee." Lucy and Andy enter. Lucy is carrying a pot of coffee. Cooper says, "No, Lucy," as he and Ken pull cans of Georgia Coffee from their pockets. White flashes and sound effects illustrate a series of quick cuts showing the Georgia Coffee can, a cup of coffee, and coffee beans. Andy gives Lucy a questioning glance. Cooper says, "You two have got to try this! It's rich! Man-oh-man, this Georgia is damn fine coffee!" The Log Lady enters and says, "It's true." Ken says, "What about his deer head?" Cooper points to an unusual symbol on the head—a circle with radiating lines. "Notice the symbol, Ken. I think you and I should take a drive." The scene

345

> dissolves to Big Ed's Gas Farm. The same symbol on the deer head is mounted atop the Big Ed's sign. An image of Asami appears. Cooper and Ken give each other the "thumbs up" sign.

Twin Peaks was notable, in part, because of its leisurely pace and sometimes slow scenes. When directing, David Lynch broke a number of rules regarding television pacing—his camera lingered on characters, and sometime he lengthened scenes to an uncomfortable degree. For the *Twin Peaks* Georgia Coffee commercials, however, Lynch had to recapture the world of *Twin Peaks* in 30-second segments, and sell a product at the same time. Amazingly, Lynch succeeds. The Georgia Coffee spots are wonderful little encapsulations of everything that made *Twin Peaks* unique, including humor, non-sequiturs, mystery, the supernatural, and the surreal.

To establish the quick pace of the first commercial, Lynch uses Angelo Badalamenti's "Dance of the Dream Man" as background music. (The commercial also contains bits of other *Twin Peaks* themes, particularly the main theme as the commercial opens.) With its steady, "finger-snapping" rhythm, the "Dance" piece accompanies the fast cuts and quick dialogue necessary for Lynch to introduce a number of characters (including two new ones) and to establish the backstory of Asami's disappearance. "Dance of the Dream Man" is also immediately identifiable as being from *Twin Peaks* as well as being the unofficial theme of Agent Cooper.

Kyle MacLachlan goes over-the-top in his portrayal of Agent Cooper—practically every one of his lines is a loud exclamation. But this overt characterization—and Cooper's rapid-fire dialogue—helps convey all of the commercial's information. The Georgia Coffee commercials are centered on MacLachlan. Kimmy Robertson, Harry Goaz, and Catherine Coulson do little more than react to him. The actor playing Ken has a more significant role, but he still acts as MacLachlan's straight man.

Just like every episode of *Twin Peaks*, the first Georgia Coffee commercial ends with the story unresolved. Viewers must wait for the next commercial to find out what will happen.

Commercial #2:

> Cooper and Ken have arrive at Big Ed's Gas Farm, and Ken notices Asami's automobile. As they get closer, they notice something on the front passenger seat: a wooden, triangular rack from a pool table. The rack is filled with red billiard balls. Ken says, "Red Snooker balls—I don't get it." As Cooper replies, "Let's grab a can of Georgia and figure it out." The triangular shape transitions to a matching triangular piece of cherry pie. Cooper and Ken are soon sitting at the Double R Diner. Shelly Johnson is serving them. A piece of pie is on the counter in front of Cooper, but he is more interested in the Georgia Coffee in his hand. He tells Shelly, "I'll let you in on a secret. It's Georgia." The Log Lady, sitting

a short distance away, says, "It's true." Shelly asks Cooper's companion, "Are you Ken?" He says yes, and she tells him that "a beautiful woman left this for you." She hands him a red origami bird. An image of Asami appears. The commercial ends with Cooper, Ken, and Shelly giving each other the thumbs-up.

As with the other commercials in this series, this spot contains a strange item that supposedly serves as a clue, this time the billiard balls and rack. These clues play no logical role in the investigation—there's no reason why the billiard balls are in the front seat of Asami's car, and there's no logical reason why they should lead Cooper to the Double R Diner—except, of course, the rack and balls resemble a piece of cherry pie! One might think that Lynch is constructing a parody of a detective story—but Cooper's unusual deductions are in keeping with his character (remember the rock-throwing deductive technique of intuitive mind-body coordination from the second episode of the TV series).

Commercial #3

Deputies Hawk and Andy study a chalkboard map of Twin Peaks at the sheriff's station. Cooper and Ken examine the red origami bird and discover the letter "G" printed on it. Ken asks, "What do you think it means?" Cooper replies, "I don't know, Ken. The letter G. How about a couple of Georgia Coffees while we think about it?!" Lucy enters carrying a tray of the beverage. Hawk seems confused. Cooper says, "Hawk, you're gonna love Georgia Coffee! Its brewed rich! Tastes incredible! Damn fine coffee!" Cooper turns to Ken and says, "Right?" Ken nods in agreement as the Log Lady enters. She flicks the lights on and off and says, "It's true." Andy points to the map. He has placed pins on various landmarks. "Agent Cooper, look what happens when I connect the pins." Cooper snaps his fingers and points, "The letter G! Good work, Andy!" Andy smiles. Cooper asks Hawk, "What's under that last pin?" Hawk replies, "Glastonberry Grove." Cooper says, "Home of the Black Lodge!" The commercial cuts to a close-up of the map as an image of Asami appears. Cooper and Ken give each other the "thumbs-up" sign.

Once again we see individual letters of the alphabet playing an important part in one of Lynch's works. Obviously, the letter "G" clue was intended as a take-off on the letter "J" clue from the series. But the clue is more than just satire—it works well within the contexts of both *Twin Peaks* and the commercial. The "G" has multiple meanings: it stands for both Glastonberry Grove and Georgia Coffee.

As the "Asami" story unfolds the continuity from commercial-to-commercial remains consistent. Lucy now knows that Cooper drinks

Georgia Coffee, so she brings him that instead of regular coffee. Hawk serves as the audience in the ad; his confusion about Georgia Coffee gives Cooper the opportunity to go through the product's spiel.

Lynch adds a couple of familiar *Twin Peaks* touches to the commercial. The Log Lady flicks the lights on-and-off just as she did in the pilot, and Cooper's praise of Andy results in one of Andy's child-like grins. Cooper is still a master detective, capable of piecing together totally unrelated clues. (Why would the last pin be so significant?) Obviously, the clues don't really matter—while a story does unfold across these commercials, it doesn't have to make much sense. The primary objective of the commercials is, of course, to sell Georgia Coffee.

Commercial #4

> Cooper, Ken, Andy, and Hawk approach Glastonberry Grove at night. Cooper looks ahead and says, "That's where I'll find Asami." The Log Lady appears and says, "Watch." Cooper explains, "The Black Lodge isn't in this world. Inside there's a red room." The commercial shows the footage from the series finale of Cooper entering Glastonberry Grove then disappearing into the red curtains. Inside he sees Asami, who says "Cooper" in backwards talk. He reaches for her and we see a close-up of their hands clasping over the zig-zag floor of the Red Room. There is a bright flash of light and both Cooper and Asami return, lying on the ground outside Glastonberry Grove. Ken rushes to Asami, who says something in Japanese. Ken replies they should have a Georgia Coffee. Cooper says, "Great idea, Ken! Brewed rich! Tastes incredible! Georgias all around!" The commercial ends with all the characters drinking from cans of Georgia Coffee as Cooper gives the "thumbs-up" sign.

The fourth and final Georgia Coffee commercial is much different from the others. Cooper and the deputies leave the Sheriff's station and travel to Glastonberry Grove—the doorway to the Black Lodge. Even though this is only a commercialized version of the Black Lodge, Lynch—and Cooper— still treat the subject with a certain amount of gravity. Cooper is far more subdued here than in previous ads. He describes some detail about the Black Lodge, telling his companions (and the viewer) that the Lodge is not of this world and that it contains the Red Room. While these are not great revelations, Lynch, through Cooper, is being more direct than usual.

Lynch is aware that this is the climax of the story. Cooper is more cautious, and the Log Lady changes her standard line from "It's true" to the simple—but vague—command of "Watch." Something is about to happen and, indeed, Cooper succeeds in rescuing Asami by simply pulling her out of the Black Lodge! We never find out how or why Asami got trapped in the Black Lodge, but these, and other story points, are secondary to the commercial's primary purpose of selling the product.

Catherine Coulson and Kimmy Robertson shared some memories of making the Georgia Coffee commercials with *Wrapped in Plastic*:

Kimmy Robertson: It felt more like *Twin Peaks* [on set]. It was because, I think, the Japanese clients were there and they were so excited. They were such huge fans and they brought us all gifts. So I felt like we were required to make sure we all had fun. And, of course, we were all thrilled to get a big chunk of money—and be with David again. It was wonderful.

Catherine Coulson: They're very tasteful commercials. They're not parodies at all. They're in the style of *Twin Peaks*, but like a "no-play," that kind of Japanese play. It's very simple. I think that is one of the reasons why *Twin Peaks* appealed to the Japanese mind so much; there's a certain kind of clean line about the way the show unfolded. These commercials are extremely simple and very beautiful. There's lightning flashing outside the window, and the Log Lady says, "It's true" a lot. And I understand that people in Japan now say, "It's true."

ACKNOWLEDGMENTS

This book exists because of Craig Miller. *Wrapped In Plastic* exists because of Craig Miller. He was the driving force behind the publication: He did the layout, handled the orders and mailing, administered the printing and distribution. He was the foundation of the magazine.

Craig approached me in 1991 about producing a *Twin Peaks* magazine. (He was adamant that it would be a *magazine* and not a "fanzine.") He had known about my fervor for *Twin Peaks*, and wanted me to join him in making a publication (I soon proposed the name, *Wrapped In Plastic,* and it stuck). That was the beginning of a strong, productive and special friendship.

Craig and I shared the editing tasks for each issue and we conducted interviews together. We both wrote extensively for the magazine, often trading off "the big essays" every-other-issue or so. I happened to be the author of much of the material regarding *Twin Peaks* and *Fire Walk With Me*; Craig often wrote about David Lynch's other films, and subjects about which he was passionate (Mark Frost, Stanley Kubrick, Peter Weir, *The X-Files*). We edited each other's work, polishing the writing and adding our own bits. Craig always kept us on schedule, firmly but gently reminding me of deadlines. He was the perfect co-editor, smart, committed, and thorough. The look, feel, and longevity of the magazine were due to Craig's tireless effort. Because of Craig's diligence, a new issue of *Wrapped In Plastic* was published every two months for over ten years.

Craig loved television, film, comics and science fiction. I shared his passion. He and I would talk endlessly of these things we treasured. Phone calls between us would last hours as we dissected a scene in *Twin Peaks*, or analyzed an issue of *Cerebus*, or examined the themes of *Blade Runner,* or pored over the writing of David Foster Wallace. I'd end these conversations feeling exhausted—and invigorated.

Craig passed away on November 7, 2012. His was a devastating loss— for family, friends, and for the *Twin Peaks* community. Craig's vast knowledge and insight were gone. In describing the death of her father, the

350

musician Laurie Anderson said, "It was like a library had burned down." That was what Craig's death was like. That huge mind—that endless curiosity—was no more. The world became a smaller place.

But Craig's work lives on—in the pages of *Wrapped In Plastic*, *Spectrum Magazine*, and *Following Cerebus*. And his work lives in the pages of this book, too; Craig Miller was the guiding spirit on the pathways to *Twin Peaks*. I can never thank him enough.

***

I want to give a special thanks to Howard Miller, Craig's father, who gave his blessing on this book. Howard was supportive from the beginning, and I am grateful for his help. (To order back issues of *Wrapped In Plastic* from Howard, visit www.wrappedinplasticmag.com.)

***

Brad Dukes gave me crucial advice about making this book a reality as he helped me understand the tricky world of self-publishing. Brad had already blazed a trail with his wonderful book, *Reflections*, and I followed humbly behind. Thanks Brad!

A great many people helped me through various stages of book production. Joel Bocko provided invaluable feedback, from spotting typos to asking questions about larger thematic concepts. His comments and ideas helped make this a sharper book.

Scott Ryan also provided generous feedback and helped me see certain pieces of this book in a new way. I am glad I had his perspective.

New and old friends alike acted as sounding boards for me. Nick Hyman has been a good friend since the early days of *Wrapped In Plastic*, and is always happy to bounce ideas back and forth. Ben Durant and Bryon Kozaczka at the podcast, *Twin Peaks Unwrapped*, and the aforementioned Scott Ryan with his podcast partner, Joshua Minton, at *The Red Room Podcast*, lent welcoming voices as I started putting the pieces of the book together. Thanks to all of them.

A special thanks to Bill Abelson, Jason Allan Haase, and John J. Pierce, who gave permission to use excerpts from various interviews they conducted for *Wrapped In Plastic*. The book is stronger for the work they did.

Back in the day, *Wrapped In Plastic* had the support of a number of *Twin Peaks* personalities. Catherine Coulson was always an advocate for the magazine. I, like all *Twin Peaks* fans, miss her greatly, and I am forever indebted to the support she provided. Mark Frost and David Lynch and Harley Peyton and Robert Engels provided valuable insights to *Wrapped In Plastic* over the years. Those interviews were the highlights of my time working on the magazine. I owe them all a special debt of gratitude. And thanks, of course, to everyone who granted *Wrapped In Plastic* an interview during its run. You helped us document the greatest television show in history.

The curiosity of a few good friends allowed me to think out-loud on more than one occasion. That kind of environment is rare and valuable when you're trying to visualize a book that doesn't yet exist. So, thanks to Courtney and Tony Jewitt, Clayton and Bonny Olney, Don and Beth Menzies, and Ann and Allen Honaker. You'd be surprised how much help you were!

Finally, a special *thank you* to my family: Laura, Sarah and Daniel (and, yes, Juno) for tolerating my obsessions all these many years. *"We embraced: a warm and loving embrace, nothing withheld. We were in this moment one. That was my vision; it was of you. I'm so glad to have had this opportunity to share it with you. I wish you nothing but the very best, always."*

END NOTES

Chapter One (Cult Buster)

1. David Lavery, "Introduction: The Semiotics of Cobbler *Twin Peaks'* Interpretive Community," in *Full of Secrets: Critical Approaches to Twin Peaks,* edited by David Lavery, (Wayne State University Press, 1995), p. 4.

2. Umberto Eco, "*Casablanca*: Cult movies and Intertextual Collage," in *Travels in Hyper Reality*, translated by William Weaver, (Harcourt, Brace Jovanovich, 1986), pp. 197-211. (Because an online version of this work—without page numbering—was used as a reference for this essay, this will be the only citation listed.)

3. Martha Nochimson, "Desire Under the Douglas Firs: Entering the Body of Reality in *Twin Peaks,*" in *Full of Secrets: Critical Approaches to Twin Peaks,* edited by David Lavery, (Wayne State University Press, 1995), p. 158.

4. María M. Carrión, "*Twin Peaks* and the Circular Ruins of Fiction: Figuring (Out) the Acts of Reading," in *Literature, Film Quarterly*, Volume 21, #4, 1993, p. 243.

5. Martha Nochimson, *The Passion of David Lynch: Wild at Heart in Hollywood*, (University of Texas Press, 1997), p. 75.

6. *Ibid.*, p. 77.

7. Gregg Rickman, "Moving Through Time: The *Twin Peaks* Cycle," *Wrapped In Plastic* #20 (December, 1995), p. 20.

8. Lavery, p. 6.

9. *Ibid.*, p. 7.

10. "The Mark Frost Interview," Interview conducted by Craig Miller and John Thorne; *Wrapped In Plastic* #9 (February, 1994), p. 2.

11. Martha Nochimson, *The Passion of David Lynch: Wild at Heart in Hollywood*, (University of Texas Press, 1997), p. 17.

12. *Lynch on Lynch*, edited by Chris Rodley, (Faber and Faber, 1997), p. 158.

13. *Ibid.*, p. 183.

14. *Ibid.*, p. 175.

15. Tad Friend, "Creative Differences," *The New Yorker*, September 6, 1999, p. 64.

353

16. *Ibid.*, p. 66.

17. *Lynch on Lynch*, p. 159.

Chapter Two (Dreams, Donuts, and Dancing Men)

1. *Lynch on Lynch*, edited by Chris Rodley, (Faber and Faber, 1997), p. 167.

2. *Ibid.*, p. 165.

3. "Peyton's Place: An Interview with *Twin Peaks* Writer/Producer Harley Peyton!"; Interview conducted by Craig Miller and John Thorne; *Wrapped In Plastic* #17 (June, 1995) p. 6.

Chapter Three (The Summer of 1990)

1. *Lynch on Lynch*, edited by Chris Rodley, (Faber and Faber, 1997), p. 180.

2. "Sheryl Lee Interviewed Again"; Interview conducted by Robert Getz; *Wrapped In Plastic* #16 (April, 1995); p. 22.

Chapter Four (Season Two (and the Supernatural))

1. Marc Dolan; "The Peaks and Valleys of Serial Creativity: What happened to/on *Twin Peaks*"; *Full of Secrets: Critical Approaches to Twin Peaks,* edited by David Lavery, (Wayne State University Press, 1995), p. 40.

2. *Ibid.*, p. 41.

3. "The David Lynch Interview," Interview conducted by David Hughes, *Wrapped In Plastic* #57 (Feb. 2002); p. 4.

4. *Lynch on Lynch*, edited by Chris Rodley, (Faber and Faber, 1997), p. 171.

5. Mark Altman; *Twin Peaks: Behind the Scenes*, (Pioneer Books, 1990), p.88.

Chapter Five (Second Season Slump)

1. "The Mark Frost Interview," Interview conducted by Craig Miller and John Thorne; *Wrapped In Plastic* #9 (February, 1994), p. 2.

2. Jacobs, John, with Craig Miller and John Thorne; "Patterns and Conflicts: An Analysis of the Windom Earle/Dale Cooper Chess Game", *Wrapped In Plastic* #4 (April 1993), p. 8.

Chapter Six (Second Season Rebound)

1. "David Bianculli Takes Television Seriously"; Interview with David Bianculli conducted by Craig Miller and John Thorne; *Wrapped In Plastic* #5 (June 1993), p. 17.

2. Gregg Rickman; "An Interview with Tim Hunter"; *Film Quarterly*, Vol 47, Number 1, p 13.

3. "Harley Peyton Interview"; Interview conducted by Craig Miller; *Wrapped In Plastic* #29 (June 1997), p. 13.

Chapter Seven (The Last Episode)

1. "Peyton's Place: An Interview with *Twin Peaks* Writer/Producer Harley Peyton!"; Interview conducted by Craig Miller and John Thorne; *Wrapped In Plastic* #17 (June, 1995) p. 6.

2. "The Mark Frost Interview"; Interview conducted by Craig Miller and John Thorne; *Wrapped In Plastic* #9 (Feb., 1994) p. 2.

3. *Ibid*; p.2.

Chapter Eight (Half the Man He Used to Be)

1. *Lynch on Lynch*, edited by Chris Rodley, (Faber and Faber, 1997), p. 183.

2. *Ibid.*, p. 168.

3. *Ibid.*, p. 182.

4. It is interesting that Laura Palmer never does anything "bad" to anyone else, nor is she ever "good" to herself; her behavior fluctuates between extreme self-gratification and extreme altruism. Laura never finds a balance, a way to satisfy her desires while being generous to others. In effect, Laura Palmer becomes a non-entity existing either entirely outside herself (through the opinions of others) or entirely inside herself (through her own base impulses). She cannot find a way for these two worlds to merge.

5. *Lynch on Lynch*, p. 182.

6. There is, arguably, a similar scene in *Fire Walk With Me*. Early in the film, Dale Cooper, acting on a premonitory dream, walks back and forth between a security camera and a video monitor. At one point in the sequence, Cooper seemingly divides—he remains rooted in front of the camera while his other self walks away to look at the monitor. This incident occurs during the arrival of the mysterious Phillip Jeffries, a long-lost FBI agent who apparently visited the Red Room. Jeffries walks past "Cooper-at-the-camera" while "Cooper-at-the-monitor" watches. As Cooper-at-the-monitor pursues Jeffries, he momentarily pauses in front of the camera as if to reunite with his (invisible) other self. Does this separation of Cooper foreshadow a division into "good" and "bad" selves? If so, one possible reason for Jeffries' appearance may be to warn Cooper about his impending division.

7. Martha Nochimson, *The Passion of David Lynch: Wild at Heart in Hollywood*, (University of Texas Press, 1997), p. 251.

8. Richard Beymer's behind-the-scenes photos reveal that Sheryl Lee—as Maddy—was wearing white contact lenses, confirming Maddy's presence as a doppelgänger in the Red Room.

9. *Lynch on Lynch*, p. 19.

10. *Ibid.*, p. 182.

11. During the time Lynch was shooting the finale, ABC Television had already placed *Twin Peaks* on a six-week hiatus. The ratings for the show were dropping, and the future of the series looked gloomy. But Lynch did not know what the fate of *Twin Peaks* would be; the series could have been renewed or

moved to another network. There was no reason to abandon the show to frivolous improvisation.

12. "David Lynch's *Twin Peaks: Fire Walk With Me*, The Press Conference," *Cinema Papers* #89, August 1992, p. 30.

Chapter Eleven (The Realization of Laura Palmer)

1. Michel Chion, *David Lynch*, (BFI Publishing, 1995), p. 157.

2. *Lynch on Lynch*, edited by Chris Rodley, (Faber and Faber, 1997), p. 184.

3. *Ibid.*, p. 183.

4. *Ibid.*, p. 185.

5. *Ibid.*, p. 19.

6. Lynch quoted in Martha Nochimson, *The Passion of David Lynch: Wild at Heart in Hollywood*, (University of Texas Press, 1997), p. 251.

7. *Ibid.*, p. 188.

8. In the script, the first scene following the dream shows Laura meeting James outside her house the next morning. James asks Laura where she was the previous night and says, "We were supposed to be together." Laura responds, "How can I be together when I'm not together?" This odd remark reinforces the divided nature of Laura's psyche and speaks to Lynch's intent regarding Laura's dream. (An edited version of this James/Laura scene was used in a later part of the theatrical version of *Fire Walk With Me*.)

9. David Foster Wallace, "David Lynch Keeps His Head"; in *A Supposedly Fun Thing I'll Never Do Again*, (Little, Brown & Co., 1997), p. 204.

10. Nochimson, p. 188.

11. It is unclear what, if any, conclusions Laura comes to about the ring. An argument could be made that she now suspects Leland of Teresa Banks's murder. Earlier, at Partyland, Ronette remarks about Teresa's death and potential blackmail scheme. Jacques then remembers that Teresa asked him about Laura's and Ronette's fathers, which startles Laura. Knowing that Teresa was killed, and then hearing the One Armed Man say, "It's your father!" could lead Laura to the conclusion that Leland killed Teresa.

12. *Ibid.*, p. 189.

13. John Alexander, *The Films of David Lynch*, (Charles Letts and Co. Limited, 1993), p. 140.

14. *Ibid.*, p. 140.

15. Nochimson, p. 158.

16. David Breskin, Interview with David Lynch, in *Inner Views*, (Faber and Faber, 1992), p. 86.

17. Nochimson, p. 152.

18. It is unclear whether the One Armed Man throws the ring into the car or whether the ring finds its own way into the car. In an interview in *Wrapped In Plastic* #11 (p. 6), Al Strobel, the actor who played Mike, the One Armed Man,

seems to confirm that the ring left of its own volition: "If the ring leaves Mike's finger and rolls on the floor of the car, it wasn't a deliberate thing [on Mike's part]. Mike was only trying to stop Bob."

19. "We're Gonna Talk About Judy—And A Whole Lot More! An Interview with Robert Engels," Interview conducted by Craig Miller and John Thorne; *Wrapped in Plastic* #58 (April 2002), p.8.

20. The series confirms that Laura and Cooper shared the same dreams, and the film establishes that Cooper and Laura were aware of one another through the Red Room realm.

21. Wallace, p. 210.

22. *Ibid.*, p. 211.

23. It should be noted, however, that Wallace considers *Fire Walk With Me* one of Lynch's "best movies," as he claims on p. 167 of his essay in *A Supposedly Fun Thing I'll Never Do Again*.

24. "An Interview with David Lynch: The Mind Inside the Mind Inside *Eraserhead*," Interview conducted by Craig Miller and John Thorne; *Wrapped In Plastic* #65 (June 2003), p. 5.

25. David Lynch interviewed on the television program, *Independent Focus*, Copyright 2000, The Independent Film Channel.

26. Stephen Pizzello, "Laura Palmer's Phantasmagoric Fall from Grace," *American Cinematographer*, Vol. 73 #9, p. 60.

27. It is significant that we do not see Al Strobel (who played the One Armed Man) throw the ring, nor do we see Sheryl Lee (who played Laura Palmer) put the ring on.

28. *Lynch on Lynch*, p. 190.

29. "*Twin Peaks*, Weak Language and the Resurrection of Affect" by Sheli Ayers in *The Cinema of David Lynch: American Dreams, Nightmare Visions*, ed. by Erica Sheen and Annette Davison, (Wallflower Press, 2004), p 101.

30. Wallace, p. 210.

Chapter Twelve (Dreams of Deer Meadow)

1. *Lynch on Lynch*, edited by Chris Rodley, (Faber and Faber, 1997), p. 26.

2. Even before *Mulholland Drive*, there is precedence in Lynch's work for taking "real world" scenes and recasting them as dreams—this precedence is found in *Twin Peaks*, itself. The "European version" of the pilot concludes with about fifteen minutes of material that was designed to "resolve" the Laura Palmer murder. Some of these scenes took place "twenty-five years later" in the Red Room. For the second episode of the television series, however, these Red Room scenes with the Little Man From Another Place, his "cousin" (who looked like—or was—Laura Palmer), and an aged Dale Cooper were re-positioned as parts of Cooper's dream, and the "twenty five years" designation removed. In effect, scenes that were originally presented as real events were re-interpreted as a dream.

3. Another purpose of the Teresa Banks prologue would be to mirror the future investigation into Laura's death. In this way, new viewers would know that the FBI would later attempt to discover what really happened to Laura. Unfortunately, this interpretation implies that the FBI will fail to solve Laura's murder, just as they failed to solve Teresa's.

4. It is clear that Lynch and Engels were trying to remain faithful to *The Autobiography of Dale Cooper* because the book mentions Deer Meadow as Teresa's home town (in the pilot, Cooper merely noted "a town in the southwest corner of this state"). The "local and apparently only authority" is a man named Cable (he's not specifically identified as a sheriff). The cause of death roughly matches Sam Stanley's report in *Fire Walk With Me*. Sam is not mentioned in the book, but Cooper is accompanied by someone (not named) while he examines the body.

5. A similar scenario occurs in *Mulholland Drive*. The dreaming Diane imagines herself as Betty, someone who has better success than she, Diane, did in "reality." But, like Cooper, Diane's dreaming mind cannot avoid reality forever. At a certain point Betty ceases to have any function in the dream and she disappears.

6. "We're Gonna Talk About Judy—And A Whole Lot More! An interview with Robert Engels," Interview conducted by Craig Miller and John Thorne; *Wrapped in Plastic* #58 (April 2002), p.9.

7. Martha Nochimson, *The Passion of David Lynch: Wild at Heart in Hollywood*, (University of Texas Press, 1997), p. 251.

8. There is no evidence in the film to definitively say whether Chet Desmond is real or imaginary in the *Twin Peaks* world. Desmond could very well be an FBI agent who works with Cooper, Albert and Gordon Cole. Cooper may be dreaming of Desmond simply because Cooper believed Desmond could solve the Teresa Banks case. Future episodes of *Twin Peaks* could easily accommodate the presence of Desmond, while still allowing the dream interpretation of the *Fire Walk With Me* prologue to stand.

9. *Lynch on Lynch*, p. 27.

10. *Ibid.*, p. 227.

11. To viewers unfamiliar with series, Annie Blackburne would seem as baffling a character as Phillip Jeffries.

12. "The David Lynch Interview," Interview conducted by David Hughes; *Wrapped in Plastic* #57 (February 2002), p. 5.

13. *Ibid.*, p. 4.

14. *Lynch on Lynch*, p.227.

15. *Ibid.*, p227.

Appendix 1: Notes

1. Tim Kreider, letter to the editor, *Wrapped In Plastic* #62, (December 2002), p.23
2. *Lynch on Lynch*, edited by Chris Rodley, (Faber and Faber, 1997), p. 185.

SOURCES

Books:

Alexander, John; *The Films of David Lynch*; (Charles Letts and Co. Limited, 1993)

Altman, Mark; *Twin Peaks: Behind the Scenes*; (Pioneer Books, 1990)

Bianculli, David; *Teleliteracy; Taking Television Seriously*; (Continuum, 1992)

Breskin, David; *Inner Views*; (Faber and Faber, 1992)

Chion, Michel; *David Lynch*; (BFI Publishing, 1995)

Eco, Umberto; *Travels in Hyper Reality*; William Weaver (trans.); (Harcourt, Brace Jovanovich, 1986)

Lavery, David (Ed.); *Full of Secrets: Critical Approaches to Twin Peaks;* (Wayne State University Press, 1995)

Lovece, Frank; *The Television Yearbook: Complete Detailed Listings for the 1990-1991 Season*; (Perigree Books, 1992)

Nochimson, Martha; *The Passion of David Lynch: Wild at Heart in Hollywood*; (University of Texas Press, 1997)

Rodley, Chris (Ed.) *Lynch on Lynch*; (Faber and Faber, 1997)

Sheen, Erica and Annette Davison (Eds.); *The Cinema of David Lynch: American Dreams, Nightmare Visions*; (Wallflower Press, 2004)

Wallace, David Foster; *A Supposedly Fun Thing I'll Never Do Again*; (Little, Brown & Co., 1997)

Periodicals:

Carrión, María M.; "Twin Peaks and the Circular Ruins of Fiction: Figuring (Out) the Acts of Reading"; *Literature, Film Quarterly*, Volume 21, #4, (1993)

Chisholm, Brad; "Difficult Viewing: The Pleasures of Complex Narratives"; *Critical Studies in Mass Communications*, 8.4, (1991)

Friend, Tad; "Creative Differences"; *The New Yorker*, September 6, (1999)

Getz, Robert; "Sheryl Lee Interviewed Again"; *Wrapped In Plastic* # 16 (April 1995)

Hughes, David; "The David Lynch Interview"; *Wrapped in Plastic* #57 (February 2002)

Jacobs, John, with Craig Miller and John Thorne; "Patterns and Conflicts: An Analysis of the Windom Earle/Dale Cooper Chess Game"; *Wrapped In Plastic* # 4 (April 1993)

Kreider, Tim; letter to the editor; *Wrapped In Plastic* #62, (December 2002)

Lynch, David, (*et al.*); "David Lynch's *Twin Peaks: Fire Walk With Me*, The Press Conference," *Cinema Papers* 89; August 1992

Miller, Craig, and John Thorne (Eds.); *Wrapped In Plastic* 1-75; (1993-2005)

Pizzello, Stephen; "Laura Palmer's Phantasmagoric Fall from Grace"; *American Cinematographer*, Vol. 73, #9

Rickman, Gregg, "An Interview with Tim Hunter"; *Film Quarterly*, Vol 47, #1

Rickman, Gregg, "Moving Through Time: The *Twin Peaks* Cycle," *Wrapped In Plastic* #20, (December, 1995)

Thorne, John (Craig Miller, ed.); "Transcending Cult Status: *Twin Peaks* as a Work of Art"; Wrapped In Plastic #49, (October, 2000)

Thorne, John (Craig Miller, ed.); "Half the Man He Used to Be: Dale Cooper and the Final Episode of *Twin Peaks*"; *Wrapped In Plastic* #53, (June 2001)

Thorne, John (Craig Miller, ed.); "Dreams of Deer Meadow"; *Wrapped In Plastic* #60, (August, 2002)

Thorne, John (Craig Miller, ed.); "Subject of Choice: The Realization of Laura Palmer"; *Wrapped In Plastic* #71, (September, 2004)

Thorne, John (Craig Miller, ed.); "*Fire Walk With Me*: Three More Observations"; *Wrapped In Plastic* #75, (September, 2005)

Audio/Visual Media

Twin Peaks Season One DVD; audio commentaries; Artisan, (2002)

Independent Focus; David Lynch interview; Copyright 2000, The Independent Film Channel

LIST OF INTERVIEWS

Anderson, Michael J., *Wrapped In Plastic* 15, (Feb. 1995)

Ashbrook, Dana, *Wrapped In Plastic* 69, (Mar. 2004)

Augustine, Phoebe, *Wrapped In Plastic* 71, (Sep. 2004), (Interview by Craig Miller at Alamo Drafthouse Cinema "Twin Peaks Marathon," Austin , TX.)

Beymer, Richard, *Wrapped In Plastic* 38, (Dec. 1998)

Boylan, John, *Wrapped In Plastic* 14, (Dec. 1994); Interview conducted by Bill Abelson.

Bullock, Gary, *Wrapped In Plastic* 63, (Feb. 2003)

Coulson, Catherine, *Wrapped In Plastic* 5, (Jun. 1993); *WIP* 49, (Oct. 2000); *WIP* 65, (Jun. 2003); *WIP* 75, (Sep. 2005)

Cruise, Julee, *Wrapped In Plastic* 7, (Oct 1993)

Davis, Don, *Wrapped In Plastic* 26, (Dec. 1996)

Engels, Robert, *Wrapped In Plastic* 58, (Apr. 2002); *WIP* 75, (Sep. 2005)

Ferrer, Miguel, *Wrapped In Plastic* 35, (June 1998)

Frost, Mark, *Wrapped In Plastic* 9, (Feb. 1994); *WIP* 18, (Aug. 1995); *WIP* 36, (Aug. 1998); *WIP* 52, (Apr. 2001); *WIP* 61, (Oct. 2002); *WIP* 75, (Sep. 2005)

Frost, Scott, *Wrapped In Plastic* 73, (Mar. 2005)

Gidley, Pamela, *Wrapped In Plastic* 20, (Dec. 1995)

Graham, Heather, *Wrapped In Plastic* 24, (Aug. 1996)

Lee, Sheryl, *Wrapped In Plastic* 16, (Apr 1995)

Lynch, David, *Wrapped In Plastic* 64, (Apr. 2003); *WIP* 65, (Jun. 2003); *WIP* 75, (Sep. 2005)

Lynch, Jennifer, *Wrapped In Plastic* 73, (Mar 2005)

Marshall, James, *Wrapped In Plastic* 72, (Dec. 2004)

McGill, Everett, *Wrapped In Plastic* 44, (Dec. 1999)

Mulkey, Chris, *Wrapped In Plastic* 45, (Feb. 2000)

Nance, Jack, *Wrapped In Plastic* 27 (Feb. 1997); Interview conducted by John J. Pierce.

Olkewicz, Walter, *Wrapped In Plastic* 24 (Aug. 1996); Interview conducted by Jason Allan Haase.

Peyton, Harley, *Wrapped In Plastic* 17, (Jun. 1995); *WIP* 55, (Oct. 2001)

Raimi, Ted, *Spectrum* 12, (Jan. 1998)

Robertson, Kimmy, *Wrapped In Plastic* 43, (Oct. 1999); *WIP* 71, (Sep. 2004), (Interview by Craig Miller at Alamo Drafthouse Cinema "Twin Peaks Marathon," Austin , TX.)

Silva, Frank, *Wrapped In Plastic* 8, (Dec. 1993)

Stewart, Charlotte, *Wrapped In Plastic* 65, (Jun. 2003)

Strobel, Al, *Wrapped In Plastic* 11, (Jun. 1994)

Struycken, Carel, *Wrapped In Plastic* 24, (Aug. 1996)

Sweeney, Mary, *Wrapped In Plastic* 75, (Sep. 2005)

Von Dohlen, Lenny, *Wrapped In Plastic* 62, (Dec. 2002)

Welsh, Kenneth, *Wrapped In Plastic* 20, (Dec. 1995)

Zabriskie, Grace, *Wrapped In Plastic* 40, (Apr. 1999)

ABOUT THE AUTHOR

John Thorne has a Bachelor of Science from Clarkson University in Potsdam, New York, and has a Master of Arts in TV/Radio/Film from Southern Methodist University in Dallas. (His thesis was a study of the television series, *Homicide, Life on the Street*.) For thirteen years, John was co-editor and co-producer of *Wrapped In Plastic* magazine, where he wrote extensively about *Twin Peaks* and associated film and television. He was also a contributor to the magazines, *Spectrum* and *Following Cerebus*. He is co-editor and contributor to the Kindle book, *Twin Peaks in the Rearview Mirror*. John lives in Dallas, Texas, with his wife and family. When he is not out geocaching, he can be reached through the website, abovethestore.blogspot.com.